Marketing Briefs: A Revision and Study Guide

Marketing Briefs: A Revision and Study Guide

Second edition

Sally Dibb and Lyndon Simkin
Warwick Business School
University of Warwick

ELSEVIER
BUTTERWORTH
HEINEMANN

AMSTERDAM BOSTON HEIDELBERG LONDON NEW YORK OXFORD PARIS
SAN DIEGO SAN FRANCISCO SINGAPORE SYDNEY TOKYO

Butterworth-Heinemann is an imprint of Elsevier
Linacre House, Jordan Hill, Oxford OX2 8DP, UK
30 Corporate Drive, Suite 400, Burlington, MA 01803, USA

First edition 2001
Second edition 2004
Reprinted 2007

British Library Cataloguing in Publication Data
A catalogue record for this book is available from the British Library

Library of Congress Cataloging-in-Publication Data
A catalog record for this book is available from the Library of Congress

ISBN–13: 978-0-7506-6200-0

For information on all Butterworth-Heinemann publications
visit our website at books.elsevier.com

Printed and bound in *Hungary*

07 08 09 10 10 9 8 7 6 5 4 3 2

Contents

Preface

Marketing Briefs: A Revision and Study Guide has been especially designed to help students studying for all kinds of marketing examinations. The collection of bite-sized Briefs is particularly suitable for those facing Chartered Institute of Marketing, college and business school marketing examinations.

So what can the book do for you? The main objective of *Marketing Briefs* is to help you understand the key marketing concepts and frameworks. It also aims to guide you through the difficult revision period, providing plenty of opportunities for you to test your knowledge and practise writing exam answers. These objectives are achieved by combining short, sharp overviews of marketing concepts with mini-cases, definitions, examination-style questions and suggestions for additional reading.

The punchy and concise overviews at the front end of the Briefs explore key marketing concepts and frameworks, and explain core terms in an easy-to-remember format. Mini-case examples are provided to help you better understand the theory and to provide ideas for when you sit your exams. Each Brief includes four examination-style questions, to which answer schemes are provided. If this does not give you enough practice, a later section of the book includes sample examination papers. There are also suggestions to help with your revision and examination performance. All in all, this is a resource designed to help you through the entire process of revising and sitting your exams. In this respect, *Marketing Briefs* is your exam survival guide.

In practice, of course, being an effective marketer is not just about remembering the stand-alone concepts described in the Briefs. It is also necessary to understand the marketing process, by appreciating the connections between the different concepts. This marketing process should endeavour to satisfy customers now and in the future, facilitate the product or service exchange with the customer, combat competitors, differentiate the particular product or service, identify emerging business opportunities, while bringing financial benefit to the business or organization in question.

To be effective, marketing requires: (i) a shrewd and objective understanding of the marketplace, the trading environment, customers' requirements and buying characteristics, competition, and the organization's capabilities; (ii) a clear target market strategy, brand positioning and the creation of a competitive edge; (iii) marketing mix tactics to implement the determined marketing strategy and operational controls to ensure implementation of these marketing programmes. This approach to actioning the marketing process (analysis – strategy – programmes for implementation) is adopted by marketing oriented businesses launching new brands or products, entering new target markets or market territories, creating defensive responses to competitor inroads, seeking an answer to poor performance, or by businesses simply striving for the next solution to satisfying their customers. This process also reflects the content of leading marketing textbooks.

This revision aid has been structured to reflect this approach to successful marketing. It begins by examining the marketing remit and the core marketing analyses. The Briefs then review aspects of marketing strategy and marketing management. This is a marketing process that the authors have successfully adopted in their MBA and undergraduate lecturing and in their consultancy with a variety of blue chip businesses. While you may welcome the bite-sized revision aid summaries provided in *Marketing Briefs*, try not to lose sight of the overall marketing process and the need for marketing practitioners to integrate these themes.

Marketing Briefs is not intended to be a fully comprehensive textbook. There are many lengthy texts available that provide detailed explanations of the key marketing concepts. This book is different: it provides brief, topical, conceptual summaries of the essential facets of modern marketing for revision purposes. These are broken down into fifty chapters – the Briefs.

In more detail, each of the Briefs:

- begins by providing a series of relevant definitions;
- provides a bulleted concise overview of the theme;
- supplements this overview with a more detailed explanation of the core relevant concepts;
- offers a selection of illustrative examination-style examples to help explain the key points;
- sets a mix of examination-oriented self-test questions: essay-style, case-based and applied to specific market situations;
- recommends further readings for each concept;
- provides full cross-referencing to related Briefs.

All of these attributes are delivered in four or five pages per Brief! The intention is to provide concise but complete revision-oriented summaries.

With revision and examinations in mind, *Marketing Briefs* also features:

- A glossary of key definitions.
- Tips and 'golden rules' concerning revision and examination techniques.
- Specimen sample examination papers with answer schemes.
- Case studies for those examinations that feature case study questions.

Our many years of experience of CIM examinations, MBA and undergraduate business school courses, college examinations and practitioners' use of the marketing toolkit, are the basis for the materials provided in this revision aid. We hope you will find it useful.

May your examinations prove successful. Good luck!

S.D.
L.S.

About the Authors

Sally Dibb and Lyndon Simkin have been at the leading UK university management centre, Warwick Business School, since the mid-1980s, teaching undergraduates, MBAs – full-time, part-time and distance learning – and executives the basics of marketing, advanced strategic marketing, buyer behaviour, marketing communications and marketing research. Sally and Lyndon's research focuses on services marketing, market segmentation, marketing planning, retail modelling, marketing communications and teaching methods, in which areas they have published extensively in the academic journals in the UK and USA. Consultancy principally addresses marketing planning and target market strategies in a host of UK and North American blue chip businesses. Married, Sally and Lyndon live in Kenilworth with their five children, Becky, James, Abby, Miranda Mae and Samantha Rose.

Sally is a former Chief Examiner with the Chartered Institute of Marketing and Associate Dean at Warwick Business School. She is chair of the Academy of Marketing's special interest group in segmentation. Her first degree and MSc were from UMIST in Manchester and her PhD was awarded in 1988 by the University of Warwick. Lyndon's background was in economic geography and his first degree was gained at the University of Leicester. His PhD in retail modelling was awarded in 1986 by the University of Bradford Management Centre, after he had joined Warwick Business School. Lyndon is an acknowledged expert witness in corporate litigation cases.

In addition to being joint authors of *Marketing Briefs*, they have authored the innovative *The Marketing Casebook: Cases and Concepts* (London: Thomson), the market leading textbook *Marketing: Concepts and Strategies* (Boston: Houghton Mifflin, now in its fifth edition) with US marketing colleagues Bill Pride and O.C. Ferrell, as well as the practitioner-oriented *The Market Segmentation Workbook* and *The Marketing Planning Workbook* (both London: Thomson), aimed at assisting marketing managers to re-assess their target markets and understand the complexities of marketing planning. These workbooks were based on their consultancy experiences with organizations as diverse as Accenture, the Audit Commission, Calor, Conoco, Courtaulds Textiles, DRA (MoD), Forte, Fujitsu, ICI, JCB, McDonald's, PowerGen, Raytheon, Standard Chartered, Tesco and Zeneca.

About the Briefs

Each Brief is a concise, revision-oriented overview of the topic featured. The Briefs, fifty of them, cover the core ingredients of marketing, commencing with a definition of the marketing concept. The running order continues to explore the essential aspects of marketing analysis, marketing strategy and marketing management, before presenting summaries of marketing's deployment in specific market situations, and concluding with some of the discipline's emerging 'hot topics'.

The structure for each Brief is deliberately similar, in order to aid revision and use:

- Core definitions
- Bulleted key point conceptual summaries
- More detailed explanation citing pertinent examples
- Caselet topical illustrations
- Selected examination-style and assessment-type questions
- Recommended additional readings

Within each Brief, associated Briefs are fully cross-referenced. The set questions include case-based, essay style and applied questions. The answer schemes for the four set questions in each Brief are presented in the section following the Briefs.

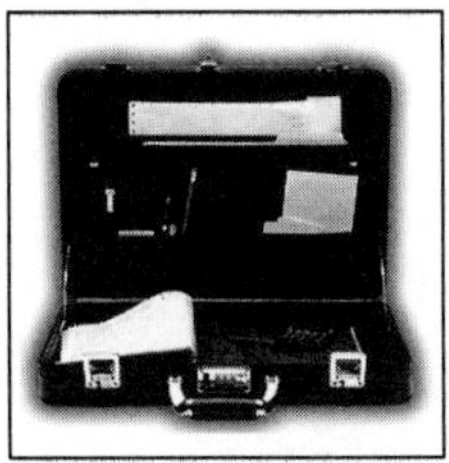

The Marketing Briefs

Concise, revision-oriented overviews of essential topics, including:

- Core definitions
- Bulleted key points conceptual summaries
- More detailed explanation citing pertinent examples
- Caselet topical illustrations
- Selected examination-style and assessment-type questions
- Recommended additional readings

1: Defining Marketing

Key definitions

Marketing consists of individual and organizational activities that facilitate and expedite satisfying exchange relationships in a dynamic environment through the creation, servicing, distribution, promotion and pricing of goods, services and ideas.

Marketing is the management process responsible for identifying, anticipating and satisfying customer requirements profitably.

Key issues

- It is often stated that business has passed through various eras: *production*, following the Industrial Revolution (1850s to 1920s), when products were developed with little consideration for customers' needs or competition; *sales* (1920s to 1950s), with the emphasis on the 'hard sell' through personal selling and advertising; and the *marketing era* (post-1950s), as a customer orientation emerged and customer needs increasingly were determined before products were developed.
- Marketing is not a science: there is no single universally adopted definition of marketing. Marketing aims to satisfy customers, understand their future requirements, differentiate a product or service from competitors' offerings, identify emerging market opportunities and provide an organization with financial viability. If customers are treated properly, they will complete their transaction and be satisfied that their payment or donation was worthwhile.
- Marketers seek new customers for their products or services. In addition, increasingly they are seeking ways to maintain on-going longer-term relationships with their existing customers. This is known as relationship marketing.
- For marketing to be effective in an organization, there must be an analytical process that involves: (a) developing a shrewd understanding of a market; (b) creating marketing strategies that seek the most viable opportunities and compete effectively against rivals; (c) developing tactical marketing programmes designed to satisfy target markets; and (d) controlling internal operations to ensure implementation of the devised marketing strategies and marketing programmes. This process incorporates marketing analysis, marketing strategy and marketing management. The core ingredients of each of these facets of marketing are explored in *Marketing Briefs: A Revision and Study Guide*.

Conceptual overview

Marketing is not a science: there is no single definition or approach to undertaking marketing. The following commonly cited definitions illustrate this variation:

> The aim of marketing is to make selling superfluous. The aim is to know and to understand the customer so well that the product or service fits him/her and sells itself.
>
> (management guru Peter Drucker)

> Marketing is the management process responsible for identifying, anticipating and satisfying customer requirements profitably.
>
> (the UK's Chartered Institute of Marketing)

> Marketing consists of individual and organizational activities that facilitate and expedite satisfying exchange relationships in a dynamic environment through the creation, servicing, distribution, promotion and pricing of goods, services and ideas.
>
> (the American Marketing Association)

Drucker argues that if a business takes the time to first properly determine customer requirements and expectations, the products that it develops are more likely to be deemed desirable by the customers the business is targeting. The Chartered Institute of Marketing adds that marketing involves understanding customer requirements both now and in the future. Businesses must strive to satisfy their customers and make profits to invest in future products and market developments. The American Marketing Association's definition hinges on the economic exchange that occurs when an interested customer purchases a product or service in return for payment or a donation. The AMA adds that marketing occurs in a dynamic environment, and that the exchange at the heart of marketing is made possible through the marketing mix (cf. Brief 32): product, people, price, promotion and place. The trading environment is prone to external pressures (cf. Brief 3), competitive threats (cf. Brief 34) and ever-changing customer demands (cf. Briefs 6 and 7), causing a set of dynamics rarely encountered by other business disciplines such as production, finance or human resources.

There are, though, common themes in most explanations of marketing. The most important are:

- The ability to satisfy customers.
- The exchange of a product or service for a payment or donation.
- The need to create an edge over competitors.
- Identification of favourable marketing opportunities.
- Profits or financial surpluses to enable a viable future for the organization.
- Shrewd utilization of resources to maximize a business's market position.
- The aim to increase market share in priority target markets.

If the 'right' opportunities are pursued, customers are properly researched, the 'right' customers targeted with a marketing proposition designed to give a business an edge over its rivals, it is highly likely that customers will be satisfied, market share will rise in core target markets and profitability will support a viable future. Conversely, if a business develops a product or service which fails to reflect customer expectations and needs, is no better than competing offers and takes no account of evolving market conditions, it is unlikely that the future will be prosperous for such an organization. These sentiments are equally applicable to consumer or industrial markets, products or services.

Definitions of marketing count for little if businesses do not develop a process, culture and set of operational procedures to actually practise marketing. The textbooks promote a process hinging on marketing analysis, marketing strategy, marketing mix tactics and internal programme controls, typified by Figure 1.1. Recent research indicates that the majority of large UK businesses do now practise marketing and that when undertaking the more defined tasks of market opportunity appraisal, market segmentation/target marketing, or marketing planning, they do proceed through an analysis–strategy–programmes process as represented in Figure 1.1.

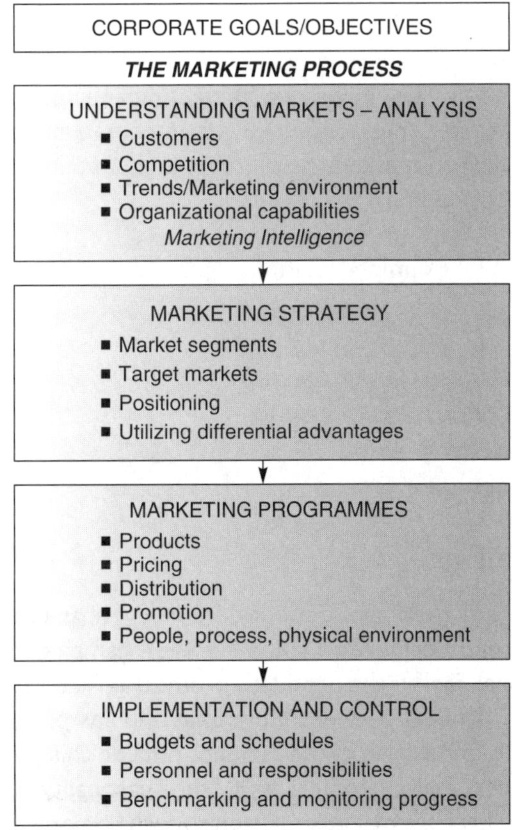

Figure 1.1 The marketing process

Marketing is a process intended to identify market opportunities, satisfy customers today and in the future, create an edge over rivals, differentiate the product or service being marketed, while generating suitable financial rewards for the business. Marketing requires analysis, strategy formulation, tactical marketing mix programmes and operational controls to ensure their implementation. Marketing is one of the core disciplines of management.

Business is widely deemed to have passed through various stages of evolution:

1 Production Era: 1850s to 1920s
Mass production was brought about by the Industrial Revolution. Products were designed and developed without much thought for customer needs or competitive pressures.
2 Sales Era: 1920s to 1950s
The focus of business switched to personal selling and advertising. Customers were 'persuaded' to buy products.
3 Marketing Era: 1950s to the present
A customer orientation replaced the 'hard sell' of the sales era. Customer needs and wants increasingly were determined before a product was brought onto the market.
4 Relationship Marketing Era: 1990s onwards
Some business experts believe that marketing itself has undergone a transformation. The emphasis of marketing apparently was on attracting new customers to make a transaction. Now many companies, while still seeking new customers, devote marketing resource to maintaining good relationships with existing customers.

Brief 2 examines relationship marketing in more detail.

Examples

Cadbury *Crème Eggs*

The marketing of Cadbury *Crème Eggs* has two distinctive characteristics. The first is that the 'How do you eat yours?' campaign launched in 1988 gives a highly 'personal' feel to the product's promotion. The second is that consumers can only buy the product between Christmas and Easter each year. Attempts during the 1970s to extend sales of the product outside this period were shelved when sales fell. It seems that customers enjoy the seasonality of the product and that awareness of the brand is maintained even though it is only on retailers' shelves for four months a year. The enduring fondness that the brand attracts is all the more impressive when it is considered that marketing activity for *Crème Eggs* is also focused during its four-month availability.

(*Source:* Emma Reynolds, 'Is Cadbury silly to keep Crème Eggs seasonal?', *Marketing*, 19 April 2001, p. 17)

Nectar

Throughout the 1990s the growth of loyalty cards was rapid. Most consumers soon had a purse or wallet jam-packed with brand-led or retailer-focused loyalty cards, such as the Boots *Advantage Card*, DIY chain Homebase's *Spend & Save*, *Marriott Rewards* from the hotel chain, *More* from music store MVC, *Recognition Frasercard* from department store group House of Fraser, and *Clubcard* from supermarketer Tesco. These cards enabled customers of these businesses to claim price discounts, special offers or to build up 'points' which could be redeemed against subsequent purchases or be used to claim prizes such as short holidays or theatre tickets. Irrespective of a scheme's detail, these various loyalty programmes were all designed to enable the host company to build up on-going customer loyalty and to learn more about their customers' spending habits and characteristics. With the notable exception of the BA-inspired Air Miles loyalty scheme, the vast majority of customer loyalty card schemes were linked solely to one brand or retailer. Air Miles were awarded by a host of member consortium businesses to their customers.

Marketing research at the start of the current millennium, however, revealed increasing levels of consumer dissatisfaction with these schemes. Consumers felt that the rewards were often minimal and that the schemes were unwieldy to use, claiming the expected reward was often far from straightforward, and – above all – consumers voiced the opinion that their purses and wallets could no longer cope with the number of cards. Many consumers stated that they no longer utilized loyalty cards in their possession and many refused to accept newly offered cards even from retailers they visited frequently. One response has been the 'collective' loyalty card, with simplified and automated rewards, such as *Nectar*. Now with additional partners such as Thresher and Ford, the original launch was jointly led by Sainsbury's, Barclaycard, Debenhams and BP. *Nectar* businesses discarded their existing loyalty card schemes in preference for *Nectar*. By enabling the consumer to present *Nectar* at many retailers and in numerous transactions across a range of purchases, *Nectar* was a direct response to consumers' desires for a different type of loyalty card. *Nectar* is an example of marketers identifying consumer wishes and responding to dislikes, with a product more in tune with evolving consumer usage than the previous generation of loyalty schemes.

(*Sources:* Sainsbury's; Nectar/Loyalty Management; Mark Kleinman in *Marketing*, 6 November 2003, p. 70)

Test yourself

Case question

1 How did marketing research of consumers' use of loyalty cards impact on the formation of *Nectar*?

Quick questions

2 How can *marketing* be defined?
3 Explain the major components of a marketing strategy.

Applied question

4 You have been appointed as marketing manager for a small business that previously did not have a formal marketing function. In order to educate other senior managers about the application of marketing principles, prepare a report explaining the underlying principles of the marketing concept and detail how these could be applied in the business. The business can trade in an area of your choice.

Extra readings

Baker, M. (2002) 'What is Marketing?', in M. Baker (ed.), *The Marketing Book*. Oxford: Butterworth-Heinemann.

Day, G.S. (1999) *The Market Driven Organization: Attracting and Keeping Valuable Customers*. New York: Free Press.

Dibb, S., Simkin, L., Pride, W. and Ferrell, O.C. (2001) *Marketing: Concepts and Strategies*. Boston, MA: Houghton Mifflin.

Hart, S. (2003) 'Marketing Changes', in M. Baker (ed.), *The Marketing Book*. London: Thomson Learning.

Kotler, P. (2003) *Marketing Insights from A to Z: 80 Concepts Every Manager Needs to Know*. Hoboken, NJ: Wiley.

2: Relationship Marketing

Key definitions

Relationship marketing develops on-going relationships with customers by focusing on maintaining links between marketing, quality and customer service.

The six markets of relationship marketing are customer markets, influencers, referral, employee recruitment, suppliers and internal markets within the business.

Key issues

- Relationship marketing has become popular in recent years. It emphasizes maintaining on-going relationships with existing customers, rather than focusing only on attracting new customers. The intention is to gain a greater proportion of an existing customer's purchases over a prolonged period.
- While not revolutionary – marketers have always sought brand loyalty from their customers – the relationship marketing concept has forced marketers to more properly develop customer service initiatives and programmes for maintaining links with existing customers.
- The supporters of relationship marketing argue that most traditional marketing activity is 'transaction-based', primarily seeking new customers or brand switchers from competing brands. Relationship marketing puts more focus on enhancing the relationship with existing customers and on the lifetime value of the relationship.
- The need to develop long-term relationships with customers has encouraged marketers to more overtly examine ways in which such relationships can be fostered. In addition, relationship marketers believe such customer relationships will not readily materialize without efforts to also market to (a) influencers, (b) referral markets, (c) employment/recruitment markets, (d) suppliers, and (e) the internal workforce.

Conceptual overview

Relationship marketing has recently attracted considerable attention in the marketing literature. It focuses on the interaction between buyers and sellers and is concerned with winning and keeping customers by maintaining links between marketing, product/service quality and customer service. The term 'relationship marketing' was first proposed by Berry in the early 1980s, who defined it as 'attracting, maintaining and – in multi-service organizations – enhancing customer relationships'. Berry described relationship marketing as a 'new–old concept': merchants have always endeavoured to maintain customer favour and loyalty and many marketers anyway devote huge marketing resource to seeking customer brand loyalty.

The basic proposition of relationship marketing is that selling organizations should take a longer-term view of customer relationships to ensure that those customers converted are also retained. The implication is that for too long marketing has focused only on attracting new customers. While it is obviously financially crucial to attract new customers, there is a logic in also devoting marketing expertise to retaining customers. Effective customer service and a commitment to provide effective and reassuring on-going support to current customers are pivotal to the relationship marketing concept.

The origins of relationship marketing, therefore, are in services marketing, the network approach to industrial marketing and the field of quality management. Recently, relationship marketing has had a major impact upon the marketing discipline. There has been a shift from transaction-based marketing towards an on-going relationship focus. According to Cranfield's Adrian Payne, 'transaction marketing of the 1980s placed the emphasis on the individual sale: relationship marketing of the 1990s placed the emphasis on individual customers and sought to establish a long-term relationship between customer and company'.

The emphasis of relationship marketing is on the share of the individual's purchasing rather than the share of the overall market, with concentration on customer retention and repeat buying through an on-going responsive dialogue. The focus is on extracting more sales from existing customers through marketing activity, rather than marketing programmes designed to attract new customers. Marketers develop a more detailed, on-going understanding of the customer, engaging in a dialogue that aims to enhance the buyer–seller relationship and to continually offer product and customer service in an attractive proposition that is regularly updated. Customer relationship management (CRM), supported significantly these days by IT-based systems, is closely linked to the concept of relationship marketing (cf. Brief 8).

On-going, longer-term relationships are essential for a business's viability and market performance. While marketers are encouraged to devote greater resources to developing such customer relationships, the relationship marketing literature explains that such long-term commitment stems not only from treating customers differently, but also from addressing other audiences. To emphasize this, Cranfield's Martin Christopher and colleagues proposed *the six markets* model (cf. Figure 2.1).

Figure 2.1 The markets of relationship marketing

(*Source:* M. Christopher, A. Payne and D. Ballantyne, *Relationship Marketing*, Second Edition, Oxford: Butterworth-Heinemann, 2002)

The rationale for the *six markets* model – the domains of relationship marketing – is that while customer markets should remain the core focus for marketing activity (to attract new customers and satisfy existing ones), to facilitate the organization's on-going commitment and success, attention should be given to developing marketing and communications programmes which convey corporate goals and marketing strategies to a variety of other audiences and stakeholders. These other 'domains' include influencers (such as the EU, government or financial bodies), those referring customers (such as brokers and advisers), employment agencies, suppliers and the internal workforce. In highlighting this final 'market', relationship marketers are acknowledging the damage that can be done if employees do not understand their role in ensuring marketing recommendations are adequately actioned (cf. Brief 40). Without the commitment and understanding of these other markets, a business will find it more difficult to look after its priority market customers effectively.

The buyer behaviour literature is full of calls to ensure customer loyalty, so the relationship marketing concept is not totally revolutionary, more evolutionary. It has made clear the importance of addressing not only new customers, but many other target audiences including suppliers and internal employees. Perhaps it is more that relationship marketers are redressing something of an imbalance. Until recently too much of marketing effort concentrated on attracting customers as opposed to retaining them. Most marketing-led businesses now have customer service teams and customer handling programmes designed to foster a positive relationship post purchase (cf. Briefs 8, 40 and 50). Relationship marketing has forced businesses to work harder to maintain customer satisfaction and to strive to keep the interest and loyalty of their present customers.

Examples

British Gas

For many years, gas and electricity suppliers operated in a competition-free zone. In recent times deregulation of national markets has meant that providers must trade in a competitive environment giving customers a choice about their energy provider. In the UK gas market, within the first five years of deregulation approaching one third of customers decided to switch to a new supplier. For British Gas, previously the sole provider of gas to the UK market, the loss of around six million customer accounts highlighted the importance of relationship building and customer retention programmes. In response to this threat, the company launched a major customer retention programme, involving an advertising campaign that focused on the number of people deciding to switch back to British Gas as a provider. By 2004, the company's strategy had worked: 12 million accounts and top ranking in research firm JD Power's customer satisfaction survey.

(*Sources:* Sonoo Singh, 'British Gas to launch defensive ad campaign', *Marketing Week*, 12 April 2001, p. 8; JD Power, 2003; British Gas website, 2004)

Chrysler

Relationship marketing is not simply about an organization 'getting to know' its customers. As car company Chrysler realized, it is also essential to build strong relationships with suppliers. There is considerable evidence that when an organization develops close ties with its partners, the enhanced level of understanding that results allows all parties to respond better to the needs of each other. For Chrysler, developing its partnerships with supplying organizations had a clear and substantive impact upon its competitiveness and profitability. The full impact of the process can be understood by considering four particular outcomes from the efforts to develop supplier links.

First, the company reduced the timeframe for product development by around 40%. Supplying companies were also involved at a much earlier point in the cycle. Second, the costs of vehicle development were cut. This outcome is related to the first, with costs being reduced because of the shorter timescale of product development and the greater level of supplier involvement. For example, by seeking opinions from partners at an early stage, fewer changes were required late on in the process. Many of the company's models are highly price-competitive as a result, such as the whacky MPV the PT Cruiser. Third, the company reduced its number of suppliers, developing a leaner purchasing system. This reduced the number of buying staff required and therefore lowered procurement costs. Finally, the changes that Chrysler made led to increases in market share and profitability. With profit-per-vehicle figures rising from just $250 to $2000 over a ten-year period, it is easy to see why Chrysler took the trouble to invest in its supplier relationships. A range of innovative models that are highly price-competitive emerged from the process, including the Neon, Crossfire, Voyager and PT Cruiser.

(*Sources:* J.H. Dyer (1996) 'How Chrysler created an American Keiretsu', *Harvard Business Review*, 74 (July/August), pp. 46–7; *What Car?* website, 2004)

Test yourself

Case question

1 Supplier relationships are just one type of linkage at the heart of relationship marketing. What other relationships must Chrysler develop and why?

Quick questions

2 What is relationship marketing?
3 Why is customer retention so important to relationship marketing and what is the link with loyalty programmes?

Applied question

4 Prepare a report that explains the key features of the *six markets* model and explain the implications for a company with which you are familiar.

Extra readings

Berry, L.L., Shostack, G.L. and Upah, G. (eds) (1983) *Emerging Perspectives on Services.* Chicago, IL: American Marketing Association.

Buttle, F. (1996) *Relationship Marketing: Theory and Practice.* London: Chapman.

Chaffey, D., Mayer, R., Johnston, K. and Ellis-Chadwick, F. (2000) *Internet Marketing.* Harlow: Pearson/FT.

Christopher, M., Payne, A. and Ballantyne, D. (2002) *Relationship Marketing: Creating Shareholder Value.* Oxford: Butterworth-Heinemann.

Cram, T. (1994) *The Power of Relationship Marketing: Keeping Customers for Life.* Harlow: Pearson/FT.

Gummesson, R. (2002) *Total Relationship Marketing: Rethinking Relationship Marketing Management.* Oxford: Butterworth-Heinemann.

3: Marketing Orientation

Key definitions

A *marketing orientation* involves a clear customer focus, understanding and staying in touch with customer needs and buying behaviour so that appropriate product offerings can be developed.

Marketing orientation entails customer orientation, competitor orientation and interfunctional coordination.

Key issues

- There are various philosophical approaches to business. Some companies have a marketing orientation, while others are financially, sales or production oriented.
- Businesses that are marketing oriented are different from those with a production orientation. Those with a marketing orientation assume that being customer focused drives organizational performance. Production oriented businesses emphasize production capabilities and tend to be cost focused. Scale economies are sought so that production costs can be minimized. A considerable sales effort is then devoted to selling as many products as possible.
- Companies with a marketing orientation are widely believed to enjoy enhanced business performance. Research suggests that such performance improvements are brought about by a combination of customer orientation, competitor orientation and interfunctional coordination (communication between and integration of different business functions).
- Businesses that are marketing oriented understand that customer needs are dynamic and are ready to respond innovatively to their changing requirements. This requires excellent marketing intelligence from a variety of internal and external sources. A clear understanding of the business's competitive position is also needed. By balancing all of this information with the company's distinctive competencies, appropriate opportunities can be pursued and a suitable competitive advantage developed. Close attention to implementation requirements is then required to ensure that the strategy is enacted.

Conceptual overview

Companies have different philosophical approaches to doing business. Some have a marketing orientation, while others have a financial, sales or production orientation. A marketing orientation involves a clear customer focus, understanding and staying in touch with customer needs and buying behaviour so that appropriate product offerings can be developed. While businesses with a marketing orientation put customers at the centre of their activities, those that are financially oriented seek short-term returns above all else. Businesses with a sales orientation are motivated by the desire to sell as many products as possible and are concerned with sales volumes rather than customer value.

A marketing orientation is different from a production orientation in a number of key ways. Businesses with a production orientation tend to be highly cost focused, striving to attain scale economies and minimize production costs. The production capabilities of the company are at the core of the philosophy. Once products have been made, a heavy sales effort is instigated to persuade customers – who may or may not have expressed a desire to do so – to buy. Often these businesses define themselves in terms of the products that are produced. For example, some telecommunications companies did not initially realize the competitive threat posed by mobile phones because most customers retained their domestic land line telephone. If these companies had considered their business in a more marketing oriented manner, they might have recognized that they were competing in the communications rather than the land line telephone market.

Companies with a marketing orientation are primarily concerned with understanding and satisfying customer needs, then responding with an appropriate marketing offer. Some marketers even use the terms customer orientation and marketing orientation interchangeably. A marketing oriented business recognizes the dynamic nature of customer needs and understands that it must remain closely in touch with its customer base. Excellent marketing intelligence is a key requirement, whether obtained from company records and contacts, marketing research or other sources (cf. Brief 9). This intelligence helps businesses to identify marketing opportunities so that the products that customers want to buy can be manufactured.

The business argument for this approach, supported by a growing body of research, is that companies adopting a marketing orientation achieve improved business performance. Much of this research highlights the behavioural components that make up marketing orientation. Customer orientation, competitor orientation and interfunctional coordination (communication between and integration of different business functions), are all seen to contribute to making businesses marketing oriented.

It is reasonably straightforward to identify businesses with a marketing orientation. According to Jobber, such companies exhibit the following characteristics:

- Customer concern shown throughout the business.
- Customer choice criteria known and matched with a marketing mix.

- Segmentation by customer differences.
- Investment in marketing research and market changes tracked.
- Welcome change.
- Try to understand competition.
- Marketing spend is regarded as an investment.
- Innovation rewarded.
- Search for latent markets.
- Fast to innovate and to undertake marketing tasks.
- Strive for competitive advantage.

As this list indicates, a marketing orientation involves much more than just being customer focused. Once an excellent and up-to-date understanding of customers has been achieved, the information must be disseminated to all parts of the business. The intention is that irrespective of where they are made, all decisions will be informed by an understanding of the customer. The interfunctional coordination that helps this communication to be achieved can also facilitate other interactions between functions. This is important because barriers between departments inhibit the innovative thinking associated with a marketing orientation (cf. Brief 37).

The marketing oriented business must also adopt a market-led approach to its activities and strive to develop a competitive advantage. Achieving this requires the business to combine its customer understanding with a realistic view of its competitive position as well as the general trading environment. At the same time, a careful appraisal of company assets is required to ensure a suitable match with the opportunities pursued. Once decisions about which opportunities to pursue have been made, the role of marketing implementation in achieving marketing orientation comes to the fore. This is where carefully considered and marketing oriented strategies are put into practice. Failure to attend to the detailed issues associated with actioning the strategy will negate the benefits of being marketing oriented in the first place.

Examples

Perrier

Most people are familiar with the traditional green glass *Perrier* bottle that has for so long been a feature of the mineral water market. Following an 11-year development process, Nestlé, owner of the *Perrier* brand, launched a plastic alternative. While being excited by the development, the company was also keen to protect the image of its existing packaging, explaining that the more formal glass container would continue to be available in a range of sizes. This helped ensure that the brand maintained its connections with the restaurant market, for which this packaging style is appropriate. However, Nestlé is also keen to make *Perrier* more easily available to consumers on the move. The new 50 cl plastic bottle, which adopts a modern take on the traditional green styling, should make the product more accessible to this sizeable market. The innovation will also help *Perrier* compete more effectively against rivals already serving these consumers with plastic bottles. Nestlé is hopeful that initial sales of around 16 million of the new bottles may eventually rise to almost ten times that amount. Innovations with packaging are integral to Nestlé's business philosophy: the packaging aims for *Perrier*, now established in over 160 countries, are to conform to health regulations in its markets, ensure product quality and to meet the expectations of consumers in a way that favourably compares with its competitors. Recently, reflecting consumer desires for flavoured water and more healthy lifestyles, Nestlé has introduced *Perrier Fluo*, a range of bubbling low-sugar drinks mixing *Perrier* with plant and fruit natural extracts.

(*Sources:* 'Nestlé ready to roll out Perrier in plastic bottles', *Marketing Week*, 3 May 2001, p. 7; Nestlé Waters website, 2004; www.cokepubsandbar.co.uk, 2004)

Ziploc

DowBrands knows that being customer oriented is a key part of marketing orientation. So when Dow bought the rights to produce plastic bags with a zip, the company applied itself to making the best product that it could. Branded as *Ziploc*, the premium priced bags with the leak-proof seal were launched in the US in 1972. By the mid-1970s, *Ziploc* was clear leader for storage bags, with market share of a third. On-going consumer research demonstrated that the bags were being used in a variety of ways: for storage in fridges and food cupboards, to carry pre-packed food and for freezer storage. Once it understood consumers' usage patterns, the company was able to emphasize the applications of its bags in its promotional material. The increasing importance of freezer use later led Dow to introduce a new product line particularly for these conditions.

Being customer oriented has been all the more important to Dow because of its stated aim to command a premium price for its storage bag brand. The company's philosophy has been to protect *Ziploc*'s price by adding value to the product. This philosophy continued to prevail when Dow acquired First Brands/Europe (FBE), with the intention of growing international sales. A full assessment of the European potential for *Ziploc* was made, following a detailed programme of consumer research that studied the use of packing materials in different countries. The research revealed, for example, that the 'air-tight' features of *Ziploc* would be popular, but that the best opportunity for entry into the British market was through sandwich-bags, whereas the German market might respond more to the *Ziploc* freezer bags. By understanding the subtleties of consumer needs in these countries, Dow was improving its chances of a successful competitive assault.

(*Source:* M. Kotabe and K. Helsen, *Global Marketing Management*, New York: Wiley, 2001, pp. 644–61)

Test yourself

Case question

1 What role is customer orientation playing in helping Dow develop a marketing orientation?

Quick questions

2 What is a marketing orientation?
3 Using examples to illustrate your answer, explain the connection between marketing orientation and company profitability.

Applied question

4 You have recently been appointed as Marketing Director for a company that manufactures and fits double-glazing and conservatories. The company has previously not employed a Marketing Director and has adopted a sales oriented approach to its business. You have been asked to make a presentation to your fellow Board members explaining the difference between a sales and a marketing orientation. Your presentation should also contain some recommendations about how the business could become more marketing oriented.

Extra readings

Day, G.S. (1999) *The Market Driven Organization: Attracting and Keeping Valuable Customers.* New York: Free Press.
Jobber, D. (2004) *Principles and Practice of Marketing.* Maidenhead: McGraw-Hill.
Kotler, P. (2003) *Marketing Management.* Englewood Cliffs, NJ: Pearson.
Levitt, T. (1986) *The Marketing Imagination.* New York: Free Press.
Narver, J.C. and Slater, S.F. (1990) 'The Effect of Market Orientation on Business Profitability', *Journal of Marketing*, 54 (4), pp. 20–35.

4: The Marketing Environment

Key definitions

The *marketing environment* is defined as the external forces that directly or indirectly influence an organization's capability to undertake its business.

The *macro marketing environment* consists of six core forces: political, legal, regulatory, societal/green, technological, plus economic/competitive issues.

The *micro marketing environment* includes more company-specific forces: types of competition, supplier power, buyer power, and a business's other publics.

Environmental scanning is the process of collecting information about the forces of the marketing environment.

A *strategic window* is a major development or opportunity triggered by change in the marketing environment.

Key issues

- The marketing environment consists of trading forces operating in a marketplace over which a business has no direct control, but these forces will shape the manner in which the business functions and is able to satisfy its customers.
- Owing to the 'beyond direct control' aspect, too many organizations fail to adequately monitor the key forces of their marketing environment. Those businesses that do assess evolving trends and the implications from environmental change, tend (a) not to encounter as many market-driven crises, and (b) often gain a competitive advantage over rivals that have failed to understand the implications from a particular environmental occurrence.
- The macro marketing environment forces are the 'big' issues that affect all businesses active in a particular market and indeed all customers in a target market segment. While individual businesses or customers may well be better placed to accommodate such issues and their implications, these forces do affect everyone in a market.
- The macro forces were first identified by economists in a PEST analysis (cf. Brief 5): Political, Economic, Social, Technological factors. Marketers more commonly discuss six components, with the addition of Regulatory and Legal forces.
- The micro forces owe much to the work of Michael Porter in the 1970s and include all aspects of competition – direct rivals, new entrants, substitute competition – plus the relative power of buyers and suppliers, and the influence of an organization's many other publics (employees, shareholders, financial backers, regulatory authorities, etc.). While the macro forces impact on all players in a market, the micro forces have a more variable impact on separate businesses trading in a particular market.
- An understanding of macro and micro marketing environment forces may help a business to compete more effectively against its rivals, but in addition may enable an organization to take advantage of emerging strategic windows and opportunities.

Conceptual overview

Many organizations strive to understand customer requirements and some evaluate their competitors. A core marketing analysis commonly not conducted is an assessment of the marketing environment and the associated implications for a business. Organizations that do effectively monitor their marketing environment tend not to fall foul of unexpected regulatory, political, economic, legal, social or economic change. More proactive businesses that devote some resource to tracking the forces of their marketing environment may well find they identify an emerging opportunity in the market – caused by environmental change – before their rivals. They can thus take advantage of this strategic window.

The very broad forces operating around all suppliers and customers in a marketplace are termed by marketers as the macro marketing environment forces. These include:

1 Political forces. Different political parties have varying stances which impact on certain markets, products or services: capital projects may benefit under the Conservatives, whereas health and education services have grown under Labour.
2 Legal forces. Pro-competitive legislation, such as the role in the UK of the Competition Commission or Office of Fair Trading, is in operation in most countries and is enacted by the EU. Similarly, legislation protecting the consumer.
3 Regulatory forces. Government ministries, local authorities or councils and trade bodies – such as television's ITC – all create and enforce regulations or codes of practice.
4 Societal forces. Consumers increasingly stand up for their rights, often through key campaigning individuals or groups. The green movement has seen consumers become more aware of pollution and ecological concerns, with resulting implications for many producers.
5 Technological forces. Technological advances impact on products, producers, consumers, society, regulators and therefore on marketers.
6 Economic forces. General business trends, prosperity, recession, buying power, wealth, willingness to spend, consumer spending patterns are just some of the broader economic concerns of marketers. The nature of competition – monopoly, oligopoly, monopolistic, perfect – and the impact of competitors are fundamental issues for marketers and their development of strategies and marketing programmes.

Michael Porter has taken this final ingredient of the macro marketing environment and researched the more micro elements of competition, recognizing that while micro forces – as with the broader macro forces – are beyond a business's direct control, they have a more variable impact on separate businesses in a particular market. Each business has different strengths, weaknesses, resources, cultures, management structures and philosophies. Each is differently placed to respond to these micro forces. Suppliers are integral to a business's viability, but one supplier may be more favourably disposed to one of its customers than to the others, and in times of short supply may safeguard the fortunes of its favoured customer. This applies also to the marketing intermediaries (cf. Brief 28) – such as dealers, distributors, agents, brokers, wholesalers, retailers – on whom most businesses depend for the delivery of their products to the consumer. Buyers, too, have a fickleness and variable loyalty to suppliers. Porter's prime concern is the nature of competition. A new product launch by a major rival will impact to variable degrees on its competitors. Most businesses consider only like-for-like competitors (cf. Brief 34). It is important to watch out for new entrants coming into a market: Daewoo in the European car market or Dyson stealing leadership from Hoover in the vacuum cleaner wars. Substitute solutions to a customer's problem should also be studied: micro-bore tunnelling moles negating the need for a JCB backhoe digging a trench.

Marketing oriented businesses often allocate the separate forces of the marketing environment to individual managers or to small work teams. These personnel snip press cuttings, collate customer, dealer or salesforce feedback, occasionally commission bespoke research, interview media pundits or technical experts, and generally 'keep their ears to the ground' in an effort to understand the emerging issues. Company intranets, mail systems and Web-based information searches, have helped speed up these activities in recent years.

Knowledge of these trends and emerging environmental issues may help a business understand the potential of new technology, target new markets, utilize innovative distribution channels, redefine market priorities, keep abreast of new legislation and technology, while avoiding financial or political shocks. An understanding of the marketing environment will assist a business in identifying strategic windows and opportunities.

Examples

BMW

BMW is one of many organizations that has responded to consumer concerns about the environment. This important social issue increasingly shapes the kinds of products that people are willing to buy and use. By stressing the 'recyclability' of its cars in its promotional activity, BMW is attempting to be responsive to what customers want. The company highlights that its *3 Series* is manufactured to high environmental standards and that production processes are friendlier to the environment. Many of the car's components can be recycled. BMW has even built its own recycling factories, which specialize in disposing of vehicles that have reached the end of their usable life. The company has also lobbied for a Europe-wide initiative for enforced recycling, where certificates must be issued to confirm that cars have been disposed of through authorized recycling companies.

(*Source:* John Eisenhammer, 'Where cars will go when they die', *The Independent on Sunday*, 21 February 1993, pp. 24–5)

F1 Grand Prix motor racing

The no-smoking lobby has resulted in considerable restrictions on the promotion of tobacco products. Many governments no longer allow television advertising and increasing numbers of employers are restricting smoking on their premises. Entertainment venues, restaurants and travel operators are also moving against smoking. Recent EU rules to outlaw tobacco advertising of all kinds look set to have a major impact on F1 Grand Prix motor racing. For decades, much of the sport's sponsorship has come from the tobacco industry. The reason for the tobacco industry's love affair with F1 is straightforward. Sponsorship and the advertising opportunities that accompany it, allow companies like Gallagher and BAT to promote their brands to a huge world-wide audience. Trackside advertising and cars designed to depict leading cigarette brands are just some of the promotional routes that have been open to these businesses.

From 2006, the situation will change. From then, European law demands that all tobacco advertising must be removed from the F1 cars. However, these restrictions only apply to EU members and it seems that governments in other parts of the world may be more relaxed about cigarette advertising. FIA, the F1 governing body, has therefore nurtured hopes that it might relocate the sport to new venues. After all, the current F1 circuit already includes venues outside of Europe. Unfortunately for FIA, many of the new venue options are located around the Pacific Rim region, where economic problems have seriously restricted the governing body's options. Whether these environmental difficulties will abate to allow F1 to overcome its current problems, remains to be seen. The new Malaysian circuit, though, bodes well of FIA.

(*Sources:* Roger Baird, 'Winning formula', *Marketing Week*, 4 March 1999, pp. 37–8; Richenda Wilson, 'Race against time', *Marketing Week*, 21 January 1999, pp. 51–3)

Test yourself

Case question

1 In what ways is the marketing environment impinging upon F1?

Quick questions

2 Why is it important for organizations to have a sound understanding of the marketing environment?

3 What are the elements of the marketing environment? Give examples of each, using an industry of your choice.

Applied question

4 Write a report that describes the marketing environment forces impacting upon the airline industry. You should provide a detailed explanation of which are the key forces and state why.

Extra readings

Brownlie, D. (1994) 'Organising for Environmental Scanning: Orthodoxies and Reformations', *Journal of Marketing Management*, 10 (8), pp. 703–24.

Dibb, S., Simkin, L. and Bradley, J. (1998) *The Marketing Planning Workbook*. London: Thomson.

Drucker, P. (1981) *Management in Turbulent Times*. London: Butterworth-Heinemann/Pan.

Jain, S.C. (1999) *Marketing Planning & Strategy*. Cincinnati, OH: South Western.

Porter, M. (1979) 'How Competitive Forces Shape Strategy', *Harvard Business Review* (March/April), pp. 137–45.

Peattie, K. (1995) *Environmental Marketing Management*. London: Pitman.

5: PEST and SWOT Analyses

Key definitions

Economists conduct *PEST analyses* of markets, examining political, economic, social and technological forces.

The *macro marketing environment* includes: political, legal, regulatory, societal/green, technological, economic and competitive forces.

The *SWOT analysis* is an evaluation of an organization's strengths, weaknesses, opportunities and threats.

Marketing assets are capabilities that managers and the marketplace view as being beneficially strong.

Key issues

- Marketers examine the forces of the macro and micro marketing environment. The macro forces are the broad forces that impact on all businesses trading in a particular market (cf. Brief 4).
- Analysis of the macro environmental forces enables the unexpected to be pre-empted and strategic windows to be turned into tangible business opportunities.
- The SWOT analysis makes use of the understanding of the marketing environment in its examination of opportunities and threats. These are issues external to the business in question. The strengths and weaknesses of the SWOT analysis are internal operational, marketing mix, resource, skill and management issues.
- Many SWOT analyses are too subjective and quickly produced to be meaningful. Nevertheless, with rigour applied, this very simple analysis can prove invaluable to marketing strategy development and marketing planning (cf. Brief 36).
- The examination of marketing assets breaks down an organization's strengths in terms of (a) customer-based assets, (b) distribution-based assets, and (c) internal marketing assets. This classification of marketing assets is part of an attempt to encourage marketers to identify and maximize their capabilities *vis-à-vis* competitors (cf. Briefs 33 and 34).

Conceptual overview

An understanding of the marketing environment can pre-empt crises occurring as a result of changes in the broader trading environment and should enable a business to take advantage of emerging strategic windows of opportunity. The well-known PEST analysis examines four core ingredients of the macro marketing environment: political, economic, social and technological forces. However, it is important to also monitor the additional forces of the marketing-defined macro and micro marketing environment (cf. Brief 4). Individual managers in conjunction with other line tasks, project teams or senior strategists can be deployed to monitor these forces, utilizing press clippings, fieldforce, distributor and customer feedback, the views of colleagues, expert opinion, information libraries, Web searches, the media and their own experiences. Emergent key issues can then be evaluated in more detail.

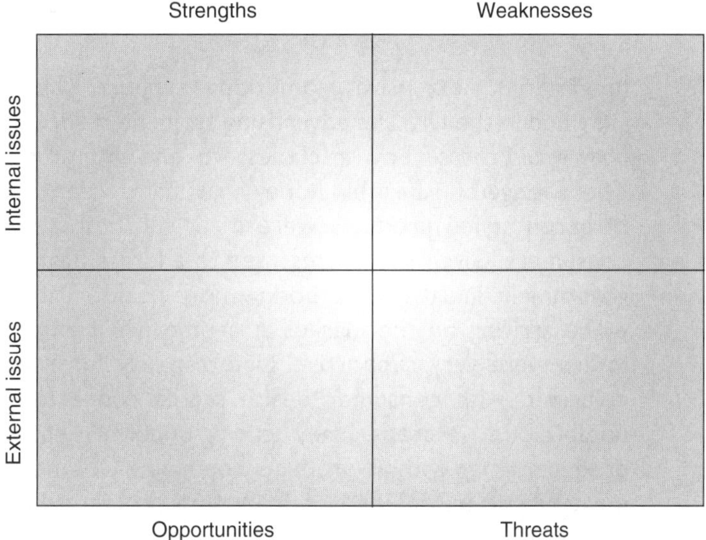

Figure 5.1 The SWOT grid

The SWOT analysis examines a business's position, resources, management and trading practices, product, people, promotion, pricing and distribution in terms of internal operational, resource and organizational strengths and weaknesses. Those issues that are visible to targeted customers and place the business at a disadvantage versus competitors should be prioritized for remedial action. The SWOT utilizes a marketing department's understanding of the marketing environment to identify key externally oriented opportunities and threats. In any SWOT, the points cited must be objectively considered with supporting evidence to justify their inclusion, they should be presented in ranked order of importance, while their implications for the business should be identified and stated.

The notion of marketing assets is not widely adopted in practice, but it usefully breaks down an organization's strengths in terms of (a) customer-based assets – brand image and reputation, for example, (b) distribution-based assets – density of dealerships, geographic network coverage, in-store shelf space allocation, and (c) internal marketing assets – skills, experience, economies of scale, technology and resources. Hugh Davidson created this popular classification of marketing assets in an attempt to encourage marketers to identify and maximize their capabilities *vis-à-vis* competitors (cf. Brief 33). The concept relates strongly with the notion of developing a competitive edge or differential advantage (cf. Brief 35).

Examples

Khero

In 1999, with extensive promotional support, Khero meat-free products were launched in the UK. The advertising strapline read, *well, well, well, the new food your body would choose*. Low in cholesterol and saturated fat and rich in protein, the Khero range of wafer thin honey roast ham, wafer thin roast chicken and rashers of bacon styled products were meat substitutes targeted at health-conscious consumers. Given social pressures to address health and to improve diets, plus government initiatives promoting more healthy eating, the Khero range seemed to be arriving on the market at a time when external marketing environment forces were very supportive. Unfortunately for Khero, the high profile launch coincided with consumer health scares connected with GM-modified foods, notably of soya crops. Many leading supermarket chains withdrew soya-based products, along with all products containing GM-modified ingredients. Khero, the meat substitute, was derived from soya protein isolate. Despite months of planning, Khero's marketers had not anticipated the sudden eruption of consumer aggression towards GM-modified foods, with the associated implications for soya-based products.

(*Sources:* Khero's advertising; Sally Dibb and Lyndon Simkin, *The Marketing Casebook*, London: Thomson, 2001)

Cruise missiles

A leading defence business attempted to diversify into non-defence markets in order to leverage its perceived competencies. The sensors and motor drives it manufactured were seen as state-of-the art in the defence market, for weapons systems and radar. While a global leader in these fields, outside of the defence sector, the multinational was not well known. The company targeted three sectors it thought had opportunities for its skills and products: oil drilling, hospital monitoring equipment and alarm – security and fire – sensors. Marketing managers undertook SWOT analyses for these three sectors, with results that surprised senior managers.

The oil drilling market was in decline and had established suppliers already battling for the shrinking sales. The opportunities for the business to enter this sector were not great, while the competitive pressure and declining market were significant threats. The business had few strengths with which to pursue this target market and insurmountable weaknesses in terms of poor brand awareness amongst targeted companies, no track record and a steep learning curve for its personnel. In the other two sectors, however, there was real growth potential owing to expanding markets, synergies with existing products and the existing use by targeted customers of some of the company's other technologies. Although this defence business needed to create a more favourable brand attitude and establish brand awareness more widely in these markets, the SWOT analyses revealed very strong prospects.

(*Sources:* Sally Dibb and Lyndon Simkin, *The Marketing Planning Workbook*, London: Thomson, 1996; the UK defence industry, 2001)

Test yourself

Case question

1 Why was it important for the missile and radar producer to properly analyse the non-defence possible marketing opportunities identified by its senior managers?

Quick questions

2 What is environmental scanning?

3 Outline the core ingredients of the marketing environment and how they might impact on a marketing strategy.

Applied question

4 As a marketing manager, you have been tasked to evaluate the sales potential for your company's products in a newly identified overseas market. Why should you conduct PEST and SWOT analyses? Prepare a report explaining the roles of these analyses and why you have opted to conduct them.

Extra readings

Aaker, D. (2001) *Strategic Marketing Management*. New York: Wiley.
Adcock, D. (2000) *Marketing Strategies for Competitive Advantage.* Chichester: Wiley.
Brownlie, D. (1994) 'Organising for Environmental Scanning: Orthodoxies and Reformations', *Journal of Marketing Management*, 10 (8), pp. 703–24.
Dibb, S., Simkin, L. and Bradley, J. (1998) *The Marketing Planning Workbook.* London: Thomson.
Jain, S.C. (1999) *Marketing Planning and Strategy*. Cincinnati, OH: South Western.
Peattie, K. (1995) *Environmental Marketing Management.* London: Pitman.

6: Consumer Buying Behaviour

Key definitions

Consumer buyer behaviour focuses on the decision processes and acts of individuals involved in buying and using products for personal or household use.

Routine response behaviour occurs when purchasing frequently bought, low-cost, low-risk items, requiring little search and decision effort.

Limited decision-making is for products purchased occasionally, for which some information gathering and deliberation are needed.

Extensive decision-making occurs for unfamiliar, expensive, infrequent or high-risk purchases where much information gathering and deliberation will be required.

Impulse purchases involve little conscious planning and result from a powerful urge to make the purchase.

The *consumer buying decision process* involves five stages: problem recognition, information search, evaluation of alternatives, purchase, and post-purchase evaluation.

Possible *influences* on the consumer decision process include: personal, psychological and social.

The *level of involvement* is the level of interest, emotional commitment and time spent on a particular purchase.

The *evoked set* is the group of products a buyer views as possible alternatives after conducting the information search.

A *reference group* is that with which a consumer identifies and to which he/she looks for his/her values. An *opinion leader* is a member of the reference group who appears knowledgeable about the particular product in question.

Key issues

- Consumer buyer behaviour is a core understanding for marketers, who must know the thought processes, influencing factors, expectations and perceptions of consumers as they go through the buying decision-making process.
- For some frequently purchased, cheap, low-risk products such as newspapers, beverages or cigarettes, there is hardly any decision-making and such purchasing is known as routine response.
- For most products there is some information search prior to a purchase as consumers deliberate between options. In more truncated situations, the purchase is known as limited decision-making, whereas in more risky situations – high cost, product longevity, unfamiliar product category, infrequent purchasing – the process is regarded as exhibiting extensive decision-making.
- Impulse buying is at odds with all of these options. This is when the consumer is driven by an instantaneous and irrepressible urge to buy!
- The buying decision process for consumer products involves: (1) problem recognition (identification of product need); (2) a search for information (from internal memory of previous purchases

and external sources such as peers, the media or sales personnel) to assist in the decision-making and selection of product options; (3) evaluation of the possible options (the evoked set) against personal criteria; (4) the purchase; (5) post-purchase evaluation of the product's benefits and suitability.

- Various influencing factors play a role during the consumer's decision-making: (1) person-specific, such as demographic and situational issues; (2) psychological influences, including individual perceptions, motives and attitudes, plus knowledge of a product and the consumer's personality; (3) social influences, with social class, culture and behaviour playing their part, strongly affected also by family roles, reference groups and messages in the media.
- The consumer buying process is affected by the individual's level of involvement in making a purchase: his/her interest, emotional commitment and time allocation.
- Marketing research, particularly qualitative 'under the skin' research (cf. Brief 9) is very important to marketers striving to properly understand consumer buying behaviour.

Conceptual overview

Marketing exists to identify and satisfy consumer requirements for goods or services (cf. Brief 1). Without an understanding of buying behaviour, it is not possible to be an effective marketer. Marketers should endeavour to understand consumers' decision-making, the influences on this process, and in what way they can manipulate their marketing programmes to reflect these consumer needs and expectations. The 'standard' consumer buying behaviour decision-making process involves (cf. Figure 6.1): (a) recognition by a consumer that there is a problem for which the purchase of a product or service is the likely solution; (b) the seeking of information to assist in selecting viable product or service options; (c) the evaluation of the evoked set of likely options; (d) the final selection and purchase of one product or service; and (e) the on-going post-purchase subjective assessment of whether the specific item purchased was the 'right' one. This final stage will impact on the process next time around.

It is important to recognize that not all purchases pass through all five stages. A brand loyal and contented consumer may start at stage (c). For low-risk, cheap, frequently purchased items such as cigarettes or a newspaper, there will be a quick progression from stage (a) to stage (d), with possibly no utilization of stages (b) or (c). The greater the risk – cost, duration of consumption, unfamiliarity, uncertainty – the more likelihood there is of all five stages coming into play. By understanding which stages feature, a marketer can better tailor a marketing mix programme to appeal to the targeted consumers.

All consumers are different, however, and this in part is a result of their social influences: social class, culture, family roles, reference group membership and grasp of marketing messages in the media. Person-specific influences such as

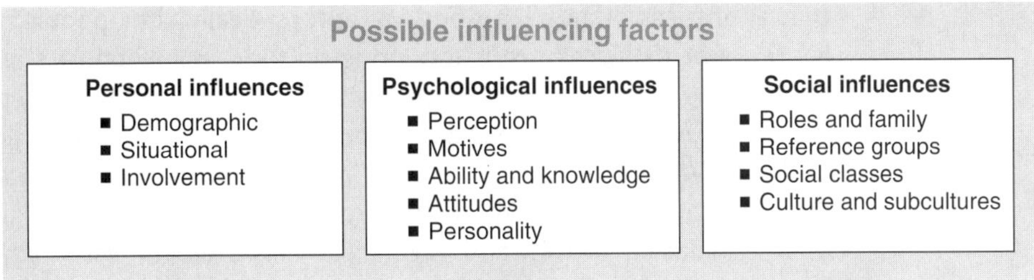

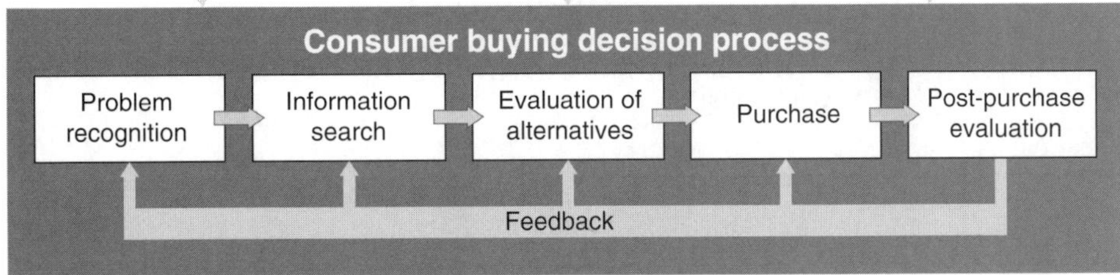

Figure 6.1 The consumer buying decision process

(*Source:* Figure 4.1 in Sally Dibb, Lyndon Simkin, Bill Pride and O.C. Ferrell, *Marketing: Concepts and Strategies*, Boston, MA: Houghton Mifflin, 2001)

demographics and situational factors are very important, as are psychological influences such as perceptions, motives, attitudes towards what and how they purchase, plus the personality of the consumer.

To be successful, a marketer should be able to: (a) profile and describe the targeted consumers; (b) identify their key customer values and needs; (c) understand who else – family members, friends, colleagues – might be involved in the decision-making and in conducting the purchase; (d) identify the stages of the buying decision-making process in the case of their product or service; (e) properly comprehend the influencing factors at play during the decision-making. Armed with this information, a marketer should be better placed to deliver a marketing programme that will satisfy the targeted consumers and in a manner that provides an edge over competing businesses.

Examples

Walkers

A trend in recent years has been towards greater awareness of the importance of healthy eating. While concerns about obesity, particularly among children, imply that awareness of an issue does not automatically alter people's behaviour, there is no doubt that pressure is mounting on food manufacturers and consumers to alter eating habits. Market leading snack food brand Walkers, part of the giant PepsiCo business, has responded by printing nutritional information and advice on packs of Walkers crisps. Tips on multipacks aim to advise parents on how to prepare healthy and balanced lunch-boxes for their children. This includes guidance on the inclusion of fruit and vegetables. This step will assist consumers with an interest in healthy eating in their information search during their buying decision-making and may even help to avoid consumer dissonance amongst Walkers' customer base as health concerns grow.

Sources: Mark Kleinman, *Marketing*, 20 November 2003, p. 1; Walkers, Leicester; *Marketing Week*, 27 November 2003, p. 6)

IKEA

Swedish retailer IKEA has brought a new dimension to the UK furniture market. Founded around 60 years ago, the company has built its success on the sale of good value, stylish products. At the heart of this strategy is the need for a low cost base on which to build competitive prices. By manufacturing in bulk, the company is able to develop significant economies of scale and scope that can then be passed on to the consumer. So long as the company maintains the necessary sales volume, it can continue to offer a wide range of competitively priced products.

IKEA, however, does more than simply sell good value products. The retailer has also managed to capture the imagination of consumers by trying hard to appeal to the consumer reasoning which underlies furniture buying. The company undertakes marketing research to ensure that it understands the practicalities and emotional side of this kind of shopping. IKEA has used this understanding of its customer base in developing its product assortments and designing its stores. In the UK, for example, research has shown that consumers are relatively conservative in their furniture buying and do not frequently alter the style of their living environment. IKEA has attempted to address this directly through a provocative advertising campaign. In terms of store design, IKEA outlets are located close to major motorways and roads and are laid out to ensure the shopping experience is fun. Furniture is set out in room style settings to include everything from the expensive lounge suite and wall cupboards, to carpets, curtains, lighting and low-priced knick-knacks. The intention is to offer consumers inspiration as they are guided through the shopping experience, giving plenty of time to browse and make selections. To make life easier, the stores also have plenty of free parking, childcare, toilets and inexpensive restaurant facilities.

(*Sources:* 'IKEA', *Retail Business – Retail Trade Reviews*, 33, March 1995; Peter Wingard, 'A study of six Swedish firms' approach to marketing', Warwick Business School MBA Programme, 1991; IKEA Birmingham, 2001)

Test yourself

Case question

1 Why is it important for IKEA to have a good understanding of how customers buy its products and how has it used this information to good effect?

Quick questions

2 Why is it important for marketers to understand consumer buying behaviour?
3 What are the different stages of the consumer buying process?

Applied question

4 A shoe retailer is interested in finding out more about the factors that influence the purchase of footwear. Using examples to illustrate your answer, review the different personal, psychological and social influences that might impact upon someone buying a pair of shoes or boots.

Extra readings

Assael, H. (1998) *Consumer Behaviour and Marketing Action.* Cincinnati, OH: South Western.

Blackwell, R.D., Miniard, P.W. and Engel, J.F. (2001) *Consumer Behaviour.* Fort Worth, Tx: West.

Foxall, G., Goldsmith, R.E. and Brown, S. (1998) *Consumer Psychology for Marketing.* London: Thomson Learning.

Lambkin, M., Foxall, G., Van Raaij, F. and Heilbrunn, B. (eds) (1998) *European Perspectives on Consumer Behaviour.* Harlow: Pearson.

Solomon, M., Bamossy, G. and Askegaard, S. (2001) *Consumer Behaviour.* Harlow: Pearson/FT.

7: Business-to-Business Buying Behaviour

Key definitions

Business-to-business buying behaviour is the purchase behaviour of producers, resellers, government units and institutions.

Organizational, or *industrial*, or *business-to-business marketing* is marketing activity targeting other organizations rather than end-user consumers. The customers are manufacturers; channel members such as retailers, wholesalers, agents, brokers, distributors and dealers; public sector bodies; not-for-profit organizations, or government departments.

An *organizational business-to-business market* is made up of individuals or groups that purchase a specific type of product for re-sale, for use in making other products, or for their use in daily operations.

Types of *business-to-business purchases* are: new task, modified re-buy, straight re-buy.

Derived demand is demand for industrial products arising from demand for consumer products (a surge in house building creates demand for construction equipment purchased by house builders).

Inelastic demand is demand that is not significantly affected by a price increase or decrease (a manufacturer requires electricity and telecommunications, irrespective of the price).

Joint demand is demand occurring when two or more products are used in combination to produce a product (a PC producer requires joint supplies of keyboards, chips and VDUs in order to produce a single PC).

The *buying centre* is the group of people within an organization who are involved in making business-to-business purchase decisions.

The business-to-business buying decision process includes six key stages: (a) problem recognition; (b) product/requirement specification; (c) search for suitable products/suppliers; (d) evaluation of options *vis-à-vis* the specified requirement; (e) selection of a supplier and order placement; and finally, (f) evaluation of product and supplier performance.

Principal influencing factors on members of the buying centre include environmental, organizational, interpersonal and individual factors.

Key issues

- The terms industrial marketing, organizational marketing and business-to-business marketing are utilized somewhat interchangeably. The key point is that the customer is not the end user consumer (you). The customer – and target for the marketing programme – is instead another organization.
- Because organizations require supplies in order to operate, their buying decision-making is often more formalized, more drawn out and involves more personnel than the buying decision-making of the private individual consumer.

- Business-to-business buying behaviour relates to the buying decision-making of manufacturers; channel members such as retailers, wholesalers, agents, brokers, distributors and dealers; public sector bodies and institutions; not-for-profit organizations, or government departments.
- An organization's first time purchase for a new product or new problem is known as a new task purchase, and often involves extensive decision-making and search for possible options.
- Most business-to-business purchases are on-going replenishment re-buys, falling into one of two categories. Modified re-buys are when the specification is modified slightly, for example when Ford slightly re-vamps the Mondeo and alters trim designs. The straight re-buy is the purchase of similar products on terms more or less identical to the previous order placed.
- Demand for business-to-business products stems from customer replenishment needs, changing customer requirements, product innovation creating demand, or derived demand from related products (hot weather creates consumer desire for ice cream and soft drinks, requiring Wall's and Pepsi to purchase greater quantities of raw materials in order to boost production). Marketers identify the degree of elasticity in the demand for their products relative to price changes. Many products are jointly demanded: flavourings, dairy produce and packaging for increased ice cream production.
- An understanding of the buying centre is very important in business-to-business marketing: the roles, characteristics, seniority, functions/departments, differing requirements and varying brand perceptions of those personnel within the client organization involved in selecting a supplier and product specification.
- The buying decision-making process involves: (a) problem recognition; (b) product and supplier specification; (c) search for a supplier and product; (d) evaluation of both the supplier and the offered product; (e) selection of the supplier and ordering of the specified product; and (f) evaluation of both the supplier and the product. Do note, the additional importance of specification versus consumer buying (cf. Brief 6), plus the formal assessment throughout of not only the product but also the supplier.
- Influencing factors include environmental, organizational, interpersonal and individual factors, and differ significantly from those impacting on consumer buying decision-making (cf. Brief 6).

Conceptual overview

Some companies market their products or services only to the end user consumer (you). Most, though, market to other organizations either exclusively – such as a component supplier to BMW – or in conjunction with marketing programmes targeted at consumers. For example, Mars has marketing programmes and advertising aimed at the ultimate consumer, but also has campaigns aimed at retailers and wholesalers in order to gain greater distribution coverage, shelf space in-store and exposure to purchasing consumers.

Unlike consumer buying behaviour (cf. Briefs 6 and 42), often several individuals or departments are involved in making the purchase decision. For example, selling chemicals into a manufacturer may involve the manufacturer's production manager, technical department, purchasing manager, financial controller and even Board members. To be successful, the supplying producer of chemicals must develop marketing programmes to appeal to all of these parties.

The buying process is similar to the consumer decision-making process, but because the process is more formal and the risks of selecting a poor supplier or product can be high, there are additional issues. The product required is more extensively specified than in most consumer purchases and its performance – along with that of its supplier – is carefully evaluated over the duration of the supply relationship.

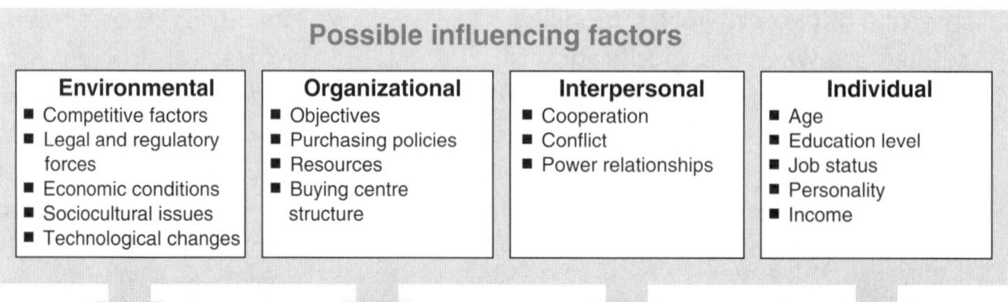

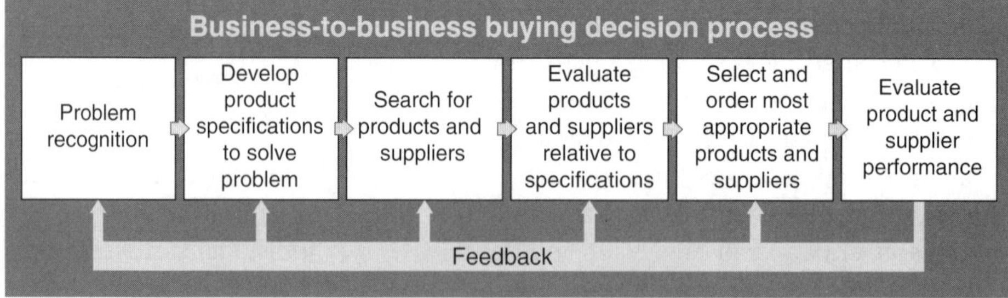

Figure 7.1 The business-to-business buying decision process

(*Source:* Figure 5.4 in Sally Dibb, Lyndon Simkin, Bill Pride and O.C. Ferrell, *Marketing: Concepts and Strategies*, Boston, MA: Houghton Mifflin, 2001. Adapted from Frederick Webster and Yoram Wind, *Organizational Buying Behaviour*, Englewood Cliffs, NJ: Prentice Hall (Pearson), 1972, pp. 33–7)

The relevant influencing factors vary compared with consumer buying decision-making. Key influences include: (a) environmental, such as political, economic and competitive, social and technological; (b) organizational objectives, purchasing policies, resources and buying centre structure; (c) interpersonal human resource and corporate issues of cooperation, conflict and power; and (d) individual characteristics of those involved, such as age, education, status, personality.

It is imperative for any marketer to understand the requirements and expectations of the target market, but in business-to-business transactions, the buying process is often perceived to be more risky and therefore is often formal and involves several different players within the buying centre. A marketer should understand the expectations of these personnel as well as the client organization's product needs. A current business trend is towards long-term relationships (cf. Briefs 1 and 2) and partnershipping programmes between organizations and their suppliers (cf. Briefs 2, 8 and 50), promoted partly by just-in-time manufacturing practices demanding security of supply and on-going commitment from suppliers. Without a thorough grasp of the business-to-business buying behaviour issues outlined in this Brief, it is unlikely a business customer's needs will be adequately met by a supplier and a long-term relationship is improbable.

Examples

Fujitsu Services

As with most companies marketing IT services, Fujitsu Services focused on marketing its specific products and services, such as mobile office technologies, customer relationship management systems, e-commerce solutions or data warehouses. With 165 000 staff in 65 countries, Fujitsu is the world's third largest IT services group, maintaining over two million PCs, managing 350 000 distributed systems and employing 12 500 consultants to assist organizations such as Aegon, the Ministry of Defence, npower and the Post Office with their IT infrastructure and data management. Recently, Fujitsu has worked closely with current and potential clients in its key target markets – including public utilities, government, health, retailing, financial services and manufacturing – to fully understand the external market drivers that are directing its clients' business planning. By properly understanding its clients' marketing environments (cf. Brief 4), Fujitsu has redefined its business propositions. The company no longer only produces CRM or mobility brochures; instead it markets service propositions that reflect the concerns of the Boards of directors of its clients, such as customer retention, reducing operating costs and effectively managing branch networks. This change of emphasis – focusing on clients' problems rather than Fujitsu's core products – has enabled Fujitsu to reinvent itself in the eyes of the marketplace and to more readily engage with its clients in a manner directly relevant to clients' senior management.

(*Sources:* 'An Energised Business', Fujitsu Services, 2003; Ian Hunter, Marketing Director, Fujitsu Services; David Olney, Marketing Director, Fujitsu Services Public Sector)

Courtaulds Textiles

Courtaulds Textiles, now part of Sara Lee Inc, manufactures clothing and fabrics. One of the challenges for the company is that the nature of its products means that it must deal with a variety of different buyers. The business is split into two areas: fabrics and garments. The fabric side of the business is characterized by the fact that in most cases consumers will not be aware that they are wearing a fabric created by Courtaulds Textiles. For this side of the business the prime customers are garment manufacturers: those that take the Courtaulds product and turn it into something else. A key part of Courtaulds' business is ensuring that it has an innovative range of fabrics to offer.

The garment side of the company's business is quite different. Many of the garments manufactured are sold as retailer own-label products. For example, Courtaulds Textiles makes clothes for big high street names Marks and Spencer, Tesco and Bhs. For these customers, the company must usually provide all of the necessary accompanying packaging, hangers, tickets/labelling and marketing support materials. In most cases the requirements are tightly specified by the retail chain, so Courtaulds ensures that it is closely in touch with buyers from these businesses. Also on the garment side of its business, the company manufactures a number of well-known clothing brands such as lingerie labels Aristoc, Berlie and Gossard. For these brands, although the products are sold through retailers, the company is responsible for maintaining the brands in the eyes of consumers. A key challenge for Courtaulds Textiles is to reflect the differing needs and wants of business-to-business customers such as Marks and Spencer, and end-user consumers in its marketing activity.

(*Source:* Courtaulds Textiles, 2000)

Test yourself

Case question

1 In what ways would the buying behaviour of a consumer shopping for a Berlie bra and a retailer's buying manager purchasing a new line of underwear for a high street retailer differ?

Quick questions

2 What is business-to-business buying behaviour?
3 List three ways in which business-to-business buying is different from consumer buying?

Applied question

4 A builder's merchant is reviewing how its customers buy its products. One of the managers working for the company has recently taken an MBA course and is familiar with a model of business-to-business buying behaviour. She decides to explain how the model works to her colleagues. What would be the key steps in the buying process that she describes and what would be the factors that influence the buying process?

Extra readings

Ford, D. (2001) *Understanding Business Marketing and Purchasing.* London: Thomson Learning.

Ford, D., Gadde, L-E., Hakansson, H. and Snehota, I. (2003) *Managing Business Relationships.* Chichester: Wiley.

Hutt, M.D. and Speh, T.W. (2003) *Business Marketing Management: Strategic View of Industrial and Organizational Markets.* Cincinnati, OH: South Western.

Webster, F.E. (1995) *Industrial Marketing Strategy.* New York: John Wiley.

8: Customer Relationship Management (CRM)

Key definitions

Customer relationship management (CRM) uses technology-enhanced customer interaction to shape appropriate marketing offers designed to nurture on-going relationships with individual customers within an organization's target markets.

Relationship marketing develops on-going relationships with customers by focusing on maintaining links between marketing, quality and customer service amongst the 'six markets' of relationship marketing: customer markets, influencers, referral, employee recruitment, suppliers and internal markets within the business.

One-to-one marketing is the segment of one: bespoke marketing messages and propositions targeted at individual customers.

Key issues

- Different authors have adopted various terms to describe one-to-one marketing, notably the 'segment of one' or 'customer-centric marketing'. The underlying rationale stems from the basis of relationship marketing and customer relationship management (CRM), popularized during the 1990s.
- Customer relationship management (CRM) has adopted recent advances in database management and customer communications to develop on-going dialogues tailored to nurture one-to-one relationships with specific customers.
- CRM utilizes improved customer data and MISs to focus on customer retention, claiming a greater share of an individual customer's purchases, the database as a device for managing direct communications, and integrated use of channels.
- Database analysis has led marketers to identify the individual existing customers worth keeping and nurturing. Specific programmes of communication and bespoke marketing programmes can be developed for these customers in order to manage these on-going relationships.
- Recent advances in technology have enabled better database management and the capture of information about customer characteristics and purchasing behaviour. Coupled with increasing use by customers of technology in buying – such as e-commerce – there has been a recent move to one-to-one marketing.
- CRM involves: analysis of customers' experiences and of their value to the business; planning of the interactions with and handling of customers; proposition development in line with customers' needs; the use of IT to manage customer data and facilitate engagement with customers; the deployment of bespoke customer management personnel; management of these personnel and the customer-facing

activities of the business; customer management activity; and measurement of the CRM activity.

- CRM activities include: targeting; enquiry management; welcoming of new or upgrading existing customers; understanding customer characteristics and issues; customer development so that customers requiring higher or different levels of service are so served; the managing of problems customers may have with the business; win-back activity to redress problems with lost customers.
- CRM activity should be benchmarked against customer expectations, competitors' standards and industry best practice.

Conceptual overview

The processes inherent in managing on-going customer relationships – particularly database, technology and communications tools – have led to a growth in marketing of customer relationship management (CRM). Database advances and direct marketing, in particular, have led to a focus on customer retention, share of the customer's purchasing, the database as a device for managing direct communications and integrated use of channels. The concept of CRM has grown out of relationship marketing (cf. Brief 2).

According to Cram, relationship marketing is the consistent application of up-to-date knowledge about individual customers to product and service design, which is communicated interactively in order to develop a continuous and long-term relationship between customers and suppliers that is mutually beneficial. The emphasis of relationship marketing is on the share of the individual's purchasing rather than the share of the overall market, with concentration on customer retention and repeat buying through an on-going responsive dialogue. The focus is on extracting more sales from existing customers through marketing activity, rather than marketing programmes designed to attract new customers.

One-to-one marketing is a more recent extension of this concept, depending on a dialogue with individual customers (cf. Brief 50). One-to-one depends on using technology to achieve communication, a continuous dialogue leading to a learning relationship, clear incentive for such a dialogue, plus acknowledging the privacy of the customer and other demands on his/her time. One-to-one marketing allows partnerships to be developed between suppliers and customers and these interactions can be used as the basis for deep and adaptive relationships. This aspect of relationship marketing is currently more commonly referred to as customer relationship management, which uses technology-enhanced customer interaction to shape appropriate marketing offers.

The development of customer databases, the decreasing costs of collecting, storing and using information, better information systems technology, plus the desire to build on-going relationships with existing customers, have led to the growth of interest in customer relationship management. Database advances have enabled marketers to identify which customers they particularly want to keep and with whom to nurture on-going loyalty. The quality of captured information in many businesses permits bespoke product and marketing communications packages to be specified to appeal to individual customers. Promotional mix developments – particularly the growth of direct marketing techniques, notably Web-based communication – have facilitated the more accurate and timely delivery of the customized message to these customers.

Taken to their logical conclusion, these advances in data capture and management allow marketers to record and respond to the needs and wants of *individual* customers. The impact of this development on market segmentation theory is potentially substantial. Now, marketers can apparently target the individual needs of customers in markets where previously it was only possible to satisfy the requirements of an entire segment or group (cf. Brief 11). The terms *customer-centric marketing*, the *segment of one* and *one-to-one marketing* have all been used to describe this development (cf. Brief 50).

To ensure CRM is effective, practices in a company must be assessed. Exponent Merlin Stone argues that robust CRM involves:

1 Analysis of the behaviour and value of different customers or customer groups and the development of an appreciation of what really are the customers' experiences of dealing with the company.
2 Planning activity and interactions with the customer in order to maximize the value of the customer base, focusing on retention, efficiency, acquisition and penetration of the customer.
3 Proposition development to ensure the customer's needs are met and new customers attracted.
4 The use of information and technology to store customer information, facilitate customer engagement and enable CRM practices to flourish.
5 The recruitment, development, motivation and deployment of bespoke customer management personnel, not just in the company but also amongst suppliers and channel members.
6 Process management to ensure customer management personnel are operating effectively and are harnessed by the rest of the business.
7 Customer management activity, including targeting, enquiry management, welcoming of new or upgrading customers, understanding customer characteristics and issues, the development of customers so that customers who require it receive a higher or different level of service, the managing of problems customers may have with the business, win-back activity to redress problems with lost customers.
8 Measurement of the value of the CRM function and personnel. All of the CRM activity should be benchmarked against customer expectations, competitors' standards and industry best practice.

Examples

Egg

One of the key objectives of customer relationship management (CRM) is to use the principles of a learning relationship to develop a deep understanding of the customer. The banking sector has, for example, been attracted by the benefits of CRM. In this sector, any implementation of CRM is dependent upon the ability to record details of customer contacts. This can be achieved by dealing in person with the customer, over the telephone, by mail or via the Internet. Thus, when Prudential launched its banking service *Egg*, the interaction with customers was seen to be vital. According to *Egg*'s website, 'every conversation and interaction with a customer needs to set up the opportunity for the next – this creates the opportunity for the relationship to develop as the customers' financial and lifestyle needs change, i.e. when moving house, having children or retiring'.

(*Source:* http://www.egg.com)

Tesco *Clubcard*

Some businesses have been attracted to customer relationship management (CRM) because of its ability to maximize customer value. The rationale is that it should be possible to improve the effectiveness of marketing spend by modifying the content and level of marketing effort on the basis of customer value. Supermarket retailer Tesco has the capability to send hundreds of different permutations of offers to customers, based on an individual's particular purchase preferences. Information about customers' buying habits is collected using the company's loyalty card. Each time a customer visits a Tesco store, s/he presents the card and is rewarded with *Clubcard* points. Each quarter, the company mails cardholders with information about the rewards they have accrued. In exchange for their points, customers are issued with money-off vouchers. These can be redeemed either against a subsequent shopping bill, or exchanged for a wide range of leisure-related offers.

In addition, customers earn *Clubcard 'Keys'* according to their level of spending. In any year, once a certain level is reached and 50 *Keys* are earned, the customer becomes a *'Keyholder'*. Once 100 *Keys* are earned, their status is enhanced to *'Premium Keyholder'*. This gives access to an improved range of offers. Although this facility is available to all *Clubcard* holders, Tesco also sends out a range of additional 'money-off' vouchers that are designed to match a shopper's buying profile. It is this capability to vary the particular offers that customers receive that demonstrates the benefits of CRM. By building a relationship with customers via their loyalty card, the company is able to tailor its marketing activity more effectively.

For example, *Clubcard*-holding new parents purchasing baby-related items are identified by Tesco's analysis of shopping trolley purchases and are mailed with baby-related offers. As the child grows, Tesco alters the lines recommended to reflect the changing needs of the child.

Tesco's international expansion has focused on central Europe (Poland, the Czech Republic, Slovakia and Hungary, with over 200 stores) and Asia-Pacific (Thailand, South Korea, Taiwan and now Malaysia, with 80 stores), as well as the Republic of Ireland and Turkey. A significant challenge for the company is to harness its *Clubcard* loyalty-building strategy in these international markets. In Asia-Pacific markets, such loyalty cards are a new phenomenon and Tesco hopes to be a trend-setter with its CRM programmes.

(*Sources:* www.tesco.com investor relations, 2004; Tesco marketing materials, 2001; Fujitsu Services, 2003)

Test yourself

Case question

1 What are the benefits of customer relationship management (CRM) to a retailer such as Tesco?

Quick questions

2 What is customer relationship management?

3 From where have the principles of customer relationship management originated?

Applied question

4 You work for a government organization that provides business advice. Your organization is currently preparing a series of fact sheets relating to a variety of business issues. Assume that you have been asked to prepare a fact sheet providing guidelines for a business considering implementing a customer relationship management approach. Prepare a draft fact sheet.

Extra readings

Chaffey, D., Mayer, R., Johnston, K. and Ellis-Chadwick, F. (2000) *Internet Marketing.* Harlow: Pearson/FT.

Cram, T. (1994) *The Power of Relationship Marketing: Keeping Customers for Life.* Harlow: Pearson/FT.

Jenkinson, A. (1995) *Valuing Your Customers: From Quality Information to Quality Relationships Through Database Marketing.* Maidenhead: McGraw-Hill.

Peppers, D. and Rogers, M. (1999) *The One-to-One Manager.* New York: Currency Doubleday.

Peppers, D. and Rogers, M. (1993) *The One-to-One Future.* London: Piatkus.

Sheth, J.N., Sisodia, R.S. and Sharma, A. (2000) 'Customer-Centric Marketing', *Journal of the Academy of Marketing Science*, 28 (1), pp. 55–66.

Stone, M. and Foss, B. (2001) *Successful Customer Relationship Marketing: New Thinking, New Strategies, New Tools for Getting Closer to Your Customers.* London: Kogan Page.

Tapp, A. (2000) *Principles of Direct and Database Marketing.* Harlow: Pearson/FT.

Zikmund, W. (2003) *Customer Relationship Management.* Hoboken, NJ: Wiley.

9: Marketing Research

Key definitions

Marketing research is a formalized means of obtaining/collecting information to be used to make sound marketing decisions when addressing specific problems.

The *marketing research process* involves: (a) defining the problem or task; (b) developing associated hypotheses to be examined; (c) data collection; (d) analysis and interpretation of the findings; (e) the reporting of the findings to the decision-makers.

Intuition is the use by marketers of their experiences and instincts to make decisions, often negating the use of marketing research.

Primary data collection is the act of acquiring bespoke information for specific marketing research requirements: observation and surveys.

Secondary data are 'second hand' information previously collected or published for another purpose but readily available to consult: internal reports or external sources such as information libraries or websites.

Quantitative marketing research involves findings that can be analysed and expressed numerically: large sample surveys from mailed questionnaires or telephone interviewing, Web-based surveying, or analysis of sales data and market forecasts.

Qualitative marketing research deals with information too difficult or expensive to reliably quantify: value judgements typically stemming from focus groups and depth personal interviews.

Sampling is the selection of survey targets that reflect their overall larger populations.

Probability sampling can be random, stratified or area, while judgemental sampling is more subjective and is often quota based.

The marketing information system (MIS) is the framework for managing and accessing internal and external data, utilizing data processing, retrieval and transmission technology.

Marketing intelligence is the composite of all the data, findings, ideas and experience available within a marketing function.

Key issues

- Many decisions in marketing are based on managers' experiences and instincts. Riskier decisions generally involve marketing research.
- Marketing research is the *ad hoc* collection of information to provide a basis for addressing a specific problem or dilemma. The marketing research process involves: (a) specifying the problem; (b) generating likely causes – hypotheses – to help focus the research activity; (c) data collection; (d) analysis and interpretation of the findings; and (e) reporting of the findings and conclusions.
- Secondary sources – previously published material or information in the public domain – tend to be examined first in order to save time and money. If the resulting search does not satisfy the

decision-makers' concerns, bespoke primary research will be specified and conducted.

- Observation – mechanical and personal – is a possibility, but more often surveys are conducted. These surveys may be mail questionnaires, telephone interviews, personal interviewing or Web-based. Although there are limitations in the availability of e-addresses, these are being overcome, with an associated growth in e-surveying. Personal interviewing includes face-to-face depth interviews, pavement intercepts, focus group discussions and quali-depth interviews. In most marketing research, a mix of tools is deployed to tackle the problem and to explore the hypotheses.
- Marketing research that generates findings that can be stored, analysed and reported numerically is quantitative. Larger samples in telephone interviews, postal questionnaire studies and the examination of sales records often permit quantitative analysis. The in-depth examination of respondents' opinions and perceptions, often from relatively small samples, is qualitative marketing research. The two are often utilized in conjunction with each: qualitative research helps generate hypotheses and finally appraise findings and options, with quantitative research providing the detailed and statistically verifiable findings.
- Sampling is typically required, as most markets are too large to permit census studies. Probability sampling includes random, stratified and area samples. Judgemental sampling often involves quotas. Good marketing research should be reliable, relevant, robust and communicable.
- IT is important in today's marketing research, enabling automated response capture and transmission of findings to analysts and clients. Touch-screen data capture, in-home bar scanners, Web cameras, are commonly deployed in consumer surveys. The use of databases is integral to the effective use of marketing research findings. Such databases are of fundamental importance to customer relationship management (CRM) programmes and to the effectiveness of the MIS.
- The marketing information system (MIS) is the framework for managing and accessing internal and external data. Typically, the MIS is IT-based, utilizing data processing, retrieval and transmission technology. There are many proprietary MIS packages now on the market. Marketing intelligence is the composite of all the data, ideas and experience available within a marketing function.

Conceptual overview

Not all decisions in marketing are based on extensive marketing research programmes: far from it. Most decisions require spontaneity and decisiveness, and cannot await the specification, commissioning, undertaking and delivery of marketing research activity. On the whole, marketers base most of their decision-making on their experience, instinct and the reaction from immediate colleagues. For more risky topics – such as a new brand identity, new product development, innovative advertising campaign, entry into a new market, determination of a strategy to combat a specific competitor, adoption of a new marketing channel, radical new pricing or warranty policy, or the withdrawal of a product – marketers tend to prefer to collect evidence to support their thinking and recommendations. This results in marketing research. Consumer, services and business-to-business marketers all utilize marketing research at some time (cf. Briefs 6 and 7, plus 42 and 43).

The first step in marketing research is to identify the problem to be examined, then secondly to hypothesize what might be the causes. In this way, the research brief can be more focused, saving on time and expense. For example, the problem may be a surprisingly sharp dip in sales. The marketers in question may hypothesize the cause to be the in-road of one particular competitor or a major flaw in their product. Either theme could then be examined through marketing research. The third stage is the collection of information that is analysed and interpreted in stage four of the marketing research process, before being summarized in a presentation or report in stage five.

Marketing research tends to commence with an examination of already published material that is readily available: library reports, Web searches, previous marketing research reports. Such secondary information is not going to be bespoke to the current problem under examination, but coupled with the marketers' experience and intuition, may provide an adequate basis for decision-making, saving the time and cost of primary data collection.

Primary data collection is the fresh, customized collection of information pertinent to the problem being researched. Observation can be personal or mechanical, such as superstore managers watching queuing behaviour of their customers or video cameras in a burger bar monitoring customer behaviour. Surveys are the most common part of marketing research and along with observations constitute primary data collection. Surveys include mail or postal questionnaires, telephone interviewing, personal interviews and Internet surveying. In most marketing research situations, a mix of data collection tools is selected.

Mail surveys are simple and mailing lists are increasingly cheaply and readily available. They lack interviewer bias and expenses. Costs are minimal – copying and postage. However, they are inflexible, cannot include probing or lengthy questions and lack the presence of an interviewer to explain questions or seek clarification of responses. Rates of response can be disappointing, with typical responses of 30% in consumer surveys and 1–2% in business-to-business surveys. Telephone surveys are very popular given the ownership rates of telephones, out-of-hours access and saving on face-to-face interviewer expenses. They are more costly, though, than postal questionnaires and lack the face-to-face interview advantages of personal interviewing and focus groups. Telephone interviewing is quick, can rapidly survey a large sample, is automated and provides very fast results. Teleselling has impeded the use of telephone interviewing, with many respondents suspecting a 'hard sell' and declining to partake in the survey.

Web surveys are becoming more common. They tended to be restricted to a company's 'home site' only, questioning visitors to the business's own site or surveying those registered in some way as users of the website. Distribution lists of people's private Web addresses are not widely available, unlike telephone or street address lists. However, companies have started to pool their lists of e-subscribers, making commercially available these e-addresses for marketing research and e-commerce. Many newspapers and consumer magazines solicit their readers' e-contact details and some demographic information, subsequently making available such e-populations to their advertisers and to marketing researchers for surveying. In business-to-business marketing, it is far more common for a company to have e-addresses for its customers or businesses in its field of operation, permitting greater use of e-surveys. While the relative newness of this research format may deter some respondents, e-surveying is growing dramatically, with benefits of speed of response and ease of data capture/input to the MIS.

Personal interviews permit the most probing of respondents, and for core issues of brand perceptions, advertising campaign design and product testing, are crucial. In-home interviews provide the respondent with the security of 'home territory', but are costly, time consuming and no longer widely deployed. Shopping mall intercepts – the person with the clipboard on the street corner – are very widespread, relatively cheap and large samples can be surveyed in a matter of weeks. Some rapport may be built up between the interviewer and the respondent, with limited clarification of questions and answers possible. Such interviews are restricted by a 4 to 5 minute ceiling, however, and only limited stimulus material can be utilized. Focus groups are 1.5 hour or 2.5 hour discussion groups, generally single sex and comprising around eight respondents. The moderator focuses in on a particular product, brand, advertising campaign or marketing proposition as the discussion proceeds. Focus groups are very popular for examining in-depth subjective opinions and perceptions. Quali-depth interviews are a hybrid approach, lasting around 25 minutes, permitting reasonable probing and use of stimulus material, but not to the extent of in-home interviews or focus groups. Quali-depths generally take place in rented meeting rooms in town centres, with respondents enticed off the streets to participate.

Sampling is necessary in most marketing research, except a few industrial markets comprising very few customers. It is important to select respondents who reflect the composition and make up of the overall, larger population. For example, if Tesco ran eight focus groups around the UK, it would probably seek to ensure the composition of the 64 participants reflected the UK's overall supermarket consumer population. There are three types of probability sampling: (a) random, when everyone in a population has an equal chance of inclusion in a survey, (b) stratified, where each group identified in the population warrants proportionate representation, and (c) area, typically geographic units. The principal type of judgemental sampling is quota-based, for example where a mall intercept researcher is briefed to interview 'fifty ladies aged between forty and fifty-five from a good background'. There is room for error in this subjective but popular approach to sampling in marketing research.

The use of technology within marketing research is hugely important and has both speeded up the process of undertaking surveys and permitted marketers to utilize findings to greater effect. For example, telephone interviews are often automated, with responses being captured by interviewers on touch-screens or even voice-response software removing the need for a 'live' researcher. The information is instantly stored in a database, enabling almost immediate statistical analysis. Even with focus groups, IT has played a greater role, with multi-unit cameras recording the discussions and 'behind-the-mirror' analysts being able to zoom in on individual respondents as they discuss. Such images are invaluable to brand managers as they strive to interpret the feedback from the group discussions. Depth interviews and pavement intercepts make use of touch-screen clipboards to quickly record responses and data can be emailed directly to analysts. In-home diary records are now automated, with respondents utilizing bar scanners to record their consumption of FMCGs and Web cameras observing consumption patterns with the agreement of participating respondents. Perhaps one of the most important uses of IT, though, has been in the creation of databases that allow marketers efficient access to marketing research findings. The manipulation and mining of such databases are at the core of effective customer relationship management processes (cf. Brief 8).

Good marketing research should be: reliable – if repeated capable of generating similar findings; valid – relevant to the problem and hypotheses; robust – not likely to crash through poor design; and communicable – the findings must be easily related to the client audience and decision-makers. The results from marketing research should be stored for easy access and up-dating on a business's MIS. Customer relationship management (CRM) and one-to-one marketing (cf. Briefs 8 and 50) depend on the effectiveness of the MIS.

Examples

Whirlpool

White goods manufacturer Whirlpool is using customer research in an innovative way. When customers telephone the company they are asked a series of questions. An operator enquires about a range of demographic criteria, then asks about the features the customer seeks when purchasing a major appliance. For example, a customer who is interested in buying a refrigerator might be asked about their kitchen colour scheme or about features such as shelf-space, freezer compartments or external size. This information is then fed into the company's database from where a server collects the data and assembles it into a template. Brochure-building software is then used to develop a full colour printed brochure specifically tailored to satisfy the customer's requirements. The company claims that the customer can receive the brochure plus a customized letter within a 35 hour period.

(*Source:* Patrick Fultz, pfultz@onebox.com)

Pivco

When Norwegian plastics company Pivco developed a one-piece plastic car body, it seemed an ideal basis for an electrically powered car. As a result, the Pivco CityBee was born. At the time, consumers were relatively unfamiliar with the idea of electrically powered vehicles and Pivco had little understanding of the sector. The company therefore commissioned some marketing research to address a series of key questions:

- How do consumers feel about electrically powered vehicles (EVs)?
- What features would consumers expect an EV to provide?
- What problems might the company face in effecting successful market entry?
- What would be the key competitive threats?

A programme of qualitative marketing research seemed the ideal avenue, to provide the kind of in-depth understanding that Pivco was pursuing. Following a period of secondary data collection, a programme of *focus group* research was undertaken. These two-hour discussions involved eight individuals, male and female, aged 20–64, from social classes ABC1. The six focus groups that took place can more accurately be described as *clinics* because they allowed participants the opportunity to look at the Pivco CityBee prototype alongside other manufacturers' cars. The qualitative marketing research provided a wide range of insights into how consumers feel about EVs and how easily they might adapt to a non-petroleum-powered car. For example, the company learned that certain groups of older consumers might consider the vehicle as a 'second car', urban runaround. There was also a great deal of useful feedback on the CityBee prototype. The outcome of the story is that Ford took over Pivco's interest in the CityBee concept in 1999, later launching its EV *Think* model.

(*Sources:* Pivco, Oslo; Sally Dibb and Lyndon Simkin, *The Marketing Casebook: Cases and Concepts*, London: Thomson, 2001)

Test yourself

Case question

1 Why was it important for the Pivco study to be based on qualitative data collection?

Quick questions

2 What are the differences between qualitative and quantitative research?
3 Explain what is meant by sampling and list three different types.

Applied question

4 Your company has a database of names derived from guarantee cards that have been returned by customers. A decision has been made to send a questionnaire to those on the database to investigate what they think about the product they purchased and the standards of customer service received since. Suggest the broad issues that the questionnaire should cover. Make sure that you explain why you have included particular issues. Base your answer around a company/industry you think appropriate.

Extra readings

Birn, R. (1999) *The Effective Use of Market Research*. London: Kogan Page.
Chisnall, P. (2001) *Marketing Research*. Maidenhead: McGraw-Hill.
Edmunds, H. (1999) *The Focus Group Research Handbook*. Lincolnwood, Ill: NTC Business Books.
Malhotra, N.K. and Birks, D.F. (2002) *Marketing Research: An Applied Approach*. Harlow: Pearson.
McQuarrie, E.F. (1996) *The Market Research Toolbox: A Concise Guide for Beginners*. London: Sage.
Tull, D.S. and Hawkins, D.I. (1993) *Marketing Research*. New York: Macmillan.

10: Forecasting in Marketing

Key definitions

Forecasting is the prediction of future events on the basis of historical data, opinions, trends or known future variables. There are three core categories of marketing forecasting: judgemental, time series projections and causal.

Judgemental forecasting is the use of subjective opinions of managers, aggregated and averaged, to predict future events and sales levels. Sales force composite, expert consensus and the delphi approach are types of judgemental forecasting.

Time series forecasting is based on a set of observations, such as monthly or annual sales returns, that is examined and extrapolated to produce predictions for the future.

Causal forecasting is the set of techniques used to examine changes in sales due to fluctuations in one or more market variables: barometric, surveys of buyer intentions, regression analysis and other econometric models.

Key issues

- Forecasts in marketing are integral to marketing planning, but also to the analysis of market attractiveness, the monitoring of marketing performance, resource allocation, production and stock management. Marketing opportunity analysis is at the heart of marketing and this requires accurate sales forecasts.
- There are forecasting models that examine product class, brand sales and market share.
- There are three core forecasting methods: (a) judgemental, (b) time series projection and (c) causal.
- Judgemental forecasting involves sales force composite, expert consensus and the delphi techniques.
- Time series models involve graphing sales patterns and trends to extrapolate for the future.
- Causal forecasting includes:
  (a) barometric, (b) buyer intention surveys, plus (c) regression and other econometric models.

Conceptual overview

Without sales forecasts and predictions of market events, marketers would be unable to properly evaluate emerging marketing opportunities or plan for the future. This would limit profitability and reduce the appropriateness of resource allocation. Forecasts are core to effective marketing plans (cf. Brief 36), to target marketing (cf. Brief 12) and to the assessment of marketing performance (cf. Brief 39). Marketers have forecasting models that examine product classes, individual brands and market shares.

There is no such occurrence as a totally accurate forecasting approach in marketing. By the very nature of the core constructs – customer fickleness, competitor aggression, marketing environment pressures – marketing faces many imponderables that cannot be incorporated within forecasts with total certainty. Nevertheless, forecasting is necessary.

Judgemental forecasts are based on the often subjective opinions of managers. The sales force composite forecast hinges on the predictions of the sales force. The views of individual sales executives are totalled and averaged. Some sales managers are very aware of impending changes, whereas others are not so well tuned in. This approach is more accurate for short-term predictions. Many companies poll the forecasts from experts outside the business, notably trade associations, journalists, financial analysts, consultants and government officials. The delphi approach is very widely deployed. Participants, such as field managers, make separate, individual forecasts. A central analyst then aggregates these views, revises the forecast accordingly, before returning the new figure to the participants for their final opinions.

Time series forecasting is widespread, with most organizations tracking sales or market shares over time, plotting these on graphs and extrapolating the curve to predict the future. It is important to establish the underlying trend, standardized for cyclical or seasonal movements. This approach is more accurate for short-term predictions based on recent sales history.

Causal forecasts examine changes in sales caused by fluctuations in one or more market variables, such as competitor activity, price changes, supply shortages, etc. Unlike time series analysis, time is not the only factor examined. The barometric approach uses trends in one variable to predict the performance in another. For example, house-building levels affect the demand for JCB's equipment. Correlations can be far from perfect, however, and only a general impact should be deduced. Marketing research may survey buyers' stated purchase intentions. If repeated over time, these figures can be plotted to help make forecasts. The more sophisticated causal forecasting techniques utilize multivariate statistical tools such as AID, factor analysis and particularly regression analysis. Multiple regression can develop an equation incorporating many independent variables that collectively cause the dependent variable, for example sales.

Forecasters tend to prefer the accuracy and reliability of causal techniques to the judgemental ones. Of the judgemental approaches, no one technique is said to be preferable, but the delphi approach is very popular. Of the causal techniques, no single approach has been demonstrated to be superior. The barometric and buyer intention survey tools are often used to help explain forecasts made from the multivariate statistical approaches and based on time series graphs. Of the statistical techniques, multiple regression analysis is well regarded. The overall conclusion is that no single forecasting tool is superior and most organizations adopt a mix of these tools.

Examples

The 2001 Census

Many countries conduct a periodic census of the people living in them. The objective is simple: to take a snapshot of the number of people living in the country at a particular point in time. For example, the UK's 2001 Census addressed a range of questions concerned with household occupancy, ethnic and religious groups, health, employment, housing and transport. A key purpose of the UK Census, which is conducted every ten years, is to assist government and businesses to forecast the future need for health, housing, education, law and order and other services. For example, by knowing how many people live in each area of the country, the government can decide how best to allocate funds for local services. It can also make decisions about required changes to the country's housing stock, transport network and health provision and identify changing employment patterns.

(*Source:* Count me in Census 2001, This is your Census!, 2000, National Statistics)

SLAM

SLAM stands for Store Location Assessment Model, a device created to help retailers identify the best locations for their stores. The model was developed following retailer research that showed the major determinants of retail performance to be competition, trading area composition, catchment demographics, store accessibility and site/store characteristics. The rationale for the model was that by collecting and modelling this information for all stores in a company's portfolio, it would be possible to determine the store location at which trading performance could be maximized for new branch openings. When applied in practice, a period of data collection was involved which was specifically tailored to the retailer involved. For example, the competition that a retailer faced might be broken down into:

- Number of direct competitors within a specified area (e.g. Burger King, Wendy's, McDonald's, Wimpy, for hamburger retailers).

- Number of indirect competitors within a specific area (e.g. any other eateries competing with the hamburger retailers. This might also include the likes of bakeries and delicatessens that sell food for people to 'eat on the go').

Once the data had been collected, they were analysed using a multiple regression approach, and a model that helped pinpoint optimum retail location was developed. The recession of the early 1990s identified another purpose for SLAM – helping retailers to rationalize their existing branch network. Once again, the principle was to collect data relating to the factors influencing store performance, before using a regression modelling approach to forecast the turnover of different branches. More rational decisions could then be made about the most appropriate outlets to close.

(*Sources:* L. Simkin, 'SLAM: store location assessment model – theory and practice', *OMEGA*, 1989, 7, pp. 53–8; S. Dibb and L. Simkin, 'Retail store performance model the impact of own-branch "friendly fire"', *International Transactions in Operational Research*, 1994, 1 (4), pp. 479–87)

Test yourself

Case question

1 Why is it important for retailers to be able to forecast required stock levels in their stores?

Quick questions

2 What is forecasting and why is it used in marketing?

3 Explain the key elements of two different methods of forecasting. Use appropriate examples to illustrate your answer.

Applied question

4 Your management consultancy business specializes in projects related to house building. In conjunction with other industry players, your company provides twice-yearly forecasts on house prices. What forecasting approaches might you have used to develop these forecasts?

Extra readings

Diamantopoulos, A. and Schlegelmilch, B.B. (1997) *Taking the Fear Out of Data Analysis*. London: Thomson.

Hooley, G.J. and Hussey, M.K. (1999) *Quantitative Methods in Marketing*. London: Thomson.

Leeflang, S.H., Wittink, D.R., Wedel, M. and Naert, P. (2000) *Building Models for Marketing Decisions*. Amsterdam: Kluwer.

Makridakis, S., Wheelwright, S.C. and Hyndman, R. (1998) *Forecasting: Methods and Applications*. Hoboken, NJ: Wiley.

11: Market Segmentation

Key definitions

A *market* is an aggregate of people who as individuals or as organizations have a need for certain products and the ability, willingness and authority to purchase such products.

Heterogeneous markets are markets in which all customers have different requirements.

An *undifferentiated* or *total market* approach assumes that all customers have similar needs and wants and can be served by a single marketing mix.

Market segmentation involves grouping heterogeneous customers in a market into smaller, more similar homogeneous customer groups. The customers in a specific segment should share similar product needs and buying characteristics.

The *market segmentation process* involves (a) grouping customers into segments, (b) targeting those segments a business deems to be the focus for its sales and marketing activity, and (c) positioning the product or service with a distinctive image in the minds of those customers targeted.

Segmentation *base variables* are the dimensions or characteristics of customers and their buying behaviour used to divide a total market into market segments.

Descriptor variables are those used to describe or label the determined market segments.

Key issues

- A market (not market segment) is an aggregate of people who as individuals or as organizations have a need for certain products and the ability, willingness and authority to purchase such products. A market may be a single market segment or consist of several segments.
- In adopting an undifferentiated or total market approach, a business is assuming that all customers have similar needs and wants that can be served with a single marketing mix. This 'take it or leave it' approach is not now often adopted. More and more organizations instead adopt a market segmentation approach.
- Market segmentation is the process of grouping customers together who share similar needs and buying characteristics. It is an effective way of sub-dividing a larger market.
- Market segmentation is now commonly practised and generally enables an organization to better serve a more homogeneous and tightly defined set of customers, to compete more effectively, utilize its resources more coherently and develop well-defined marketing programmes.
- The process of market segmentation involves the identification of market segments (the breaking down of the overall market into customer groups derived from an analysis of customer needs and buying characteristics), the prioritization of which segment(s) to

target, and the determination of a suitable brand/product positioning for the segment(s) targeted.

- Two types of variables are involved in segmentation: base and descriptor. Base variables – customer attributes and buying behaviour characteristics – are utilized to produce the segments, while descriptor variables describe or profile the resulting segments in order to help sales and marketing staff and activities differentiate between the segments. Each segment targeted should require a unique marketing mix programme.
- Developments in IT are increasing the opportunities for businesses to capture and manage data about customers in business-to-business marketing and consumers in consumer marketing. This use of technology has led to more complex segmentation studies, with resulting segmentation schemes using more variables.
- Resulting segments must be (a) measurable, (b) substantial, (c) accessible to marketing activity, (d) stable for the foreseeable future, (e) useful for focusing marketing activity and sales force efforts.
- Segmentation is based on customer buying behaviour characteristics: their needs, buying decision-making criteria and the influencing factors impacting on their choices. The concept was first established by the fast moving consumer goods (FMCG) brands. Many industrial companies tended to adopt customer classification schemes based on their customers' industrial sectors of activity. In recent years, many industrial business-to-business marketers have instead adopted true segmentation schemes based on how their customers buy and their needs.

Conceptual overview

The days of Henry Ford's undifferentiated approach for the Model T Ford – 'any car you like, so long as it's black' – have long gone. The car industry now adopts a more sophisticated approach, with models such as the Rav 4 or MX5 appealing to people with very specific lifestyles: BMW or Saab vehicles satisfying 'techno-motorists', Seat aiming at a 'sporty' value for money segment, with Volvo and VW striving to promote their cars on the basis of safety and security.

Consumer and business-to-business markets are segmented. There is no one correct way to produce segments. A large range of options exists (cf. Figure 11.1). Most businesses examine numerous aspects of their customers: their needs, buying decision-making and the influencing factors involved in their buying behaviour (cf. Briefs 6 and 7). They identify a number of base variables which are then used to aggregate customers in groups – segments – of consumers or businesses sharing similar characteristics. It is important that the analysis is robust so that all customers deemed to be in one particular segment do in fact have similar needs and buying behaviour. Descriptor variables are used to describe the resulting segments.

Consumer	Business-to-business
■ Customer characteristics • Demographics • Socio-economics • Geographic location • Personality, motives and lifestyles ■ Product related • Purchase behaviour • Purchase occasion • Benefits sought • Consumption behaviour • Attitude to product	• Geographic location • Type of organization • Trade category • Customer size • Product usage • Business sector • Buying 'personalities' • Brand loyalty • Processes adopted

Figure 11.1 Segmentation variables: *bases* (creation) and *descriptors* (profiling). A requisite for effective segmentation is a full knowledge of consumer or customer buying behaviour

Typically, a combination of these variables is used by a marketing team in order to produce a segmentation scheme for a given product or service. It is essential that the customers placed in a specified segment have similar product needs, expectations and buying characteristics to each other. Customers deemed to be in a segment together should share similar buying behaviour (cf. Briefs 6 and 7). In this manner a business such as Ford can develop one marketing mix programme for segment X and a different marketing mix programme for segment Y's customers. As IT capabilities increase, so do the opportunities to develop more complex segmentation schemes mixing many base variables. The growth of one-to-one marketing reflects this (cf. Brief 50).

The segmentation process enables a well-developed marketing programme to be produced in order to attract and satisfy a tightly defined group of like-minded customers. This should lead to enhanced customer satisfaction, greater likelihood of fending off competitors, and prudent use of resources, particularly those supporting the sales and marketing activity within a business. The effective use of resources results from the second facet of market segmentation: targeting (cf. Brief 12). The final part of the segmentation process is positioning (cf. Brief 13).

Examples

Life cycle segmentation in banks

Consumers of all types require banking facilities, although their needs may be diverse. Many banks have found that it makes sense to offer different sorts of products to consumers at different stages in their life cycle. Young children opening their first account may be seeking a reasonable rate of interest, but might also be motivated by free gifts of book or CD vouchers. University students, whose finances are often at a rather precarious stage, may require the provision of preferential overdraft facilities. Young families might require access to good value credit facilities to allow them to cope with the demands of growing children. Older consumers with savings might seek a particular kind of bank account: some US banks have developed special saving accounts for this older age group, offering preferential rates of interest.

(*Source:* Meadows, M. and Dibb, S. (1998) 'Assessing the Implementation of Market Segmentation in Retail Financial Services', *The International Journal of Service Industry Management*, 9(3), 266–85)

LEGO

Most parents and children are familiar with the products of LEGO, the Danish toy business formed more than 60 years ago. Today, with more than 10 000 employees worldwide, the company is among the world's top ten toy manufacturers. Achieving this position has been made possible by LEGO's ability to enchant children of all ages. Dealing with so wide an age range is demanding, particularly as the mix of children's activities grows and technology – such as the Web and computer games – opens up exciting play opportunities. To assist the process LEGO has segmented the market, dividing its play materials accordingly.

LEGO has themed its products in four groups, reflecting a mix of segmentation variables. These include the age and educational development of children, the spending power of the age group, and the evolution of children's imaginations and cognitive prowess. The importance of external influences on children's and parents' decision-making also has been central to LEGO's strategy, as parents are better informed about the developmental requirements for their children, and branded characters such as *Bob the Builder* or *Harry Potter* have become ever more a part of children's daily lives. LEGO has also considered how its product development can assist in broadening its distribution away from toy departments into hobby shops and educational learning displays of museum stores. LEGO EXPLORE, with the *Intelli-train* and *Story Builder* ranges, targets toddlers and younger children, encouraging children with their journey of discovery pre-school. LEGO MAKE & CREATE, based on *Advanced Designer*, *Inventor* and *Technic* ranges, enables children from ages four to ten to build basic robots, 'construct whacky inventions and discover how LEGO is infinitely creative'. LEGO STORIES & ACTION includes *Belville*, *Bionicle*, *Harry Potter*, *Racers* and *Sports*, such as the Skatepark Street Park with ramps and stunt challenges. For older children developing an interest in technology, LEGO NEXT includes 'cool tech-gadgets' and programming of the creations, featuring the *Spybotics* and *Mindstorms* ranges. There is a related *Mindstorms for Schools* range of educationally oriented products.

(*Source:* LEGO: www.lego.com, 2004)

Test yourself

Case question

1 LEGO has apparently segmented its market on the basis of age and educational development. What other base variables might the company have used to segment its market?

Quick questions

2 What is a market segment?
3 What are the potential benefits of a market segmentation approach?

Applied question

4 You work in the marketing research department of one of the large retail banks. Your company is considering alternative ways to segment its customer base. It is particularly interested in the varying service requirements of different types of customers. You have been asked to collect some customer data using a mailed questionnaire to assist with the process. What kinds of questions would you include in your questionnaire and why?

Extra readings

Dibb, S. and Simkin, L. (1996) *The Market Segmentation Workbook*. London: Thomson.

Hooley, G., Saunders, J. and Piercy, N.F. (2004) *Marketing Strategy and Competitive Positioning*. Harlow: Pearson/FT.

Hutt, M.D. and Speh, T.W. (2003) *Business Marketing Management: A Strategic View of Industrial and Organizational Markets*. Cincinnati, OH: South Western.

McDonald, M. and Dunbar, I. (1998) *Market Segmentation*. London: Palgrave Macmillan.

Webber, H. (1998) *Divide and Conquer: Target your Customer through Market Segmentation*. Hoboken, NJ: Wiley.

12: Targeting

Key definitions

Targeting is the task of prioritizing the segment or segments on which an organization should focus its sales and marketing activities.

A *concentration strategy* is a process by which a business directs its marketing effort towards a single market segment through one marketing mix.

A *multi-segment strategy* is a process by which a business directs its marketing effort towards two or more market segments by developing a bespoke marketing mix for each separate targeted market segment.

Key issues

- In a mass marketing strategy a business offers one product concept to most of the market, ignoring the individual requirements of separate market segments. The diversity of customer needs in most markets means this is not now a common approach.
- A business adopts a single segment strategy or concentration strategy when it concentrates its resources, product development and marketing activity on a single target market segment. Success can result from this approach, but it also has its risks.
- Although a multi-segment strategy demands more resources, a business may opt to spread its risk and seek opportunities across several different segments. Many organizations adopt this approach, developing separate products and marketing mix programmes for each segment targeted.
- A variety of factors should be considered by a business in determining which market segments to target. Until market segments have been identified (cf. Brief 11), it is not possible to consider which targeting approach to adopt for target market segment prioritization.
- The factors used to assess the attractiveness of segments should include financial, operational and external market factors, plus immediate performance issues and longer-term predictions of market conditions.

Conceptual overview

Mass marketing (cf. Brief 11) may provide scale economies, but there is a risk of few customers fully being satisfied by such a 'scatter-gun' approach. Hence, the popularity of market segmentation. Under this approach, customers with similar needs and buying behaviour are grouped together in market segments. Some businesses, such as Porsche Cars, concentrate on a single segment or concentration strategy. If customers value the proposition and are satisfied by the product, such businesses can be very successful. They run the risk, though, that their targeted customers progress to different products owing to evolving needs. Or, rivals active in other markets decide to also compete in the same segment but with the benefit of greater scale economies. Under a multi-segment strategy, businesses spread their risks by trading in several different segments. However, the development of various product offers and marketing mix programmes can require substantial resources. This is the more commonly adopted approach to target market selection.

Various factors impact upon an organization's assessment of target market attractiveness, including:

- The company's existing market share and market homogeneity – a company's knowledge of an existing market.
- Product homogeneity – a company's expertise, on which it can build, in an existing product field.
- Likelihood of production and marketing scale economies.
- Level of competition.
- Capability and ease of matching customer needs.
- Segment attractiveness in terms of size and structure.
- Available company resources.
- Anticipated profitability and market share.

As companies face increasing pressure from stakeholders and the media to perform well, marketers are placed under greater pressure to identify viable target markets and growth opportunities for the future. The use of analytical tools such as those described in Brief 17 becomes even more important, but it is essential that a balanced set of target market attractiveness criteria is identified.

Various models, such as the *Directional Policy Matrix*, have been developed to assist managers' decision-making regarding market attractiveness (cf. Brief 17). Best practice suggests 'a basket' of variables should be considered, including short-term and long-term impacts on attractiveness, internal forces (financial rewards, budgeting costs, operational requirements) and external forces (customer satisfaction considerations, competitive intensity, marketing environment factors).

Examples

Chester Zoo

When the marketing manager at Chester Zoo decides how to spend his marketing budget, he must carefully consider the distance prospective visitors are prepared to travel. Around three-quarters of the budget is spent on television advertising, which is focused on the Granada, Carlton/Central and Harlech (HTV) ITV regions. These television regions are chosen to fit with the home locations of visitors. Regular consumer research carried out by zoo personnel helps pinpoint from where visitors have travelled and the length of time they are prepared to spend driving to such an attraction. In recent years, the improvement of the motorway network has resulted in the zoo extending its target catchment. With a relatively limited amount of money available for marketing spend, it is crucial that the marketing function targets prospective customers as efficiently as possible. In this case, it seems that travel times and the home location of visitors are key.

(*Source:* Chris Vere, Marketing Manager, Chester Zoo)

CACI

CACI specializes in providing clients with segmentation and targeting assistance. The company is particularly well known for its expertise in lifestyle segmentation and has created a database which classifies 44 million UK consumers according to the way in which they live and spend their time. In all, around 300 different characteristics are covered in the database. These include everything from personal details and domestic arrangements to interests, leisure pursuits, hobbies, readership/viewing habits, buying behaviour and shopping preferences.

CACI's lifestyle database can be used to identify potential customers with a particular profile. Clients seeking to identify those who might be interested in their products can specify variables that they believe will help pinpoint the consumers. For example, a holiday tour operator wishing to expand sales of holidays over the Internet may have identified that existing consumers have certain lifestyle characteristics. CACI could use this information about the tour operator's customer profile to track-down new potential customers from the 44 million individuals on the lifestyle database.

(*Source:* CACI website; *Marketing Systems Today*, 13 (1), 1998, p. 11)

Test yourself

Case question

1 Why might a company choose to use the services of a company like CACI to help with its targeting instead of collecting its own customer data?

Quick questions

2 What is targeting?

3 What are the advantages/disadvantages of concentration and multi-segment targeting strategies?

Applied question

4 The research and development function of an agrochemicals company has developed an insecticide that is suitable for use on fruit or flower farms. However, the company only has the marketing resource to target one of these groups of prospective customers. What factors should the company take into consideration when deciding on which type of customers to target?

Extra readings

Dibb, S. and Simkin, L. (1996) *The Market Segmentation Workbook.* London: Thomson.

Dibb, S. and Simkin, L. (1998) 'Prioritising Target Markets', *Marketing Intelligence and Planning*, 16 (7), pp. 407–17.

Hooley, G., Saunders, J. and Piercy, N.F. (2004) *Marketing Strategy and Competitive Positioning.* Harlow: Pearson/FT.

Stone, M. and Foss, B. (2001) *Successful Customer Relationship Marketing: New Thinking, New Strategies, New Tools for Getting Closer to Your Customers.* London: Kogan Page.

Webber, H. (1998) *Divide and Conquer: Target your Customer through Market Segmentation.* Hoboken, NJ: Wiley.

13: Brand and Product Positioning

Key definitions

Product positioning is the activity directed towards creating and maintaining a company's intended product concept and image in the minds of targeted customers.

Brand positioning is the creation of a clear and distinctive image for the brand.

Market positioning is arranging for a brand or product to occupy a clear, distinctive and desirable place in the minds of targeted customers relative to competing products or brands.

Positioning is the process of creating an image for a product in the minds of targeted customers.

A *positioning statement* is a plausible, memorable image-enhancing summation of a product's or brand's desired stature.

Key issues

- Positioning is the place occupied by a product or brand in a given market as perceived by the target market customers. It is based on the product's or brand's attributes, standing, quality, the types of users, its strengths and weaknesses, price and value, plus any other memorable characteristics, as perceived by the targeted customers.
- A positioning must be created. It should be distinctive, memorable, plausible and desirable for the targeted market(s) and be relevant in the longer term.
- Perceptual mapping is a tool used by marketers to visually depict consumer perceptions, their prioritizing of brands and the perceived attributes of these brands. It enables the relative standings of competing brands to be comprehended.
- Positioning must stem from consumer perceptions and a business should endeavour to determine a positioning that sets its proposition apart from competitors' positionings.
- To be effective, a positioning must be readily communicated to the intended target market in a manner that is plausible, distinctive and differentiated from rivals. *The Ultimate Driving Machine* is a perfect example, utilized by BMW for many years.
- Hand-in-hand with the creation of a brand positioning strategy – how a company wants its brand or product to be perceived *vis-à-vis* rival offerings by target customers – is the creation of a desirable and viable brand with a shrewdly managed brand image.

Conceptual overview

In the market segmentation process (cf. Brief 11), positioning is the final stage. Positioning follows the identification of market segments and the prioritization of target markets. Positioning is the creation of a distinctive image for a product or brand that enhances the appeal of the product in question for the targeted customers and helps differentiate it from rival products.

There are a number of steps involved in determining a positioning:

1. Define the segments in a particular market (cf. Brief 11).
2. Decide which segment or segments to target (cf. Brief 12).
3. Understand what the target consumers expect and believe to be most important when deciding on a purchase (cf. Briefs 6 and 7).
4. Develop a product or retail brand that caters specifically for these needs and expectations (cf. Brief 14).
5. Evaluate the positioning and images, as perceived by the target customers, of competing products/retail concepts in the selected market segment or segments.
6. With the understanding achieved in steps 1 to 4 (knowledge of a product/brand, the needs and expectations of target customers, their perception of competing brands' positioning), select an image that sets the product or brand apart from the competing brands. Ensure the chosen image matches the aspirations of the target customers. The selected positioning and imagery must be credible.
7. Communicate (cf. Briefs 15 to 27) with the targeted customers about the product using the promotional element of the marketing mix as well as making the product readily available at the right price and place. This necessitates the associated development of the full marketing mix (cf. Brief 32). The ingredients of the marketing mix must all reflect the desired positioning image.

Perceptual mapping of customers' views of a brand's attributes and its standing *vis-à-vis* rivals is a common approach adopted by marketers as they strive to identify how customers perceive their brand in the context of their needs and perceptions of competing brands. The brand positioning statement (Peugeot's *Drive of Your Life*) and visual identity (McDonald's *Golden Arches*) are often the manifestation of the positioning strategy. The positioning should be given to the advertising agency and marketing communications expert, who must effectively convey the determined positioning to the target audience.

While a positioning strategy, part of the market segmentation process, focuses on deciding how a company wants its targeted consumers to perceive its brand or

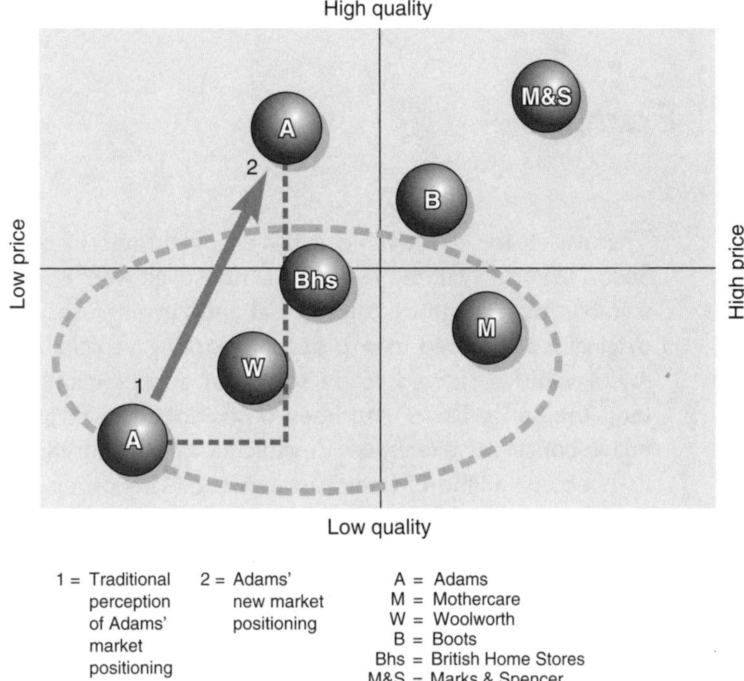

Figure 13.1 A perceptual positioning map: positioning of major UK retailers of children's wear, featuring the repositioning of Adams

(*Source: adapted from* Lyndon Simkin and Jens Maier (as WBC), as presented in Sally Dibb, Lyndon Simkin, Bill Pride and O.C. Ferrell, *Marketing: Concepts and Strategies*, Boston, MA: Houghton Mifflin, 2001)

product *vis-à-vis* competitors' positionings, there is an implicit link with the management of the brand. BMW's brand positioning – *The Ultimate Driving Machine* – is plausible and desirable to its targeted consumers because of the years of careful brand management and product development that have made such a positioning credible. Marketers invest significant time and resource to managing their brands, seeking brand recognition, preference, insistence and loyalty as they strive for a strong and successful brand. A carefully constructed brand positioning strategy, taking full account of customer views and perceptions, competitors' brand positionings and market trends, is an important facet of effective brand management (cf. Brief 14).

Examples

Range Rover

The market for 4 × 4 vehicles has changed radically over the years. Following the Second World War, the Jeep and Land Rover were sold as hard-working vehicles, suitable for a range of commercial and farming uses. The Range Rover was also originally positioned as a practical working vehicle. However, during the 1980s 4 × 4 vehicles started to be sought after as exciting executive vehicles. Before long, the Range Rover had been repositioned to target wealthy country folk and image-conscious executives. A vehicle originally intended as a reliable workhorse had become a kind of fashion statement. Many other car manufacturers, including Toyota, Ford and Vauxhall, were quick to try to emulate the Range Rover success by launching their own 4 × 4 models. Today, there is a full range of 4 × 4 offerings offered at a range of price points and targeting all kinds of customers, many of whom will never take their 4 × 4 off a tarmac surface! The Rav 4 and the Land Rover Freelander are 4 × 4 models whose positionings aim to appeal to buyers in the affluent suburbs rather than to working farmers.

(*Source:* Sally Dibb, Lyndon Simkin, Bill Pride and O.C. Ferrell, *Marketing: Concepts and Strategies*, Boston, MA: Houghton Mifflin, 2001, pp. 241–3)

Budget hotels

The emergence of the 'no-frills', good-value hotel chain was a feature of the 1990s. Aimed at business and leisure travellers on a budget, the development offered an alternative to traditional bed and breakfast accommodation. *Campanile*, *Travel Inn* and *Travelodge* are just some of the offerings to emerge in an increasingly crowded marketplace. French hotel operator Accor, perhaps best known for *Novotel*, has gone further than most, developing five different budget offerings including *Formule I* and *Ibis*.

One of the most interesting features of this trend is that the providers of the new genre of budget hotels typically also operate in other segments of the hotel market. Whitbread Hotels, one of Europe's largest hotel groups, has a range of four-star deluxe establishments trading under the franchised *Marriott* brand. At the other extreme, the company offers an extensive network of motel-style budget-priced *Travel Inns*, located on or close to major routes or in large conurbations. Whitbread Hotels keeps its *Marriott* and *Travel Inns* quite separate and has created distinctive brand positioning images for each separate hotel chain. As well as its budget brands, Accor has upscale and mid-scale brands, such as *Sofitel*, *Novotel* and *Mercure*. The only realistic way to manage such diversity is for Accor to ensure that the different brands are clearly positioned within their respective segments:

- **Sofitel:** The premium brand of Accor. Now more than 150 prestige hotels, 'offering a varied taste of the French Art of living, throughout the world'. Top architects, interior designers and chefs combine for the discerning business and leisure traveller.
- **Novotel:** 'Innovative, harmony, freedom and consistency – 350 hotels and resorts in 56 countries', offering informality, meeting and leisure amenities – 'a relaxing spot for people travelling on business as well as for families on week-ends or holidays'.
- **Mercure:** Now with a network of over 750 hotels in 45 countries, operating under various four- and mainly three-star brands: Mercure, Libertel, Parthenon, All Seasons and Orbis, primarily serving the business traveller.
- **Parthenon:** A new lodging concept: comfort and convenience in apartments with hotel services.
- **Suitehotel:** A new and small three-star chain. Guest rooms are 30 square metre modules that can be re-arranged during the day to cater for meetings, desk work or to provide sleeping accommodation. The brand welcomes guests 24 hours per day.
- **Thalassa:** Seawater and spring spas, in twenty locations.
- **Ibis:** Round the clock service and budget prices at 550 hotels worldwide. Bars, choice of restaurants, comfortable bedrooms, typically in the city centre.
- **Etap:** Over 200 'basic-service budget hotels' in France, Germany, Great Britain, Belgium, Hungary, Switzerland and Israel. Limited amenities, buffet breakfast, comfortable rooms.
- **Formule 1:** Over 350 budget hotels in ten countries offering simple and functional comfort. Best value accommodation, 'setting the standard for economy hotels'.

(*Sources:* Whitbread Hotels' marketing material; Marriott website, 2004; Accor website, 2003; AA, 2003)

Test yourself

Case question

1 Why is it important for Accor and Whitbread to have separate positionings for their various hotel chains?

Quick questions

2 What is a positioning statement?
3 What steps should be followed to establish a clear positioning?

Applied question

4 As an independent marketing consultant you have been retained by a specialist manufacturer of large luxury cars. The company is considering developing a small luxury car to compete with the BMW *Compact 3-Series*. However, the company is concerned that the image of its larger current models is not adversely affected by the new offering. You have been asked to prepare a report that outlines the problems that might be faced in positioning the new model.

Extra readings

Dibb, S. and Simkin, L. (1996) *The Market Segmentation Workbook.* London: Thomson.

Hooley, G., Saunders, J. and Piercy, N.F. (2004) *Marketing Strategy and Competitive Positioning.* Harlow: Pearson/FT.

Keller, K.L. (2003) *Building, Measuring and Managing Brand Equity.* Englewood Cliffs, NJ: Pearson.

Ries, A. and Trout, J. (2000) *Positioning: The Battle for Your Mind.* New York: McGraw-Hill.

14: Branding

Key definitions

A *brand* is an established product name, term, symbol, design, wholly of a proprietary nature, usually officially registered.

Brand positioning is the creation of a clear and distinctive image for the brand.

Branding types are manufacturer, retailer own label and generic.

Brand loyalty is a strongly motivated and long-standing decision to purchase a particular product or service.

A customer's awareness that a brand exists and is an alternative purchase option is *brand recognition*.

Brand preference is the degree of brand loyalty and preference for the brand over competing brands.

The degree of brand loyalty persuading a customer to accept no substitute is *brand insistence*.

Brand attributes are the specific benefits to the consumer from purchasing or using the brand. *Brand values* are the emotional benefits associated with the brand. *Brand personality traits* are the psychological and less tangible desirable facets of a well-presented brand.

Brand equity is the marketing and financial value associated with a brand's strength in the market.

Branding policies include individual branding, overall family branding, line family branding and brand extension.

Brand extension is a company's use of one of its existing brand names for an improved or new product, usually in the same product category.

Successful brands require prioritization on quality, superior service, first mover advantage, differentiation, unique positioning, strong marketing communications, consistency and reliability.

Levels of a brand are the tangible product, the basic brand and the augmented brand.

Key issues

- Marketing requires product or service differentiation, often using branding. Differentiation entails product design, features and attributes, customer service, branding and the other ingredients of the marketing mix.
- Branding enables customers to readily identify their favoured products and marketers to more easily communicate their advantages.
- There are manufacturer brands created and controlled by the producers of products, retailer-originated own label brands and a few generic brands featuring only the product's constituents or description as the name.
- Brand loyalty is highly desirable and marketers invest vast sums in persuading targeted customers to prefer their products over and above those supplied by competitors. In order to achieve brand loyalty there must be brand recognition on the part of targeted

customers. Brand preference and brand insistence are examples of customers strongly desiring a particular brand ahead of rival options.

- Branding experts believe that well-managed, strong and desirable brands should identify a set of specific tangible benefits to attach to the brand, known as brand attributes, a set of reassuring and more emotive brand values, plus a set of appealing and desirable brand personality traits. Implicit in this view is the importance of effectively creating a well-differentiated and memorable image for the brand that is carefully controlled.
- Brand equity is increasingly important in many Board rooms and results from the financial and marketing value that can be placed on a brand owing to its market position and standing. Brand awareness, brand loyalty, perceived brand quality and brand associations create brand equity.
- A brand name must be selected with care and be memorable, distinctive, plausible, relevant to the product's usage and customer need, easily communicable and synergistic to the selected brand positioning. The brand name should be registered and legally protected. Its application occasionally may be licensed for use by third parties.
- There are various branding policy options, including individual branding, overall family branding, line family branding and brand extension.
- Successful brands often prioritize quality, offer superior service, are innovative or have first mover advantage, are differentiated, develop strong positioning, receive extensive marketing communications support and over time are consistent and reliable.
- Brand strength is a function of the product's attributes and functionality, its differentiation, plus any demonstrable added value to the purchaser or user.
- The three levels of a brand are the tangible product, the basic brand and the augmented brand.

Conceptual overview

Most marketers believe a key focus for their activity is the differentiation of their product offer versus competing products and services. For many consumer, service or industrial products, such differentiation entails a mix of product design, features and attributes with the creation of a distinctive image (cf. Brief 15). This generally involves creating a brand and brand identity for products or services (cf. Brief 13). Indeed, without distinctive branding, many service products in particular would struggle to differentiate themselves against rivals (cf. Briefs 19 and 44).

With the exception of a few generic products such as some pharmaceuticals, paper products or ironmongery, most products are these days branded to create an image and differentiation, enabling customers to readily identify their desired products and to compete against rival products and services. There are (a) manufacturer brands, such as Heinz, IBM or JCB; (b) retailer brands, including Boots' *No. 7*, *Saisho* in Dixons, Tesco *Finest*, or simply lines carrying the retailer's trading name, such as Sainsbury-labelled products; and (c) generic brands, for example paracetamol, rather than *Panadol.* Irrespective of the type of brand, the brand should 'say' something positive and relevant to the targeted customer and strive to be distinctive. Many shoppers have their favourite brands, and many observers believe that branding therefore makes shoppers more efficient: they seek only these favourites in the shops and distributors rather than 'clogging up' the aisles in lengthy deliberation.

The notion of brand loyalty is closely linked to branding. Brand loyalty is a strongly motivated and long-standing decision to purchase a particular product or service. It implies customer satisfaction and that marketers have effectively communicated product benefits to these retained customers. All marketers strive for brand loyalty and hope to switch customers away from competing brands. This involves the creation of brand recognition, so that targeted customers are at least aware that a brand exists and is an alternative to purchase. Brand preference is the term used to describe a situation that is stronger than basic brand loyalty: here a customer definitely prefers a particular brand over competitive offers and will only purchase this favoured brand, if it is available. If there is such strong brand preference that stock-out or limited availability make purchase difficult but the consumer continues to seek the preferred brand and will not accept a substitute, there is brand insistence.

Brand values are defined as the less tangible identifiers attached to the brand that provide reassurance and credibility for targeted consumers. They supplement the specific brand attributes in making the brand attractive to current or potential purchasers. For example, IT services company Fujitsu has many brand attributes, including its ability to manage clients' IT infrastructure, offer the latest technology and thinking, be cost-effective and reliable. Its brand values are defined as offering knowledge, dependability, technical excellence, reassurance and passion. These values are far more emotional than the brand attributes. Together, the brand values and brand attributes constitute a more compelling proposition in the marketplace. Many branding experts argue that in addition to brand attributes and brand values, an effective brand strategy should identify brand personality variables in order to facilitate greater differentiation versus competitors and to form a stronger affinity with customers. In Fujitsu's case, the brand personality variables include having friendly, customer-focused personnel who are confident, state-of-the-art and passionate about assisting clients to improve their businesses. In the market for IT services to large corporations, these are desirable traits. Implicit in this discussion is the need to determine a strong and relevant brand image that is managed effectively (cf. Brief 13).

A notion receiving much attention in recent years in the marketing and financial journals is that of brand equity. This is a marketing and financial value placed on a brand resulting from its strength and desirability in the marketplace. Indeed, some brands have been given a financial book value on companies' balance sheets. A well-managed brand is an asset to a company. Brand equity stems from (a) brand name awareness, (b) brand loyalty, (c) perceived brand quality and (d) brand associations, such as Volvo's safety or BMW's *Ultimate Driving Machine* innovation.

A company must select a brand name that enhances its product's image, is easily communicable (in other countries, too), is memorable, relates to the product's usage/image and to customer needs, and sets the product apart from rivals. Marketers generate brand names internally through brainstorming, by extrapolating names already used in the company, through customer feedback and focus group discussions (cf. Brief 9), or by commissioning external branding consultants. The name selected and its associated logos/designs should be registered and protected: McDonald's rigorously protects the use of *Mc* and its *Golden Arches*. Brands sometimes are licensed for use by other businesses, such as construction equipment brands JCB and CAT for clothing.

In terms of branding policies, a company has three core choices: (a) individual branding, giving each product its own identity, such as Proctor & Gamble's *Tide*, *Bold*, *Daz* and *Dreft* washing powders; (b) overall family branding, when all of a business's lines share a common name in part, as in Heinz, Microsoft or Ford branding; and (c) line family branding, which is family branding but only within a single line: Colgate–Palmolive uses *Ajax* for many cleaning products but the *Colgate* brand for its dental products. Brand extension branding occurs when an existing brand is used for a different but related product: *Timotei* extended from shampoos to other skin care products.

Research has shown that to have a successful brand, a company must:

- Prioritize quality.
- Offer superior service and support.
- In the minds of targeted customers, be a first mover or innovator.
- Differentiate its brand.
- Develop a unique positioning concept (cf. Brief 13).
- Support its brand and positioning with strong marketing communications.
- Deliver consistency and reliability over time.

The notion of brand strength relates to a function of (a) the product itself and its attributes or functionality, (b) how it is shown to have differentiation in the view of customers versus competing products, plus (c) any added value attributes marketers have been able to attach through aspects of the augmented product (cf. Brief 15), reputation and image building programmes and market presence.

There are three levels of brands suggested by the branding experts: (a) the tangible product or degree of quality, performance, features and actual attributes; (b) the basic brand made up of the identity, differentiation and positioning; and (c) the augmented brand, which is the aggregated impact from supplementary products and service support.

Examples

Heinz

Heinz uses overall family branding to identify its products. This means that the company uses the name Heinz in conjunction with a generic description of the particular item, such as *Heinz Tomato Ketchup*, or *Heinz Salad Cream*. This approach is beneficial to the company because consumers are familiar with the Heinz name, which they associate with quality. For consumers, there is the reassurance that they are buying a trusted brand, which increases their confidence in the purchase they are making. For Heinz, which was at one time renowned for its '57 varieties' (there are now many more!), this consumer trust allows the company to extend its brand further. For example, the Heinz soup in a cup range. The company can therefore launch new Heinz products which can benefit from the place in the consumer's shopping basket already secured by other Heinz lines.

(*Sources:* Heinz UK; Tesco Stores, 2003)

BMW

BMW cars are a familiar sight around the world, as is the blue and white BMW badge that adorns them. This well-known logo, which is based on a spinning aeroplane propeller, dates back to the company's early days when Bayerische Motoren Werke was producing aircraft engines. The design principles on which the company's cars are now manufactured have, however, remained remarkably consistent over time. According to BMW:

> The BMW badge is far more than just a design feature: its changing form symbolises how BMW has evolved over time whilst remaining true to the original design philosophy of those who founded the company over 80 years ago. We have always believed that form should never take precedence over function. Achieving perfection in car design is not simply a matter of conforming to temporary fashions. Rather, it means consistently adhering to standards that will retain their original appeal for many years to come. (BMW *3-Series Coupe* brochure, 2001)

Today, the BMW brand has become synonymous with quality and prestige. Marketing experts agree that the company's positioning statement (or strap line) – *BMW, The Ultimate Driving Machine* – powerfully depicts the key brand values. BMW is aware that if it is to protect this valuable brand, it must continue to produce cars that deliver the quality and prestige that customers expect.

(*Source:* BMW marketing materials 2001)

Test yourself

Case question

1 Why is it important that BMW protects its brand? What can the company do to achieve this?

Quick questions

2 What are the customer and organizational benefits of branding?
3 What are the different levels of a brand?

Applied question

4 Your company is in the process of recruiting an advertising agency to help manage and market its portfolio of brands. The company has reached the stage where it has short-listed three agencies. Each agency has been asked to prepare a presentation describing what it believes are the key elements of brand equity. What elements would you expect the agencies to include in their presentations?

Extra readings

Aaker, D. (2002) *Building Strong Brands.* New York: Free Press.

Aaker, D.A. and Joachimsthaler, E. (2002) *Brand Leadership.* New York: Free Press.

De Chernatony, L. and McDonald, M. (2004) *Creating Powerful Brands.* Oxford: Butterworth-Heinemann.

Doyle, P. (2002) *Marketing Management and Strategy.* Harlow: Pearson/FT.

Keller, K.L. (2003) *Building, Measuring and Managing Brand Equity.* Englewood Cliffs, NJ: Pearson.

Ries, A. and Ries, L. (2002) *The 22 Immutable Laws of Branding: How to Build Any Product or Line Into a World Class Brand.* London: Harper Collins.

15: Products

Key definitions

A *product* is a core ingredient of the marketing mix and is everything – favourable and unfavourable, tangible and intangible – received in the exchange of an idea, service or a good.

Consumer products are items purchased to satisfy personal or family needs. There are convenience products, shopping goods, speciality products, unsought products and consumer services products.

Business-to-business or *industrial* products are items bought for use in a company's operations or to produce other products. There are raw materials, major equipment, accessory equipment, component parts, process materials, consumable supplies and industrial services.

Levels of a product are the core product, actual product and the augmented product.

A *product item* is a specific version of a product that can be designated a distinct offering amongst a company's portfolio of products.

A *product line* is a group of closely related product items that are considered a unit through marketing, technical or end-use considerations.

The *product mix* is the composite group of products that a company makes available to target markets.

Managing product involves new product development, product modification and product deletion.

The *new product development process* entails idea generation, screening, concept testing, business analysis, product development, test marketing and commercialization.

Product development newness presents four options: radical product development, routine product development, new style product development, extended product development.

The *product adoption process* is awareness, interest, evaluation, trial and then adoption (purchase).

Key issues

- At the heart of marketing is an exchange: a marketer's product in return for payment or a donation. The product is pivotal to a business's marketing mix and can be a physical good, service or an idea.
- Consumer products include convenience goods, shopping goods, speciality products, unsought goods and consumer services.
- Business-to-business products include raw materials, major plant and equipment, accessory equipment, component parts, process materials, consumable supplies and industrial services.
- The three levels of a product are the core product, the actual product and the augmented product. The core product is the benefit to the customer, the actual product is the product's features and capabilities, while the augmented product consists of customer service and support facilities.

- A product item is a specific version of a product aimed to satisfy particular customer needs and expectations. A product line is a group of closely related product items. The product mix is the composite group of products made available to a company's target markets.
- Marketers must specify product quality and augmented product characteristics.
- Owing to product life cycles, changing customer expectations and market conditions, and product performance within the product mix, marketers must constantly alter their product portfolios. This involves product modification in terms of quality, functionality or styling, product deletion and new product development.
- The new product development process involves idea generation, screening, concept testing, business analysis, product development, test marketing and, finally, full commercialization.
- There are positive links between business performance, strong brands and product innovation. Effective product development requires access to market information and a set of organizational and operational requisites.
- Product and market 'newness' must be considered: radical product development, routine product development, new style product development or extended product development.
- Successful product introduction requires product adoption by sufficient targeted customers. The product adoption process involves awareness, interest, evaluation, trial and adoption by the targeted customers.

Conceptual overview

Marketing involves an exchange of a customer's money or donation in return for an organization's good, idea or service. In the marketing mix (cf. Brief 32), the product ingredient is the most important and 'product' is widely defined to include physical goods, ideas and services. There typically is a distinction made between products aimed at consumer markets and those targeting business-to-business markets (cf. Briefs 42 and 43), and between the more intangible service product (cf. Brief 44).

Consumer products include: (a) inexpensive, frequently purchased, low involvement convenience products, such as bread, drinks, cigarettes or newspapers; (b) more carefully selected shopping goods, such as lower-priced appliances, stereo equipment and clothing; (c) speciality goods demanding much deliberation owing to their value, length of ownership, visibility to peers or novelty, including expensive jewellery, cars, holidays and computing equipment; (d) unsought goods purchased when a sudden problem occurs or when aggressive selling generates interest, for example pension policies or life insurance.

Business-to-business or industrial products include: (a) raw materials; (b) major plant and equipment; (c) accessory equipment used in production; (d) component parts; (e) process materials; (f) consumable supplies; and (g) industrial services. Marketing tends to treat services in a different category as their intangibility and other characteristics require a different set of marketing mix ingredients from those applied to the marketing of physical consumer or business-to-business goods (cf. Brief 44).

Marketing's understanding of the product ingredient of the marketing mix used to focus on the tangible design features and styling of the product. In order to create a competitive edge over rival products (cf. Brief 35), marketers have increasingly turned to the support service aspects of the product offer. This has encouraged marketers to define three levels of the product:

- The core product is the level that provides the perceived or real core benefit or service. For the BMW *3-Series* this is transportation.
- The actual product is the composite features and capabilities offered in a product's design, styling, quality, durability, packaging and brand name. BMW's *Ultimate Driving Machine* innovative design provides many such elements.
- The augmented product is made up of the support elements now frequently demanded by customers: customer service, warranty, delivery, credit, personnel, installation and after-sales support. The three-year warranty and full free recovery service offered by BMW are good examples.

Marketers must take various decisions about the product mix to make available to the specified target markets. A product item is a specific version of a product that can be designated a distinct offering amongst a company's portfolio of products. A product line is a group of closely related product items that are considered a unit through marketing, technical or end-use considerations. The product mix is the composite group of products that a company makes available to target markets. Marketers must also determine product quality in order to satisfy customer expectations, compete effectively, but minimize production costs: the ideal life span for a VCR may be five years. The augmented product must be specified, and for many products these aspects may provide a differential advantage over competitors (cf. Briefs 35 and 44). A key concern for marketers is what is termed the product life cycle, discussed in the next Brief.

Owing to life cycle considerations, evolving customer expectations, competitors' product mixes, market forces and the desire for brand differentiation, marketers must constantly modify their portfolios. The analytical techniques available to assist in this process are discussed in Brief 17, but the result is that products must be modified or deleted and new products created to add to the product mix.

The new product development (NPD) process involves: (a) idea generation; (b) screening or short-listing of ideas; (c) concept testing for those short-listed; (d) business analysis to examine commercial viability; (e) product development of any product deemed potentially viable; (f) test marketing to check for customer acceptance; and (g) commercialization, the full roll-out, of any product successfully making it through the test marketing stage.

Much has been published in recent years connecting the NPD process, product innovation and competitive success. Research into strong and successful brands (cf. Brief 14) has demonstrated that these strive to innovate. Research into commercial success reveals a similar link with the ability to bring to the market innovative, desirable and credible products that are seen by targeted consumers to offer advantages over existing products. In order to achieve such innovation and effective NPD, an organization must be able to access market information concerning products' advantages, customer needs and expectations, and aspects of market attractiveness trends (cf. Brief 12). It is also necessary to match other requisites, including senior management support; synergy or familiarity between the new project and existing products; proficiency in pre-development activity, marketing programme activities and technological acquisition or utilization; the integration of R&D and marketing functions; plus, speed in the NPD process. There must also be an understanding about the degree of 'newness' in terms of the intended customer base and the proposed product:

- Radical product development: NPD aiming at the existing customer base.
- Routine product development: old product development aiming at the existing customer base.
- New style product development: NPD aiming at extending the customer base.
- Extended product development: old product development aiming at extending the customer base.

Any product launched successfully depends on enough target customers adopting the product and being satisfied. This involves the product adoption process:

- Awareness: the buyer becomes aware of the product.
- Interest: the buyer finds out more.
- Evaluation: the buyer considers the product's benefits and whether to test it out.
- Trial: the buyer examines or tests the product.
- Adoption: the buyer makes the purchase and consumes the product.

Products nearing the end of their life cycles or commercial viability are deleted from the product mix, immediately if they are seriously draining resources, through a run-out exploiting any remaining marketing strengths or through phasing out. Often, though, products are modified many times in order to 'kick start' their sales and add to their life expectancy. Modification can be through quality, functionality, or style changes. A company that fails to up-date its product mix to reflect changes in its marketplace will not survive.

Examples

Robinsons

No matter how successful a product may be, if it remains unchanged the likelihood is that over time its fortunes will decline owing to a mix of factors such as changing customer needs, market trends and competitor activity. Most businesses must continually review their product mix, introducing new products, modifying existing ones and possibly withdrawing some. Britvic drinks brand Robinsons has recently reassessed its portfolio, deciding to modify its range of fruit dilutables and to introduce two new products. Until now, the company's dilutables have been every-day and added-value squashes, but a new range of flavours is dilutable with milk. *Robinsons for Milk* had Wimbledon tennis tournament tie-ins and was primarily aimed at children aged 3 to 12. The second new product, *Fruit Spring*, is a range of fruit-based soft drinks targeted at adults, especially the 42% of office workers who take a packed lunch to work. The Robinsons brand is well known for soft drinks, but these new product launches demonstrate the company's commitment to maintaining its success in this sector.

(*Sources:* agency Jones, Knowles, Ritchie; Britvic promotional materials; Emily Rogers in *Marketing*, 30 October 2003, p. 4)

Disney

Wherever you travel in the world, people have heard of Mickey Mouse. Initially, the loveable Disney character achieved his global recognition with friends Minnie Mouse, Donald Duck and Pluto through Disney movies and television cartoons. Today, Disney has built on its entertainment expertise to extend the brand that surrounds its well-known characters into theme parks, hotels and retail outlets. The company has also capitalized on opportunities to develop merchandizing based on its famous brand, leading to an extensive array of Disney-related products. Visitors to Disney theme parks in France, Japan and the United States can use their spending money in a host of retail outlets. Disney Stores have also appeared in most major cities around Europe. In these stores, customers can buy anything from 101 Dalmatian nightwear and Minnie Mouse clothing, to stationery, games, computer software and even their own soft-toy version of their favourite character.

The commercial viability of the company's diverse product and service range relies on the continued recognition of its ever-popular characters. Disney goes to great lengths to ensure regular appearances for Mickey and friends at hospitals, in parades and at shopping malls. Snow White and the Seven Dwarfs even celebrated their 50th birthday with a visit to the New York Stock Exchange. The continued success of the Disney brand is not just dependent upon its existing business interests.

The company is also continually developing new characters and pursuing new business opportunities, so that it can further increase its market presence.

(*Sources:* Gail DeGeorge, 'A theme park you can live in', *Business Week*, 25 September 1995, p. 57; Stanley Bing, 'More magic from Mickey's and Michael's kingdom', *Fortune*, 15 January 1996, p. 51; Disneyland Paris, 1999)

Test yourself

Case question

1 Why has Robinsons added to its product mix? What impact might a narrower product mix have on the company?

Quick questions

2 Name five different types of industrial (business-to-business) products and give an example of each type.
3 Using an example to illustrate your answer, explain what is meant by the core, actual and augmented product?

Applied question

4 You are preparing a lecture for undergraduates that aims to explain the classification of consumer products. Prepare an outline of your slides for the session. Make sure that your slides explain the key features of convenience, shopping, speciality and unsought products.

Extra readings

Baker, M. and Hart, S. (1998) *Product Strategy and Management.* Harlow: Pearson/FT.

De Chernatony, L. and McDonald, M. (2004) *Creating Powerful Brands.* Oxford: Butterworth-Heinemann.

Doyle, P. (2002) *Marketing Management and Strategy.* Harlow: Pearson/FT.

Lehmann, D. and Winer, R. (2001) *Product Management.* Boston, MA: McGraw-Hill.

Rosenau, M.D., Griffin, A., Castellion, G. and Anschuetz, N. (eds) (1996) *The PDMA Handbook of New Product Development.* New York: John Wiley.

Trott, P. (2002) *Innovation Management and New Product Development.* Harlow: Pearson/FT.

Wind, Y.J. (1982) *Product Policy: Concepts, Methods and Strategy.* Reading, MA: Addison-Wesley.

16: The Product Life Cycle (PLC)

Key definitions

The *product life cycle* (PLC) emulates the human life cycle: introduction, growth, maturity and decline.

Introduction denotes a product's first appearance in the marketplace, before any sales or profits develop.

Growth is the PLC stage at which a product's sales rise rapidly and profits reach their peak.

Maturity is the stage at which a product's sales curve peaks and starts to decline, profits continue to decline.

Decline denotes the final stage of the PLC during which sales fall rapidly.

PLC options are product deletion, modification or new product development.

Key issues

- The product life cycle (PLC) emulates the human life cycle, with introduction, growth, maturity and decline. It is a difficult concept to utilize in practice, but is very useful in allocating resources, assessing market attractiveness or managing product portfolios. Marketers must track sales and benchmark performance against rivals' products and market conditions in order to deploy the PLC concept.
- The introduction stage is when sales are zero, the product is first offered to the target segment and profits are negative owing to the product development and marketing costs incurred before sales commence.
- Assuming the product satisfies target market needs and is adequately resourced in terms of marketing, it should enter the growth stage. Sales take off, but the number of competitors is likely to be low, leading to a peak in profits. Towards the end of this stage, competitors enter, increasing the number of rival products and reducing profitability.
- During the maturity stage of the PLC, sales level and then decline. Customers switch to new technologies or simply no longer desire the product. Gradually, companies withdraw their products in the face of declining sales. Those competitors remaining must modify their marketing mix tactics in order to rejuvenate their sales performance.
- By the decline stage, most customers have moved on, preferring alternative products or solutions to their needs. Most suppliers will have withdrawn their products. The few companies remaining may make a reasonable return as niche players in a much smaller marketplace.
- For the marketer, the key task is to identify the maturity stage before it is too late, modifying the marketing mix accordingly to encourage continued sales. The decline stage, too, must be recognized to avoid heavy financial losses or in order to consciously alter to a

niche marketing strategy, utilizing little marketing resource.

- Occasionally, the life cycle is distorted from the norm owing to market conditions, such as long-term patent protection, a player dropping out, new applications or uses for the product being discovered, a lack of competitor innovation/substitution or customer dissonance reducing sales, or the introduction of product innovations and style changes kick-starting the marketplace's interest in the product.

Conceptual overview

As discussed in Brief 17, companies must often manage more than a single product or brand, allocating their marketing resource to support products generating the most benefit for the business. There are many considerations in such decision-making, including the attractiveness of a market, the business's strength and performance and evolving market conditions. Important aspects are the product life cycle (PLC) and the associated likely sales curve.

People are born, develop, mature, then decline in old age until death. The product life cycle builds on this human cycle, assuming that a successful product is created, launched, builds up a sales base, faces increasing competition or changing customer needs and declines, until the company withdraws it from the marketplace and kills it off. The marketer's PLC concept has four stages, therefore: introduction, growth, maturity and decline. Not all products pass through all of these stages, as on-going analyses (cf. Brief 17) may identify problems that

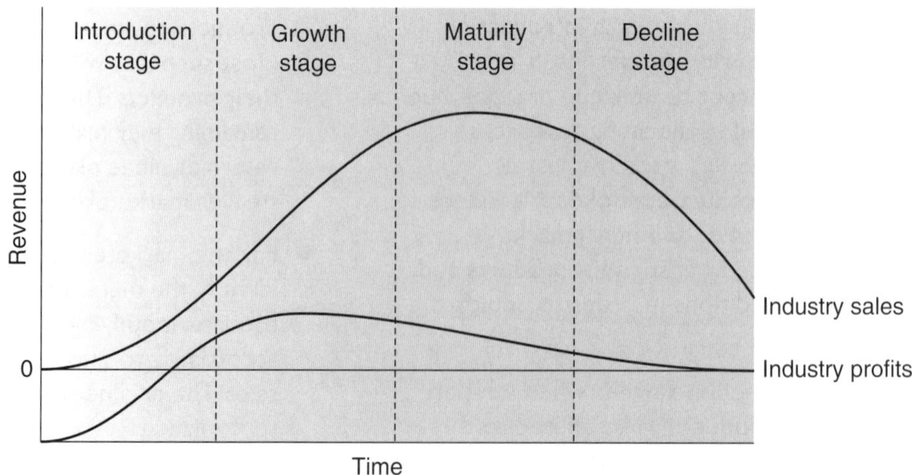

Figure 16.1 The product life cycle (PLC)

persuade decision-makers to withdraw a product before it reaches the growth or maturity stages.

The curves for some products, for example pharmaceuticals and IT products, exhibit slightly modified curves, but the stages of the PLC apply to all products and services. While the PLC concept is particularly helpful as part of a market attractiveness study, resource allocation, or marketing planning programme, the difficulty arises in practice in determining which stage a product has reached. Introduction and decline are readily apparent, but how does the marketer know when maturity is reached until sales already have levelled off? On-going tracking of sales and benchmarking against rival products assist in recognizing growth and maturity stages, but without such thorough and continual analysis, the PLC concept cannot be of real benefit to marketers. Shrewd use of the concept enables marketers to take remedial action to remedy premature declines, maximize profit opportunities and re-allocate sales and marketing resources to reflect sales levels.

The introduction stage commences with the product's first appearance in the marketplace, with zero sales and negative profits: new product development expenses and launch costs have not been recouped from any sales revenue at this stage in the PLC. Potential buyers must be made aware of the product and enticed to try it: costly marketing activities. Few competitors will have developed similar products or have the required marketing resource. Philips and Sony alone developed CD players, but had to spend heavily to persuade software producers and consumers to consider the product.

Assuming the product satisfies customers' requirements and is given the right image to appeal to the target market, the growth stage will occur when sales start to take off. Many products fail to reach this stage of the PLC. Profits peak during this stage as sales rise but are shared by the few active producers or retailers. Towards the end of the growth stage, competitors have witnessed the rise in demand and have brought out copycat products that increasingly fight for market share.

During the maturity stage, sales level off and eventually decline. Innovative products may be stealing customer demand, customers may have found alternative solutions or simply no longer require a product of this nature. The increasingly hostile battlefield of a marketplace requires rival producers to increase their marketing spend in order to defend their market shares. The result is a sharp drop in profitability and some suppliers will be forced out of the market. Those that remain must renew their promotional and distribution efforts, along with their pricing policies, in order to invigorate the market. In order to 'kick start' the product fortunes in mature markets, marketers may need to modify their products in terms of quality, functionality or style.

During the decline stage, new technology or social trends lead to drastically reduced sales and often negative profitability. Many remaining suppliers withdraw from the market or introduce the next generation of a product, so commencing a new PLC. A few niche producers may remain and in a less competitive market, albeit much smaller, reasonable profitability may be possible. Product deletion may be immediate if financial losses are catastrophic, or the product may be run out or phased out (cf. Brief 16).

The marketer must strive to identify the decline stage before the harsh realities of declining sales and profitability cause problems. In reality, few companies are single-product, so marketers constantly juggle a portfolio of products all at differing stages in the product life cycle. This is termed managing a portfolio (cf. Brief 17).

Research has shown that while the shape of the life cycle in Figure 16.1 is generally applicable to most products and sectors, there are product categories for which the shape varies slightly, such as for pharmaceuticals and high-tech products. Certain market conditions may also distort the life cycle. For example, an unsuccessful competitor may enter the market, initially gaining sales but then losing them as customers switch from this player's inferior product, creating a second growth stage for the other players. There may be a highly cyclical pattern of several peaks and troughs caused by the discovery of new uses or applications leading to sequential improvements of sales. Occasionally, there is no decline stage owing to a lack of competition or customer dissonance. Very often, the decline stage is halted early on, as new product launches or style changes rekindle the market's interest.

Examples

Whiter teeth

Caring for teeth used simply to involve regular brushing and periodic visits to the dentist. Yet tooth care has recently undergone a change. Consumers' preoccupation with their appearance is creating enormous marketing opportunities in this and other areas. Glossy magazines are full of advertisements for cosmetics designed to improve the way we look. In recent years some consumer concern has become focused upon the whiteness of their teeth. Perhaps the increasing fascination with celebrities, most of whom display flawless, dazzling teeth, is partly to blame? Whatever the cause, the outcome has been the appearance of a wide range of tooth whitening products. The *Rapid White* system is just one of many available through pharmacists and other retail outlets. According to the marketing material promoting the system, consumers can expect a safe and gentle tooth whitening system, promising great results in just one week. Many dentists are also offering cosmetic treatment of this type. At a time when dental hygiene is improving and tooth decay is declining, consumers' concern about the whiteness of their teeth is providing a new source of business.

(*Source: Rapid White* marketing material)

Thorntons

Even well-known and well-loved brands such as Thorntons reach the maturity phase of the product life cycle. At such times, businesses must do what they can to avoid the decline in sales that can follow. Despite the popularity of its *Continental* chocolates and other confectionery products, Thorntons' financial results suggested that the company had hit turbulent times. In 2000, the company's full-year profits were around 40% down, causing the company to review its marketing and change the advertising agency handling its account. As a result of this review, Thorntons reconsidered its core message to consumers, which had been to encourage individuals to buy their indulgent chocolates for themselves rather than only as gifts. Customer marketing research suggested that rather than persuading individuals to engage in a self-indulgent purchase, the company should shift its emphasis to marketing chocolates as a gift item. The company knew that achieving this positioning shift required a new advertising campaign, emphasising the gift-buying possibilities, as well as the introduction of new products.

Thorntons also examined the design and layout of its 410 retail outlets, in order to develop a more suitable environment for displaying qualities of its varied product range and promoting gift ideas. The company has also been considering whether it should develop its café outlets, as well as ways to develop on-line e-commerce sales. As part of its shift in emphasis to gift provision, the company has expanded its on-line division, focusing on the gift market, with offers for hampers, flowers, gift ideas, seasonal treats, a wedding service, and even corporate gifts. *The perfect way to say thank you*, is the on-line message.

(*Sources:* Cordelia Brabbs, 'Thorntons unwraps its brand rescue strategy', *Marketing*, 29 March 2001, p. 15; www.Thorntons.co.uk, 2004)

Test yourself

Case question

1 What options are open to Thorntons to prolong the life cycle of its chocolate products?

Quick questions

2 What are the different stages of the product life cycle?
3 Once a product reaches the 'maturity' stage of the product life cycle, will it inevitably go into decline?

Applied question

4 Assume the role of a Marketing Director explaining the product life cycle to a Board of Directors unfamiliar with the concept. Using an industry of your choice, explain how company strategy should vary at different stages of the product life cycle.

Extra readings

Aaker, D. (2001) *Strategic Marketing Management.* New York: Wiley.

Adcock, D. (2000) *Marketing Strategies for Competitive Advantage.* Chichester: Wiley.

Baker, M. and Hart, S. (1998) *Product Strategy and Management.* Harlow: Pearson/FT.

Dhalla, N.K. and Yuspeh, S. (1976) 'Forget the Product Lifecycle Concept', *Harvard Business Review* (Jan/Feb), pp. 102–12.

Doyle, P. (2002) *Marketing Management and Strategy.* Harlow: Prentice Hall/FT.

Majaro, S. (1995) 'Product Planning', in Thomas, M.J. (ed.), *Gower Handbook of Marketing.* Aldershot: Gower.

Rosenau, M.D., Griffin, A., Castellion, G. and Anschuetz, N. (eds) (1996) *The PDMA Handbook of New Product Development.* New York: John Wiley.

Wind, Y.J. (1982) *Product Policy: Concepts, Methods and Strategy.* Reading, MA: Addison-Wesley.

17: Product Portfolios

Key definitions

Product portfolio analysis is a strategic planning tool that analytically takes a product's performance and market standing into consideration when determining a marketing strategy and allocating the marketing budget.

The BCG growth-share matrix is a proprietary portfolio model that considers market growth rate and the product's relative market share.

The directional policy matrix (DPM) market attractiveness–business strength model helps to determine growth and divestment opportunities by considering many aspects of market attractiveness and business position.

The ABC sales : contribution analysis examines the financial worth to a company of its products, brands or target markets.

Key issues

- Most businesses are not single product entities and must decide how best to support a portfolio of products. This decision-making is supported with a range of portfolio planning models and analyses, the most popular of which are the BCG growth-share matrix and the directional policy matrix (DPM).
- The BCG growth-share matrix assumes a marketing strategy should take account of a product's relative market share and the growth rate of the market. When all of a company's products are plotted on the growth-share matrix, it is possible to identify star products, cash cows, dogs and problem children. Strategic options include building market share, maintaining share, harvesting or divesting.
- The market attractiveness–business strength model is commonly known as the directional policy matrix (DPM). Instead of using single measures for the matrix axes as with the BCG growth-share matrix, the DPM enables several criteria to be assessed on both axes: market attractiveness criteria and business strength/position criteria. For this reason, it is increasingly popular in marketing oriented businesses. Each company adopts its own set of specified criteria, but utilizes the same variables and weightings over time in order to track changes in the fortunes of strategic business units (SBUs) or individual products.
- The ABC sales : contribution analysis assesses the financial worth to a company of individual products, customers, market segments or strategic business units. A plot of sales and financial contributions enables marketers to judge where to devote their sales and marketing resources, which products, customers or market segments require more attention, and which no longer warrant resourcing.

Conceptual overview

Most organizations have a portfolio of brands or products. One marketing team may control the whole portfolio or separate groups of marketers may be responsible for one or a family of brands. Either way, the company's senior managers must know which particular products have the greatest chance of success, where they are in terms of the product life cycle, how each will be affected by changes in the marketplace and market attractiveness, which exhibit business strengths and where best to allocate sales and marketing budgets for the overall benefit of the business. The product portfolio approach to marketing management presents marketers with a set of analytical tools to help facilitate this complex task. The most popular of these techniques include the ABC sales : contribution analysis, the BCG growth-share matrix, and the directional policy matrix (DPM).

These models allow strategic business units (SBUs) or products to be classified and visually displayed according to the attractiveness of various markets and a business's relative performance within those markets. In addition, the product life cycle concept (cf. Brief 16) is an important tool often utilized in determining future strategies for brands and products: options differ for the growth or mature stages and markedly for the introduction and decline stages. The Boston Consulting Group (BCG) growth-share matrix builds on this suggestion.

The Boston Consulting Group (BCG) growth-share matrix

The Boston Consulting Group (BCG) approach is based on the notion that a product's market growth rate and its relative market share are important considerations in determining its marketing strategy. All the company's products are integrated into an overall matrix and evaluated to determine appropriate strategies for individual SBUs and products. A balanced product portfolio matrix is the end result of a number of actions, not just the analysis. Options include building market share, maintaining share, harvesting share, or divesting. Managers can use this matrix to determine and classify each product's expected future cash contributions and future budget requirements.

The BCG growth-share matrix (Figure 17.1) enables a marketing manager to classify a company's products into four basic types: (a) *stars* are products with a dominant share of the market and good prospects for growth, but they use more cash than they generate to finance growth, add capacity and increase market share; (b) *cash cows* have a dominant share of the market but low prospects for growth, generating more cash than is required to maintain market share and funding the stars and problem children; (c) *dogs* are struggling, having a subordinate share of the market and low prospects for growth, so they should be phased out or withdrawn immediately; and (d) *problem children* – 'question marks' – have a small share of a growing market and generally require a large amount of cash to build share: will they be future star products or dogs?

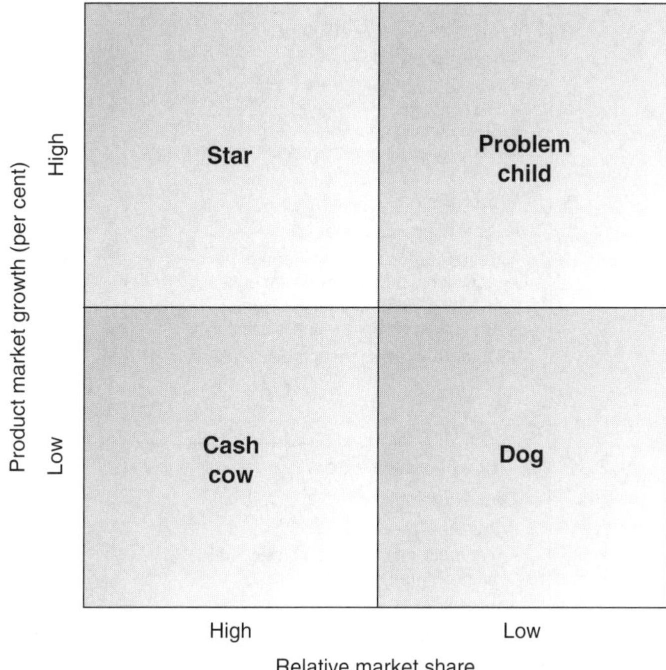

Figure 17.1 The BCG growth-share matrix

The BCG growth-share matrix can be expanded to show a company's whole portfolio by providing for each product: (a) its cash sales volume, illustrated by the size of a circle on the matrix; (b) its market share relative to competition, represented by the horizontal position of the product on the matrix; and (c) the growth rate of the market, indicated by the position of the product in the vertical direction. It should be noted that relative market share is a company's own market share relative to the biggest competitor's. Figure 17.2 summarizes marketing strategies appropriate for cash cows, stars, dogs and problem children.

Market attractiveness–business strength model

Rather than using single measures to define the vertical and horizontal dimensions of the portfolio matrix, the market attractiveness–business strength model employs multiple measurements and observations. It is an increasingly popular tool, particularly in businesses producing detailed annual marketing plans and is commonly known as the directional policy matrix (DPM). The vertical dimension – market attractiveness – includes all aspects that relate to the market, such as seasonality, economies of scale, competitive intensity, industry sales and the overall cost and feasibility of entering the market. The horizontal axis – business strength – is a composite of factors such as sales, relative market share, research and development, price competitiveness, product quality and market knowledge. Each company deploying

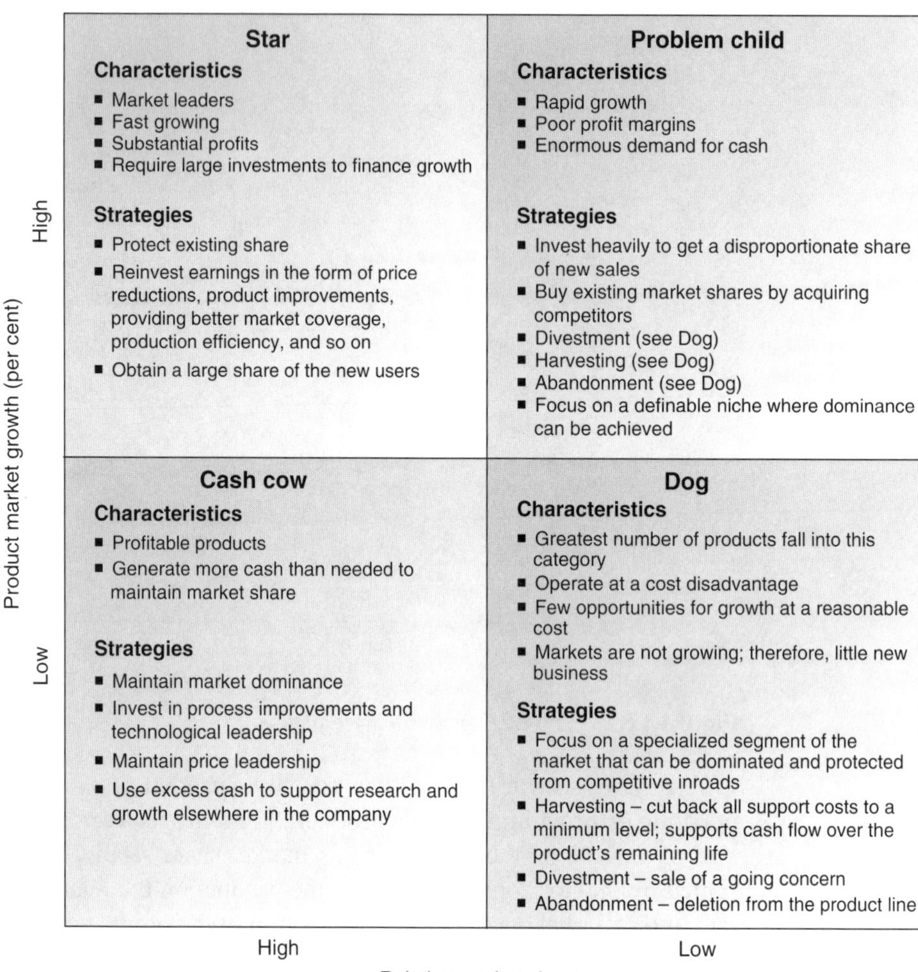

Figure 17.2 Actions resulting from the BCG analysis

this tool selects its own criteria, but uses these same ones over time to monitor changes. A slight variation of this matrix is called General Electric's strategic business planning grid because General Electric is credited with extending the product portfolio planning tool to examine market attractiveness and business strength.

The best situation for a company is to have a strong business position in an attractive market. The upper left area in Figure 17.3 represents the opportunity for an invest/grow strategy, but the matrix does not indicate how to implement this strategy. The purpose of the model is to serve as a diagnostic tool to highlight SBUs or products that have an opportunity to grow or that should be divested or approached selectively. SBUs or products that occupy the invest/grow position can lose their position through poor marketing strategies. Decisions on allocating resources to SBUs or products of medium overall attractiveness should be arrived at on a basis relative to other SBUs/products that are either more or less attractive.

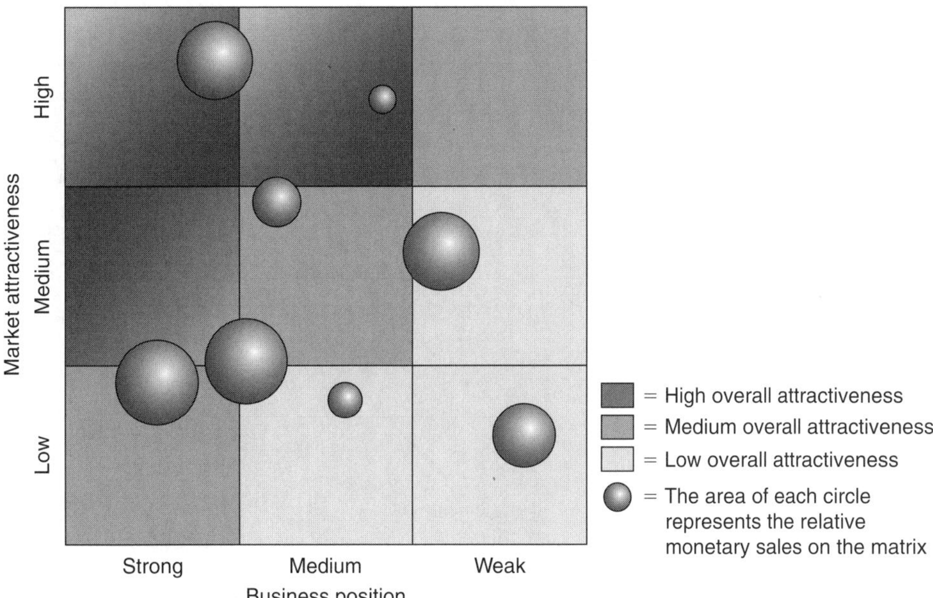

Figure 17.3 The DPM market attractiveness–business strength matrix

The lower right area of the matrix is a low growth harvest/divest area. Harvesting is a gradual withdrawal of marketing resources on the assumption that sales will decline at a slow rate but profits will still be significant at a lower sales volume. Harvesting and divesting may be appropriate strategies for SBUs or products characterized by low overall attractiveness (cf. Brief 33).

The ABC sales : contribution analysis

The ABC sales : contribution analysis can be conducted at either product group or product line level; for the total market, territories or sub-markets; for customer groups/market segments; or for individual customer accounts. The aim is to show both the amount of sales and the financial worth from these sales to the company's fortunes. Financial success is not confined to sales volume figures; a business must have an adequate level of contribution (sales revenue minus all variable costs) from its sales. This analysis helps companies to identify the relative value of different products, markets or even individual customer accounts, assisting with the allocation of resources.

The 45 degree diagonal line from bottom left to top right (see Figure 17.4) is the optimum. It is a straightforward ruled line, not a regression line. In an ideal world, the dots (products or customers) on the chart would be located on the line (good sales and contribution) and be at the top right of the graph (high sales and high contribution). These 'sell a lot, make a lot' are the 'A' class. Typically, however, this is not the case. The majority of products, customers or markets fall at the bottom left of the graph (low sales and low contribution: the 'C' class), or they have mediocre sales and contributions (the 'B' class).

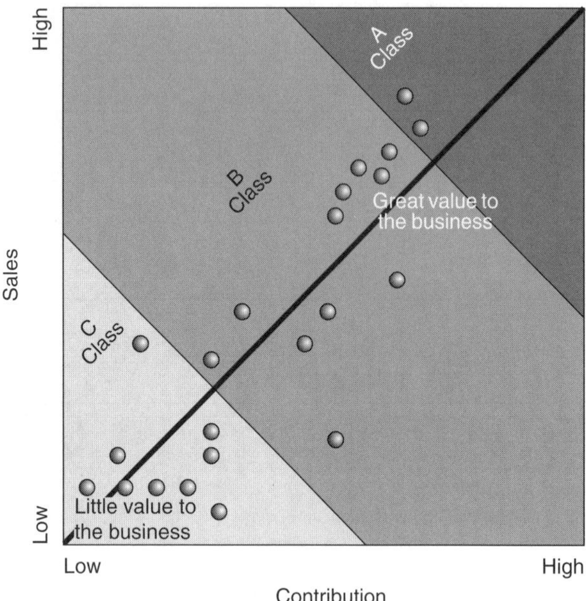

Figure 17.4 ABC sales: contribution analysis

(*Source: adapted from* Sally Dibb, Lyndon Simkin, Bill Pride and O.C. Ferrell, *Marketing: Concepts and Strategies*, Boston, MA: Houghton Mifflin, 2001)

Three important conclusions can be drawn from an ABC analysis. (a) It can identify highly attractive customers, markets or products in terms of the associated contributions, but where sales are relatively low. For such cases, an increase in sales (no matter how slight), with associated high prices and good financial returns, will be highly rewarding. (b) It can determine accounts with high sales figures but low or pitiful contributions. Cash flow may be good, but profitability is not helped: even a slight increase in contribution is most desirable. (c) It can challenge the historical perspective that often clouds managers' judgement as to what constitutes a 'good' product, market or customer. Often, managers still believe the historical rhetoric rather than recognize that the situation has moved on; new priorities must benefit from the available resources and marketing effort.

Examples

AVENT

AVENT is well established as an international provider of high-quality baby equipment. Using the positioning *AVENT Naturally*, the company has developed its expertise as a manufacturer of a range of gadgets designed to make life with a baby easier. These include baby bottles, bottle warmers, bottle bags and sterilizers. Now AVENT has developed its brand to include a range of new products targeted at pregnant women. The premium-priced AVENT *Future Mother* range offers Indulgent Body Cream, Moisturising Light Oil, Relaxing Bath & Shower Essence and Leg and Foot Reviver. This extension to the brand continues to promote the 'natural' characteristics of the company's products with hypoallergenic products, including a variety of natural oils and vitamins. The result is a more diverse portfolio for AVENT to manage.

(*Source:* AVENT marketing material)

JCB

Privately owned construction giant JCB has become synonymous with the backhoe loader. Originally designed by company founder Joe Bamford, the 'digger' has become a familiar sight on country roads and building sites. With around one-quarter of the world's backhoe loader market and approximately 40% share in Europe, the importance of this product to the company is beyond dispute. Not surprisingly, JCB is continually trying to improve the mechanical and other characteristics of the backhoe loader to ensure that it maintains its market position. However, the backhoe loader is just one of a range of products in JCB's portfolio. In all, the company has eight main product areas, covering a wide range of construction equipment. In addition to backhoe loaders, JCB manufactures crawler and wheeled crawler excavators, fork lifts, rough terrain fork lift trucks, skid steer loaders, mini-excavators, telescopic handlers and wheeled loading shovels.

In construction industry terms, JCB has chosen to focus primarily on medium-sized and compact equipment, leaving the very large earth-moving equipment to US competitor Caterpillar and Japanese companies such as Hitachi and Komatsu. Even so, JCB is clear about the need for variety in its product portfolio, seeking to avoid over-reliance on one particular product group. Many of JCB's customers from sectors such as plant hire, house building, manufacturing, contracting, civil engineering, agriculture, waste disposal, landscaping, public utilities and extraction, expect to be able to source a range of products from the company. It is also the case that in different international markets, the popularity of particular types of construction equipment varies. For example, some customers in Germany use mini-excavators for jobs that UK customers might carry out with a backhoe loader. JCB must continually assess the whole of its product portfolio in order to ensure resources are allocated to the 'stars of tomorrow' and to identify declining products that must be harvested.

(*Sources:* Sally Dibb and Lyndon Simkin, *The Marketing Casebook*, London: Thomson; *The JCB Experience*, JCB, 2001)

Test yourself

Case question

1 Why does JCB need a mix of products in its portfolio?

Quick questions

2 What is a product portfolio?
3 Using examples to illustrate your answer, explain why businesses need to manage their product portfolios?

Applied question

4 You are advising a camera manufacturer about its product portfolio. The company in question has become very reliant on a camera type that is now in danger of becoming obsolete. Prepare some notes to accompany a presentation to the company that explains how portfolio management might help them plan for the future.

Extra readings

Day, G.S. (1986) *Analysis for Strategic Marketing Decisions.* St Paul, MN: West.

Dibb, S., Simkin, L., Ferrell, O.C. and Pride, W. (2001) *Marketing: Concepts and Strategies.* Boston, MA: Houghton Mifflin.

Doyle, P. (2002) *Marketing Management and Strategy.* Harlow: Pearson/FT.

Macrae, C. (1999) *The Brand Chartering Handbook.* London: Thomson.

Majaro, S. (1995) 'Product Planning', in M.J. Thomas (ed.), *Gower Handbook of Marketing.* Aldershot: Gower.

McDonald, M. (2002) *Marketing Plans.* Oxford: Butterworth-Heinemann.

Rosenau, M.D., Griffin, A., Castellion, G. and Anschuetz, N. (eds) (1996) *The PDMA Handbook of New Product Development.* New York: John Wiley.

Wensley, R. (1981) 'Strategic Marketing: Beta, Boxes or Basics', *Journal of Marketing,* 45 (Summer), pp. 173–83.

Wind, Y.J. (1982) *Product Policy: Concepts, Methods and Strategy.* Reading, MA: Addison-Wesley.

18: Packaging

Key definitions

Packaging is the development of a product's container, label and graphic design.

Labelling is a packaging ingredient that is used to distinguish a product and to convey product or legally required information to customers and distributors.

Key issues

- The requirement to effectively communicate product benefits and brand differentiation includes a product's packaging and labelling, both primary packaging and the shipping (secondary) packaging.
- Packaging should be functional, for the end users and also for the stockist or distributor. Packaging must protect the product while facilitating its easy use and storage. Packaging needs also to support the product's branding and differentiation, while adhering to legal requirements and ethical considerations.
- Increasingly, packaging must pay attention to the environmental concerns of the 'greening' consumer and to the regulations addressing its manufacture and waste disposal. Tamper-resistant packaging is also desirable.
- Packaging should reflect the needs and expectations of targeted customers, differentiate the product from rivals and adhere to the adopted branding.
- Packaging development involves aesthetical and structural choices. Other considerations include: material selection, surface graphics, typography, information layout and hierarchies, front-of-pack versus back-of-pack detailing, language and jargon, photography and illustrations, use of colour, symbols and icons, final finishes and effects, labelling practicalities and bar-coding/tracking.
- There are numerous primary packaging options: cartons, bottles, tubes, cans, tubs and jars, multi-packs, clamshells, blister-packs, CD boxes, gift packs and a host of innovatory solutions for storing, displaying and dispensing products.
- There are many strategic issues connected with packaging, including when and to what extent to alter packaging, secondary use packaging, category consistent packaging, innovation, multiple packs and product handling.
- Labelling is integral to packaging, but must increasingly conform to regulations and ethical controls. Labelling should be informative, truthful and – to assist in product differentiation – distinctive.

Conceptual overview

Packaging and labelling are also part of the marketing process. Packaging includes the immediate container (the primary packaging) and the shipping packaging (the secondary packaging). Both need to exhibit functionality in order to protect and easily convey the product inside and facilitate its easy use and storage. Additionally, packaging should support the product's branding and differentiation. The packaging design and display properties are often integral to the brand identity being marketed, particularly for fast moving consumer goods (FMCGs). As with the product's design, the packaging must also reflect the needs and expectations of the customer.

Packaging design should consider customer requirements but also the needs of the retailers, wholesalers and distributors who will be required to handle and stock the products, and in many circumstances display and deliver the products. Tamper-resistant packaging is often desirable to both channel members and customers, but in all packaging executions, cost is an issue. When developing packaging, a business must consider not only the functionality for the end-user, but for the retailer or distributor, too. Failure to consider the ease of use, movement and storage considerations of marketing channel members may result in them deciding not to stock the product.

The promotional application of packaging is a major issue for marketers who aim to utilize their packaging designs to convey a strong brand identity and assist in differentiating their products from rival products. Colour choice is important, as some colours suggest danger, neutrality, calm, luxury and so forth. Many design experts believe that good packaging design is fundamental to consumers making speedy product selections in retail environments, particularly as self-selection by shoppers becomes the norm. For brands offering ranges, wishing to benefit from cross-promotional activity and increased joint brand awareness, packaging design is particularly important. Increasingly, environmental concerns are more to the fore in marketers' packaging decisions, with consumers and regulators becoming alarmed about waste disposal and emissions during manufacture.

Packaging development requires a mix of aesthetical considerations and structural necessities to guarantee the functionality of the design. There are cartons, bottles, tubes, cans, tubs and jars, multi-packs, clamshells and blister packs, CD boxes, gift packs, plus many innovative formats for storing, displaying and dispensing products in a manner that is ahead of the competition. Material selection is an important stage in the design process, as are the specification and application of surface graphics, and typography. Decisions must be made concerning information layout and the hierarchy of messages, front-of-pack versus back-of-pack detailing, choice of language and jargon, the photography and images to be selected, illustrations and use of colour, deployment of symbols and icons, final finishes and effects. There are often practical requirements, such as weights, measures, ingredients, nutritional information and bar-coding.

In terms of marketing strategy, packaging raises a number of issues:

- Alterations to packaging. Innovations from rivals may lead to changes in order to keep abreast of market developments. Where this is not the case, change should be made with caution as some consumers are surprisingly change-averse. Changes should be consistent with the branding and brand positioning strategy and ensure the heritage advantages of existing brand recognition (cf. Brief 14) are not lost. Changes could be for safety reasons, improved customer use or to feature more prominently product benefits: these explanations should be communicated to the target market.
- Secondary use packaging. Jars and ice cream tubs are used as domestic storage: this may be harnessed to persuade customers of additional purchase benefits.
- Category consistent packaging. Consumers, but particularly channel members such as retailers and distributors, often welcome packaging that is consistent with existing product category norms: familiarity leads to reassurance.
- Innovative packaging. In many cases, a break from the norms, so long as consumers perceive a benefit, creates a competitive edge over rivals: non-drip Tetra Paks or easy-to-squeeze ketchup containers.
- Multi-packs. Multiple packages such as six-packs of beer or nine toilet rolls conveniently packaged together, appeal to stockists and to consumers, but have pricing policy implications (cf. Brief 31).
- Product handling. Some packaging innovations are designed to facilitate easy handling during the distribution process or by customers.

Labelling is an integral part of packaging that can be used effectively to convey product information and benefits to customers and to promote a brand's positioning image. There are increasing legal considerations that marketers must address, such as EU regulations in terms of food sourcing, ingredient content, weights and measures, as well as cooking or application instructions. Ethical marketing requires that consumers are not misled or 'over-sold' owing to the information provided on labels.

Examples

Phileas Fogg

When United Biscuits re-launched its Phileas Fogg Tortilla Chips in new pyramid bags, the company believed it had discovered an innovative way to boost market share. The concept was simple: a pyramid bag, with a wider opening, allowing the company to promote the fact that the snack was ideal for sharing. From a production viewpoint, the new design could be manufactured relatively easily, with only small changes to the production line. The innovative design also meant that the packs were eye-catching on supermarket shelves. Although customers responded positively and sales increased, United Biscuits soon had to withdraw the new packaging because retailers found the merchandising trays in which the snacks were displayed difficult to stack. Ultimately the company could not afford to alienate the supermarkets and risk declining shelf space. Instead, United Biscuits undertook a new re-launch, putting the Tortilla Chips back into pillow packs, but with an updated graphic design.

(*Source:* Pamela Buxton, 'Brave moves into radical redesigns', *Marketing*, 22 March 2001, pp. 33–4)

Tetra Pak

For decades, households in the UK received morning doorstep deliveries of milk in glass pint bottles. Competition to doorstep deliveries emerged from the national supermarket chains, which increasingly turned to non-glass packaging. Initially, alternative packaging was in the form of card-based cartons. These became rather infamous for being hard to open. Retailers, therefore, looked to packaging alternatives, with many deciding to use plastic one- and two-litre containers with twist-open tops. These containers were easier to open than the cartons and less fragile than the original glass bottles. The largest manufacturer of the cartons responded by developing similarly easy-to-open tops, which compared favourably to the plastic rival and shared the safety advantages over glass.

Now the manufacturer, global packaging giant Tetra Pak, is challenging the plastic-based competition on environmental grounds. High profile advertising has targeted consumers in an attempt to persuade them to choose non-plastic cartons. Tetra Pak's aim is to stem a switch in the dairy industry to plastic-based packaging. As the world's largest producer of liquid food packaging, the company is behaving sensibly in striving to compete more effectively, but its environment-friendly message also fits well with increasing consumer concerns about green issues. In addition, Tetra Pak plans to orientate consumers to the food preservation benefits of its packaging option. Advertisements featuring a carton boldly display the Tetra Pak name and the strapline *protects what's good.* The losses to plastic rivals reflected consumer dissatisfaction with the old-style cartons. The reaction by Tetra Pak, in modifying its openings and now in highlighting other consumer and environmental benefits, reflects the forward-thinking of this manufacturer.

(*Sources: Marketing*, 30 October 2003, p. 5; Tetra Pak; Tesco Stores; Sainsbury's; Tetra Pak advertising, January 2004)

Test yourself

Case question

1 Why did Tetra Pak have to modify its packaging concept and subsequently promote its product benefits?

Quick questions

2 What are the key purposes of packaging?
3 Using examples to illustrate your answer, explain two ways in which packaging can be used strategically.

Applied question

4 As a consultant working for a consultancy specializing in packaging design, you have been asked to develop a brochure for prospective clients which explains the factors to be considered when developing new packaging.

Extra readings

Calver, G. (2004) *What is Packaging Design?* Mies, Switzerland: RotoVision SA.

De Chernatony, L. and McDonald, M. (2004) *Creating Powerful Brands.* Oxford: Butterworth-Heinemann.

Lehmann, D. and Winer, R. (2001) *Product Management.* Boston, MA: McGraw-Hill.

Macrae, C. (1999) *The Brand Chartering Handbook.* London: Thomson.

Rosenau, M.D., Griffin, A., Castellion, G. and Anschuetz, N. (eds) (1996) *The PDMA Handbook of New Product Development*. New York: John Wiley.

Trott, P. (2002) *Innovation Management and New Product Development.* Harlow: Pearson/FT.

19: Service Products

Key definitions

A *service* is an intangible product involving a deed, performance or effort that cannot be stored or physically possessed.

Service characteristics include intangibility, a direct organization–client relationship and inseparability, consumer participation in the production process and complexity.

Service quality is a customer's perception of how well a service meets or exceeds expectations.

Key issues

- The marketer's definition of product suggests that 'product' includes physical goods, services and ideas. Services differ from other products in marketing because of the core characteristics: intangibility, a direct organization–client interaction and inseparability, consumer participation in production, and complexity.
- Consumer services comprise education, health care, government administration, sports and recreation, entertainment and leisure, tourism, finance, personal and professional services, plus charitable activities.
- Business-to-business services include computing and telecoms, media, consultancy, legal and professional, financial, technical, personnel and recruitment, catering, janitorial and maintenance.
- The economy of most developed countries has witnessed a switch in emphasis in the past 30 years, with the service sector increasingly dominant over manufacturing. Close to two-thirds of gross domestic product (GDP) in Europe, the United States and Japan stems from services and in the UK approaching 70% of the workforce is now employed in providing services.
- The core implications for marketing are the extension of the traditional product-focused marketing mix to include further ingredients and the difficulty in creating brand differentiation and a competitive advantage.
- Service quality is of paramount importance, resulting from the provider properly understanding customer expectations, service quality specification, employee performance and the management of service operations.

Conceptual overview

Brief 15 examined physical products. The service product is different. A service happens, it is intangible and results from human activity. It cannot be stored, physically possessed or repeated in an absolutely identical manner or set of circumstances. The same medical practitioner may give slightly differing advice to two patients apparently suffering the same disease. The chef in a favourite restaurant may well add a different ingredient or vary the presentation of the food. A lecturer delivering a repeat performance may re-order the slides used the second time the lecture is presented. Largely owing to the human factor and the intangibility of the service product, there can be marked variations in service delivery. To the customer, this may alter product quality, product satisfaction and even the customer's perception of the brand. The manufacturers of baked beans, cars, mobile phones or televisions do not face these issues, so long as they have incorporated stringent quality control procedures within their production and distribution systems.

Services include consumer and business-to-business activities. Consumer services comprise education, health care, government administration, sports and recreation, entertainment and leisure, tourism, finance, personal and professional services, and charitable activities. Business-to-business services include computing and telecoms, media, consultancy, legal and professional, financial, technical, personnel and recruitment, catering, janitorial and maintenance. Given such variety of coverage, it is not surprising that the service sector now accounts for more GDP and employment than manufacturing, and is a key recruitment ground for marketers.

The growth in consumer services has resulted from a mix of factors, including greater personal wealth, increased leisure time, smaller families creating spending and consumption opportunities, technological complexity demanding assistance from experts, the consumer's desire for more variety and extra challenges, and political parties promising more service provision. In businesses, decision-makers buy in expert advice, contract out routine services to free up working capital, desire flexibility in their operations and require help with increasingly complex technology.

The service characteristics create a unique set of circumstances for marketers. The key characteristics include:

- The intangibility of the service product: services cannot be stockpiled, mass produced in identical fashion or remove the human factor.
- There is a direct relationship between the service customer or client and the service provider or producer. Usually the customer meets or has contact via telecommunications with the service provider who in turn must be proficient, pleasant and appealing. There is little inseparability.
- The consumer partakes of the service at the time of its production: the theatre show or dental appointment takes place at the time of consumption. Service

quality, therefore, partly depends on the capability of the customer to understand and to conform to the service provider's operational needs.

- Services, compared with most consumer or industrial goods, are complex. The people factor – as customers and service providers – is largely responsible for these product and operational complexities and the difficulty in supervising product quality.

The dominant theme is that people are fickle, difficult to motivate and control as staff, while being hard to satisfy repeatedly as service customers.

Marketers must devote significant management time and resources to controlling service quality. This involves: (a) proper understanding of customer expectations; (b) thorough specification of service quality criteria; (c) monitoring of the delivery of the service, benchmarked against these criteria; (d) employee performance control, motivation and remedial activity; and (e) management's control of the service's operational requirements.

For services marketers, the implications are that the traditional marketing mix – product, price, place and promotion – is inadequate. The services marketing mix has thereby been extended to include additional ingredients: people, physical evidence and process (cf. Brief 44). The marketers of these 'products' must also strive harder to create strong brand identities and a differential advantage over competitors (cf. Brief 44). These issues apply equally to services marketers responsible for commercial services, such as financial services or tourism, and to those in the not-for-profit sector such as government departments or charities (cf. Brief 45).

Examples

Diabetes UK

It is estimated that the UK has 2.5 million sufferers of diabetes, one million of whom do not know. As more sufferers are diagnosed, there are increasing numbers of people requiring support, information and networking opportunities with other sufferers and health carers. Diabetes UK is the leading charity addressing these requirements amongst diabetes sufferers. The charity funds research, campaigns and endeavours to help people to live with the condition. In order to further help sufferers and families of those worried about the condition, the charity has decided to increase its membership from its current level of approximately 200 000. The charity's current marketing is mainly in conjunction with third parties such as pharmacies and medical practitioners, but this activity is now under review as the charity has appointed its first Marketing Director. In this role, Dawn Jackson oversees marketing, corporate affairs, community fundraising and supporter relations. A revised strategy is evolving which includes appraising target audience selection, the development of messages and propositions relevant to the target market and consideration of the choice of marketing communications.

(*Sources:* Diabetes UK website; Ben Bold in *Marketing*, 27 November 2003, p. 6; *Marketing Week*, 27 November 2003, p. 7)

Aer Lingus

Irish airline Aer Lingus competes against large and small operators on domestic, European and transatlantic routes. In order to secure its place in this competitive arena, the company views itself primarily as a service provider and has developed a service proposition based on friendly and professional customer care. Aer Lingus is clear that this proposition must extend to all aspects of its service delivery, including the recruitment, training and motivation of personnel, plus the airport and airline environment in which customers encounter the company. The Aer Lingus *Programme for a Better Airline* initiative was set up to ensure that the company stays customer-focused. Regular programmes of customer research and staff feedback enable the airline to understand and respond to changing needs and wants in the marketplace. The programme has already helped Aer Lingus begin dealing with customer anxieties associated with airport facilities, queuing, baggage handling, the in-flight experience and punctuality.

The Aer Lingus brand is built on a series of customer-focused values:

- Professionalism: this signals the company's desire to offer a service that reflects increasing professionalism within business.
- Intuition: in an industry where so much of the service experience is intangible, the airline seeks to ensure that its personnel can look beyond the obvious and be sensitive to customer needs that lie beneath the surface. This includes a desire to be proactive and ready to meet the unexpected.
- Intimacy: this refers to the need to build customer relationships based on the customer's point of view. There is an emphasis on being friendly, empathetic and caring.

So far, customers have responded well to Aer Lingus' efforts to be a responsive, high-quality service provider. There has been an 8 per cent rise in passenger numbers, cargo has increased by 10 per cent and new destinations are being added to the company's routes.

(*Sources:* David Bunworth, Aer Lingus; Aer Lingus Annual Reports, Aer Lingus Media Relations, 1999)

Test yourself

Case question

1 Why has Aer Lingus chosen to emphasize the brand values described in the case?

Quick questions

2 'Some services are more tangible than others.' Discuss this statement.
3 Using appropriate examples, explain the four characteristics of services that distinguish them from tangible goods.

Applied question

4 Assume that you work in the marketing department of a company owning several themed restaurant chains. You are currently working on the launch of a new chain and are giving careful consideration to an appropriate differential advantage. Your boss cannot understand why the process is taking you so long. You arrange to have a meeting to discuss the problems associated with creating a differential advantage in a service business. Prepare some notes summarizing the discussion you need to have.

Extra readings

Berry, L. (1995) *On Great Service.* New York: Free Press.
Gilmore, A. (2003) *Services Marketing and Management.* London: Sage.
Glynn, W.J. and Barnes, J.G. (1995) *Understanding Services Management, Integrating Marketing, Organisational Behaviour, Operations and Human Resource Management.* Chichester: Wiley.
Gronroos, C. (2000) *Service Management and Marketing.* Chichester: Wiley.
Kasper, H., van Helsdingen, P. and de Vries Jr, W. (1999) *Services Marketing Management: An International Perspective.* Chichester: Wiley.
Lovelock, C.H. (2001) *Principles of Services Marketing and Management.* Englewood Cliffs, NJ: Pearson.
Palmer, A. (2000) *Principles of Services Marketing.* Maidenhead: McGraw-Hill.

20: Advertising

Key definitions

Advertising is a paid form of non-personal marketing communication about an organization and/or its products that is transmitted to a target audience through mass media.

The *target audience* is the marketing communications practitioner's term for the target market segment intended as the principal recipient of the advertising's message.

An *advertising campaign* is a series of advertisements, utilizing various media, to reach a target audience.

The *promotional mix* comprises advertising, public relations, personal selling, sales promotion, direct mail, sponsorship and the Internet.

AIDA is a persuasive sequence aimed at the target audience: attention, interest, desire and action.

The *product adoption process* is awareness, interest, evaluation, trial and adoption.

The five *communications effects* are category need, brand awareness, brand attitude, brand purchase intention and purchase facilitation.

A *push policy* is promotion to only the next stage in the marketing channel and a *pull policy* is promotion directly to the intended ultimate consumer.

IMC (integrated marketing communications) is the coordination and integration of all marketing communication tools, avenues and sources within a company into a seamless programme that maximizes the impact on consumers and other end-users at a minimal cost.

Key issues

- Advertising is the most costly ingredient of the promotional mix, owing largely to high production and media expenses.
- The finished advertisement should be in harmony with target market buying behaviour, customer expectations and the company's brand positioning strategy. The advertising should facilitate the brand's differentiation and emphasize any differential advantages over rivals' brands or products.
- Advertising is part of the promotional mix, which traditionally included advertising, public relations, personal selling and sales promotion, but more recently has been expanded to include direct mail, sponsorship and the Internet.
- Advertising has many purposes over and above simply promoting a brand or an institution, including stimulating demand, combating competitors, supporting the field force, educating customers, increasing uses for a product, reminding and reinforcing attitudes, reducing sales fluctuations and conveying a brand's positioning.
- Although expensive, on a per capita basis, advertising's costs are relatively low. Media selection can be very specifically related to the target audience. The effectiveness of advertising

is very difficult to assess. Advertising is generally deployed in conjunction with other ingredients of the promotional mix.

- A series of advertisements, often using a mix of media, forms an advertising campaign. The key stages of developing a campaign are target audience identification, definition of advertising objectives, determination of an advertising platform, specification of the budget, development of the media plan, creativity, execution of the campaign and performance tracking.
- Marketers attempt, through marketing communications, to persuade the target audience to pass through a persuasive sequence of attention, interest, desire and action: AIDA.
- Advertising is often pivotal to creating sufficient brand awareness in the early stages of the product adoption process and in persuading the target audience to view a particular brand positively.
- Marketers adopt a push or a pull policy, or a combination: push is promotion to only the next stage in the marketing channel; pull is promotion directly to the intended ultimate consumer.
- There has been a proliferation of media, reducing the costs of placing specific advertisements but making the skill of media buying all the more important. The advertising industry has identified more targeted and cost-effective techniques, such as ambient advertising and viral marketing.
- Integrated marketing communications (IMC) is the coordination and integration of all marketing communication tools, avenues and sources within a company into a seamless programme that maximizes the impact on consumers and other end-users at a minimal cost. It is integration of the whole promotional mix and business-to-business, marketing channel, customer-focused and internally directed communications.

Conceptual overview

The promotional mix is the marketing communications ingredient of the marketing mix, comprising advertising, public relations, sales promotion, personal selling, direct mail, sponsorship and the Internet. Owing to the significant costs and lead times associated with advertising, it occupies much of a marketer's time and is a heavy burden on an organization. When a company is facing hard times, the advertising budget is an all too easy target for cuts, partly owing to the difficulty in proving a causal link between an advertisement and sales. It is important, therefore, that marketers plan advertising with care, having a full understanding of their target market and how customers perceive their product and competitors' products. The finished advertisement should reflect the needs and expectations of the target audience (cf. Briefs 6 and 7), support the business's determined brand positioning (cf. Brief 13) and emphasize any differential advantage over rivals (cf. Brief 35).

Advertising has many purposes in marketing:

- Promoting products, brands and organizations.
- Stimulating primary and selective demand.
- Off-setting competitors' advertising.
- Supporting the sales force's endeavours in the field.
- Educating the marketplace/target consumers.
- Increasing uses for a product.
- Reminding and reinforcing attitudes.
- Reducing sales fluctuations.
- Communicating a brand's positioning.

Advertising is more expensive than the other promotional mix ingredients, largely due to the associated production costs and the high charges demanded by the principal media: television, radio, press, magazines, websites, cinema and outdoor advertising media. Despite the high cost, owing to the large numbers of viewers, listeners or readers, per capita costs are relatively low, certainly lower than face-to-face personal selling or many forms of sales promotion. Shrewd media selection can target very specifically defined target audiences, although effectiveness feedback is notoriously slow and imperfect. Even if a targeted consumer claims to like an advertisement, it does not mean s/he was persuaded to make a purchase.

In terms of the product adoption process (cf. Brief 15) – awareness, interest, evaluation, trial and adoption – advertising is particularly important for creating brand awareness. The exponents of marketing communications, including advertising, believe in five communications effects: (a) category need; (b) brand awareness; (c) brand attitude; (d) brand purchase intention; and (e) purchase facilitation. Advertising plays a role in the first four effects, but particularly in creating brand awareness and a favourable attitude to the brand.

Marketers adopt a push or a pull strategy, or a combination. A push policy is when a producer promotes a product only to the next stage in the marketing channel, who in turn promotes the product. A pull policy is when a producer promotes directly to the intended ultimate consumer in order to create strong demand for the product to encourage stockists to source the product. A major manufacturer such as Mars will deploy both policies, promoting its products to consumers and trade channel members.

A series of advertisements, often utilizing a mix of relevant media, aimed at a target audience is an advertising campaign. There are eight core stages involved in creating an advertising campaign:

1 Identification and profiling of the target audience.
2 Definition of clear campaign objectives in synergy with the brand's marketing strategy.
3 Determination of a distinctive platform or advertising proposition: BMW's *Ultimate Driving Machine*, the Andrex puppies or L'Oreal's '*Because you're worth it*'.
4 Specification of the advertising budget.
5 Development of a media plan: detailed print or broadcast titles and timings.

6 Creativity to produce oral and visual vehicles for the advertising message.
7 Execution of the advertising campaign.
8 Evaluation of the advertising's effectiveness.

When preparing advertising copy, marketers strive to move the target audience through a persuasive sequence termed AIDA: attention, interest, desire and action. Marketers should test out several creative ideas with small samples of the target audience, often with the use of focus groups (cf. Brief 9) before commissioning an advertisement's production, and the eventual campaign's effectiveness should be monitored during and after its execution. An advertising agency consists of client services personnel, who coordinate strategy and production; creative, responsible for concept, art direction and copywriting; a media department that plans and buys media slots; and account planning, controlling research and strategy development. Advertising generally is deployed in conjunction with other ingredients from the promotional mix.

Advertising budgets account for a large part of the overall marketing budget, but in recent years there has been a proliferation of media, reducing the costs of placing specific advertisements. Companies have also extended their use of an increasingly diverse set of promotional mix ingredients, often at the expense of mainstream advertising, such as sales promotions, PR, Internet applications and sponsorship. The advertising industry has fought back, identifying more targeted and cost-effective techniques, such as ambient advertising and viral marketing. Advertisements appearing on huge buildings, as texts to mobiles or pop-ups on the Web, are just some examples.

Currently popular is the concept of integrated marketing communications (IMC). This is the coordination and integration of all marketing communications tools, avenues and sources within a company into a seamless programme that maximizes the impact on consumers and other end-users at a minimal cost. It is integration of the whole promotional mix (cf. Briefs 20–25), but also all business-to-business, marketing channel, customer-focused and internally directed communications. Rather than treating all aspects of the promotional mix and internal marketing (cf. Brief 40) separately, often utilizing many different departments and external agencies in an uncoordinated manner, the company instead opts to fully harmonize these activities. The benefits include greater clarity, reduced costs, stronger impact in the marketplace and more effective branding.

Examples

Marmite

Different advertising campaigns have different objectives. Bestfoods, makers of the yeast extract spread *Marmite*, have adopted a novel approach to encouraging people who like the product to buy more. The '*love it or hate it*' campaign, which is quite open about the fact that many people dislike the product, started running in 1996. One television advertisement featured a young man handing an elderly tramp his last *Marmite* sandwich. Initially grateful for the kindness, the tramp soon spits out the sandwich in disgust, throwing the remainder in the direction of his benefactor. The account director for the campaign from agency BMP explains the rationale by stating that *Marmite* is unusual: few brands attract such polarized views from consumers. The implication is that those who 'hate' the product will never be persuaded to eat it. Instead, the campaign aims to encourage those who enjoy the strong-tasting spread to use it more often. Bestfoods is even hopeful that consumers who have forgotten they enjoyed the product and who have not bought it for a long time, will be reminded and may start to buy it once again.

(*Source:* Emma Reynolds, 'Marmite develops "love it or hate it" theme in new ads', *Marketing*, 22 March 2001, p. 24)

KFC

Advertising, along with the rest of the promotional mix, exists to help implement a brand's target market strategy by communicating the product appeal and the brand positioning image to intended customers. Occasionally, a creative execution can be sufficiently memorable and strike a chord so well with the target audience, that a business re-thinks its whole marketing mix for a brand or product. New KFC advertising agency BBH, renowned for its creativity, launched the 'Soul Food' campaign in an attempt to break away from standard fast food chain advertising and to reflect recent menu changes at KFC.

In 2003, KFC spent over £16 m on its UK advertising, depicting a soul food positioning through moody, relaxed and vivid advertisements that promoted the sharing of food. Now new-look interiors, using large refectory-style 'sharing' tables and atmospheric décor, are being introduced to the company's restaurants. The aim is to provide a relaxing, friendly, contemporary ambience in which to enjoy music, food and the company of family and friends. This positioning is quite different from the original no frills, quick meal on the go imagery of the chain adopted the past. The ground-breaking soul food advertising has led to the reformulation of KFC's entire marketing mix.

(*Sources:* KFC website; Emily Rogers in *Marketing*, 6 November 2003, p. 7 and 13 November 2003, p. 5)

Test yourself

Case question

1 Why did KFC adopt a different style of advertising?

Quick questions

2 Why is it important to develop clear advertising objectives?
3 Explain the different stages in developing an advertising campaign.

Applied question

4 In your role as marketing manager for a conference centre, you are developing an advertising campaign to promote the venue to business clients. Explain the steps you will need to follow in developing the advertising campaign.

Extra readings

Belch, G. and Belch, M. (2003) *Advertising and Promotion: An Integrated Marketing Communications Perspective with Powerweb*. New York: McGraw-Hill.

Fill, C. (2003) *Integrated Marketing Communications*. Oxford: Butterworth-Heinemann.

FitzGerald, M. and Arnott, D. (2000) *Marketing Communications Classics*. London: Thomson Learning.

Percy, L., Rossiter, J. and Elliott, R. (2001) *Strategic Advertising Management*. Oxford: Oxford University Press.

Rapp, S. and Collins, T. (1999) *New Maximarketing*. New York: McGraw-Hill.

Shimp, T.A. (2002) *Advertising, Promotion and Supplemental Aspects of Integrated Marketing Communications*. Cincinnati, OH: South Western.

21: Public Relations

Key definitions

Public relations is the planned and sustained effort to establish and maintain goodwill and understanding between an organization and its publics.

Target publics in public relations are the organization's target audiences: customers, employees, shareholders, trade bodies, suppliers, referral bodies, financial institutions, government officials and society in general.

Publicity is communication in news story form about an organization and/or its products that is transmitted through mass media at relatively no charge.

A *PR programme* is an on-going, lengthy duration, awareness building or awareness maintaining multi-technique PR activity.

Crisis management is a process in which a company responds to negative events by identifying key target publics for which to provide publicity, developing a well-rehearsed contingency plan, reporting facts quickly and accurately with no attempt to cover up, and providing access for journalists.

Key issues

- Public relations (PR) used to be something of the 'Cinderella' in the promotional mix, but in recent times has become more professional and plays a greater role in the promotional activity of a wide variety of profit and not-for-profit organizations.
- Corporate PR is activity intended to promote goodwill towards the organization, its various activities and its place in society. A sub-set of corporate PR is the lobbying of regulators and politicians. Marketing PR is more tactical and is viewed as an integral component of the promotional mix for a specific product or brand.
- A great deal of PR activity hinges on publicity: the communication of information about an organization or its products in news story form designed to appeal to journalists in the print and broadcast media.
- A PR event is a one-off PR activity, such as an open day or single press release. A PR campaign is a period of activity involving several different activities. A PR programme is an on-going, sustained, awareness building set of PR activities.
- It is often argued that PR is 'free'. Compared with the production and media costs of advertising, the production of sales promotions or the expenses of the field force, PR is low cost. The inclusion of a press release in a newspaper's editorial or within a local television channel's news bulletin is free, but the PR activity that resulted in the press release involved time and people, and thereby some costs.
- A core benefit of PR is that unlike the other ingredients of the promotional mix, PR output often does not need to overtly identify the sponsoring organization or brand. Many viewers and readers fail to appreciate that a story

grabbing their interest stemmed from a business's press release or use of journalist contacts. PR activity tends to enjoy inherent credibility, but the same activity, unlike advertising, cannot be repeated uniformly over time.

- PR activity includes many activities, ranging from the common press release, to in-company visits for VIPs, media training for staff and internal marketing activity such as newsletters. PR activity is capable of promoting many issues, including company developments, social issues, or combating negative publicity about the organization or its products.
- The use of third party endorsement by a figure reputable in the view of the target publics – newsreaders, politicians, entertainers – enhances the credibility of the organization, product or its PR output.
- To be effective, PR must be properly managed, continuously undertaken, be accountable, develop strong links with journalists and the media, produce targeted material and monitor its on-going effectiveness.
- There are limitations: no payment fails to guarantee use by the media of publicity, the publicity must be deemed newsworthy, plus there is no control over how a journalist may utilize the publicity material. PR in general has suffered image problems only now being rectified.
- PR is commonly deployed to combat negative publicity. This involves the organization defending itself having the means to react: identification of key target publics, the need for a well-rehearsed contingency plan of action, the ability to quickly and accurately report facts, plus the provision of immediate access to company personnel for journalists and interested parties.

Conceptual overview

Public relations (PR) hinges to a large extent on the use of publicity, but there is much more to PR than the creation of a press release or its tactical deployment as part of the promotional mix for a brand. PR activity can be the one-off event, a campaign or an on-going programme. Marketers use PR routinely as part of the promotional mix. To be effective, PR should be on-going; professionally managed with accountable, bespoke personnel; develop strong links with journalists and interested parties; present carefully produced and targeted output; while continually monitoring the effectiveness of its endeavours. Third party endorsement by a reputable figure, such as an impartial TV personality, can be very supportive, but selection should be with care (cf. Brief 22).

Corporate and strategic PR are used to present the organization and its activities in a favourable light and to lobby independent decision-makers. Marketing PR is the use of the PR toolkit within the promotional mix to achieve marketing communications objectives for the product or brand. Therefore, many organizations use the PR toolkit at two levels: (i) to promote a positive corporate image and to communicate the policies and activities of the overall business, and (ii) to help raise awareness of specific products and brands, leading to greater numbers of purchases. Marketing managers tend to be concerned with the latter aspect of PR, while Boards of Directors and those responsible for the Corporate Affairs department are interested in the former.

PR is not totally free, as someone has to produce the publicity material or arrange the PR activity, but compared with advertising, PR is low cost. Unlike the other ingredients of the promotional mix, PR is able to target a host of target publics other than simply customers or marketing channel intermediaries. Unlike other promotional activity, PR does not overtly represent a brand, creating an air of impartiality and credibility. However, compared with many of the other promotional mix activities, PR cannot be uniformly repeated over time, minimizing economies of effort and adding to its complexity. Lack of payment for publication or transmission results in a lack of control over how some PR output, particularly publicity, is used and reported. Publicity must be newsworthy to be included in a news story or editorial, while all PR activity must effectively find a spin that appeals to its target publics.

PR activity includes many activities, ranging from the common press release, to in-company visits for VIPs, media training for staff and internal marketing (cf. Brief 40) activity such as newsletters. PR activity is capable of promoting many issues, including company developments, social issues, or combating negative publicity about the organization or its products (cf. Table 21.1).

Table 21.1 Public relations – types and issues

Types	Issues
• Press release (1 page)	• Marketing developments
• Feature article (1000 words) for a specific title	• Company policy
• Captioned photos	• General interest
• Editorials	• Current developments
• Press conferences	• Personalities
• Films and tapes	• Slogans/symbols/endorsements
• In-company publications	
• Interview techniques	
• Visits/VIPs	

The use of the PR toolkit and process to overcome the effects of adverse publicity is one of the most popular uses of public relations. This is unfortunate, as on-going and well-managed PR is capable of much more. In terms of negative publicity and crisis management, PR is particularly useful owing to its understanding of how journalists behave, contacts with the media and other target publics, plus the processes for effective communication inherent in good PR activity. Tackling adverse publicity or handling an unwelcome event involves the identification of key target publics, the need for a well-rehearsed contingency plan of action, the ability to quickly and accurately report facts, no 'covering up', plus the provision of immediate access to company personnel for journalists and interested parties.

Examples

British Gas

A key task for public relations is to maintain a positive ethos and image around a brand or company, particularly as perceived by key stakeholders such as customers, employees, investors and suppliers. For decades, gas producer and distributor British Gas was the butt of comedians' jokes about poor customer service and easy prey for campaigning consumer journalists. Towards the end of 2003, the headlines in the news bulletins were very different. British Gas was rewarded for changing its operating practices and image by being named as the best supplier of gas in terms of customer satisfaction. Market analyst JD Power's survey polled close to 3000 consumers and British Gas was placed top. For the energy company, this good news was the response to the business's £400 m investment in customer service systems, staff training and – according to its Managing Director – its strategy of 'putting the customer at the heart of everything' the company does. For British Gas and its public relations advisors, the award was perfect source material for its publicity activity.

(*Sources:* British Gas; Ben Carter in *Marketing*, 11 December 2003, p. 5)

Perrier

The Perrier crisis of 1990 has become a well-known example of effective public relations. Following the discovery of benzene contamination in some of its bottles, the company moved swiftly to minimize damage to its well-known brand. By using established procedures for handling public relations issues, Perrier was able to deal with distributor, retailer and consumer anxieties. A crisis team was established and an independent organization employed to carry out product tests so that the full extent of the problem could be properly understood. Fast and honest information provision for all of the company's publics were seen as key. A telephone information service was set up and full information was provided to anyone requiring it. In-depth meetings were held with journalists. Perrier also took an early decision to recall its products from supermarket shelves worldwide.

Within a very short space of time, the company was able to re-launch its mineral water. This was accompanied by new packaging, bottle sizes and a 'Welcome Back' advertising campaign. The company's effective handling of the crisis, combined with its obvious commitment to dealing with the production problems causing it, paid dividends. Despite the potentially huge competitive risk that Perrier had taken in so dramatically withdrawing its product, before long consumers were back and buying its products once more. Although the company's long-term market share was obviously affected by the crisis, with rival mineral waters gaining access to supermarket shelves, Perrier still enjoys substantial market share and strong brand awareness among consumers.

(*Sources:* Greg Prince, 'In hot water', *Beverage World*, March 1995, pp. 90–5; John Tylee, 'Publicis extends "eau" theme for Perrier blitz', *Campaign*, 19 May 1995, p. 7)

Test yourself

Case question

1 What are Perrier's various publics and why must they be carefully managed?

Quick questions

2 How is publicity different from advertising?
3 Describe some of the key problems associated with using public relations.

Applied question

4 You work for a public relations agency. Your latest assignment is to help a client company to develop a procedure for handling negative publicity. Write a report containing some recommendations for the client company to follow.

Extra readings

FitzGerald, M. and Arnott, D. (2000) *Marketing Communications Classics.* London: Thomson.

Hunt, T. and Grunig, J.E. (1997) *Public Relations Techniques.* Fort Worth, Tx: Harcourt Brace.

Kitchen, P.J. (1997) *Public Relations: Principles and Practice.* London: Thomson.

Moss, D. and Desanto, B. (2001) *Public Relations Case.* London: Routledge.

Theaker, A. (2001) *The Public Relations Handbook.* London: Routledge.

22: Sponsorship

Key definitions

Sponsorship is the financial or material support for an event, activity, person, organization, product or cause by an unrelated organization or donor. Funds are made available to the recipient of the sponsorship deal in return for the prominent exposure of the sponsor's name or brands.

A *reputable partnership* in sponsorship is the requirement for reputable and ethical dealings between a recognized, welcome and acceptable recipient organization and a sponsoring organization.

Key issues

- Sponsorship is used by many businesses to increase awareness of their brands or to persuade the target audience to think more positively about the organization and/or its products. There are examples of organizations that are truly philanthropic, expecting no benefits from donations or sponsorship arrangements, but in general sponsorship is a commercial arrangement.
- The arts, sports, television programmes, medical services and education facilities are sponsored. Sponsorship is a spin-off from public relations but now has its own specialist consultants and advisers.
- It is essential when selecting a sponsorship partner that a marketer identifies a recipient with which his or her target market customers have a positive affinity. Reputable partnerships are crucial: if the image of one partner is tarnished, the fall out will impact detrimentally on the other partner(s).
- Sponsors seek the benefits of media coverage and exposure for the activity being sponsored. In some cases, this overcomes advertising restrictions and ensures the target audience is still exposed to the brand. The second principal benefit is internal: marketers and senior managers hope external sponsorship and image boosting will improve employee morale.

Conceptual overview

Once part of the endeavours of public relations to build among its target audience positive perceptions of a client's brand, sponsorship has grown into an industry in its own right, with specialist sponsorship bodies and media guidelines. Sports events and the arts, where the donor's logo and brand will be exposed to large audiences and viewers of broadcast events, are still the largest receivers of commercial sponsorship, but even hospital facilities and education establishments benefit from sponsorship. Recently, relaxed regulations have permitted sponsorship of individual television programmes.

The primary benefits for the sponsoring organization are: (a) increased brand awareness; (b) enhanced media coverage; (c) a refined corporate image and community standing; and (d) improved employee morale. Some sponsorship arrangements are still philanthropic, but most have commercial motives: the recipient requires funding or material support, while the donor wishes to improve brand and corporate perceptions.

When selecting a sponsorship partnership, it is essential that both parties are at ease with each other's standing and that the target audience would not be surprised or alienated by the choice of partner. It is important to avoid contentious issues and to seek partners unlikely to face probes into their ethical behaviour, moral fibre or social responsibility (cf. Briefs 47 and 48).

Examples

Zurich

When Jonny Wilkinson's extra time kick won the Rugby Union World Cup for England, an estimated 15 m UK viewers were watching the early morning match live and perhaps up to another 10 million saw various programmes of highlights. A few weeks later, when the victorious team paraded the trophy around the streets of London, the capital's streets were grid-locked as close to 750 000 well-wishers thronged to offer their congratulations. For many weeks, the media's usual exhaustive coverage of football was over-shadowed by a new interest in rugby. Local 'grass roots' rugby clubs reported increased crowds, requests for membership and demands for the creation of more junior teams. Satellite TV broadcaster Sky Sports had signed the broadcast rights for rugby's Heineken Cup, to show up to forty live games. While the cup competition already had a sponsor in the form of Heineken, Sky's TV coverage did not. In stepped a very willing Zurich Financial Services, believing the viewing audience to fit its target market customer profile very closely. For £500 000, Zurich FS had credits around all of the coverage and features in the many Sky trailers and programmes of highlights.

(*Sources:* Sky Sports; *Marketing*, December 11 2003, p. 6; Daniel Thomas in *Marketing Week*, November 27 2003, pp. 24–7)

Nestlé *Milkybar*

TV sponsorship links with chocolate companies are not new. Cadbury's sponsorship of the popular TV soap *Coronation Street* is well known to the UK public. The Cadbury credits that precede the programme have become a familiar feature of ITV's evening schedule, enabling the chocolate manufacturer to feature a number of its branded products. Now Nestlé Rowntree is seeking a slice of the TV sponsorship action, using *Milkybar* – its white chocolate bar targeted at children – as the basis for a new deal. The company is paying £750 000 for the privilege of sponsoring Telly Tots, a CiTV (children's ITV) programme for toddlers. Nestlé views sponsorship very positively and apparently sees the deal as a way of extending its promotion of the brand beyond the usual television advertising. Nestlé believes the choice of television programme is an ideal match for its well-loved *Milkybar*. As well as being the market leading white chocolate product, *Milkybar* is the favoured brand for youngsters.

The details of the sponsorship are that two different animated credits will be used at the start of the television programme. The 15-second executions will focus on the Milkybar and Milkybar Buttons products and will use an animated version of the Milkybar Kid character, who has featured in advertising for the confectionery line for the past 25 years. On this occasion, the blond-haired hero will be joined by his pals the Dog and the Horse. Nestlé hopes that its new sponsorship venture will fit well with the strong positioning that has already been achieved for the Milkybar brand.

(*Source:* Tania Mason, 'Nestle Milkybar makes TV sponsorship debut', *Marketing*, 6 March 2001, p. 7)

Test yourself

Case question

1 Why is sponsorship a suitable form of promotion for the *Milkybar* brand?

Quick questions

2 For what purposes can sponsorship be used?
3 Why is the popularity of sponsorship increasing?

Applied question

4 You play soccer for an amateur football team seeking sponsorship. Your colleagues on the team have asked for advice about the factors that should be considered when choosing a prospective sponsor. What advice would you give?

Extra readings

Belch, G. and Belch, M. (2003) *Advertising and Promotion: an Integrated Marketing Communications Perspective.* New York: McGraw-Hill.

Bovee, C.L. and Thill, J.V. (1998) *Excellence in Business Communication.* Englewood Cliffs, NJ: Pearson.

FitzGerald, M. and Arnott, D. (2000) *Marketing Communications Classics.* London: Thomson.

Hunt, T. and Grunig, J.E. (1997) *Public Relations Techniques.* Fort Worth, Tx: Harcourt Brace.

Kitchen, P.J. (1997) *Public Relations: Principles and Practice.* London: Thomson.

Kolah, A. (2003) *Improving the Performance of Sponsorship.* Oxford: Butterworth-Heinemann.

Rapp, S. and Collins, T. (1999) *Maximarketing.* New York: McGraw-Hill.

23: Personal Selling and Sales Management

Key definitions

Personal selling is a process of informing customers and persuading them to purchase products through personal communication in an exchange situation.

Teleselling uses telecommunications for sales and marketing activity, focusing on one-to-one communication between the sales person and the customer prospect.

Sales management is the determination of sales force objectives, forecasting and budgeting, sales force organization and sales territory planning, sales force selection, recruitment, training, reward and motivation, and sales force evaluation and control.

Key issues

- Personal selling is the passing of information and persuasion with face-to-face communication. More loosely defined, it can include telesales, which still involves direct customer–sales person interaction facilitated via telecommunications.

- The specialist area of sales management focuses on the importance of preparation, the techniques for introducing sales personnel to prospective customers, the requisites for effective presentations and written proposals, the skills required to turn a potential customer's interest into commitment, how to negotiate, the skills necessary to capture an order, and the ability to close the sale.

- Sales personnel not only seek new customers but they often handle the on-going requirements of existing customers, ensuring repeat orders are won and handled competently.

- Personal selling is narrowly focused often on only the individual customer prospect and bespoke messages easily may be targeted.

- Sales force time, salaries and expenses are costly and personal selling is one of the most expensive components of the promotional mix.

- The personal selling exchange heavily depends on language: verbal, kinesic, proxemic and tactile. These languages require much skill and the management, recruitment, training and motivation of the sales force are specialist activities. Sales is often a separate business function to marketing, but marketers direct the messages offered by the sales force, the brand positioning and choice of target markets.

- The personal selling sequence involves various stages: prospecting and evaluating, preparation, approaching the customer, making a sales pitch, the production of a sales proposal document, overcoming objections, negotiation, closing the deal, internal liaison to ensure the order is actioned, and following up. The growth of relationship marketing has placed increased emphasis on post-purchase customer handling, often involving the sales force and customer relationship management (CRM) processes.

- There are various types of salespeople, including order creators, order getters, order takers and support personnel.
- Management of the sales force involves establishing clear objectives, determining sales force size and allocating sales territories, recruiting and selecting the right staff, training, rewarding and motivating, and controlling performance.
- Inter-personnel skills are pivotal to the effectiveness of the field sales force.

Conceptual overview

Marketers include personal selling as a component of the promotional mix. However, most businesses with sales forces have a Sales Director and the sales function is treated as a stand-alone operation from the marketing function. The sales function links strongly with the marketing function, notably with sales personnel providing marketing intelligence (the sales force learns much about customers, market trends and competitors' activities) and in terms of sales personnel delivering the devised target market strategy and product propositions to the target market customers or marketing channel partners.

The literature assisting sales management is extensive and tends to focus on the sales management process: (a) the importance of preparation (understanding the products and prospective customers, predicting sales and developing systems for recording sales-related data); (b) the techniques for introducing the sales personnel to prospective customers either face-to-face or via telecommunications; (c) the requisites for effective presentations (or pitches) and written sales proposals; (d) the skills required to turn a potential customer's interest into commitment; (e) how to negotiate; (f) the skills necessary to capture the order; and (g) the ability to close the sale (win the order).

Sales personnel do not only address prospective customers: they are often involved with managing on-going client relationships and in ensuring repeat orders are won and handled competently. These days, there are strong links with customer relationship management (CRM) techniques (cf. Brief 8).

From a marketing perspective, owing to the high costs of staff salaries and expenses, the sales force is an expensive ingredient within the promotional mix. The skills required to be effective are considerable, placing high demands on management processes, recruitment, training and motivation of sales staff. In many businesses, the bulk of business-to-business orders are won by the sales force and the sales manager is a senior member of the management team. Increasingly, sales and marketing are separate functions, but the marketing department still directs the message to convey and specifies the priority target markets for the sales force.

Personal selling involves direct customer–sales person contact, but in addition to face-to-face interaction, personal selling now often benefits from improved telecommunications and telesales. Unlike other forms of promotional activity, personal selling can customize messages for individual customer prospects and build ongoing relationships with existing customers. The per capita cost, however, is high. The growth of relationship marketing to nurture the goodwill and repeat business of existing customers (cf. Briefs 2 and 8) has given fresh impetus to the role of personal selling and post-purchase contact.

Effective personal selling, owing to the direct customer–seller interaction, requires a shrewd understanding of verbal clues, kinesic (body) language, proxemic distance issues, and when tactile (physical) contact will assist or hinder the contact. There is a core sequence of activity at the heart of personal selling, involving:

1. Prospecting and evaluating potential customer targets (often initially undertaken by the marketing or business development functions in the organization).
2. Preparation before the sales pitch.
3. The approach to the potential customer.
4. A presentation or sales pitch.
5. The production of a formal sales proposal document and costings.
6. The overcoming of any resistance or objections.
7. A period of negotiation (over product specification, logistics, customer support, exclusivity or price and payment terms).
8. The deal closure to clinch the sale.
9. Liaison internally to ensure the order is handled effectively by the organization.
10. The follow-up to ensure customer satisfaction and to seek repeat orders.

There are various types of salespeople, including order creators, order getters, order takers and support personnel. Management of the sales force involves establishing clear objectives, determining sales force size, recruiting and selecting the right staff, training, rewarding and motivating, managing sales territories and controlling performance. These activities require specialist skills and they are generally undertaken by professional sales managers. Effective selling hinges to a large extent on the inter-personnel skills, motivation and abilities of the individuals involved in the field sales forces: these areas warrant specialist management within the organization. For marketing, personal selling impacts in two primary guises: as the field sales force and as staff interfacing with customers, as illustrated in the following examples.

Examples

IBM

Sales personnel have always played a key role in IBM's marketing activity. Throughout its history, the company has invested substantial resources in developing responsive sales professionals with a clear understanding of customer needs.

However, following IBM's difficulties during the 1980s and early 1990s, the company decided that the way its sales force was organized was just as important as the quality of the individuals employed. The company therefore undertook a restructuring programme, redefining its sales areas on the basis of industry rather than geography. As a result, sales staff were able to specialize, concentrating on selling the company's products to customers in one particular industry area. The move was designed to extend the capability of sales staff as business advisers and lead to closer customer links. The level of industry expertise that individuals developed as a result of the changes helped IBM's sales force to become more in-tune with the company's customer base.

(*Sources:* Sally Dibb, Lyndon Simkin, Bill Pride and O.C. Ferrell, *Marketing: Concepts and Strategies*, Boston, MA: Houghton Mifflin, 2001; L. Hays, 'IBM chief unveils top-level shake-up, consolidating sales arm, software line', *Wall Street Journal*, 10 January 1995, p. B6)

TGI Friday's

The restaurant chain TGI Friday's is a familiar sight around the world. The expansion of the themed restaurant concept to new countries relies particularly upon the recruitment of suitable employees. Anyone who has visited a TGI Friday's restaurant will appreciate that the staff who wait on the tables and manage the outlets have particular characteristics. They are generally gregarious and fun, enjoying interacting with customers. As they go about their work in bright and informal uniforms that feature belts, braces and an array of pin badges, employees must be prepared to engage in the vibrant atmosphere associated with the restaurant concept. This might involve dancing, distributing balloons, juggling glasses or simply singing 'Happy Birthday' to a young customer.

As TGI's extends its operation to new countries, it therefore follows a systematic process to ensure that appropriate employees are recruited. This involves selecting a partner in new countries to help route the business through the local bureaucracy. A local management team then runs the new TGI outlets. However, although the company wishes to benefit from local knowledge, it is also keen to ensure that those recruited into management positions are familiar with US business standards and the parent company's ethos. For this reason, TGI's often recruits foreign nationals who are working or studying in the US, but who would like the chance to return to their home country. This balanced approach provides TGI's with the benefits of local knowledge while ensuring that its service standards are maintained.

(*Source:* M. Hamstra, 'Operators bullish about opportunities in overseas markets, despite turmoil', *Nation's Restaurant News*, 5 October 1998, p. 86; Sally Dibb and Lyndon Simkin, *The Marketing Casebook*, London: Thomson, 2001).

Test yourself

Case question

1 Why is TGI Friday's so concerned about the criteria it sets for selecting staff?

Quick questions

2 What is personal selling and what does it aim to achieve?
3 Explain the different elements of the personal selling process.

Applied question

4 A regional sales director working for an agrochemicals business is deciding how best to organize his/her sales territory. List and explain the key factors that he/she should take into account.

Extra readings

Clay, J. (2003) *Successful Selling Solutions.* London: Thorogood.

Dalrymple, D.J., Cron, W.L. and DeCarlo, T. (2000) *Sales Management.* Hokboken, NJ: Wiley.

Dibb, S., Simkin, L., Pride, W. and Ferrell, O.C. (2001) *Marketing: Concepts and Strategies.* Boston, MA: Houghton Mifflin.

Honeycutt, E.D., Ford, J.B. and Simintiras, A. (2003) *Sales Management: A Global Perspective.* London: Routledge.

Jobber, D. and Lancaster, G. (2003) *Selling and Sales Management.* Harlow: Pearson Education.

Kitchen, P.J. (ed.) (1998) *Marketing Communications: Principles and Practice.* London: Thomson.

Shimp, T.A. (2002) *Advertising, Promotion and Supplemental Aspects of Integrated Marketing Communications.* Cincinnati, OH: South Western.

24: Sales Promotion

Key definitions

Sales promotion is activity and/or material inducing sales through added value or incentive for the product to resellers, sales people or consumers.

Consumer sales promotion encourages or stimulates consumers to patronize a specific retailer or to try/purchase a particular product.

Trade sales promotion encourages wholesalers, retailers or dealers to carry and market a producer's products.

Key issues

- Sales promotion is activity that encourages, by offering transient added value, customers to 'bring forward' sales that often may anyway have occurred.
- Consumer sales promotions include coupons, free samples, demonstrations, competitions, loyalty cards, frequent-user incentives, trading stamps and discounted merchandise.
- Trade sales promotions are aimed at wholesalers, retailers and sales people, such as sales competitions, free merchandise subject to sales levels being exceeded, buy-back allowances, point-of-sale display materials, trade shows and conferences.
- There are sales promotions from manufacturer to distributor: trade sales promotion. From manufacturer to the sales force: sales force sales promotion. From manufacturer to end-user consumers: consumer sales promotion. There are retail/distribution sales promotions, from distributors to consumers.
- Sales promotions are often used to support the activities of the sales force or in conjunction with advertising.

Conceptual overview

Sales promotions do not, on the whole, grow a market: instead their added-value inducements persuade regular or infrequent purchasers to bring forward their acquisition to take advantage of the promotion, such as a price reduction, two for the price of one deal, competition or other incentive. They are costly activities, often involving free or discounted merchandise and the provision of prizes or other materials. Sales promotion is deployed to level out sales peaks and troughs or to rectify unexpected dips in sales. Sales promotions tend to be short term, *ad hoc* and irregular. They provide a short-term benefit to the recipient in order to entice purchase.

The recent growth of frequent-user incentives (such as Air Miles) and reward cards (as with Tesco's *ClubCard*), have added significantly to the use of sales promotions. The menu of sales promotions targeting consumers available to marketers is extensive: coupons, free samples, demonstrations, competitions, loyalty cards, frequent-user incentives, trading stamps and discounted merchandise. Sales promotions are rarely deployed in isolation of other promotional mix ingredients: they often support sales force activities and feature in associated advertising (cf. Figure 24.1).

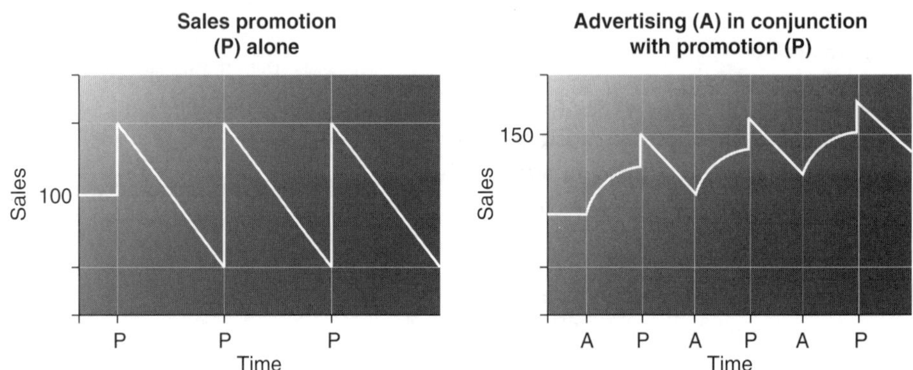

Figure 24.1 The use of sales promotion and advertising in conjunction

(*Source: adapted from* W.T. Moran, 'Insights from pricing research', in E.B. Bailey (ed.), *Pricing Practices and Strategies*, New York: The Conference Board, 1978, pp. 7 and 13)

Sales promotions are not confined to consumer targets. There are trade sales promotions aimed at distributors, sales force sales promotions to motivate sales personnel, retail sales promotions instigated by retailers targeting consumers. Some brands may be subject simultaneously to various types of sales promotions. Mars runs competitions for *Snickers* and *Mars* bars aimed at consumers, while also offering prizes for increased sales to its field force and trade customers. Some retail stockists may also feature Mars' products in their sales promotions targeted at consumers.

Examples

Slimfast

After sales dropped by close to 25% in just 3 months, Unilever diet brand Slimfast turned to new products and increased marketing communications activity to change its fortunes. *Yoghurt Muesli, Fruits of the Forest* and *Chocolate Crunch* bars were added to the Slimfast range of meal-replacement bars. The launch was supported with point-of-sale communications and in-store promotions. Simultaneously, Slimfast decided to offer its range of frozen evening meals additional support, with TV advertising and direct mail: 300 000 consumers were targeted on the Jigsaw database, plus existing Slimfast customers. Six million leaflets were also inserted into women's lifestyle magazines, challenging people to fit back into their jeans within three weeks by following the Slimfast plan after their Christmas time eating excesses. While the TV campaign required the lion's share of the promotional budget, the exposure to in-store sales promotions proved particularly effective given the target customer profile.

(*Sources:* Slimfast, 2004; Emily Rogers in *Marketing*, 8 January 2004, p. 4; Ben Bold in *Marketing*, 11 December 2003, p. 8)

Air Miles

The market for travel incentives, a popular form of sales promotion, is buoyant. Leading player Air Miles was established in 1988 and currently enjoys a turnover in excess of £200 million. Although the business attracted some bad publicity after separating its Executive Club frequent flyer members from the scheme (they now collect *BA Miles*), the company's turnover is still more than ten times that of its closest rival. The travel incentive provider competes with a range of others, including Landround, Thomas Cook Vouchers and Virgin Vouchers. Variety and customer choice are clear keys to success in the business. As the dominance of Air Miles illustrates, brand loyalty also plays an important role.

Air Miles has recently increased the scope of its travel incentives by adding additional airlines, such as American Airlines, as redemption partners. This move fits with the widely held industry view that breadth of opportunity for redemption is key. Virgin Vouchers group, for example, allows its vouchers to be exchanged for a wide range of goods, services and travel options, provided by Virgin, Virgin Holidays and a variety of partner businesses. British Midland (BMI), which has frequent-flyer incentive programmes aimed at the business market, also aims for variety. According to the company's marketing agency, 'Branded merchandise and gadgets such as penknives work extremely well in increasing response and make a significant difference to whether people respond to a campaign or not'.

(*Source:* Sharon Greaves, 'Customised travel offers hit the spot', *Marketing*, 1 March 2001, p. 41)

Test yourself

Case question

1 Why did Slimfast use more than only advertising in its promotional mix?

Quick questions

2 What is sales promotion?
3 What are the principal consumer and trade sales promotion techniques? Give examples of each.

Applied question

4 As marketing manager for one of the major supermarkets, you have been asked to investigate the possibility of implementing a consumer loyalty programme. You are required to make a presentation to members of the Board exploring the possible role of such a programme and identifying its possible key features. Draft out the areas that your presentation would cover.

Extra readings

Belch, G. and Belch, M. (2003) *Advertising and Promotion: an Integrated Marketing Communications Perspective*. New York: McGraw-Hill.

Cummins, J. and Mullin, R. (1998) *Sales Promotion: How to Create and Implement Campaigns that Really Work*. London: Kogan Page.

Percy, L., Rossiter, J. and Elliott, R. (2001) *Strategic Advertising Management*. Oxford: Oxford University Press.

Shimp, T.A. (2002) *Advertising, Promotion and Supplemental Aspects of Integrated Marketing Communications*. Cincinnati, OH: South Western.

25: Direct Mail

Key definitions

Direct mail is printed advertising material delivered to a prospective customer's or donor's home or work address.

The *direct mail package* is the mailing envelope, attention-getting device, explanatory letter, response and return devices.

Key issues

- Direct mail has suffered through its associations with unsolicited 'junk' mail, but is a very well used ingredient of the promotional mix for consumer goods, services and also in business-to-business marketing.
- Direct mail can generate orders, pre-sell prior to a sales call, qualify prospects for a sales call, screen out non-prospects, follow up a sale, announce special sales or localized selling initiatives, or help raise funds for charities.
- Direct mail requires careful planning, production expertise and an understanding of the target market. There are specialist providers of this expertise and growing professionalism in this industry.
- To be effective, direct mail must incorporate up-to-date and bespoke mailing lists of relevant target consumers or business personnel; attention-grabbing devices to entice the recipient to read the contents; skilful copywriting; and a well-conceived direct mail package.
- The direct mail package is the mailing envelope, attention-getting device, explanatory letter, response and return devices. The bulk of direct mail is discarded unread because of failings to properly construct the package and up-date mailing lists.

Conceptual overview

A well-used ingredient of the promotional mix, direct mail is deployed to promote goods, services and ideas in consumer and business-to-business markets. There is now growth of direct mail using e-mail addresses. Direct mail can generate orders, pre-sell prior to a sales call, qualify prospects for a sales call, screen out non-prospects, follow up a sale, announce special sales or localized selling initiatives. It is also popular in the promotional activity for not-for-profit organizations, such as fund raising charities.

Junk mail has alienated many recipients of unsolicited selling material and has made the direct mailer's task even more difficult. To be effective, the direct mail vehicle, generally the envelope, requires an attention-getting flash that encourages the recipient at home or at work to open the mailing: 'Prize details inside' or 'This is not a circular' are common choices. The direct mail package is the composite of envelope, attention-getting flash, covering letter, circular or promotional information, response device and a return device, such as a pre-paid envelope or freephone number. Professional copywriting, by people familiar with the product in question and the intended target audience, is important. Direct mailings can be customized to reflect target market behaviour to good effect.

In-house mailing lists must be regularly up-dated and screened for redundant data, or commercially available lists must be bought from database houses known to regularly up-date their lists. One-third of names on a list change each year, so topical lists are essential. The suppliers of lists often will, for a fee, undertake the entire direct mailing operation for a marketer, including design, production, mailing and sales prospecting.

Examples

John Lewis

Debenhams (through *Nectar*) and House of Fraser have both been involved in relationship-building drives in order to build customer loyalty. Now department store rival John Lewis Partnership has also turned to relationship-building programmes to increase sales. John Lewis has analysed customer spending patterns and characteristics, including examining the profiles of its account card holders and on-line shoppers. Part of the relationship marketing drive is being handled by its non-store arm, *John Lewis Direct*. In the run-up to Christmas, five catalogues were produced, mailed directly to customers' homes, featuring bed and bath, home furnishings, gifts, flowers and hampers. Other direct mail campaigns have focused on health and fitness – a brochure was mailed to customers immediately post Christmas – and on e-gadgets, targeted primarily at male customers.

(*Sources:* Mark Kleinman in *Marketing*, January 8 2004, p. 8; John Lewis Partnership, 2004; John Lewis Direct, 2003)

John Smith's Bitter

Marketers at brewer Scottish Courage have successfully used direct mail to promote John Smith's Bitter. During 2000, the company's *A Gift to the Working Man* campaign received an extremely positive response. Now the company intends to capitalize on the success of 2000, with a new campaign targeting 250 000 individuals. The company has good reason to be optimistic about the success of its new campaign. The mailing in 2000 enjoyed a particularly high response rate from customers, as well as enthusiastic accolades from the industry. In total, 80 000 beer drinkers were targeted in the Midlands and the North of the UK by the direct mail shot. Scottish Courage was particularly pleased with the return on investment for the campaign.

The principle of the mailing was simple – seven money-off vouchers were included that were to be used over a six-month period. Individuals could redeem the vouchers, worth £5 in total, at retailers around the country. By introducing a time-sensitive element to the campaign, the intention was to spread the effect of the promotion over a longer time period than might otherwise have been possible. Eight per cent of those receiving the mail-out redeemed all of the vouchers provided; 18% of those targeted redeemed at least one of the promotional vouchers. Scottish Courage cited an improvement in sales and market share for the beer brand in the regions targeted by the campaign. This has provided the back-drop for the company's continuing use of direct mail.

(*Source:* Rachel Miller, 'Taking stock of DM campaigns', *Marketing*, 22 February 2001, pp. 37–8)

Test yourself

Case question

1 For what reasons was a direct mail campaign suitable for promoting John Smith's Bitter?

Quick questions

2 What is direct mail?
3 Describe three purposes for which direct mail might be used.

Applied question

4 You have recently been appointed as an external marketing consultant to a college that has traditionally used a variety of promotional tools to promote its courses. While reviewing the college's previous marketing activity, you discover that relatively little use has been made of direct mail. Write a memo to the head of the college explaining the role direct mail might have in the college's future marketing activity.

Extra readings

Belch, G. and Belch, M. (2003) *Advertising and Promotion: An Integrated Marketing Communications Perspective.* New York: McGraw-Hill.

Bird, D. (2000) *Commonsense Direct Marketing.* London: Kogan Page.

FitzGerald, M. and Arnott, D. (2000) *Marketing Communications Classics.* London: Thomson.

O'Malley, L., Patterson, M. and Evans, M. (1999) *Exploring Direct Marketing.* London: Thomson Learning.

Rapp, S. and Collins, T. (1999) *Maximarketing.* New York: McGraw-Hill.

Shimp, T.A. (2002) *Advertising, Promotion and Supplemental Aspects of Integrated Marketing Communications.* Cincinnati, OH: South Western.

Thomas, B. and Housden, M. (2001) *Direct Marketing in Practice.* Oxford: Butterworth-Heinemann.

26: Direct Marketing

Key definitions

Direct marketing is a decision by a company's marketers to select a marketing channel that avoids dependence on marketing channel intermediaries, and to focus marketing communications activity on promotional mix ingredients that contact directly targeted customers.

Key issues

- Originated in the 1960s to describe direct mail and mail order, direct marketing is now one of the 'hot topics' of marketing, enabled largely by the growth of e-commerce.
- Direct marketing includes all of the marketing communications tools that permit a marketer to deal directly with targeted customers, including direct mail, telemarketing, direct response television advertising, door-to-door and personal selling, plus Internet-based marketing.
- Direct marketing is more than promotional mix activity: it involves a decision by marketers to avoid or minimize the role of marketing intermediaries in the distribution channel, preferring instead to contact customers directly.
- Direct marketing evolved from the mail order industry. Database improvements, telecommunications and recently the Internet have facilitated a rapid growth in direct marketing for all types of profit and not-for-profit organizations.
- All core facets of direct marketing are increasing: direct mail, telemarketing, personal selling, door-to-door marketing, direct response advertising and more than any other facet, Web-based marketing.
- Direct marketing must still reflect customer expectations and buying behaviour, offer differentiated and competitive propositions, reflect the organization's brand positioning and corporate objectives, and be professionally managed and executed.

Conceptual overview

The recent advances in media, telecommunications and computing use have facilitated a massive increase in what has been termed direct marketing. This is the use of promotional mix ingredients that communicate directly with the targeted customer and the selection of a direct distribution channel that negates or reduces the role of marketing intermediaries such as wholesalers, retailers or distributors. The origins of direct marketing, though, stem from the 1960s and the roll-out of mail order home shopping and direct mail promotions. Direct marketing has grown because of:

- The desire by marketers to identify alternative media and promotional tools.
- The need to improve the targeting of potential customers.
- Improvements in marketing data and databases.
- Advances in technology and systems permitting cost-effective direct and interactive contact with certain types of consumers.

The choice by a marketer of direct marketing may be intended to supplement other marketing mix programmes or may be substituting traditional channels of distribution and marketing communications (cf. Briefs 28 and 25). While many 'dot.com' businesses do not deploy marketing channel strategies utilizing channel intermediaries, most businesses practising direct marketing have in fact adopted it alongside other marketing channels and promotional mix applications.

The core activities of direct marketing in terms of marketing communications are all currently increasing, led by the surge in Web-based marketing. Direct mail, telemarketing, personal selling and door-to-door marketing, and direct response advertising – largely as a result of satellite and cable television growth – have all witnessed significant increases in activity. The core requirements for effective marketing still apply, however. Direct marketing must reflect customer expectations and buying behaviour, offer differentiated and competitive propositions, reflect the organization's brand positioning and corporate objectives, and be professionally managed and executed. Many business-to-business transactions are now via e-commerce: direct marketing is not by any means solely focused on consumer markets.

Examples

William Hill

Betting business William Hill has joined the growing on-line gambling industry very successfully, but aimed to acquire 200 000 new on-line customers. Integral to its strategy was the use of direct marketing. e-CRM agency RedEye was employed to help William Hill. Over half of consumers who registered on-line to gamble did not do so, or they waited some time before spending anything. So RedEye developed a programme that contacted newly registered consumers with a follow-up email. Three different email executions, using different messages, timing and creative designs, were tested against a control sample that did not receive any email follow-up. In all cases, those receiving an e-follow-up were five times more likely to convert to being a real user, placing bets on-line. RedEye also tackled high-value customers, targeting them with specific e-messages so that website content of no interest to the remainder of the client base could be removed from the site, with significant cost savings. However, despite the loss of website content, this direct engagement with these high-value customers avoided any client dissatisfaction with the William Hill on-line service.

(*Sources: Marketing Direct, Data 2003*, Haymarket Publishing and the Royal Mail, 2003, p. 14; William Hill, 2004)

L'Oreal

Café Society is L'Oreal's new range of brown hair colourants in the *Recital* product range. The range includes shades like Café au Lait, Espresso and Mocha and is targeted at women in their 30s who colour their hair at home. The mailing, sent to 75 000 addresses, is contained in a parchment-type, see-through envelope, evocative of the new colours. A £1 money-off coupon is enclosed. This coupon is a particularly important feature of the campaign because it is being used to collect a range of marketing intelligence about users of the hair colourant. L'Oreal, it seems, is especially keen to develop a better understanding about the behaviour of users and whether they also buy other L'Oreal products.

L'Oreal is not confining its marketing activity for the new range to the mailing. This is another instance of a company using direct marketing alongside other marketing tools. In this case, the mailing is being supported by an advertising campaign. Advertising for *Recital* has typically used high-profile celebrities – such as Jennifer Aniston from the US comedy, *Friends* – and incorporates the L'Oreal strap-line *'Because I'm worth it'*.

(*Source:* Mark Kleinman, 'L'Oreal drives colourant range', *Marketing*, 15 March 2001, p. 13)

Test yourself

Case question

1 Why do you think that L'Oreal is using the mailing in combination with an advertising campaign?

Quick questions

2 What is direct marketing?
3 What kinds of communications tools are used in direct marketing?

Applied question

4 Initially, direct marketing was the term used to describe common tools like direct mail and mail order. You have been asked to make a presentation at a marketing conference explaining how direct marketing has changed in emphasis. Put together some notes to accompany the presentation that explain the wide range of communications tools that are used to allow a marketer to deal directly with his or her customers.

Extra readings

Adams, N.R., Dogramaci, O., Gangopadhyay, A. and Yesha, Y. (1999) *Electronic Commerce: Technical, Business and Legal Issues*. Englewood Cliffs, NJ: Pearson.

O'Malley, L., Patterson, M. and Evans, M. (1999) *Exploring Direct Marketing.* London: Thomson.

December, J. and Randall, N. (1996) *The World Wide Web Unleashed*. New York: Sams Publishing.

Sargeant, A. and West, D.C. (2001) *Direct and Interactive Marketing.* Oxford: Butterworth-Heinemann.

Schwartz, E.I. (1997) *Webonomics: Nine Essential Principles for Growing Your Business on the World Wide Web.* New York: Broadway Books.

Thomas, B. and Housden, M. (2001) *Direct Marketing in Practice.* Oxford: Butterworth-Heinemann.

27: The Internet

Key definitions

The *Internet* is a chain of computer networks stretching across the world, linking computers of different types to the websites of commercial businesses, not-for-profit organizations, public bodies, private individuals and social groups. Increasingly used for e-commerce.

E-commerce is the use of the Internet for commercial transactions.

Intranets are internal, in-company Internet networks for routine communications, fostering group communications, providing uniform computer applications, distributing the latest software, or informing colleagues of marketing developments and new product launches.

A *website* is a coherent document readable by a web browser, containing simple text or complex hypermedia presentations, generally promoting the views of the website host or brand.

Key issues

- Until relatively recently, only computer enthusiasts accessed the Internet for information searches or on-line discussions. The growth of home and office PCs, coupled with the Internet, has created a new media opportunity for businesses communicating with certain target audiences. In turn, this has led to an explosion in e-commerce, home shopping and direct marketing.

- Not all consumers and businesses are capable or willing to use e-commerce and marketers' target market strategies must ensure they fully understand their customers' buying behaviour and needs. Many businesses have, though, been able to successfully incorporate the Internet in their marketing channel and promotional mix activities.

- Internal marketing, increasingly prevalent in many organizations' activities, has also benefited from Web-based communication, notably through businesses' intranets.

- Website development requires clear goals, analysis of required content to reflect users' expectations, assessment of rival organizations' or brands' sites, the creation of the site, implementation using hypertext mark-up language, and on-going monitoring to ensure the site's look, usability and content continually are up-dated to reflect users' needs.

- Research has demonstrated that effective websites must be able to attract, engage, relate, learn, retain and work for returning website visitors/users and new users.

- To be effective, a website must be accessible to the intended target audience, contain relevant information, be eye-catching but easy to interpret, distinctive, consistent with the organization's branding and product positioning, have synergy with the marketing mix executions already deployed, regularly and accurately up-dated, and seek and respond to user feedback.

- The current trend of direct marketing has increased marketers' use of the Internet and heightened its value in marketing mix applications.

Conceptual overview

Once, only computer enthusiasts accessed the Internet on a regular basis, mostly for on-line discussions or to search for information. The World Wide Web is now a major focus of attention for marketers of consumer goods, services, charities and industrial products. Companies provide product and company details on their web pages. These websites tended initially to be for information purposes rather than overtly for promotional tools or selling opportunities, but e-commerce has altered the manner in which organizations and customers utilize the Web. Consumer concern about the security of making purchases on-line, divulging credit card details or bank account numbers held back progress, but investment by the Web hosts and credit card companies to instigate scrambling and coding of confidential information has led to massive growth in e-commerce.

As more and more households and businesses connect to the Internet, confidence in using this medium for consumer and business-to-business transactions is growing. This is not uniform across all consumers: just as with any product, there are those who do not find e-marketing and e-commerce appealing or do not have the necessary capabilities. Older consumers, the less affluent and less educated are now also accessing the Web. In the UK, only one in ten consumers purchase on-line and three in ten companies use the Web for business-to-business marketing. While the numbers are growing, the relevance for certain product types and brands is minimal. Fifty per cent of UK households regularly surf the Web, but in practice that is generally restricted to teenagers or professional adults. Internet access across Europe is hugely variable, with Iceland, Sweden and the UK scoring highest at around two-thirds of the population. Germany has access for just over a third of its population, France and Italy just under a third, while Spain and Portugal have a quarter of the population capable of accessing the Web, and Greece is worst placed with only 15%. The average for Europe is that 35% of the population has access to the Web.

As an ingredient in the promotional mix, the Internet is increasingly present (cf. Brief 26). Most major brands now have their own websites. Most television and press advertisements direct consumers to web addresses for further information or ordering facilities. Packaging for many consumer products identifies the presence of a website. Web pages can be quickly modified, up-dated and customized to reflect the expectations of specific target audiences. The growing activity of internal marketing (cf. Brief 40) has made use of intranets for more effective in-company communication, the provision of uniform computer applications, distribution of the latest software, and sharing information about market developments and new product launches.

There is a clear process for developing a website:

1 Planning the site's goals.
2 Analysis of the required content.
3 Evaluation of rivals' websites.
4 Designing and building of the site.
5 Implementation using hypertext mark-up language (HTML).
6 Monitoring to ensure that once up and running the site reflects user views and is regularly up-dated.

Far from being a minor task, marketers have realized that website design is a specialized activity that requires the skills of a qualified web master and the careful design of material to reflect the characteristics of the product, the brand and of the intended consumer. To be an effective website, key requisites are vital:

- Targeted customers must be prepared and able to access the Internet.
- The site has to contain information that is relevant and interesting for targeted customers.
- The pages of the site need to be stylish, eye-catching, while easy to interpret.
- The website design should be memorable and distinctive.
- Website branding and imagery must be consistent with the brand positioning of existing products, the product's packaging and other promotional mix executions such as advertising and sales promotion materials.
- The website's ethos should not contradict the work of the rest of the marketing mix or the product's heritage.
- The information on the website has to be regularly and accurately up-dated and tailored carefully to reflect the buying behaviour of the targeted customer.
- User feedback should be sought to continually up-date the website, just as with any other service or product.

Research has revealed that effective – for marketing purposes – websites must: (a) attract potential customers and respond readily to on-line searches; (b) engage with these customers or users to gain their participation and interest; (c) relate to these users by empathizing with them in terms of their usage behaviour, informational needs and expectations; (d) learn from users and non-users to up-date the site's content and navigation; (e) retain users by modifying site content in line with their desires; and (f) work smoothly for returning users and first time hits. More and more organizations are recognizing these requisites, resulting in a significant increase in the use of the Web in marketing.

There has been a trend in marketing towards direct marketing, where producers and suppliers exclude subsequent channel members and sell directly to the target market. Direct marketing (cf. Brief 26) involves a decision by a company's marketers to select a marketing channel that avoids dependence on marketing channel intermediaries. Instead, marketing communications activity is focused on promotional mix ingredients that directly contact targeted customers, such as direct mail, telemarketing, direct response television advertising, door-to-door/personal selling and the Internet. Its growth has been rapid in recent years, caused largely by home shopping and e-commerce. Such change has provided marketers with a new set of options in selecting a channel for distribution and placed greater emphasis on the Internet.

Examples

Tescowishlist.com

Leading supermarket chain Tesco was one of the first major players to start making a profit from an on-line retailing operation. *Tesco Direct* is now an integral part of the Tesco retailing strategy, enabling customers to buy their groceries while at home or in the office, with doorstep deliveries to suit the requirements of shoppers. However, Tesco retails much more than just groceries. In the run-up to Christmas, the company wanted to boost awareness of its ranges of DVDs, mobile phones, video games and electrical goods, many of which are not available inside smaller Tesco stores. Agency Profero developed the *Christmas Wish List* campaign, offering customers the opportunity to win £1000 worth of products and to create wish lists for gifts that could be emailed to friends or family. As part of the campaign, a viral email was sent to thousands of *Tesco.com* customers promoting the *Wish List* campaign and associated product offers. There were links from other websites, too, including *lastminute.com* and *Channel4.com*. *Tescowishlist.com* was also launched, with Tesco's hope to position Tesco's e-shopping service as a one-stop on-line destination. For a company that ten years ago only retailed through its store network, e-commerce has opened up a vast array of opportunities and challenges.

(*Sources:* Tescowishlist.com, 2004; Tesco.com, 2003; Tesco Stores, 2003; *Marketing*, 4 December 2003, p. 8)

Services and the Internet

The number of customers prepared to make purchases over the Internet is increasing. However, until recently, many of these purchases related to tangible products such as clothing, cars, gifts and groceries. There is now an increasing trend towards the sale of services on the Internet, with companies selling a wide range of business and marketing services. For example, *Theincentiveshop.com* is operated by Projectlink, a well-established provider in the incentives business. The website offers a readily accessible source of travel and other incentives that businesses can buy on-line. Some business customers, particularly in sectors such as financial services, telecoms and IT, apparently prefer making these kinds of purchases over the Internet. A particular advantage is that the site provides customers with an end-of-year summary of spend on incentives. As UK law requires tax and insurance to be paid on these kinds of incentives, a single catch-all service proves very useful.

Other business services available on-line include printing services; marketing research via WAP phones; direct marketing; plus a full range of marketing, technology and other professional services. There are even companies offering to help businesses manage their supplier relationships. For example, *58k.com* provides a service to match print buyers with printing companies. The site uses an auction approach, where printers can put in bids for a range of jobs on offer. The advantage to the print buyer is a keen price, while the printers can use the facility to fill periods of low demand. As time passes, the number of service businesses trading over the Web will increase, as customers become more familiar with transacting over the Internet.

(*Source:* David Murphy, 'Services advance onto the Internet', *Marketing*, 8 February 2001, p. 33)

Test yourself

Case question

1 Why might a company such as Tesco decide to support its existing activities with a website?

Quick questions

2 For what marketing purposes can an Internet presence be used?
3 Is the Internet more than just another marketing channel? Why?

Applied question

4 You work for a frozen food retailer that is considering developing an Internet presence. Write a report explaining how your company might use the Internet to support its presence on the high street.

Extra readings

Adams, N.R., Dogramaci, O., Gangopadhyay, A. and Yesha, Y. (1999) *Electronic Commerce: Technical, Business and Legal Issues.* Englewood Cliffs, NJ: Pearson.

Chaffey, D., Mayer, R., Johnston, K. and Ellis-Chadwick, F. (2002) *Internet Marketing: Strategy, Implementation and Practice.* Harlow: Pearson/FT.

O'Malley, L., Patterson, M. and Evans, M. (1999) *Exploring Direct Marketing.* London: Thomson.

December, J. and Randall, N. (1996) *The World Wide Web Unleashed.* New York: Sams Publishing.

Rouilly, J. (2002) *E-Business: Principles and Practice.* Basingstoke: Palgrave Macmillan.

Schwartz, E.I. (1997) *Webonomics: Nine Essential Principles for Growing Your Business on the World Wide Web*. New York: Broadway Books.

Zikmund, W. and d'Amico, M. (2001) *Marketing: Creating and Keeping Customers in an E-Commerce World.* Cincinnati, OH: South Western.

28: Marketing Channels

Key definitions

A *marketing channel* is a channel of distribution; a group of interrelated intermediaries that direct products to customers.

Distribution is the 'place' ingredient in the marketing mix, involving the selection of a marketing channel or channels.

A *marketing intermediary* is a 'middleman' who links producers to other middlemen or to those who ultimately use the product.

Intensive distribution is the use of all available outlets or channels for distributing a product.

Selective distribution is the use of only some available outlets or channels to distribute a product.

Exclusive distribution is the use of only one outlet in a relatively large catchment to distribute a product.

Key issues

- Marketers spend a great deal of time ensuring the 'right' product or service is offered to the target market. If the channel of distribution from supplier to customer is not properly determined and managed, however, marketers will not be successful in their endeavours.
- The marketing channel is the channel of distribution adopted within a marketing mix and is often referred to as the *place* ingredient of the '5Ps' of the marketing mix, along with product, people, price and promotion.
- The marketing channel comprises intermediaries that direct products to the targeted customers. These intermediaries fall into two broad categories: (a) merchants that re-sell, such as wholesalers and retailers, and (b) agents, brokers or dealers that receive commission or a fee for expediting exchanges.
- There are also intermediaries that facilitate the physical distribution of goods, such as transportation, storage and warehousing, marketing services businesses, finance and insurance providers, trade shows and trade markets.
- Without intermediaries, five producers serving five customers would require 25 separate transactions. With a wholesaler or retailer acting as 'middleman', only ten transactions are required between the same parties.
- When determining a channel of distribution, a business must consider its objectives, resources, the characteristics and expectations of the market, buying behaviour, product attributes and environmental forces.
- A business must decide on its desired intensity of market coverage: intensive, selective or exclusive.
- A conventional marketing channel involves discrete components: manufacturer to wholesaler to retailer to consumer. There are some vertical marketing systems, integrating manufacturing, wholesaling and retailing.
- In consumer markets, the marketing channel usually involves two or more of

these stages: producer, agents or brokers, wholesalers, retailers and then the consumer. Factory outlets have only two stages: producer direct to consumer. Confectionery products may pass through all five stages.

- Many businesses deploy various channels in parallel in order to service different customer needs and to cater for various target market segments.
- In business-to-business markets, the options include producer to agents to industrial distributors to industrial buyers. As with consumer channels, some channels include all four stages, but some products or customer accounts involve only two or three stages.
- Direct producer–customer relations, except for farm shops and factory outlets in consumer markets or component suppliers into large factories, used to be rare. Internet-based marketing and direct marketing have altered this situation, with many more direct supplier–customer relationships emerging.
- The arrival of the Internet has added a channel option for many organizations. Most e-channels of distribution are relatively recent additions to organizations' existing marketing channel choices.
- Despite the growth in direct marketing, marketing intermediaries are commonplace and numerous. These intermediaries perform key tasks: sorting out, accumulation, allocation and sorting.
- Channel leadership and cooperation are important strategic issues, stemming from various sources of power: economic and non-economic.

Conceptual overview

Marketers must distribute their products to their customers. This may be direct, such as farm shops, factory outlets, suppliers to large manufacturing sites or goods now retailed over the Internet. Often, though, distribution requires intermediaries to expedite the flow of goods from producer to customer. Occasionally a vertical marketing channel exists with integration of manufacturing, wholesaling and retailing. A marketer must select an appropriate channel of distribution (or channels) to ensure targeted customers may readily obtain the product or service.

In consumer markets, this may involve movements from producer to agent or broker, to wholesaler, to retailer, to the end-user customer, or some combination of these stages. For example, Mars distributes its confectionery products through two principal channels: direct to the warehouses of the national supermarket chains which in turn sell these products to the ultimate customers, and to wholesalers and cash and carry operators which in turn supply corner shops, CTNs (newsagents) and forecourt shops. Business-to-business channels may involve movement from producer to agent, to industrial distributor, to the industrial buyer, or may skip certain stages.

When selecting a suitable channel for a target market, a marketer should consider: (a) company objectives; (b) available resources; (c) market characteristics and expectations; (d) buying behaviour of the end-user and channel intermediaries; (e) product attributes; plus (f) marketing environmental forces. The company must decide on a market coverage policy:

- Intensive: many outlets with small catchments, such as for convenience goods.
- Selective: larger catchments, for example for shopping goods.
- Exclusive: restricted distribution, often for prestigious products or when available resources can serve only a limited number of outlets/catchments.

The intermediaries in a marketing channel: (a) sort out and classify heterogeneous goods to homogeneous groups; (b) accumulate a bank of homogeneous products to provide aggregate stock; (c) allocate homogeneous stocks into smaller units that reflect their customers' needs; (d) sort or combine products into collections, assortments or ranges that their buyers are seeking. Facilitating agencies include organizations assisting with transportation, storage and warehousing, advertising, finance and insurance provision, trade shows and trade markets, and marketing research. These issues are discussed more thoroughly in Brief 29.

The arrival of the Internet has added a channel option for many organizations, as more and more goods and services are marketed through the Web. While there are examples of businesses existing only in cyberspace, such as Amazon, most e-channels of distribution are relatively recent additions to organizations' existing marketing channels. The adoption of the Internet by a growing number of businesses has added to the complexity of channel selection and management.

A major concern in many organizations is that of channel leadership. Just-in-time manufacturing, relationship marketing, partnershipping programmes between suppliers and business customers, amongst other market developments, have led to greater cooperation and less conflict within many businesses' channels. For some organizations, however, there is still a desire to control the marketing channel and to be the most powerful player. For all businesses, even in zero-conflict channels, it is still important to recognize the driving forces and organizations that will innovate and create change. Power in the marketing channel stems from: (a) economic sources, such as resource control or business size; and (b) non-economic sources, including reward power, expert power, referent power/opinion leadership, legitimate leadership power, or coercive power.

Examples

Games Workshop

Games Workshop makes and sells fantasy games to enthusiasts via a number of distribution channels. The company's products, which are especially popular with teenagers and children, are centred on two settings. The first consists of a war-ravaged universe in the 41st Millennium. Strange creatures such as Dwarfs, Goblins, Orcs and Scaven populate the second. Games Workshop enthusiasts can buy boxed games, figures, paints, books, T-shirts and other paraphernalia from the company's 250 plus retail outlets around the world. Products are also stocked by certain other toy retailers and are available via the company's specialist mail order operation. With a database of 150 000 contacts and 40 staff, the large mail order facility is available in-store, by post, telephone or over the Internet. It is capable of responding to requests in a range of languages and can handle 1000 calls every day.

(*Source:* Jervis Johnson and Chris Prentice of Games Workshop; www.games-workshop.co.uk)

Petrol distribution

The distribution of petrol has undergone significant changes in recent years. Traditional suppliers, such as BP, Shell and Esso, have become engaged in a competitive battle with some of the major supermarkets. With customers prepared to shop around for the best price deal, retailers like Sainsbury, Safeway and Tesco have periodically reduced the price of the fuel to attract consumers to their stores. Although these retailers are prepared to go to considerable lengths to buy their petrol supplies wherever prices are lowest, they also regard fuel sales as a loss-leading mechanism for attracting customers to their stores. A further attraction for customers is that they can also use their supermarket loyalty cards for petrol purchases. This makes for challenging times for the fuel companies, who have been forced to respond to this competitive pressure while at the same time realizing that selling petrol alone may not be profitable.

The fuel companies have responded to this threat in a variety of ways. Some have focused on offering the lowest possible prices, others have attempted to develop customer loyalty schemes. Perhaps the most ironic development is that many of the fuel companies have increased the sale of grocery and other products at their forecourt shops, believing that this will act as a magnet for customers. In some cases this has been achieved through cooperative arrangements with the supermarkets. For example, BP and Safeway have rolled out a 'mini-supermarket and forecourt' concept. With around 3000 product lines available, the intention is to use the pulling power of both brands for the mutual benefit of both companies.

(*Sources:* Julian Lee, 'Clubcard move fuels price war', *Marketing,* 29 February 1996, p. 1; Martin Payne and Phillip Wisson, 'Retailscan: ads fuel petrol's risky price war', *Marketing Week,* 19 April 1996, pp. 30–1; Sally Dibb and Lyndon Simkin, *The Marketing Casebook*, London: Thomson, 2001)

Test yourself

Case question

1 Fuel companies such as Shell, Esso and BP have a distribution system based on vertical channel integration. What does this mean and does it have any particular advantages or disadvantages?

Quick questions

2 Why are shorter distribution channels seen as more efficient?
3 What are the major types of distribution channels for consumer goods? Give an example of a product distributed through each type.

Applied question

4 Having recently inherited some money, you decide to leave your job with one of the major holiday tour operators to set up your own company to sell specialist adventure holidays. You are trying to decide whether you should sell the holidays direct, or operate through a small chain of travel agents with which you have a connection. What factors should you consider when deciding on the channel of distribution?

Extra readings

Christopher, M. (2003) *Marketing Logistics.* Oxford: Butterworth-Heinemann.
Christopher, M. (1999) *Logistics and Supply Chain Management.* Harlow: Pearson/FT.
Coughlan, A., Anderson, E., Stern, L.W. and El-Ansary Adel. (2001) *Marketing Channels*, International Edition. Harlow: Prentice Hall/FT.
Friedman, L. and Furey, T. (1999) *The Channel Advantage.* Oxford: Butterworth-Heinemann.
Hines, T. (2003) *Supply Chain Strategies.* Oxford: Butterworth-Heinemann.
Rosenbloom, B. (2003) *Marketing Channels: A Management View.* Cincinnati, OH: South Western.

29: Wholesaling and Physical Distribution Management (PDM)

Key definitions

A *wholesaler* is an individual or business engaged in facilitating and expediting exchanges between producers and business-to-business customers within the distribution channel.

Facilitating agencies are organizations such as transport companies, insurers, financiers, marketing services businesses, warehouse operators, and trade market organizations performing activities that facilitate marketing channel operations.

Physical distribution is a set of activities used in the movement of products from producers to consumers: order processing, materials handling, warehousing, inventory management and transportation.

Customer service in terms of physical distribution focuses on product availability, promptness and quality.

Key issues

- Marketing requires the effective distribution of products to the targeted markets. This often involves marketing intermediaries (cf. Brief 28) and facilitating agencies. In order to ensure adequate provision of customer service, physical distribution management also impacts on marketing.
- The growth in direct marketing (cf. Brief 26) has limited the use of channel intermediaries for certain market segments and products, but not the use of facilitating agencies and physical distribution management.
- Wholesaling in marketing includes all transactions in which the purchasing business intends to re-sell the products bought. Wholesaling is broadly defined, therefore, to include merchant wholesalers, agents and brokers and manufacturers' own sales branches.
- Facilitating agencies smooth the work of the marketing channel and include a diverse mix of operations: transport and warehousing companies, insurance and finance providers, plus a wide range of marketing services businesses.
- Physical distribution management (PDM) is a separate discipline to marketing but its activities create the product availability, promptness and quality often so important to customers. PDM includes order processing, materials handling, warehousing, inventory management and transportation. Each is a complex, specialist and costly area, but collectively must be controlled to ensure the provision of customer service and customer satisfaction.

Conceptual overview

Marketers must distribute their products to their customers. This involves transportation, storage and warehousing, finance and insurance, marketing services, trade markets and an understanding of marketing environment forces. Irrespective of the selected marketing channel (cf. Brief 28), facilitating agencies will play a role: even direct e-commerce still entails delivery firms and warehousing. In channels involving many channel intermediaries and stages in the distribution process, numerous participants will be involved.

Wholesaling includes all transactions in which the purchasing business intends to re-sell the product. In marketing, wholesaling is more than cash and carry wholesaling operations. Most channel intermediaries could fall into this classification. Wholesalers therefore provide services for both producers and retailers and are involved with many activities: (a) managing wholesaling operations; (b) negotiating with suppliers; (c) promotion; (d) warehousing and product handling; (e) transport; (f) inventory control and data processing; (g) security; (h) pricing; (i) financing and budgeting; (j) providing marketing advice to clients.

Wholesalers fall into various categories:

- Merchant wholesalers: take title to goods and assume risks associated with ownership and stock handling.
  - Full service merchant wholesalers: offer the widest range of wholesaling functions. They include general merchandise wholesalers, limited line wholesalers and speciality line wholesalers.
  - Limited service merchant wholesalers: carry only a few product lines but offer extensive assortments within these lines. They include cash and carry wholesalers, truck wholesalers, drop shippers and mail order wholesalers.
- Agents and brokers: functional middlemen who perform limited marketing tasks in return for a commission. Agents represent buyers or sellers on a contractually permanent basis, while brokers are employed temporarily.
- Manufacturers' sales branches and offices: manufacturer-owned and -controlled operations selling products and providing support to sales staff and customers.

Agencies such as transport companies, warehousing operators, insurance providers, advertising and marketing research firms, financiers, operators of trade shows and trade markets perform activities that smooth the progress of goods through the distribution channel. These companies are termed facilitating agencies.

Activities used in the movement of products from producers to consumers, including order processing, materials handling, warehousing, inventory management and transportation, are termed physical distribution management (PDM). Many companies have specialist managers handling these logistical issues, but PDM is central to the provision of customer service and therefore must be monitored by marketers. Availability, promptness and quality are important customer needs that are facilitated by PDM. In order to ensure satisfactory customer service, marketers must persuade their colleagues in logistical operations to give adequate consideration to:

- Order processing.
- Materials handling.
- Selection of packaging materials.
- Warehousing and storage.
- Inventory control.
- Transportation.

The systems required for these operations are increasingly costly and specialized, so in practice there must be a balance between cost-effectiveness and the delivery of the expected levels of customer service. Orders should be handled competently and efficiently, while providing adequate customer service. Materials handling is the physical handling of products and is important for efficient warehousing, as well as in the transportation from the point of production to the point where an item is consumed. Materials handling should raise the usable capacity of a warehouse, reduce the number of times an item is handled, improve customer service and increase customers' satisfaction with the product.

Warehousing can be in-company or sub-contracted to marketing channel intermediaries. It must minimize operational costs, while facilitating the efficient and secure distribution of products. When selecting packaging material, companies must consider the functionality of the packaging for end-users, stockists and distributors; packaging must protect the product, while also facilitating its easy use, storage and handling; 'green' concerns and technological advances should be considered (cf. Brief 18). Inventory management supports the required levels of customer service while minimizing unnecessary stock-holding costs. Possible transport modes include motor vehicles, railways, inland waterways, air, and pipelines. Some of the essential criteria for selecting a mode of transport include cost, transit time, reliability, capability, accessibility, security, traceability and operational coordination.

Examples

Securicor

Courier companies such as DHL, FedEx, UPS and Securicor play an important role in the physical distribution of products, and their vans and lorries are a familiar sight. According to Securicor Distribution's marketing material, the courier company offers same and next day delivery services within the UK, as well as a range of services for further afield. The company aims to solve other businesses' distribution needs, by providing a facilitating service. Securicor also offers container transport, movement of bulk and liquid materials together with warehouse management and integrated logistics services.

(*Source:* Securicor Distribution marketing material)

Packaging materials

The selection of packaging materials for use when transporting products must be made with care. Consumers and businesses are increasingly aware of the detrimental environmental impact of many traditional packaging substances. For many years, the polystyrene peanut was the packaging material of choice for products as diverse as washing machines and video players. However, the peanuts have a number of clear disadvantages: they are produced from non-renewable resources, may release CFCs when burnt and are not biodegradable. Some sources suggest they can stay in the environment for up to 1000 years. The peanuts also attract static electricity, meaning they are not suitable for transporting all kinds of products.

There are some more environmentally friendly alternatives. Eco-Foam is made primarily from cornflower, so is biodegradable without directly resembling a foodstuff. It also looks rather like the old polystyrene peanut, so companies seeking a shift can make the switch with relative ease. Popcorn is another, quite novel new packaging material. It is biodegradable and has the necessary physical characteristics for protecting items in transit. Another advantage is that popcorn is very cheap and can be transported to where required, prior to 'popping'. The space taken for moving the material around is therefore very small. However, the more usual use of popcorn is as a food. Some governments have banned the use of popcorn in packaging, because they are concerned that people will eat it. Various ways are being considered for overcoming these difficulties.

(*Sources:* Jerry Drisaldi, 'Protective packaging: it's your responsibility', *Inbound Logistics*, November 1991, p. 39; Walter L. Weart, 'Packaging dilemmas: the sequel', *Inbound Logistics*, June 1991, pp. 27–9; Patricia B. Demetrio, 'A race against time', *Inbound Logistics*, June 1994, pp. 40–8)

Test yourself

Case question

1 What considerations must companies make when choosing a packaging material?

Quick questions

2 What is materials handling?
3 What criteria should be used for selecting a mode of transport?

Applied question

4 As a consultant specializing in physical distribution, you are preparing a report for a flower grower to explore possible transport modes. Your report should consider the advantages and disadvantages of a number of alternative transport approaches.

Extra readings

Christopher, M. (2003) *Marketing Logistics.* Oxford: Butterworth-Heinemann.

Christopher, M. (1999) *Logistics and Supply Chain Management.* Harlow: Pearson/FT.

Friedman, L. and Furey, T. (1999) *The Channel Advantage.* Oxford: Butterworth-Heinemann.

Hines, T. (2003) *Supply Chain Strategies.* Oxford: Butterworth-Heinemann.

Rosenbloom, B. (2003) *Marketing Channels: A Management View.* Cincinnati, OH: South Western.

Waters, D. (2003) *Global Logistics and Distribution Planning: Strategies for Management.* London: Kogan Page.

30: Pricing Concepts

Key definitions

Price is the value placed on what is exchanged during the marketing process.

Perceived value for money is the benefit consumers believe to be inherent in a product or service weighed against the price demanded.

Key issues

- The customer exchanges his/her money or donation in return for satisfaction or utility.
- To the marketer, price is of fundamental concern. Profitability equals price multiplied by quantities sold, less total costs. A change in price will have a direct impact on profitability. In certain markets, price modification will reduce or increase sales.
- Marketers adopt either a policy of price competition or of non-price competition. Under price competition, a marketer emphasizes price in the marketing mix and endeavours to match or beat the prices set by competitors for rival products. Under a policy of non-price competition, a marketer instead opts to emphasize other ingredients in the marketing mix rather than keen pricing.
- Marketers have several pricing objectives: survival, profitability, return on investment, market share levels, cash flow, maintaining the status quo, or product quality.
- Key factors affecting pricing include organizational and marketing objectives, pricing objectives, costs, other marketing mix ingredients, channel member expectations, buyers' perceptions, competition, legal and regulatory issues, and perceived value.
- In business-to-business markets, price discounting, geographic pricing, transfer pricing, price discrimination, and economic value to the customer, are additional pricing concerns.

Conceptual overview

Pricing is inextricably linked to a business's fortunes. Profits are a result of price multiplied by units sold, less total costs. Price is the value placed by a marketer on a product or service. The customer expects satisfaction and utility from the product in return for a payment or donation. In most markets, price is quantified in a monetary value. In markets that are highly competitive or where the product is far from an essential requisite for life, a price rise may well result in falling sales and reduced profitability. A marketer must set prices with caution, with full knowledge of target market conditions, and with the intention of maximizing the financial standing of the company (cf. Brief 31).

In most markets, price is a key ingredient in the marketing mix. Everyday low pricing (EDLP) is a concept familiar to supermarket shoppers and is an example of price competition – the emphasis on price in the marketing mix with the intention of beating rivals' prices. On occasions, marketers prefer not to emphasize price, instead focusing on the other ingredients of the marketing mix: product, people or customer service, promotion and place (distribution). This is non-price competition.

When establishing price, a marketer will have numerous pricing objectives in mind, often selected from: (a) the need for commercial viability and survival; (b) senior management's profit expectations; (c) return on investment; (d) market share requirements; or (e) cash flow levels for on-going operations. A business may be in a favourable position and simply wish to maintain the status quo. A company such as Jaguar or JCB may adopt a strategy based on superior product quality, entailing relatively high prices to cover product quality or research and development costs.

Organizational objectives will impact on pricing: Chanel's brand strategy requires premium pricing. If marketing objectives dictate a rapid market share increase, overly high prices will not be desirable. Pricing must generate enough income to cover costs, at least in the long term, otherwise the company will not survive. Pricing must permit channel members to make their margins when selling on. If a product is premium priced, its promotion, distribution, customer service and product attributes will need to be in harmony. The whole of the marketing mix should be cohesive and price cannot be at odds with the other 'Ps' of the marketing mix (cf. Brief 32).

Marketing must never lose sight of customer needs and expectations: price, too, must reflect buyers' perceptions. Customers generally have a choice of suppliers, so a marketer needs to understand competitors' pricing when determining price. Increasingly, marketers are becoming aware of how customers perceive value for money, which involves a trade-off for the customer between the price paid and the benefit inherent in adopting the product or service. Finally, in many markets, regulators dictate permitted pricing or price bands: the EU, for example, prohibits price dumping.

There are additional issues in business-to-business markets. Customers rarely pay the advertised price (cf. Brief 31). There are trade discounts, quality or bulk purchase discounts, cash discounts for prompt payment, seasonal discounts for out-of-season sales, plus allowances in price subject to the achievement of sales targets. Geographic pricing may well feature, with price modification for transport costs or costs associated with the physical distance between buyer and seller. Marketers may have to determine prices for products or services that are purchased by other business units or operations within their own organization: transfer pricing. There may be price discrimination, a policy by which different prices are charged in order to give a particular group of buyers a competitive edge. It is important that a marketer ascertains that such discrimination does not violate any laws.

In order to avoid winning orders purely on the basis of low price, which ultimately leads to financial ruin, many marketers increasingly have emphasized product quality, customer service or other aspects of the marketing mix. This has led to the notion of economic value to the customer (EVC), the underlying principle of which is that a premium price can be charged while still offering the customer better value than the competition.

Examples

Montblanc

The price of pens varies from just a few pence for a simple disposable biro, to thousands of pounds for a solid gold Montblanc. Separate customers in different contexts make purchase choices based on a wide range of dimensions that impact upon the price that can be charged. For example, a customer who spends hundreds of pounds purchasing a gold fountain pen is clearly motivated by rather more than just needing a writing instrument. When determining pricing levels, companies such as Montblanc and Parker must be prepared to take these factors into consideration. Parker, for example, determines the pricing of its various ranges by carefully analysing the requirements of a particular target market, undertaking an examination of costs and rigorously testing to discover the price level customers are prepared to pay. This systematic process allows the company to better understand some of the psychological issues underlying price. Montblanc similarly analyses the buying behaviour of its targeted customers and the pricing strategies of its rivals, particularly as it is extending its brand into deluxe giftware such as jewellery and watches.

(*Sources:* Parker Pen Co. sales literature, 1996; Chuck Tomkovich and Kathryn Dobie, 'Apply hedonic pricing models and factorial surveys at Parker Pen to enhance new product success', *Journal of Product Innovation Management*, 1995, 12 (4), pp. 334–5; Montblanc, Geneva, 2003)

Knock-down perfume prices

The high prices associated with exclusive fragrances are actually designed to attract customers. Many people, apparently, believe that expense can be equated with exclusivity and enjoy the feeling that not everyone can afford their favourite scent. Perfume houses around the world, such as Chanel, Dior and Givenchy, have attempted to protect this exclusive image by allowing a limited number of carefully chosen outlets to sell their fragrances. Controlling distribution in this manner has historically also restricted the possibilities for price discounting. However, a number of retailers, led by the Superdrug discount chain and leading supermarket chains, recently started to offer the more exclusive brands at reduced prices. Such a move was complicated by the fact that supplies of the fragrances had to be obtained from the 'grey market', as the perfume houses resisted supplying these discounting businesses. The fragrance manufacturers also tried to stir up a wave of negative opinion amongst key industry players. For example, many fashion and women's magazines refused to advertise the discounted products for fear that the perfume houses might take their advertising business elsewhere.

Ultimately, in order to maintain sales, other retailers such as Boots and House of Fraser were forced to follow the lead taken by the discounters and cut their prices. Although these moves might appear to be in the consumers' interest, there is concern in the industry that the narrowing gap between the leading perfume brands and cheaper products aimed at the mass market might reduce their exclusivity. The result could be serious damage to the complex and expensive process of brand-building that the leading perfume houses have undertaken.

(*Sources:* Sally Dibb, Lyndon Simkin, Bill Pride and O.C. Ferrell, *Marketing: Concepts and Strategies*, Boston, MA: Houghton Mifflin, 2001; Helen Slingsby, 'House of Fraser reviews scent pricing', *Marketing Week*, 18 December 1992; Suzanne Bidlake, 'Perfume firms fear wrath of retailers', *Marketing*, 29 October 1992, p. 5; Boots, 2004; Superdrug Stores, 2003)

Test yourself

Case question

1 Why have the leading fragrance houses tried so hard to maintain the premium prices of their products?

Quick questions

2 What are pricing objectives?
3 Explain the difference between price and non-price competition.

Applied question

4 Write a paper that explains to a new entrant in the hotel industry the factors affecting pricing decisions.

Extra readings

Diamantopoulos, A. and Mathews, B.P. (1995) *Making Pricing Decisions: a Study of Managerial Practice.* London: Thomson Learning.

Dibb, S., Simkin, L., Pride, W. and Ferrell, O.C. (2001) *Marketing: Concepts and Strategies.* Boston, MA: Houghton Mifflin.

Dolan, J. and Simon, H. (1996) *Power Pricing: How Managing Price Transforms the Bottom Line*. New York: Free Press.

Monroe, B.K. (2002) *Pricing: Making Profitable Decisions*. New York: McGraw-Hill.

Nagle, T. (1994) *Strategy and Tactics of Pricing: A Guide to Profitable Decision-Making.* Harlow: Pearson/FT.

Nagle, T. and Holden, R.K. (2002) *The Strategy and Tactics of Pricing: A Guide to Profitable Decision-Making.* Upper Saddle River, NJ: PHIS.

Winckler, J. (1983) *Pricing for Results.* Oxford: Butterworth-Heinemann.

31: Setting Prices

Key definitions

The *price elasticity of demand* is a measure of the sensitivity of demand to changes in price.

The *break-even point* is that at which the costs of producing a product equal the revenue made from selling the product.

Pioneer pricing is the setting of a base price for a new product. Options include price skimming and penetration pricing.

Psychological pricing is designed to encourage purchases based on emotional rather than rational responses.

Professional pricing is deployed by experts with significant experience in a particular field.

Promotional pricing is linked to the short-term promotion of a product.

Cost-oriented pricing is a process of adding a monetary amount or percentage to the cost of producing and marketing a product.

Demand-oriented pricing is based on the level of demand for a product: high prices when demand is high; low prices when demand is weak.

Competition-oriented pricing considers costs and revenue to be secondary to competing with rivals' pricing.

Marketing-oriented pricing takes into account marketing strategy, competition, value to the customer, price–quality relationships, explicability, costs, product line pricing, negotiating margins, political factors and the impact on distributors or retailers.

Key issues

- There are eight stages in establishing a price: setting objectives; assessing the target market's view of price; determining demand; analysing the relationship between demand, cost and profitability; evaluation of competitors' prices; selection of a pricing policy; developing a pricing method; and determining a specific price.
- Selecting pricing objectives is critical and involves short-term and longer-term expectations. Pricing must be based on an assessment of target market expectations and ability to pay, plus a detailed examination of likely demand at different price points.
- The understanding of the relationship between demand, cost and profit is complex but it is a core task of marketing management. Without this understanding, profitability is likely to be impaired. Within this economic evaluation, break-even analysis ensures financial viability and survival.
- The customer often has a choice of supplier options: marketers must be aware of the competitive set and the prices charged by these rivals.
- A pricing policy is a guiding philosophy. Pioneer pricing options include price skimming and penetration pricing. Psychological pricing focuses on emotional responses and includes odd–even pricing, customary pricing, prestige pricing and price lining. Professional pricing is used by

experienced managers knowledgeable in a particular field. Promotional pricing includes price leaders, special event pricing and everyday low pricing. Experience curve pricing sets a low price that high cost competitors cannot match.

- A pricing method is a mechanical procedure for assigning prices to products. Options include cost-oriented pricing, demand-oriented, competition-oriented and marketing-oriented pricing.
- Pricing objectives, policies and methods should dictate actual price selection. Of all the marketing mix ingredients, price is often the easiest and quickest to modify. Marketers must be aware, however, of the implications on business performance.

Conceptual overview

A fundamental aspect of marketing is the setting of the price within the marketing mix for a product or service (cf. Briefs 30 and 32). This will determine the viability of the marketing programme and possibly also the company. There are eight essential stages in determining the price charged: (a) setting objectives consistent with short-term and longer-term corporate goals; (b) assessing the target market's view of price; (c) determining demand; (d) analysing the relationship between demand, cost and profitability; (e) evaluation of competitors' prices; (f) selection of a pricing policy; (g) developing a pricing method; and (h) determining a specific price.

Understanding the demand for a product and how sensitive this is to different prices is a difficult but important task. Profitability is unlikely to be optimized without this understanding, or worse, the company may endure financial hardship if prices lead to a fall in demand (cf. Figures 31.1 and 31.2). Some products are highly price sensitive, while others are not so prone to fluctuations in demand caused by rising or falling prices. The analysis of demand generally also involves examining the cost base behind the product to ensure the break-even point, at the very least,

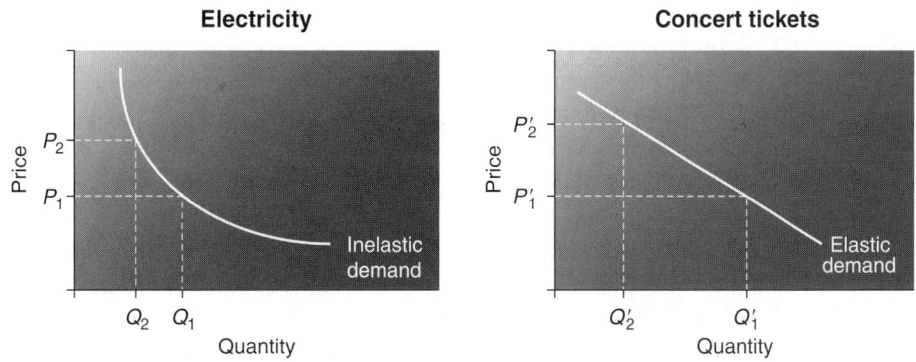

Figure 31.1 Elasticity of demand

(*Source: adapted from* Sally Dibb, Lyndon Simkin, Bill Pride and O.C. Ferrell, *Marketing: Concepts and Strategies*, Boston, MA: Houghton Mifflin, 2001, ch. 19)

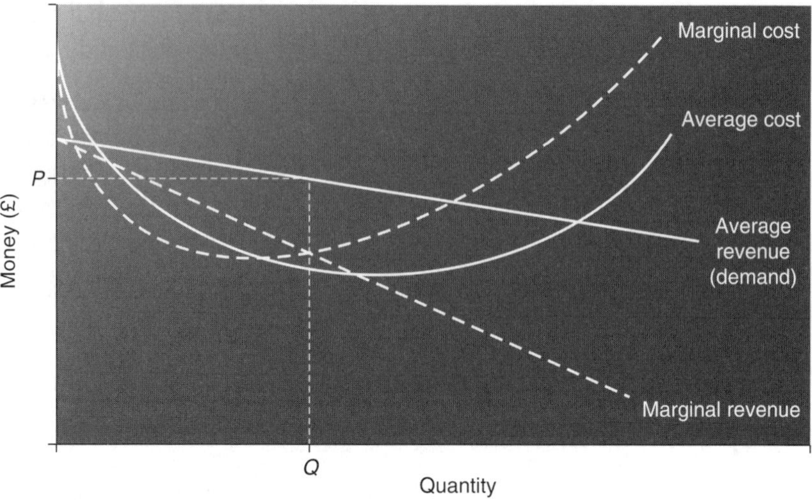

Figure 31.2 Combining marginal cost and marginal revenue for optimal profit

(*Source: adapted from* Sally Dibb, Lyndon Simkin, Bill Pride and O.C. Ferrell, *Marketing: Concepts and Strategies*, Boston, MA: Houghton Mifflin, 2001, ch. 19)

is covered by the resulting revenue at a specific price point. The break-even point = fixed costs/(price − variable costs).

Customers invariably can choose between various suppliers. A marketer must be aware of competitors' prices when selecting a price to charge for a product or service. There must also be a pricing policy: (a) pioneer pricing, the setting of a price for a new product, either through price skimming to charge the highest price that buyers who most desire the product will pay, or penetration pricing to undercut competing products and generate quick sales; (b) psychological pricing to play on customers' emotions, through odd–even pricing, customary pricing, prestige pricing or price lining; (c) professional pricing, using the experience of experts; (d) promotional pricing, such as price leaders, special event pricing, or everyday low prices; and (e) experience curve pricing, with prices fixed at a low point that rival higher cost competitors cannot match.

The most commonly adopted pricing methods include: (a) cost-oriented, cost-plus or mark-up, based on a fixed percentage margin above costs; (b) demand-oriented, featuring high prices in periods of strong demand and lower prices when demand is weaker; (c) competition-oriented, placing greater emphasis on rivals' prices than costs or revenues; and (d) marketing-oriented. The in-vogue marketing oriented method is something of a hybrid approach considering numerous factors, including the specified marketing strategy, competition, value to the customer, price–quality relationships, explicability of the price to the market, costs, product line prices for 'sister' products, negotiating margins, political factors and the implications for distributors'/retailers' pricing.

Finally, based on these seven previous stages, the marketer establishes the price to be charged. The implications on the performance of the business and of the marketing function are significant. Of all the marketing mix ingredients, price is often the easiest and quickest to alter. Unfortunately, the ramifications of such modifications to the price are not always well thought out.

Examples

Kuoni

Kuoni specializes in offering deluxe long-haul hotel and resort holidays in Africa, Australasia, the Caribbean, and the Americas, along with cruises, escorted tours, safaris and wedding packages. When a package holiday company sets the prices that appear in its brochures or on its website, it must take a number of factors into consideration. As the company is selling a product comprising a number of components (e.g. travel, transfers, board and accommodation, car hire, excursions and possibly insurance), a major consideration is to ensure that all its costs are covered and a reasonable mark-up can be achieved. However, this is not the only consideration. Kuoni must ensure that it carefully assesses its target customers so that it can make an appropriate estimation of what they might be prepared to pay. As the company will have a finite number of holidays to sell, it must also take the likely demand for its products into consideration. In addition, Kuoni must evaluate the prices being set by competing package holiday operators. After all, many customers are prepared to shop around and will base their purchase decision on a number of competing propositions.

(*Sources:* www.kuoni.co.uk, 2004; Carrick Travel, 2003)

Heinz Beans

Baked beans are one of the more interesting weapons used in the battle between supermarkets. Retailers including Tesco, Sainsbury's and Asda have used the humble bean as a loss-leader, to attract customers into their stores. Instead of charging the usual 40–50 pence for a can, prices of budget baked beans, such as Tesco's Budget range, have fallen to little more than 10 pence.

For big brands such as Heinz or HP, which have built an enviable reputation for their baked beans, these manoeuvres are threatening. Previously, Heinz had protected its position by refusing to manufacture beans for anyone else. In other words, if it did not have Heinz on the tin, it was not a Heinz product. However, in recent years, consumers have become aware that Heinz has started to supply own-label beans to the supermarkets. Although the company claims that its 'regular' recipes are not used for these purposes, there is a danger that consumers may stop believing that Heinz beans are worth the price premium. From the Heinz viewpoint, the move into own-label supply makes sound economic sense. The company can make use of spare production capacity to make budget beans for the supermarkets. However, the company must keep closely in mind the fact that customers may increasingly choose to pay just a few pence for their beans, rather than handing over the price-premium for the Heinz brand.

(*Sources:* Stephanie Bentley, 'Heinz own label hits supply snag', *Marketing Week*, 16 February 1996, p. 9; Julian Lee and Claire Murphy, 'Cracking the lookalike code', *Marketing*, 29 February 1996, p. 12; Tesco Stores, 2003)

Test yourself

Case question

1 Is price the only factor taken into consideration by customers buying baked beans?

Quick questions

2 What are fixed and variable costs? Give examples of each.
3 What steps are involved in setting prices?

Applied question

4 You have been asked to prepare a briefing sheet explaining the relationship between price elasticity and demand. The briefing sheet is to be made available to small businesses in order to help them with setting their prices. Draft out such a briefing sheet.

Extra readings

Diamantopoulos, A. and Mathews, B.P. (1995) *Making Pricing Decisions: a Study of Managerial Practice.* London: Thomson Learning.

Dibb, S., Simkin, L., Pride, W. and Ferrell, O.C. (2001) *Marketing: Concepts and Strategies.* Boston, MA: Houghton Mifflin.

Dolan, J. and Simon, H. (1996) *Power Pricing: How Managing Price Transforms the Bottom Line.* New York: Free Press.

Monroe, B.K. (2002) *Pricing: Making Profitable Decisions.* New York: McGraw-Hill.

Nagle, T. (1994) *Strategy and Tactics of Pricing: A Guide to Profitable Decision-Making.* Harlow: Pearson.

Nagle, T. and Holden, R.K. (2002) *The Strategy and Tactics of Pricing: A Guide to Profitable Decision-Making.* Upper Saddle River, NJ: PHIS.

Winckler, J. (1983) *Pricing for Results.* Oxford: Butterworth-Heinemann.

32: The Marketing Mix

Key definitions

The *marketing mix* is the tactical toolkit of product, place, price and promotion that marketers manipulate in order to satisfy their customers and implement their target market strategies.

The *product* is everything, unfavourable and favourable, received in an exchange. A product is a complexity of tangible and intangible attributes and may be a physical good, service or idea.

The *product mix* is the composite group of products made available by a company to customers.

Place is the selection of a distribution or marketing channel.

A *marketing channel* is a channel of distribution, a group of interrelated intermediaries that direct products to customers.

Price is the value placed on the product being exchanged.

Perceived value for money is the benefit consumers perceive to be inherent in a product, weighed against the price demanded.

Promotion is communication with individuals, groups or organizations in order to facilitate exchanges by informing and persuading an audience to accept the business's products.

Communication is the sharing of meaning through the transmission of information.

People provide customer service and interact with customers in order to facilitate the exchange process.

Physical evidence is the environment in which a service is offered, its ambience and physical utility.

Process is the interaction of staff with customers; flows of information to customers; ordering, delivery and payment mechanisms; and systems for handling customers.

Key issues

- The marketing mix is the set of tactical activities developed by marketers to implement their market strategy recommendations and facilitate the exchange process with targeted customers.
- Traditionally, the marketing mix included the '4Ps' of product, place, price and promotion. More recently, it has been extended by services marketers to '7Ps', including people, physical evidence/ambience and process of transaction.
- Marketers should first analyse the marketplace – notably buying behaviour, competitor activity, trends of the marketing environment and capabilities – and devise a marketing strategy before specifying a marketing mix. Each targeted market segment will require a bespoke marketing mix.
- The product is the central ingredient of the marketing mix. Marketers consider

three levels of the product: (a) core, (b) actual and (c) augmented. Other product decisions include quality, name, positioning, packaging and associated customer service issues.

- The product life cycle (PLC) and management of the product mix require a great deal of attention. The portfolio of products must be managed carefully, with new product development, product modification and product deletion.
- The place ingredient of the marketing mix involves selecting and managing a channel of distribution in order to reach and satisfy the customers in the targeted markets.
- Price is the value placed on the product being exchanged, but in the marketing mix, pricing includes consideration of payment and financing arrangements. Perceived value for money is a related concern for marketers to understand.
- Promotion is the use of marketing communications to attract targeted customers, convey a brand positioning, and persuade customers to seek out the product to try it. Key techniques include the promotional mix activities of advertising, personal selling, public relations, sponsorship, sales promotion, direct mail and the Internet. Integrated marketing communications (IMC) strives to harmonize all activities associated with marketing communications.
- People are part of the service product and their recruitment, training, motivation and control are fundamental concerns for the services marketer. More recently, in the context of providing customer service and interfacing with customers, staff have become important to all marketers, not just those dealing with services.
- The physical environment is important to many customers taking receipt of and consuming certain products, particularly services. The ambience and physical utility of the surroundings impact on the customer's perception of the product and their likely level of customer satisfaction.
- The process of the transaction – ease of dealing with staff, ordering, receiving and paying for the product – matters to many customers, particularly those acquiring services.

Conceptual overview

The marketing mix is the set of tactical activities deployed by marketers in order to facilitate the exchanges at the heart of the marketing process. The marketing mix facilitates the exchange process, seeks to ensure customer satisfaction, strives to differentiate the proposition offered to customers from rivals' products or services, and is designed to achieve the target market strategy requirements of the specified marketing strategy (cf. Brief 33). Without an understanding of customer buying behaviour, needs and expectations, an evaluation of competitors' activities, an assessment of trends in the marketplace, plus an awareness of the organization's own standing and capabilities, it is not feasible to develop the marketing mix. Until the target market strategy has been formulated – market segment priorities and brand positioning – the marketing mix should not be determined. Each separate target market segment generally requires a bespoke marketing mix (cf. Brief 11). The marketing mix activities should reflect the needs and behaviour of targeted customers, emphasize any competitive advantage held by the business (cf. Brief 35), and communicate the organization's desired brand positioning to the targeted customers.

The traditional ingredients of the marketing mix used to be known as the '4Ps': product, place (distribution channels), price and promotion decisions. The marketers of services, faced with intangible products, the integral involvement of people in service product production, delivery and consumption, plus the characteristics of the service product (cf. Brief 19), added three additional 'Ps', to create the '7Ps' of the services marketing mix: product, place, price, promotion, people, physical environment and process. The marketers of consumer goods and business-to-business products increasingly have incorporated these additional ingredients within their marketing mixes.

The product is pivotal to the marketer's ability to satisfy targeted customers (cf. Brief 15). Marketers consider three levels of product – core, actual and augmented – and typically create a brand identity for their physical products and service products. Product positioning, product name, product quality, packaging and associated customer service, are just some of the issues addressed by marketers. Major issues for the marketer are the product life cycle (cf. Brief 16) and the need to manage a product mix. The use of portfolio models helps with the managing of the product mix (cf. Brief 17). Related to these analyses are the needs to: (a) create new products; (b) modify existing ones; and (c) delete products from the product mix offered to target markets.

The place ingredient in the marketing mix involves selecting an appropriate channel of distribution (cf. Brief 28), understanding the dynamics of the marketing channel and the requirements of channel members, and assessing the leadership roles prevalent within a channel. Direct marketing, largely owing to e-commerce, has led to more direct channels without channel members, but most products pass through channels involving wholesalers and retailers, or agents and distributors (cf. Brief 26). Even for organizations that have embraced the Web as a channel, there are relatively few examples when this has been instead of more conventional marketing channels (cf. Brief 27).

Price in marketing is the value placed on the physical good, service or idea offered by the marketer to the target market. In marketing mix terms, price includes payment conditions, credit and financing, plus the notion of value for money as perceived by the targeted customer. Pricing is of fundamental importance to an organization, affecting demand for products and the financial viability of the company (cf. Briefs 30 and 31).

Promotion in the marketing mix relates to marketing communications activities that attract customers and convey the desired brand or product positioning to the target market. Key techniques include advertising, personal selling, public relations, sponsorship, sales promotion, direct mail and the Internet. These techniques are some of the most costly marketing activities undertaken by a business and must be managed to good effect (cf. Briefs 20–27). A popular concept in recent years has been integrated marketing communications (IMC), which strives to harmonize and link all facets of the promotional mix across all internal and external stakeholder groups (cf. Brief 20).

The additional marketing mix ingredients popularized by services marketers include people, physical evidence and process (cf. Briefs 19 and 44). People are integral to the service product, which tends to be an event or occurrence depending on staff to produce and provide the service and customer ability to consume the service product. Employee selection, training, motivation and control are of paramount importance. The physical environment, such as layout, décor, lighting and ambience, affects how the customer perceives the service product, and therefore impacts on likely customer satisfaction. So does the ease of the transaction: the process for attaining, consuming and paying for the service.

Examples

Private health care

The UK market for private health care has enjoyed a period of considerable growth. During the 1980s, BUPA was the leading operator, but now many of the main insurance companies offer private health insurance products. Those who operate in this increasingly competitive market must give careful consideration to their marketing mix. The complexities of the product mean that considerable efforts may be needed to explain the benefits on offer to customers. This difficulty is compounded by the fact that providers must deal with individual consumers as well as business customers seeking corporate health care contracts. For this reason, promotional materials – such as the leaflets displayed in clinics and hospitals – must emphasize benefits relevant to the different groups. The use of standard pricing systems by many private clinics and hospitals is needed to ensure inclusion on insurance companies' lists of approved hospitals. Making health care available close to patients' homes is also a priority and many new facilities have been built. In some respects the infrastructure being developed bears more similarity to comfortable hotel accommodation than to traditional hospitals: increasing competition means that patients are choosing to be treated in more convivial and relaxing surroundings. The marketing mix for BUPA's or PPP's health care plans and facilities are carefully planned.

(*Sources:* Claire Murphy, 'BUPA looks for better health', *Marketing*, 3 December 1998, p. 21, Nuffield Hospitals' marketing material)

The NSPCC

People often associate marketing with commercial business and making profits. Yet marketing has a major role to play in the non-business sector. Charities are just one type of non-profit-making businesses that are increasingly turning to marketing in order to promote their cause. In a heavily publicized campaign, the NSPCC (the National Society for the Prevention of Cruelty to Children) set a target of raising £300 million, six times more than the usual level of fundraising during that period. The *Full Stop* campaign, which attempted to raise awareness of child cruelty, used images of children's toys – such as Action Man and pop icons the Spice Girls – to grab attention. A particular feature of the campaign was that it targeted both consumers and businesses through a variety of media, inviting them to donate funds via a pledge document.

The *Full Stop* campaign originally was concentrated in the month before Easter in 1999. It began with a public relations campaign, before following up with direct mail to the charity's 160 000 'best' donors. Soon after, the NSPCC website was updated to centre around the concept and on on-line pledges. This was accompanied by a major television and poster campaign. All-in-all, around 7500 poster sites were used to display images associated with the *Full Stop* project and 60, 30 and 10 second televisions advertisements were screened. Towards the end of March more letters were mailed, this time to all of the NSPCC's existing donors. At the same time a leaflet drop to 23 million UK homes was carried out and new press advertisements appeared. During the final weekend in March, NSPCC volunteers operated 2000 'Call to Action' sites to offer yet another opportunity for the public to sign donation pledges. Within three years, 140 000 individuals signed up to the *Full Stop* campaign. It is still at the heart of the NSPCC's activity. Recently, *there4me.com*, an on-line confidential advice service for children, has been pioneered, benefiting from an 82% increase in the charity's expenditure on activities to end cruelty to children. The charity's brand positioning statement is clear: *NSPCC. Cruelty to children must stop. FULL STOP.*

(*Sources:* Jade Garrett, 'Charities snub shock tactics for subtle approach', *Campaign*, 26 March 1999, p. 10; 'Spotlight charity', *Marketing Week*, 17 December 1998, pp. 28–9; 'NSPCC aims to convert abuse anger into cash', *Marketing*, 25 March 1999, pp. 37–8; www.nspcc.org.uk/campaigning, 2004)

Test yourself

Case question

1 Why did the NSPCC decide to use a variety of different marketing components in its *Full Stop* campaign?

Quick questions

2 What are the basic elements of the marketing mix? In what circumstances is an extended marketing mix appropriate?

3 Is consistency between elements of the marketing mix important? Explain why, using examples to illustrate your answer.

Applied question

4 Assuming the role of a brand manager about to launch a new shampoo, prepare a discussion document explaining the key features of the required marketing mix.

Extra readings

Belch, G. and Belch, M. (1998) *Advertising and Promotion: an Integrated Marketing Communications Perspective.* New York: McGraw-Hill.

Berry, L. (1995) *On Great Service.* New York: The Free Press.

Christopher, M. (2003) *Marketing Logistics*. Oxford: Butterworth-Heinemann.

De Chernatony, L. and McDonald, M. (2004) *Creating Powerful Brands.* Oxford: Butterworth-Heinemann.

Diamantopoulos, A. and Mathews, B.P. (1995) *Making Pricing Decisions: a Study of Managerial Practice*. London: Thomson.

Dibb, S., Simkin, L., Pride, W. and Ferrell, O.C. (2001) *Marketing: Concepts and Strategies.* Boston, MA: Houghton Mifflin.

Fill, C. (2003) *Integrated Marketing Communications.* Oxford: Butterworth-Heinemann.

Gronroos, C. (2000) *Service Management and Marketing.* Chichester: Wiley.

Kitchen, P.J. (1998) *Marketing Communications: Principles and Practice.* London: Thomson.

Nagle, T. and Holden, R.K. (2002) *The Strategy and Tactics of Pricing: A Guide to Profitable Decision-Making.* Upper Saddle River, NJ: PHIS.

Palmer, A. (2000) *Principles of Services Marketing.* Maidenhead: McGraw-Hill.

Rosenbloom, B. (2003) *Marketing Channels: a Management View*. Cincinnati, OH: South Western.

Rosenau, M.D., Griffin, A., Castellion, G. and Anschuetz, N. (1996) *The PDMA Handbook of New Product Development*. New York: Wiley.

Trott, P. (2002) *Innovation Management and New Product Development.* Harlow: Pearson/FT.

33: Marketing Strategy

Key definitions

Marketing strategy indicates the specific markets towards which activities are to be targeted and the types of competitive advantage to be exploited.

A *strategic market plan* is an outline of the methods and resources required to achieve an organization's goals and mission within specified target markets and coordinates all of a business's functions to this end.

The *mission* is a statement of the broad, long-term tasks the organization wishes to achieve and the overall standing *vis-à-vis* its publics that it intends to cement.

Corporate strategy determines the utilization of resources in all core business functions, not just marketing: production, finance, research, personnel, sales and marketing.

Marketing assets are customer-based, distribution-oriented and internal capabilities that managers and the marketplace perceive to be beneficially strong and that can be exploited by an organization.

Marketing opportunity analysis is an appraisal of the marketplace and organizational assets to identify circumstances and timing that enable a business to effectively reach its selected target markets.

Key issues

- Marketing strategy indicates the specific markets towards which activities are to be targeted and the types of competitive advantage to be exploited. A marketing strategy should identify the most beneficial market segments to target, specify the appropriate brand positioning and seek a competitive advantage over rivals.
- A strategic market plan is an outline of the methods and resources required to achieve an organization's goals and mission within specified target markets and coordinates all of a business's functions to this end. Strategic market planning yields a marketing strategy that directs the tactical recommendations that form the core output of marketing planning.
- There must be a clear view of the organization's corporate strategy and vision to steer the development of a target market strategy. The mission is the broad, long-term tasks the organization wishes to achieve and the overall standing *vis-à-vis* its publics that it intends to create. Corporate strategy determines the utilization of resources in all core business functions, not just marketing: production, finance, research, personnel, sales and marketing.
- Without a marketing strategy, it is difficult to develop marketing programmes that will truly benefit a business and achieve its corporate mission. Without a marketing strategy, the marketing mix tactics central to the marketing plan will not be carefully constructed to maximize opportunities, fend off competitors and satisfy the most attractive customer segments.

- Marketing opportunity analysis is core to the development of a marketing strategy, involving: (a) evaluating the organization's opportunities; (b) environmental scanning; and (c) understanding the company's capabilities and assets.
- Marketing assets are capabilities that managers and the marketplace perceive to be beneficially strong: (a) customer; (b) distribution; and (c) internally based.
- Based on an assessment of opportunities, the company must determine a competitive strategy to be implemented through marketing activity: (a) intense growth; (b) diversified growth; (c) integrated growth; or (d) simply maintenance.
- Of fundamental importance to a marketing strategy is the ability to attract customers, satisfy and retain them. The market segmentation process (segmentation, targeting and positioning) is the over-riding core element of developing a robust and meaningful marketing strategy.
- A marketing strategy cannot be developed without a sound understanding of competitive forces, potential competitive threats and competitor weaknesses to exploit. The organization should endeavour to create a differential advantage over rivals in order to compete effectively. The notions of offensive and defensive warfare have been applied to good effect by marketing strategists. A differential advantage is a marketing attribute unique to one supplier and desired by the targeted customers.
- The marketing strategy must specify marketing objectives, such as target markets, customer satisfaction and loyalty measures, brand awareness measures, product and market developments, market shares, profitability and other financial measures.
- The marketing mix should not be formulated until the marketing strategy has been specified. The marketing strategy cannot meaningfully be determined until the necessary marketing analyses have been undertaken. A number of strategic planning tools have been developed to assist marketers, notably the popular portfolio models.

Conceptual overview

At the heart of a marketing strategy is the target market strategy stemming from the market segmentation process of segmentation, targeting and positioning (cf. Briefs 11, 12, 13). A marketing strategy specifies the segments to target, the brand or product positioning required to appeal to these targeted customers, plus the competitive advantage to be exploited versus rivals. Most larger organizations specify a corporate mission and strategy. The mission is a statement of the longer-term tasks the business wishes to action and its intended standing regarding its many publics. A corporate strategy determines the use and allocation of resources to achieve the organization's goals across all business functions, not just marketing. The marketing strategy must be in harmony with both the mission and corporate strategy.

A strategic market plan is an outline of the requirements for achieving the goals and mission of the organization. Strategic market planning provides the guiding marketing strategy – focusing on the target market strategy – to direct the activities specified in the marketing plan (cf. Brief 36). The marketing plan is the specification of the marketing activities, principally the tactical marketing mix tactics, that will be undertaken by the marketing function over the forthcoming one to three years. Without a marketing strategy, these marketing mix activities are unlikely to bring significant benefits to the organization and probably will fail to satisfy and retain targeted customers.

There is much more to the development of a marketing strategy than the use of target marketing (market segmentation), as summarized in Figure 33.1. Marketing opportunity analysis is integral to effective strategizing, involving (a) evaluating the business's opportunities, (b) environmental scanning (cf. Brief 5) and (c) understanding the business's capabilities and assets (cf. Brief 5). Part of this assessment is the evaluation of a business's marketing assets. These are capabilities that are, or

ORGANIZATIONAL MISSION, GOALS AND CORPORATE STRATEGY
ORGANIZATIONAL OPPORTUNITIES AND CAPABILITIES Environmental scanning Customer and competitor analysis Marketing opportunities Capabilities and resources
STRATEGIC OBJECTIVES Intense growth Diversified growth Integrated growth Maintenance
TARGET MARKET STRATEGY, BRAND POSITIONING AND DIFFERENTIAL ADVANTAGE Market segmentation Prioritization of target markets Brand positioning Differential or competitive advantage
MARKETING OBJECTIVES
MARKETING PROGRAMMES FOR IMPLEMENTATION Marketing mix tactics Operational controls and processes
PERFORMANCE ASSESSMENT AND MONITORING

Figure 33.1 The core components of marketing strategy

could be, attractive to customers, and tend to be: (a) customer-based (such as brand image or product reputation); (b) distribution-based (for example, dealer coverage or aftermarket care); or (c) internal assets (personnel skills, resources or flexibility, for example).

Core to a marketing strategy is the understanding of competition and the identification of a differential advantage – something unique to one supplier and highly desired by targeted customers. In terms of the overall competitive strategy, there are four broad options: (a) intense growth, when current products and current markets have the potential for increasing sales; (b) diversified growth, which occurs when new products are developed to be sold in new markets; (c) integrated growth, owing to forwards, backwards or horizontal integration; and (d) maintenance of the *status quo*. The marketing strategy should specify marketing objectives so that marketing performance can be monitored (cf. Brief 39).

Examples

Coca-Cola Ware

Coca-Cola has extended its brand into casual clothing and accessories. Known as *Coca-Cola Ware*, the fashion line launched at the end of the 1990s is being used by the global drinks giant to support the brand values that consumers associate with its fizzy drinks. The new products, available in department stores and boutique clothing retailers, provide the company with an opportunity to extend its licensing schemes. At a time when the market is awash with promotional clothing, the company hopes that its own particular style of jeans, knitwear and shirts will help raise the profile of the Coca-Cola brand across its global markets. In this respect, the move is an integral part of the company's strategy for the brand, which, it is hoped, will result in large numbers of consumers acting as moving adverts for the drinks brand. By 2004, designer on-line retailer *Otoko* described the range in glowing terms: 'Coca Cola is so much more than a soft drink. *Coca-Cola Ware* is produced in Italy, under licence from Coca-Cola, using the same fabrics and design processes as its sister company *Replay*. Building on the heritage of the label, and using designs from the original bottle labels, *Coca-Cola Ware* is one of the most up-and-coming clothing labels.' It seems that Coca-Cola's strategy of enhancing the brand's reputation through clothing is paying off, as its licensed clothing is now sold alongside *Armand Basi*, *Buckler*, *Diesel Style Lab*, *Etienne Ozeki* and *Moschino*!

(*Sources:* Amanda Wilkinson, 'Is Coke hip?', *Marketing Week*, 28 January 1999, pp. 26–9; Julia Day, 'Coke plans global clothing brands', *Marketing*, 21 January 1999, pp. 37–42; www.otoko.co.uk)

Ireland

How do you develop a marketing strategy for a country? This was a question faced by the Irish Government during difficult times in the 1960s and 1970s. The challenge was to build the Irish economy to match the affluence enjoyed by some of its European neighbours. The Industrial Development Authority (IDA) played an important role in developing the country's economy, moving it away from its traditional over-reliance on agriculture. Today, with over one-third of the country's GDP coming from industry, and services also accounting for approaching a third, agriculture's contribution has fallen to just 10%.

In order to instigate this change, the IDA established a clear strategy by pinpointing attractive sectors for growth and actively encouraging growth businesses in those areas. Consumer products, electronics, health care and financial services were some of the key targets. Once decisions about growth priorities had been made, the key was to develop a marketing programme based around the particular assets that Ireland was able to offer. For example, promotional material focused on – amongst others – the young, highly educated workforce, the low rates of corporate taxation, excellent digital and satellite telecommunications systems, and a stable currency with low inflation. Considerable care was taken to ensure that the propositions developed matched the requirements of the businesses targeted. This provided many overseas businesses with substantial, tangible reasons for establishing a base in Ireland, bringing with it the investment the country so badly craved.

(*Sources:* Irish Embassy, London; Industrial Development Authority (IDA); 'Facts about Ireland', IDA, 1995, 1996, 1999)

Test yourself

Case question

1 What role did targeting play in the IDA's efforts to develop the Irish economy?

Quick questions

2 What is marketing strategy?

3 Using an industry of your choice to illustrate your answer, explain why businesses should develop a marketing strategy.

Applied question

4 As a marketing manager for a manufacturer of industrial spray-painting equipment, write a report explaining the role that strategic marketing planning might play in the business.

Extra readings

Aaker, D. (2001) *Strategic Marketing Management.* New York: Wiley.

Adcock, D. (2000) *Marketing Strategies for Competitive Advantage.* Chichester: Wiley.

Baker, M. (2000) *Marketing Strategy and Management.* Basingstoke: Palgrave Macmillan.

Cravens, D. and Piercy, N. (2002) *Strategic Marketing.* London: McGraw-Hill.

Littler, D. and Wilson, D. (1995) *Marketing Strategy.* Oxford: Butterworth-Heinemann.

Porter, M.E. (1980) *Competitive Strategy: Techniques for Analysing Industries and Competitors.* New York: Free Press.

34: Competitive Forces and Strategies

Key definitions

Competitors are generally viewed by a business as those companies that market products similar to, or substitutable for, its products when aimed at the same target market.

Competing products, services and *brands* are those that a targeted customer could select as an alternative to a business's own product or service.

Competitive forces are industry rivals, new entrants, substitute solutions, plus the bargaining power of customers and of suppliers.

The *competitive positions of warfare strategy* influence marketing strategies and tactics. They are market leader, market challengers, fast movers, followers and nichers.

Defensive warfare is a policy striking a balance between awaiting market developments or competitor activity and proactively parrying competitors' actions.

Offensive warfare is a policy whereby challengers aggressively seek market share gains by identifying weaknesses in the market leader's and other rivals' marketing mixes and developing corresponding strengths.

Key issues

- Companies are not always good at monitoring their competitive environment.
- Competing products, services and brands are those that a targeted customer could select as an alternative to a business's own product or service.
- Marketers must develop marketing strategies that strive to effectively combat rivals' marketing mixes and target market strategies. Competitive strategy is a core ingredient of marketing.
- Understanding competitors' relative strengths and weaknesses, market shares and positionings is essential. Taken in conjunction with an appreciation of key customer needs, companies should have an indication of where to position their product offerings now and in the future.
- In addition to planning its own marketing activity, a business should be aware of its rivals' activities, current strategies, likely future proposals and even how key competitors will react to its own proposed marketing mix programmes.
- Companies must understand like-for-like rivals, but also the impact of new entrants, substitute solutions, and the bargaining power of buyers and suppliers. Competitors to avoid and to attack should be identified.
- Warfare strategy is an integral facet of marketing strategy. This involves offensive and defensive strategies, knowing the strengths and weaknesses of rivals and of the marketer's own organization, and modifying marketing programmes accordingly.
- Identifying competitive positions within a market is an approach ever more common: market leader, market challengers, fast movers, followers and nichers. Each has different strategic options and creates both threats and opportunities for a marketer.

Conceptual overview

Customers generally have a choice of supplier and product. Marketers must endeavour to understand the merits and deficiencies of these competing propositions and incorporate such knowledge in the development of their marketing strategies. David Aaker proposed a set of issues marketers should be able to address when examining competitors:

- Who
  - The 'usual' rivals, plus those less obvious but still committed, as well as the makers of substitute products.
  - Categorization of rivals in terms of assets, skills, strategies, level of activity or threat.
  - Any new entrants.
  - Barriers to entry and the possibility of strengthening them.
- Evaluation
  - Strategies and level of commitment.
  - Successes and failures over time: track record.
  - Strengths and weaknesses, assets and skills.
  - Leverage points over the business. Any strategic weaknesses, customer problems, unmet needs that rivals could exploit.

These issues relate to an often utilized process for undertaking competitor analysis: (a) identify competitors; (b) determine competitors' objectives; (c) identify competitors' strategies; (d) assess competitors' strengths and weaknesses; (e) estimate competitors' reaction patterns; and (f) select competitors to attack and to avoid.

A key issue in marketing is the actual identification of the competitive set. Too many businesses consider only like-for-like competitors, but for the customer there may be alternative solutions. For example, airline Aer Lingus competes for Anglo-Irish passengers with car ferries as well as other airlines. There are also substitute solutions, such as tunnelling moles replacing the use of excavators to lay pipes, plus the impact of new entrants coming into a market and stealing customers. Together with the competitive forces of buyers and suppliers, who may well have a variable impact on different rivals in a market, these are the competitive forces as popularized by Michael Porter (cf. Figure 34.1).

Many competitive strategy experts discuss competitiveness in terms of warfare strategies – offensive and defensive – based on military analogies. Different marketing strategies are appropriate for companies that occupy the various competitive positions within markets, including aspects of attack and defence. Under this scenario, competing companies represent the enemy to be defeated. The principles are based upon the concept that in any market there are five different types of competitive position that companies can occupy:

- *Market leader*. This is the highest market share company that retains its position either (a) by trying to expand the total market (market development), perhaps

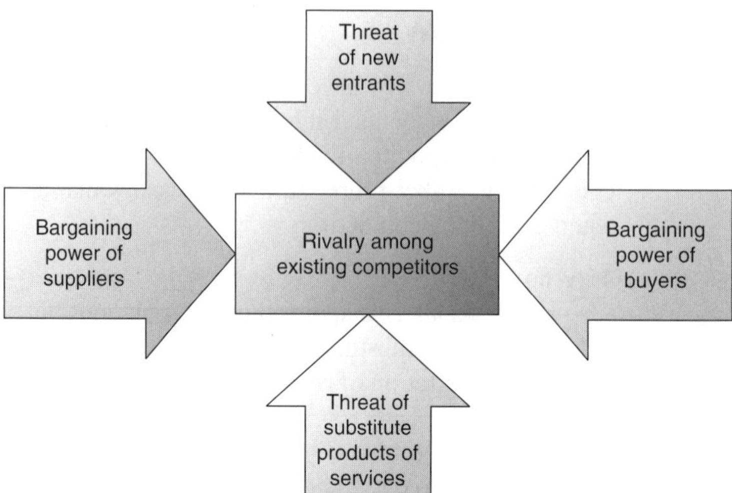

Figure 34.1 Porter's competitive forces

(*Source: adapted from* M.E. Porter, 'How competitive forces shape strategy', *Harvard Business Review*, 47 (March/April), pp. 137–45)

by finding new uses for a product, or (b) by increasing market share (market penetration), for example through an aggressive advertising campaign. The aggressive measures are balanced by a desire to protect current market share. The market leader has the most difficult job in that it has to help to grow the overall market, improve its own share and defend its existing market share against attack from rivals. Only the market leader should consider adopting a defensive role. Even in these circumstances it is necessary to combine defensive with offensive strategies. A defensive strategy still requires that strong competitive moves are blocked; the best approach to defence is attack; and the understanding that a myopic view to competition will not lead to safety.

- *Market challenger.* One or more non-market leaders that aggressively attack for additional market share. They seek rapid growth and one day perhaps market leadership. Challengers must be aware of the leader's position, capabilities and strategies; identify weaknesses to exploit in the leader and other challengers; and attack on a narrow front that fits the challenger's competencies.
- *Fast movers.* These are smaller players that are unlikely to remain minor rivals. Fast movers grow at the expense of more minor rivals in the market, so as not to antagonize the market leaders and aggressive challengers who could turn their guns on the upcoming 'upstart' before it is capable of defending itself. They must have a differential advantage and quickly establish distribution channels and a loyal customer base in readiness for eventual attack.
- *Market followers.* These are low share competitors without the resources/market position/R&D/commitment to challenge or seriously contend for market

leadership. Followers must use market segmentation carefully and concentrate only on areas where the company can cope. They should specialize rather than diversify and use R&D as efficiently as possible.

- *Market nichers.* These are companies that specialize in terms of market/product/customers by finding a safe, profitable market segment. As markets mature, increasing competitiveness tends to mean large companies become more interested in such segments, which then for a niche-only company are more difficult to retain. Nichers should find safe market segments, securing a niche by specializing on a particular market, customer or marketing mix; and, if possible, be strong in more than one niche.

With a proper understanding of the competitive arena, a marketer is then in a position to identify a differential advantage and basis for competing against rivals (cf. Brief 35). Without an awareness of competition, it is difficult to achieve success.

Examples

Marquis by Waterford Crystal

Waterford Crystal products are internationally recognized for their exceptional quality and craftsmanship. Despite its considerable expertise in the sector, in the early 1990s following the take-over of china company Wedgwood, the crystal part of the business suffered the effects of recession. The problem was that high-priced giftware, such as that produced by Waterford, is particularly susceptible to economic downturns. The number of consumers in the market for such premium-priced items is also very small. In order to grow its market, the company needed to change its strategy and alter its basis for competing. However, it did not want to jeopardize the brand standing of its Waterford ranges. So it created *Marquis*, a lower-priced, diverse line of giftware designed to make crystal products accessible to a much wider range of consumers. Despite initial concerns that the move into more mainstream markets might harm the Waterford brand, it seems that the company has been successful in broadening the appeal of crystal products, particularly in the all-important US market. Waterford has continued to pursue the 'broadening' strategy for competing in the giftware and crystal markets with the launch of John Rocha designer crystal ware.

(*Sources:* Sally Dibb and Lyndon Simkin, *The Marketing Casebook*, London: Thomson Learning, 2001; www.waterford.com, 2004; www.waterfordwedgewood.com, 2004)

Vodafone

There was a time when the mobile phone was an expensive substitute rival to land line telecommunication businesses such as BT, used primarily by business executives. Now, operators such as Orange and Vodafone are major global brands, competing with a host of rivals and offering increasingly diverse services to numerous market segments, in a quickly evolving marketplace. Plug-in cards for laptops enable travelling executives to download emails on the move without the need to hook up to landline sockets. Phones download games and Web-based consumer information, becoming hand-held entertainment systems rather than just verbal communication devices. Many mobile phones are now also handheld cameras or music players. There can be few markets in which technology has moved so quickly, continually opening up new business opportunities with customers. First mover advantage can be costly but also may result in huge rewards, though the market must be educated to accept and to desire the new service or product application.

Throughout its history, Vodafone – the global market leader – had avoided price discounting or price-based campaigns. Instead, product innovation, new services, smart target marketing, had kept its sales increasing. However, increasing competitive pressures led to the company's first price-led marketing in early 2004. Vodafone cut the price of its picture messaging service and promoted the low-cost nature of the service, with television, radio and press advertisements saying, '*Don't just talk about it. Picture it and send it for 12p*'. This was a hefty discount on the normal cost of 36p. Vodafone hoped to establish picture messaging services as a mass market medium, rather than a quirky niche market ignored by many users of mobile phones. It also intended to support the take-up by Vodafone subscribers of the *Vodafone Live!* e-service, already claiming to have over 700 000 users in the UK. With rival service providers launching competing propositions to *Vodafone Live!*, it was particularly important to tie-in users to this service.

(*Sources:* Vodafone UK, 2004; Ben Carter in *Marketing*, 8 January 2004, p. 3)

Test yourself

Case question

1 As a new entrant in the mobile phone wars, what competitive strategy would you pursue and why?

Quick questions

2 What is the competitive environment?
3 Why can an understanding of competitors' strategies improve an organization's marketing capability?

Applied question

4 As a journalist for a business magazine, you have been asked to prepare a feature that explores the use of Michael Porter's model of competitive forces. The article you write should focus on how the model works, the situations in which it can be used, as well as describing any shortcomings. Make sure that you use illustrative examples in your article.

Extra readings

Aaker, D. (2001) *Strategic Marketing Management.* New York: Wiley.

Adcock, D. (2000) *Marketing Strategies for Competitive Advantage.* Chichester: Wiley.

Hooley, G., Saunders, J. and Piercy, N.F. (2004) *Marketing Strategy and Competitive Positioning.* Harlow: Pearson/FT.

O'Shaughnessy, J. (1995) *Competitive Marketing: a Strategic Approach.* London: Unwin-Hyman.

Porter, M.E. (1980) *Competitive Strategy: Techniques for Analysing Industries and Competitors.* New York: Free Press.

Porter, M.E. (1985) *Competitive Advantage: Creating and Sustaining Superior Performance.* New York: Free Press.

Porter, M.E. (1998) *On Competing.* Boston, MA: Harvard Business School Press.

35: Competitive Advantage

Key definitions

Competitive advantage is the achievement of superior performance *vis-à-vis* rivals, through differentiation to create superior customer value or by managing to achieve lowest delivered cost.

Competitors are generally viewed by a business as those companies that market products similar to, or substitutable for, its products when aimed at the same target market.

The *generic strategies* for creating a competitive advantage are cost leadership, differentiation and focus, and are not mutually exclusive.

A *differential advantage* is an attribute of a brand, product, service or marketing mix that is desired by the targeted customer and is provided by only one suppler.

A company's *basis for competing* is a combination of strengths plus any differential advantage and should form the leading edge of a marketing strategy.

Marketing assets are capabilities that marketers and the marketplace view as beneficially strong and are customer-based, distribution-based or internal assets.

A *strategic window* is a temporary window of opportunity to take advantage of a market opportunity ahead of competitors.

Key issues

- Marketers strive to create an edge over their competitors and differentiation.
- The generic strategies proposed by Michael Porter argue that to be successful in creating a competitive edge, a marketer must create differentiation, focus or cost leadership. These are not mutually exclusive, but it is unusual to find examples of all three simultaneously. To have none courts disaster.
- A differential advantage is the term used to describe an attribute of a brand and its marketing mix that is strongly desired by the target market and not readily offered by rival businesses.
- A business must identify its basis for competing – differential advantage combined with strengths or capabilities – otherwise the target market will have no reason to prefer the organization's products and services.
- Marketing assets are a classification of a company's capabilities, generally in terms of customer, distribution and internal assets. The concept of capabilities is often linked to market opportunity analysis and the search for a strategic window ahead of competitors.

Conceptual overview

There are three related concepts that marketers may utilize in their quest for a competitive edge over rivals: (a) Porter's generic strategies; (b) defining a differential advantage; and (c) marketing assets. It is first important to understand the competitive arena (cf. Brief 34).

Porter identified three generic competitive strategies that he claimed result in success for companies competing for position in any particular market. These are: (a) cost leadership; (b) differentiation; and (c) focus. Failure to achieve these strategies can result in companies becoming 'stuck in the middle', with no real competitive advantage. It is not generally possible to follow all three generic strategies simultaneously, but it is common for businesses to gain cost leadership while also differentiating their proposition, and it is also possible to seek a focused and differentiated approach.

- *Cost leadership.* Involves developing a low cost base, often through economies of scale associated with high market share, to give high contribution. This can then be used to further develop the low cost base. Very tight cost controls are essential to the success of this strategy.
- *Differentiation.* Companies adopting a differentiation strategy strive to offer a product/marketing effort that has a distinct advantage or is different to that offered by competitors. Differentiation can be achieved on a number of fronts: creative and innovative product or brand design are possibilities, as are novel distribution channel, pricing and customer service policies.
- *Focus.* Focused companies must maintain close links with the market so that product and marketing effort can be designed with a particular target group in mind. Typically of small size, unable to achieve cost leadership or maintain significant differentiation, such companies succeed by effectively meeting customer needs that may be being missed by larger players in the market. Many such players are niching (cf. Brief 34).

In developing a marketing mix, marketers should strive to identify and maintain a differential advantage. This goes further than determining a business's strengths. A differential advantage is unique to one brand, product or organization: it is an attribute not yet matched by rivals that is highly desired by the target market's customers. If emphasized in the marketing mix, it should appeal to the targeted customer while providing the business with an edge over its competitors. Inevitably, such an advantage will be short-lived, but it should (a) bring financial rewards in the short term, (b) improve standing with customers and (c) make it much more difficult for rivals to emulate the overall proposition being marketed.

Stages in developing a differential advantage include: (a) identifying the market's segments; (b) ascertaining product and service attributes desired by each segment; (c) assessing which of these attributes the business offers; (d) understanding what the business's competitors offer; (e) identifying their genuine strengths; (f) assessing the gaps between customer expectations and competitors' offers; (g) determining if any of these gaps are matched by the business and its products; (h) checking that these advantages may be emphasized through sales and marketing programmes.

Marketing assets are often attributed to Hugh Davidson and relate to a business's strengths and capabilities. Notably:

1 Customer-based, such as brand image, reputation and service.
2 Distribution-based, stemming from the density of dealer coverage or alliances.
3 Internal assets, including skills, experience, technology and resources.

Davidson also proposed a framework for marketing assets that includes: (a) people; (b) working capital; (c) capital equipment; (d) customer franchises/loyalty; (e) sales, distribution and service networks; and (f) sales advantages.

The notion of marketing assets is usually linked with capability analysis and the fit with emerging market opportunities. When a business has assets or capabilities that permit it to take advantage of a window of opportunity ahead of its rivals, there is a strategic window.

Each of these concepts – the generic strategies, differential advantage and marketing assets – is related to the marketer's quest or 'Holy Grail': the desire to identify an edge over rivals; to be able to differentiate a product or service *vis-à-vis* competing propositions; and to satisfy customers more effectively than rivals.

Examples

ERCOL

ERCOL manufactures a variety of traditional and modern furniture in a range of wood finishes. The company's distinctive products have developed a reputation for fine quality and high standards of craftsmanship; factors that are used explicitly in the company's promotional and marketing material. Recent advertising, which carries the positioning statement '*Perfection in detail*', emphasizes that it is the company's commitment to craftsmanship and quality in all aspects of its products that sets ERCOL apart. In this respect, the company's capabilities and reputation are its competitive advantage, wrapped around the tangible features of its product range.

(*Sources:* ERCOL marketing material, 2001; www.ercol.com)

Smelly fabrics

Finding an innovative source of competitive advantage is not easy to achieve. In established markets that have already reached the maturity stage of their life cycle, this can be even more challenging. Such is the reality faced by businesses supplying the highly competitive underwear and sportswear markets. Yet recently, a technological break-through has allowed Courtaulds Textiles (part of Sara Lee) to develop a completely new kind of competitive advantage. The situation has arisen as a result of the launch of the company's Fragrance Fabrics, which have one of a range of pleasant scents built into them. Through a process known as 'micro-encapsulation' Courtaulds Jersey Underwear Ltd has shown that it is possible to 'glue' a fragrance to certain cotton jersey and cotton/Lycra fabrics. Fragrances that are currently available include the zesty scents of lemon and orange, relaxing lavender as well as forest flowers and fruity apple and strawberry.

So what might be the marketing potential for this innovation? The possibilities are considerable, ranging from sportswear that is able to overcome the results of an energetic and sweaty tennis game, to underwear that really can and does remain fresh-smelling through the challenges of the day. The signs are also that the technology used enables the scents to be retained through repeated washing of the garment. It seems that the key now is for Courtaulds Textiles to ensure that this potential source of competitive advantage is appropriately marketed to a variety of garment manufacturers and large retail groups.

(*Sources: Fragrance Fabrics and Essential Oils and their 'Well-Being' Qualities*, Courtaulds Jersey Underwear; Courtaulds Textiles, Nottingham; Sally Dibb, Lyndon Simkin, Bill Pride and O.C. Ferrell, *Marketing: Concepts and Strategies*, 2001, pp. 445–6)

Test yourself

Case question

1 In the market for underwear, what other types of competitive advantage might manufacturers use?

Quick questions

2 What is meant by the term 'competitive advantage'?
3 'Different organizations develop different bases for competing.' Explain what this means using examples of your choice to illustrate your answer.

Applied question

4 Using a detailed example as illustration, prepare a report detailing the steps to developing a competitive advantage.

Extra readings

Aaker, D. (2001) *Strategic Marketing Management.* New York: Wiley.

Adcock, D. (2000) *Marketing Strategies for Competitive Advantage.* Chichester: Wiley.

Hooley, G., Saunders, J. and Piercy, N.F. (2004) *Marketing Strategy and Competitive Positioning.* Harlow: Pearson/FT.

O'Shaughnessy, J. (1995) *Competitive Marketing: A Strategic Approach.* London: Unwin-Hyman.

Porter, M.E. (1980) *Competitive Strategy: Techniques for Analysing Industries and Competitors.* New York: Free Press.

Porter, M.E. (1985) *Competitive Advantage: Creating and Sustaining Superior Performance.* New York: Free Press.

36: Marketing Planning

Key definitions

Marketing planning is a systematic process involving assessing marketing opportunities, devising marketing strategies and specifying marketing objectives, determining marketing mix programmes, allocating resources and developing a plan for implementation and control.

The *marketing plan* is the written document or blueprint for implementing and controlling an organization's marketing activities related to the specified marketing strategy.

Key issues

- Most businesses produce a marketing plan annually, often with a three-year perspective. The annual marketing planning is a point in the hectic operations of most marketing departments when a formal appraisal of the marketplace and emerging opportunities is undertaken.
- The marketing plan is a 'call to action' and outlines to marketers, colleagues in other business functions and to senior management what marketing activity is expected to occur, at what cost, for what benefits, when and who will shoulder the responsibility of implementing the designated marketing programmes.
- Marketing planning requires marketing analyses, strategy formulation, marketing mix design and the specification of internal controls to ensure recommendations are actioned.
- The marketing planning cycle involves the assessment of marketing opportunities and resources, the revision or formulation of marketing strategy, development or revision of the plan for implementation and control, implementation of the marketing plan, and the development or revision of marketing objectives relative to performance.
- The marketing plan guides management in implementing marketing activity, orientates managers in respect of their roles, specifies how best to use resources, identifies deficiencies, problems, opportunities and threats. Fundamentally, it controls a business's marketing activities.

Conceptual overview

Marketing planning is commonly deployed by larger businesses – and increasingly by smaller firms – to 'pull together' in a more orchestrated manner the marketing strategizing and marketing programme activity within the organization. Marketing planning incorporates an analysis of marketing opportunities and of the marketplace, the recommendation of marketing strategies, the determination of a plan for implementation and control.

Marketing planning involves the essential marketing analyses: customers, competitors, the marketing environment, market trends, internal capabilities, brand perceptions and current business performance. On the basis of these analyses, the target market strategy, brand positioning and basis for competing (the essence of marketing strategy) will be revised and up-dated. The bulk of the final marketing plan will present detailed marketing mix tactics and internal operational requirements intended to implement the recommended marketing strategy.

The so-called marketing planning cycle (Figure 36.1) implies that marketing planning is never-ending. The previous year's plan provides the starting point for the current year's planning activity. Marketing analyses enable the marketing strategy and marketing mix recommendations in last year's plan to be revised to reflect changes in the marketplace, corporate objectives and on-going performance. Successes can be emulated while failures or missed opportunities may be remedied.

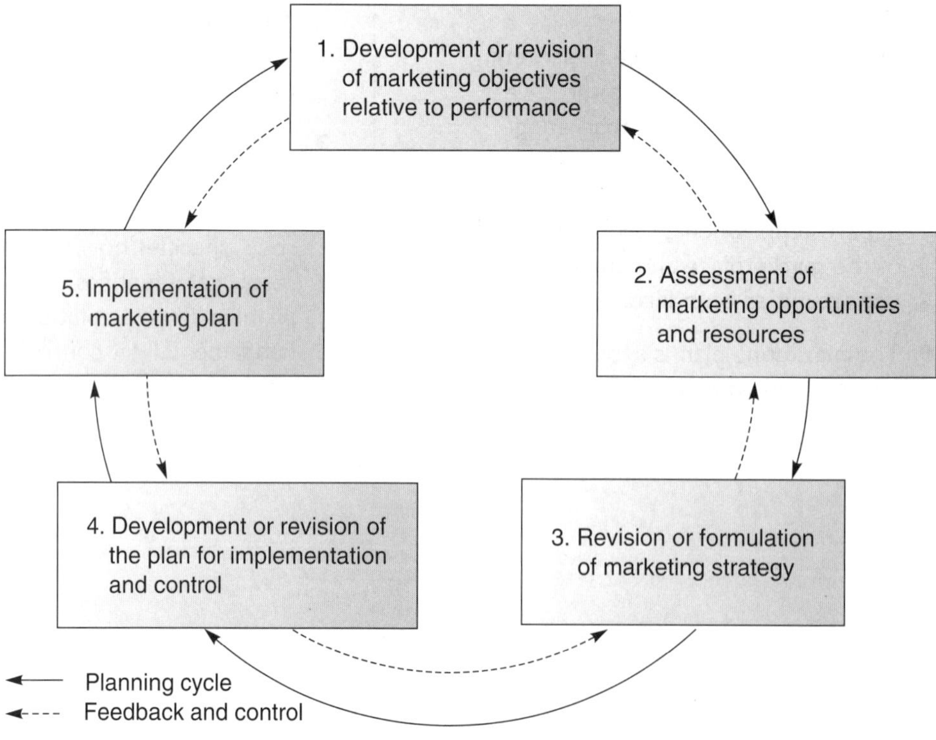

Figure 36.1 The marketing planning cycle

Marketing planning reflects the aims of marketing *per se*, with aims to serve the most appropriate target customers, beat the competition, stay ahead of market developments, maximize returns for the company, use resources to good effect, minimize threats, recognize and address the organization's weaknesses and threats, develop a clearly defined plan of action and operational controls, seek well-defined rewards in terms of sales, market share, customer retention, customer satisfaction and brand awareness.

The marketing planning process involves:

- Analysis of markets and the trading environment.
- Determination of core target markets.
- Identification of a differential advantage or competitive edge.
- Statement of specific goals and desired brand positioning.
- Development of marketing mix programmes to implement the plans and recommended strategies.
- Determination of required budgets, schedules of activity, task allocation to individual managers and performance measures.

The final document – the marketing plan – differs from company to company, reflecting 'house styles' for reports and senior management's expectations. A typical marketing plan will include key sections: (a) executive summary; (b) objectives; (c) product/market background; (d) SWOT analysis (cf. Brief 5) and other core marketing analyses; (e) target market strategy, desired brand positioning and basis for competing; (f) expected results and forecasts (cf. Brief 10); (g) marketing mix programmes, task allocation and schedules; (h) financial implications and required budgets; (i) operational implications for non-marketing functions in the business; and (j) appendices for research findings and details of the marketing analyses, forecasts and budgets.

Examples

Raytheon

US defence business Raytheon focused on radar and missile systems, but recognized that the technologies it developed could be used in many non-military applications. Its UK operation, Raytheon Systems Ltd, embarked on a programme of marketing planning activity in order to scope out the business opportunities for these technologies. This work involved identifying products that could utilize the company's sensors, semiconductors and motor drives. However, the company wanted to use its resources shrewdly, identifying market opportunities that related well to its capabilities and in which it could achieve a competitive advantage. There was also a desire to enter non-military markets with significant growth potential and to deal with clients that would build long-term relationships, something for which RSL had developed an enviable track record. Within three years, RSL had successfully entered a range of markets, providing components and technical solutions to businesses active in oil exploration, the automotive sector, alarm systems and civil aviation. The marketing planning programme first identified these opportunities and then developed the marketing mix activities required to engage successfully with the targeted business clients.

(*Sources:* Raytheon; www.raytheon.co.uk; Raytheon press releases)

Crayola Crayons

How does a manufacturer of traditional children's toys compete with computer games and other high-tech goodies? At a time when many children's heads have been turned by technology, this was the challenge faced by Binney & Smith's *Crayola Crayons*. The answer emerged from a systematic process of customer analysis and strategy development that allowed the business to update its marketing programmes.

The company had previously targeted parents in its marketing, relying on a series of educational themes. However, with children playing an increasing role in the buying process, it was clear that capturing the child's imagination would be key. A marketing research programme involving children played an important early step in the company's new strategy. One outcome was that kids prefer brighter colours. This resulted in a new brighter selection of *Crayola* colours, with exciting names to match. Ironically, resistance from parents, who liked the familiar colours, meant that the company also reissued packs of the old favourites. In addition, *Crayola* innovated with a range of exciting new colour products including *Silver Swirls* (a mix of silver and wax colours), *ColourWorks* (erasable crayon sticks) together with new products such as *Crayola Jewellery* and *Badge Bonanza* making kits and single-use cameras. The company even joined forces with their high-tech competitors by launching a range of art-related software games.

The new strategy was implemented through a carefully constructed marketing plan. The tactical marketing mix programmes needed to create a balance between appealing to children and providing reassurance to parents, who are still the primary purchaser. As a result, advertising in parenting and women's magazines continues to play an important part in *Crayola's* marketing, but the company can be more confident that the new strategy is based on a clear understanding of what its customers – children and their parents – want.

(*Sources:* E. Neubourne, 'Crayola crayons have old colors back', *USA Today*, 2 October 1991, p. 2B; K. Riddle, 'Crayola draws brighter lines in the market', *Marketing*, 21 January 1991, p. 4; Sally Dibb, Lyndon Simkin, Bill Pride and O.C. Ferrell, *Marketing: Concepts and Strategies*, Boston, MA: Houghton Mifflin, 2001)

Test yourself

Case question

1 How does the process that *Crayola* undertook relate to the steps of marketing planning?

Quick questions

2 What is marketing planning and why should businesses undertake it?
3 Describe the principles of the marketing planning cycle and explain why businesses must continually update their marketing plans.

Applied question

4 As a partner in a consultancy business specializing in marketing planning, you are currently involved in 'pitching' for new business. The potential client company, a vehicle component manufacturer, is seeking to instigate a marketing planning process for the first time. You have been asked to prepare a proposal document as part of your company's pitch for the business. Your proposal should explain the main steps in the marketing planning process, indicating the order and manner in which they should be undertaken. The document should also recommend a process for implementing the results of planning around the business.

Extra readings

Dibb, S., Simkin, L. and Bradley, J. (1998) *The Marketing Planning Workbook: Effective Marketing for Marketing Managers.* London: Thomson Learning.

Gilligan, C. and Wilson, R.M.S. (2003) *Strategic Marketing Planning.* Oxford: Butterworth-Heinemann.

Jain, S.C. (2000) *Marketing Planning & Strategy.* Cincinnati, OH: South Western.

McDonald, M.H. (2002) *Marketing Plans.* Oxford: Butterworth-Heinemann.

37: Implementation and Controls

Key definitions

Marketing implementation is a process involving activities to put marketing recommendations into action.

Implementation requires necessary infrastructure, processes and managerial controls.

Key issues

- Too few businesses recognize the link between devising marketing strategies and managing their implementation. The facilitation and management of implementation should be integral to the marketing process.
- The impediments hindering the effective deployment of marketing used to relate to industry's poor understanding of the role and scope of marketing, inappropriate use of the marketing toolkit, ineffectual marketing processes, and inadequate resourcing of marketing.
- Marketing is now widespread and the barriers impeding marketing have switched away from these misconceptions and misuse of marketing to internal operational and cultural concerns.
- Successful marketing departments recognize the importance of creating a realistic foundation for their marketing activity – infrastructure requisites – as well as adopting robust marketing processes and practices. In addition, they instigate managerial procedures to monitor and control the on-going implementation of their marketing recommendations.
- The recent popularity of relationship marketing (cf. Briefs 2 and 8) and internal marketing (cf. Brief 40) have helped address some of the core implementation hazards.

Conceptual overview

The barriers impeding effective implementation of marketing strategies and marketing plans used to hinge on (a) a lack of senior management support, comprehension and use of marketing; (b) no orientation or resourcing of marketing planning or marketing strategy initiatives; (c) separation of strategizing and planning from functional marketing activity; (d) poor marketing skills and misuse of the marketing toolkit; (e) inadequate implementation procedures for marketing strategies and plans; (f) unrealistic time, budgetary and human resource expectations placed on the marketing department; (g) a paucity of marketing analysis; (h) tactical marketing mix programmes developed in isolation of any analysis of strategizing; (i) poor internal communication and resourcing of planning. In other words, marketing *per se* was poorly comprehended within an organization or was ineffectively deployed and resourced. There are still smaller organizations displaying these traits.

An inadequate understanding of marketing's remit or the poor grasp of marketing *per se* are, on the whole, no longer impediments, with most businesses now practising marketing. The issue is not whether to embrace marketing or marketing planning, but how better to resource these activities, develop the required skills and ensure that effective associated internal marketing occurs. Little internal communication, ineffectual marketing intelligence, poor coordination, flawed managerial skills, petty internal 'politics' and inadequate marketing resources are still severe impediments to the implementation of marketing strategies and plans. Much appears to hinge on internal marketing (cf. Brief 40) – the application of marketing within the organization to internal audiences, based on communication and developing a unified sense of purpose among employees.

Underpinning any marketing activity is the need to have the right skills, resources, processes and orientation. This includes managing the expectations of senior and line managers, orientation communication and the involvement in marketing implementation of cross-functional skilled personnel. In addition, any marketing initiative requires purpose, process and robust propositions. Marketing activities will not occur by chance and must be managed: training and orientation, clear recommendations, detailed action programmes, schedules, reviews, performance assessment and remedial actions, with praise and rebuke from senior management as deemed appropriate by on-going progress. The necessary infrastructure (cf. Figure 37.1) must be in place to permit implementation of marketing recommendations.

In addition to the necessary infrastructure requisites, rigorous marketing processes are required. Figure 37.2 outlines the well-established *A–S–P* process approach to creating marketing plans and target market strategies. Any development of a marketing strategy or a marketing plan will be invasive and must be adequately resourced in terms of time, personnel, communications processes, budgets, information and systems. Busy personnel cannot be expected to take 'time out' from routine operations to undertake analysis, strategic thinking and the construction of revised

PROCESSES

1. **Participants:** Orientation, managing expectations, involvement
2. **Leadership:** Senior support, intrateam/site cooperation
3. **Clarity:** Purpose, process, propositions
4. **Progress management:** Reviews, performance monitoring, remedial action
5. **Requisite resources:** Creation and allocation, personnel, schedules, budgets, marketing information

RESOURCES AND TOOLS

1. **Process and implementation:** IT, people, funds, time
2. **Skills:** Concept comprehension, training, external support, facilitation
3. **Personnel:** Team selection, skills, functions, hierarchy
4. **Information:** Availability, storage, access, auditing
5. **Communications:** Internal and external, channels, processes, schedule, key targets

CULTURE

1. **Marketing:** Ethos, skills, role
2. **Corporate:** Vision, mission, marketing fit, change receptiveness
3. **Leadership:** Abilities, understanding, participation
4. **Awareness:** Capabilities, operational constraints and implementability, new initiative and planning impact
5. **Facilitation:** Strategy initiatives, operationalization

Figure 37.1 The barriers to implementation triad

sales and marketing tactics without being provided with the resources for tackling such tasks. Too often, senior management expects too few line managers to undertake additional weighty tasks without extra resource provision. The skills to undertake marketing analyses, facilitate a strategic review and to modify accordingly often entrenched marketing tactics must be inherent or bought-in from external agencies. Equally, implementation of resulting recommendations will require orchestrating and resourcing.

Without attention to these infrastructure and process requirements, much marketing endeavour and strategizing will fail to result in recommendations being implemented. Establishing such a foundation and the required process requisites will help overcome the obstacles still found to be impeding the implementation of marketing plans and target market strategies in marketing-oriented organizations. Marketing managers intending to address these concerns must also monitor the on-going effectiveness of the implementation of marketing recommendations.

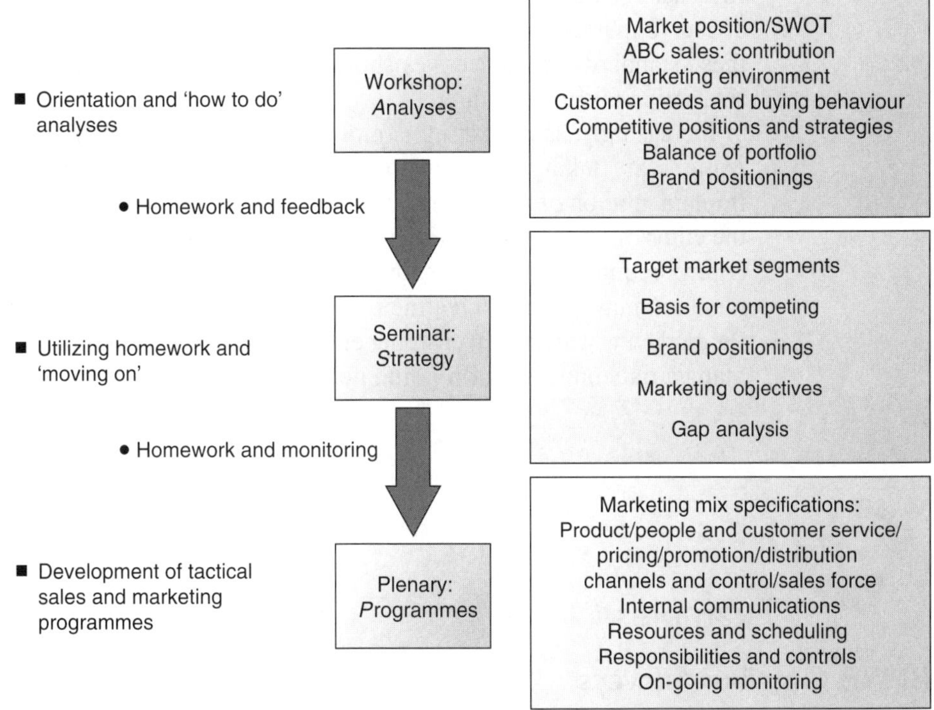

Figure 37.2 The *A–S–P* process for marketing or marketing planning

These management controls include audits, specifications, orientation, authorization and reviews:

- Audits of the business's track record for tackling marketing initiatives, available marketing intelligence, people skills, marketing expertise and ease of internal communication.
- Detailed specification of the marketing task; personnel involvement, reporting procedures, leadership schedules and resources allocated; plus external support and roll-out requirements for the resulting marketing strategy or plan recommendations.
- Set-up orientation sessions for participating line managers and their seniors, skill training, progress reviews and debriefs for final recommendations with internal marketing and communication of their requirements.
- Task authorizations and senior 'sign-off' for team selection, budgets, access to information and key personnel, time, the overall process and expected deliverables.
- On-going reviews with progress meetings, senior managerial assessments, remedial actions for evolving problems or inadequacies and determination of final recommendations. These reviews should demonstrate leadership and control, plus support and understanding of operational difficulties.

In order for marketing to be controlled, (a) objectives must first be clearly specified, (b) performance standards should be established, (c) performance relative to these standards and objectives should be monitored (cf. Brief 39) and (d) corrective action taken as required.

Increasingly, as marketing is more widely deployed, marketing-oriented organizations are taking the time to identify operational impediments hindering the implementation of their marketing recommendations. This hinges significantly on the ethos of internal marketing (cf. Brief 40) and on the infrastructure, process and control requirements for effectively operationalizing marketing. Successful implementation involves: (a) creating the necessary infrastructure, ethos and foundation for marketing activity; (b) ensuring effective processes are utilized; and (c) developing managerial controls for on-going performance evaluation.

Examples

BMRB Omnibus Surveys

Research company BMRB International offers clients access to on-going omnibus surveys. These regularly repeated surveys include questions from a range of organizations and markets. The BMRB ACCESS survey collects data in various ways and, amongst other things, provides the opportunity for businesses to test how effectively their marketing is being implemented. Each week, there are face-to-face interviews with 2000 adults and telephone interviews with 1000 individuals. In addition, the opinion of 1000 youngsters aged 7–19 is sought. The idea is simple. Companies can have a series of questions relevant to their product/market added into the survey. The approach allows them access to regular market feedback without the inconvenience of having to set up the data collection themselves. As the technology used to record and analyse the data becomes more sophisticated, the timeframe in which the results can be returned is shortened. BMRB states in its advertising material that top-line results can be available as soon as the day after the data collection is undertaken. Research findings help monitor implementation.

(*Sources:* BMRB advertising materials; www.bmrb.co.uk)

RadioLab

A recent comparative study has examined the effectiveness of radio and television advertising. Using quantitative research techniques, the RadioLab study has tracked consumer awareness and attitudes for a number of brands over a six-month period. Among the big brands included in the research were Coca-Cola,

Branston Pickle and Kwik Save. The research was conducted in two regions of the Central ITV area. Some 5500 telephone interviews were conducted with adults aged between 16 and 44. This collaboration between the Radio Advertising Bureau (RAB), research house Millward Brown and Universal McCann, cost £140 000, making it the most costly study ever carried out by the RAB.

So what have been the benefits of this expensive research? The results are highly revealing. By tracking consumer awareness and attitudes towards 17 different brands, the report suggests that radio advertising might be a very cost-effective way of reaching certain target groups. Although the levels of consumer awareness achieved on radio were only three-fifths as efficient as those achieved by television advertising, the costs were substantially lower. In some cases, the television advertising cost seven times more than the radio advertising. The conclusion of the RAB report is that when these factors are taken into consideration, radio can be considered to be around four times as cost-effective as television. For many years in advertising circles, radio has been thought of as a poor second best to television. This research suggests that the medium may have considerable potential for businesses seeking a more cost-effective communications approach. For businesses wishing to assess the effectiveness of their promotional mix activity, such research is important input to their decision-making.

(*Source:* Tania Mason, 'Research Reveals Radio's Potential', *Marketing*, 26 October 2000, p. 8)

Test yourself

Case question

1 How can research of the type outlined in the case help businesses decide whether their marketing programmes are being effectively implemented?

Quick questions

2 Why is implementation control important in marketing?
3 Using examples to illustrate your answer, explain what barriers can impede the effective implementation of marketing strategies.

Applied question

4 Assuming the role of a marketing consultant, prepare a document outlining the key infrastructure and process requirements involved in marketing implementation.

Extra readings

Aaker, D. (2001) *Strategic Marketing Management.* New York: Wiley.
Jain, S.C. (2000) *Marketing Planning and Strategy.* Cincinnati, OH: South Western.
Kotler, P. (2003) *Marketing Management.* Englewood Cliffs, NJ: Pearson.
McDonald, M. (2002) *Marketing Plans.* Oxford: Butterworth-Heinemann.
Piercy, N. (1999) *Tales from the Marketplace.* Oxford: Butterworth-Heinemann.
Piercy, N. (2001) *Market-Led Strategic Change.* Oxford: Butterworth-Heinemann.

38: The Marketing Audit

Key definitions

The *marketing audit* is a systematic examination of the marketing function's objectives, strategies, organization and performance.

Key issues

- The marketing audit is not designed to determine a business's market position. That is the function of the marketing plan and marketing analyses. The marketing audit is an implementation review process to assess how effectively the marketing department has performed its assigned functions.
- As with an accounting audit, the marketing audit should be performed regularly in order to track progress and to help remedy problems.
- The marketing audit may either focus on only one facet of a business's marketing activity (one campaign, brand or target market segment, for example) or it may be fully comprehensive, instead examining the entire marketing activity of the business.
- The results of the marketing audit can rectify staff and resource deficiencies, re-allocate marketing effort and help in re-examining marketing opportunities. Fundamentally, the marketing audit (popularized by US guru Philip Kotler) can assist in keeping marketing on track.
- The marketing audit may be conducted by senior managers, the whole marketing function or by external consultants. All core aspects of the marketing function should be examined.

Conceptual overview

In the 1970s marketing was still struggling to be widely accepted as a core management discipline. Various US marketing academics produced processes to enable companies to diagnose inherent problems and deficiencies in their marketing. One of the most widely adopted frameworks was Philip Kotler's marketing audit. This is primarily designed to review the operations of a marketing department rather than replicate the analyses central to a marketing plan, which does aim to determine a business's standing in its core target markets.

The audit can tackle the entire activity of a marketing function or be focused on a single business unit, brand or target market. Regular auditing permits on-going progress to be monitored and in this manner the marketing audit has become central to some organizations' evaluation of implementation effectiveness (cf. Brief 37). The audit, whether conducted by external consultants or company employees, provides information enabling managers to remedy problems in their marketing function, re-allocate marketing resources, appraise marketing opportunities and the business's ability to address them.

The marketing audit should:

- Describe current activities and results to sales, costs, prices, profits and other performance measures (cf. Brief 39).
- Gather information about customers, competition and environmental issues that may affect the organization's capacity to implement its recommended strategies and marketing mix programmes.
- Explore opportunities for improving the recommended marketing strategies.
- Provide a database to be used in evaluating the attainment of stated goals and objectives.
- Diagnose reasons for success and failure encountered by the business's marketers in terms of their analyses, strategies and tactical programmes.

While many businesses do not formally conduct a marketing audit, their annual marketing planning activity (cf. Brief 36) acts as a formal review of current performance benchmarked against the previous year's plan, its objectives, stated performance expectations and planned marketing activity. Through whatever mechanism, the implementation concerns discussed in Brief 37 require a process of auditing and formal evaluation in order to improve the effectiveness of marketing.

Kotler's marketing audit examines the company's markets, strategy, organization, systems, productivity and marketing mix functions, all from a marketing perspective (cf. Figure 38.1).

MARKET AUDIT

- Marketing environment forces
  - Economic
  - Technological
  - Political/legal/regulatory
  - Societal/green
- Task environment
  - Markets
  - Customers
  - Competitors
  - Distribution and dealers
  - Suppliers
  - Facilitators and marketing organizations
  - Publics

MARKETING STRATEGY AUDIT

- Business mission
- Marketing objectives and goals
- Strategy

MARKETING ORGANIZATION AUDIT

- Formal structure
- Functional efficiency
- Interface efficiency

MARKETING SYSTEMS AUDIT

- Marketing information system (MIS)
- Marketing planning
- Marketing controls
- New product development process

MARKETING PRODUCTIVITY AUDIT

- Profitability analysis
- Cost-effective analysis

MARKETING (MIX) FUNCTION AUDITS

- Product and service
- Price
- Distribution
- Promotional mix
- Sales force

Figure 38.1 Kotler's audit checklist

Examples

JCB

When construction equipment manufacturer JCB embarked on a major programme of marketing planning, one of the first activities that it carried out was a marketing audit. The aim was to ensure that the business had a realistic overview of the strengths and weaknesses of its current marketing operations. Amongst other areas, the audit reviewed the company's marketing environment, its marketing strategy and existing marketing programmes. Once JCB had a detailed analysis of these areas, it was able to identify key strengths on which the company could build its planning activity. The process also identified certain weaknesses, prompting early action to minimize their likely threat to future marketing activity.

(*Source:* Sally Dibb and Lyndon Simkin, *The Marketing Casebook*, London: Thomson, 2001)

Sky

From time to time, businesses re-think their marketing strategies and how they are organized to implement these strategies. Whether as a result of external pressures and market trends, or undertaken as a result of a formal marketing audit, the results generally help to invigorate performance and internally market a business's marketing priorities. In its early days, when there was a need to create category need and mass awareness of satellite TV availability, broadcaster Sky focused its marketing communications around television, press and print advertising, sales promotions offers and publicity. The marketing strategy also involved joint promotions with hardware providers such as rental firm *boxclever*, and the buying up of broadcast rights for major sports competitions and movies.

Recently, Sky re-jigged its marketing team in order to reflect trends in the marketplace and the findings of research it had undertaken. The Internet had been identified as a principal marketing channel. A senior executive role was created, Head of Internet Marketing, responsible for improving Sky's on-line profile and e-marketing activity. This move reflected the success rival broadcaster the BBC had enjoyed with *BBCi*. Sky's audit had revealed that already 14% of its subscribers came via the Internet, but that trends in consumer usage and competitors' successes implied the percentage should be much higher. In addition to a greater emphasis on e-marketing, Sky's review of its sales and marketing operations had revealed the need to place greater importance on the role of marketing planning and on the control of marketing operations. The audit led to the strengthening of all of these crucial roles, plus the re-orientation of the marketing communications mix.

(*Sources:* BBCi; Sky TV; *Marketing*, 8 January 2004, p. 3)

Test yourself

Case question

1 What kind of information can a marketing audit usefully collect for a company such as Sky?

Quick questions

2 What is a marketing audit?
3 Why should marketing audits be carried out on a regular basis?

Applied question

4 You have been asked to make a presentation to a car parts manufacturer to explain the different dimensions of a marketing audit. What key pieces of information would you include in your presentation pack?

Extra readings

Dibb, S., Simkin, L., Pride, W. and Ferrell, O.C (2001) *Marketing: Concepts and Strategies*. Boston, MA: Houghton Mifflin.

Gilligan, C. and Wilson, R.M.S. (2003) *Strategic Marketing Planning.* Oxford: Butterworth-Heinemann.

Kotler, P. (2003) *Marketing Management: Analysis, Planning and Control.* Englewood Cliffs, NJ: Pearson.

Piercy, N. (2001) *Market-Led Strategic Change.* Oxford: Butterworth-Heinemann.

39: Performance Measures in Marketing

Key definitions

Marketing performance is the assessment of the effectiveness of marketing programmes to implement recommended marketing strategies, satisfy marketing objectives, fulfil corporate expectations and achieve the required levels of customer satisfaction.

A *performance standard* is an expected level of performance against which actual performance can be measured.

Sales analysis is the use of sales figures to evaluate a business's performance.

Marketing cost analysis is the breakdown and classification of costs to determine which are associated with specific marketing activities to determine their worth.

Customer satisfaction is a qualitative measure of marketing performance involving surveying customer views over time and benchmarking results against competitors' scores.

Brand awareness is a qualitative measure of marketing performance that determines whether a company's brands adequately capture the attention of their target markets.

Key issues

- Marketing is an expensive activity and this activity must be justified. Marketing research, new product development and promotional activity are some of the largest expenditures within a business.
- Marketers require clear objectives against which their endeavours may be measured. Marketers must themselves be aware of specific objectives and strive to achieve them through their marketing strategies and marketing mix programmes.
- Marketers used to be judged primarily on the basis of their company's sales figures. Some businesses break down the marketing budget to allocate the costs of functional accounts to different budgets. These management accounts may be brand-based, product group-centred, oriented around markets, or focused on channels of distribution. The functional accounts include: advertising, personal selling, transport, storage, marketing research, and non-marketing expenditure.
- For most marketing departments, effectiveness is measured by senior managers and their colleagues in other management functions in terms of the business's profitability and sales figures. While these criteria are of fundamental importance to an organization desiring a viable future, there are other criteria of importance to marketers.
- Marketing exists to ensure customer needs are met and to deliver customer satisfaction. It seems only reasonable, therefore, for marketers to measure customer satisfaction and customer retention. Marketers also control the brand, and brand awareness is another performance measure that should be judged.
- A balanced set of short-term and longer-term performance measures should be adopted, including financial and non-financial marketing performance metrics.

Conceptual overview

As with all management disciplines, marketers must be judged by their colleagues. Owing to the high visibility of marketing programmes – a new advertisement rarely goes unnoticed, for example – and the high proportion of a company's budget devoted to marketing-related expenditure, marketing must be able to justify itself. Traditionally, the company's profitability and sales levels have been assumed to reflect the prowess of the business's marketing, along with other familiar financial ratios, such as return on investment or return on capital employed (cf. Brief 49). Sales analysis is the use of sales figures to evaluate a business's performance and is often adopted by senior management when judging the effectiveness of marketing. Marketing cost analysis is the break down and classification of costs to determine which are associated with specific marketing activities, in order to determine the worth of these activities, such as advertising or marketing research.

The assessment of marketing performance is a necessary part of the marketing control process. Marketers must have clearly defined objectives that subsequently can be assessed in terms of successful achievement. Marketing performance is an assessment of: how well marketers (a) implement their marketing strategies and marketing mix programmes; (b) fulfil corporate expectations, such as market share targets and profit levels; and (c) achieve the desired levels of customer satisfaction. In addition to the core financial measures such as profitability, sales and market share, marketers increasingly are judged on the qualitative measures so central to the marketing concept: customer satisfaction and brand awareness.

A company should endeavour to adopt a balanced set of performance measures, mixing the short-term view of profitability with the often longer-term perspective of market share gains. It often requires considerable resources to increase market share at the expense of rivals, which may reduce short-term profitability. However, market share increases are likely to bring longer-term security and rewards. In addition to the financial performance measures, marketers should insist on being assessed on dimensions such as customer retention, customer satisfaction and brand awareness. If marketing programmes are effective, these three customer-oriented criteria should all show signs of improvement.

Key marketing financial performance measures include:

- Revenue growth
- Return on investment
- Product profitability
- Customer profitability
- Return on sales
- Total return to shareholders
- Sales per square metre for retailers.

Leading non-financial marketing performance measures include:

- Customer satisfaction.
- Delivery performance.
- New customers gained.
- Market share.
- Customer loyalty.
- Customer dissatisfaction.
- Brand awareness.
- Lost customers.
- Price level achieved.
- Customer brand attitudes.

The first set of these, the financial performance measures, are deemed 'hard' (quantitative) measures, while the second set of marketing performance measures are often described as 'softer' (qualitative) measures. Marketers and their Boards of Directors should adopt a mix. A more recent addition to performance measures is that of value-based marketing, utilizing the concept of marketing shareholder value analysis (cf. Brief 49). Boards are devoting increasing attention to demonstrating performance outcomes to their stakeholders, including their shareholders.

Examples

First Direct

Telephone and Internet bank First Direct regularly commissions independent research to assess customer satisfaction. One such survey recently revealed that 86% of the bank's customers were 'extremely' or 'very' satisfied with the service provided, while four-fifths of customers believe that First Direct is better than its competitors. The same research suggested that existing customers demonstrate their loyalty by recommending the bank to someone else every 7 seconds. Information of this kind provides a useful measure against which First Direct can benchmark customer satisfaction in the future and assess the performance of its marketing programmes.

(*Sources:* First Direct marketing literature, 2001; NOP December 2000)

Chester Zoo

All types of businesses need to measure their marketing performance. The dimensions that are appropriate as benchmarks will vary for different organizations. For Chester Zoo, a major animal tourist attraction with around one million visitors a year, performance indicators play a key role in maintaining visitor attendance levels. Several years ago, the Zoo started to take part in a major performance monitoring programme run by the Association of Leading Visitor Attractions (ALVA). The zoo also carries out regular customer surveys and conducts focus groups to assess visitor impressions, other attractions visited and home locations. Amongst other things, this helps the marketing team to plan its promotional activity. By supplementing the ALVA study with its own programme of customer research, the Zoo has developed an array of performance indicators that can be regularly updated. These include:

- Membership growth.
- Amount of breeding of threatened species.
- Visitor 'dwell time' (number of guests remaining at the attraction for more than five hours).
- Value for money ratings.
- Value for money comparisons with competitors.
- Publicity levels.

By establishing benchmarks in these areas, the zoo is able to set targets for the future and monitor its progress towards them.

(*Sources:* Chris Vere and Chester Zoo, Annual Reports, 1998, 1999, 2000)

Test yourself

Case question

1 Why is it important for Chester Zoo to assess its performance across a number of dimensions?

Quick questions

2 What is performance measurement in marketing?
3 What is the difference between qualitative and quantitative measures of marketing performance?

Applied question

4 You work as brand manager for an international manufacturer of spirits (whisky, gin and so forth). The company is looking at ways to assess the performance of a marketing campaign for its leading brand of Scotch whisky. Prepare a report recommending the marketing performance measures that should be used.

Extra readings

Dibb, S., Simkin, L., Pride, W. and Ferrell, O.C. (2001) *Marketing: Concepts and Strategies.* Boston: Houghton Mifflin.

Gilligan, C. and Wilson, R.M.S. (2003) *Strategic Marketing Planning.* Oxford: Butterworth-Heinemann.

Jain, S.C. (1999) *Marketing Planning and Strategy.* Cincinnati, OH: South Western.

Kotler, P. (2003) *Marketing Management: Analysis, Planning and Control*. Englewood Cliffs, NJ: Pearson.

McDonald, M.H. (2002) *Marketing Plans.* Oxford: Butterworth-Heinemann.

Piercy, N. (2001) *Market-Led Strategic Change.* Oxford: Butterworth-Heinemann.

40: Internal Marketing

Key definitions

Internal marketing is the application of marketing within the company, utilizing programmes of communication and guidance targeted at internal audiences to develop responsiveness and a unified sense of purpose among employees.

Relationship marketing develops on-going relationships with customers by focusing on maintaining links between marketing, quality and customer service. The six domains of relationship marketing are customer markets, influencers, referral, employee recruitment, suppliers and internal markets within the business.

Key issues

- Internal marketing is the application of marketing internally within an organization. Marketing communications targeting the workforce ensure staff understanding and cooperation. The intention is to facilitate the implementation of marketing strategies and marketing plans.
- Increasingly, customers demand high levels of service. The staff providing this service must be fully conversant with a business's strategy, brand positioning and basis for competing. Internal marketing helps ensure this understanding pervades the organization.
- The internal marketing concepts holds that all staff have 'suppliers' and 'customers' (other staff colleagues) in the business. The expectations, needs and perceptions of these people must be managed.
- Internal marketing requires information sharing, orientation of staff, multi-functional team interaction, internal marketing communications, debrief sessions, staff motivation programmes, empowerment of line management to deal with emergent problems, plus 'success stories' to champion. Staff must be carefully selected, well trained, motivated and encouraged to provide good service.

Conceptual overview

In businesses that have fully embraced the marketing philosophy, much appears to hinge on internal marketing. This is the application of marketing internally within the organization, with programmes of communication and guidance targeted at internal audiences. Internal marketing plays a vital role in developing a customer-focused organization and in helping ensure coherent relationship marketing (cf. Briefs 2 and 8). Internal marketing is based on internal communication and with developing responsiveness and a unified sense of purpose among employees. It aims to develop internal and external customer awareness and to remove functional (human) barriers to organizational effectiveness: the workforce is harnessed to positively implement and comprehend the devised marketing strategy.

Long-term, on-going relationships are highly sought after by marketers, but such relationships require improved customer service. High levels of service depend on individuals ensuring their suppliers and customers are happy. The internal marketing concept is also concerned with ensuring that all members of staff work together, in tune with the organization's mission, strategy and goals. The aim is to ensure that all staff represent the business in the best possible way in all transactions they have with suppliers, customers and other staff. Internal marketing centres on the notion that every member of the organization has a 'supplier' and a 'customer'. Internal marketing is a philosophy for managing human resources with a marketing perspective. Relationship marketing has built on this to propose that senior managers should view non-marketing employees as 'part-time marketers' in order to better satisfy customers and employees and that all employees must recognize they are colleagues' customers. In order to achieve this internal cohesiveness, six steps have been proposed:

1 The creation of internal awareness.
2 Identification of internal 'customers' and 'suppliers'.
3 Determination of internal customers' expectations.
4 Communication of these expectations to internal suppliers.
5 Internal suppliers' modifications to their activities to reflect internal customers' views.
6 A measure of internal service quality and feedback to ensure a satisfactory exchange between internal customers and suppliers.

In the context of marketing planning, market segmentation or marketing strategy, this implies those involved in the process must be aware of their colleagues' expectations, views and understanding before, during and after producing the marketing plan, segmentation scheme or marketing strategy. An overt response is required to allay any fears, miscomprehension or resistance to the evolving recommendation. The proponents of internal marketing argue this process needs to be formalized and built into an organization's marketing culture in order to ensure ready compliance, commitment and understanding within the organization of recommended marketing strategies and programmes.

Internal marketing requires the acceptance of the need for improved internal communication, information sharing and liaison across business functions and managerial hierarchies. The core requirements are (a) information sharing of marketing intelligence, (b) orientation sessions to familiarize staff with marketing plans, (c) multi-functional team interaction, (d) formalized internal marketing communications campaigns, (e) debrief and feedback sessions, (f) incentivized staff motivation, (g) empowerment of line management to take ownership of problems, and (h) the encouragement of 'success stories' to champion. In order to effectively exploit the internal market, thought must be devoted to establishing communication channels, leadership qualities, associated resources, information and clear internally focused propositions and messages. All of this would routinely be undertaken for an external customer or target market, so why not within the business to ensure staff understanding and cooperation?

For too long, the output of most marketing functions has focused on satisfying external customers. These customers *are* undoubtedly the 'bread and butter' for an organization's survival. However, greater attention to internal smoothing of understanding will significantly reduce the organizational and cultural barriers that so often impede the effective implementation of a marketing strategy or marketing plan.

Examples

Raytheon

In 1999, leading US defence business Raytheon, manufacturer of Tomahawk Cruise Missiles and AWACS early warning systems, launched a new initiative designed to focus on quality manufacturing processes, customer service and cutting internal operational inefficiencies and wastage. *Six Sigma*, the management process concerned, had cost the company millions of dollars to create and to equip senior managers with the necessary skills to manage its implementation. Raytheon recognized, though, that without significant awareness building and orientation training programmes within the business, the impressive benefits – for customers, employees and the company's fortunes – from this *Six Sigma* process would not be forthcoming. A focus on internal marketing enabled Raytheon to maximize the benefits from introducing this management process.

(*Source:* Raytheon Inc, 2000)

Fujitsu

Ranked third in the global market for IT services behind only IBM and EDS, Japanese based Fujitsu Services has reinvented itself recently within its European operations. Instead of only marketing specific standalone products, such as CRM systems, data warehouses or mobile office solutions, the company has sat down to talk with its key clients in order to fully appreciate their business imperatives. These may include improving shareholder value, taking cost out of their businesses, attracting new customers, retaining existing customers, persuading customers to buy more than one product from them, or integrating operations and systems across multiple sites, often in many different countries. By listening to its business clients in this way, Fujitsu has been able to rethink its service propositions and how best to relate its immense capabilities with the problems causing its clients to lie awake at night.

While this market strategizing has been successful in identifying new-look Fujitsu business propositions and in moving the company much closer to its clients, the internal operational ramifications for Fujitsu were immense. Previously, the business had been structured around its capabilities and service offerings, rather than around client problems. The sales force had to be reallocated and be educated to move away from the mindset of selling separate products, such as a CRM system. Product development approaches also needed re-orientating. To make this transition effective, the Public Sector division of Fujitsu, serving local government needs, health, education, the emergency services and not-for-profit clients, organized a series of workshops. These sessions included the senior management team across all business functions and leading personnel responsible for both product development and engaging directly with customers. Through this internal marketing strategy, those ultimately tasked with modifying their working remits and foci were involved in the analyses that led up to the new-look strategy. This resulted in immediate 'buy-in' from all of the key personnel within Fujitsu, which smoothed this switch in emphasis for the company.

(*Sources:* Fujitsu promotional material and website, 2004; David Olney, Fujitsu Public Sector Marketing Director, 2003)

Test yourself

Case question

1 Why did Fujitsu include such a diverse set of personnel in its marketing strategy programme?

Quick questions

2 What is meant by internal marketing?
3 How is internal marketing linked to the beliefs inherent in relationship marketing?

Applied question

4 As a consultant brought in by a leading manufacturer of paints, what advice would you give to the Board wishing to adopt an internal marketing approach?

Extra readings

Christopher, M., Payne, A. and Ballantyne, D. (2002) *Relationship Marketing.* Oxford: Butterworth-Heinemann.

Gronroos, C. (1985) 'Internal Marketing: Theory and Practice', in Bloch, T.M., Upah, G.D. and Zeithaml, V.A. (eds), *Services Marketing in a Changing Environment.* Chicago, IL: American Marketing Association.

Gummesson, R. (2002) *Total Relationship Marketing: Rethinking Relationship Marketing Management.* Oxford: Butterworth-Heinemann.

Reynoso, J. and Moores, B. (1996) 'Internal Relationships', in Buttle, F. (ed.), *Relationship Marketing: Theory and Practice.* London: Chapman.

41: International Marketing

Key definitions

Domestic marketing is activity directed exclusively to a business's home market.

Export marketing is taking advantage of opportunities outside of the home market through exports, but focusing production and product development on domestic markets.

International marketing involves the reduction of reliance on intermediaries and the establishing of direct involvement in non-domestic target markets.

Multinational marketing is the adaptation of some of a company's marketing activities to appeal to local culture and differences in taste outside of the home market.

Global marketing is a total commitment to international marketing, in which a company applies its assets, experience and products to develop and maintain marketing strategies on a global scale.

Key issues

- International marketing used to mean marketing activity performed across national boundaries. In its loosest sense, this still holds, but the specific term 'international marketing' now is just one of several options for trading outside the home market.
- Options include: (a) domestic marketing only; (b) export marketing; (c) international marketing; (d) multinational marketing; or (e) global marketing.
- Businesses adopting international marketing strategies have decided to take their existing products and services to markets away from their domestic base, or to develop different products and services for these non-domestic markets. In doing so, they have to respond to opportunities and threats in markets exhibiting different characteristics and behaviour to the domestic market.
- The process for internationalization includes: (a) the decision by the organization to internationalize; (b) analysis of the international marketing environment; (c) the determination of an entry strategy; (d) the development of international marketing mix programmes; and (e) the implementation and control of the international marketing strategy.
- An understanding of the international marketing environment is crucial for effective non-domestic marketing, notably social, regulatory, political and competitive forces.
- Market entry strategies for addressing non-domestic opportunities include: (a) exporting; (b) licensing; (c) franchising; (d) joint ventures and strategic alliances; (e) the use of trading companies; and (f) foreign direct investment, possibly including acquisitions.
- The marketing mix ingredients invariably will require modification, from those specified for the domestic market, in order to satisfy local demands in foreign markets.

Conceptual overview

A marketer may concentrate solely on the domestic home market: domestic marketing. The company may seek out opportunities for selling its existing products outside of its domestic market through exporting: export marketing. International marketing is the reduced reliance on intermediaries and the direct involvement in countries in which trade takes place. Multinational marketing involves greater modification of the company's marketing mix to take account of cultural and taste differences in target markets outside the domestic market. Global marketing is the extreme, where companies recognize the need to establish operations in non-domestic markets, requiring significant investment and the understanding of business practices in these countries.

According to Bradley, the corporate context of international marketing involves understanding how the business responds to environmental opportunities and threats in markets of very different configurations and underlying behaviour to 'home' markets. Bradley states that, 'international marketing processes and decisions require the firm to identify needs and wants of customers, to produce assets [products or services] to give a differential marketing advantage, to communicate information about these assets and to distribute and exchange them internationally through one or a combination of exchange modalities', outside the organization's domestic market. There is a straightforward process for internationalization: (a) the decision by a business to internationalize; (b) analysis of the international marketing environment; (c) entering international markets through one or more entry strategy options; (d) the development of associated international marketing mix programmes; and (e) the implementation and control of the international marketing strategy and programme.

A core task for the marketer addressing international markets is the understanding of the international marketing environment (cf. Brief 4). Regulations, political practices and the legal environment will be different from those experienced in the domestic market. Technological and economic forces may vary, too. Generally, it is the issues under social forces from the macro marketing environment that differ greatly, notably cultural and ethical issues. The forces of the micro marketing environment (competitive challenges) are particularly relevant. International marketing intelligence is therefore of great value. Owing to these issues, the marketing mix specified for the domestic market invariably must be modified for non-domestic target markets.

A business deciding to offer its products outside its domestic home market has various entry strategy options: (a) exporting the product already produced for the home market; (b) licensing the product idea or production supplies to a third party who operates across national boundaries or in overseas markets; (c) franchising arrangements – such as McDonald's outlets in many countries; (d) a joint venture between a domestic company and a foreign company or government, or a strategic alliance to form partnerships across national boundaries; (e) the use of trading companies, that provide links between buyers and sellers in different countries; or

(f) foreign direct investment – possibly including the acquisition of an established business – which is a long-term commitment to a non-domestic market and is resource-demanding. Clearly the associated levels of commitment, resourcing, managerial complexity and risk increase through this range of options from (a) to (f).

The marketing process – analysis of the marketplace and the scoping of the opportunity, followed by the development of a target market strategy and competitive brand positioning, then the creation of a suitable marketing mix, and the control of the marketing activity – holds true for international marketers, too. However, the relative unfamiliarity of non-domestic markets places greater importance on understanding the macro and micro marketing environments (cf. Brief 2), defining the optimum target market and in selecting a channel strategy (cf. Brief 33). Plus, the lack of an established base in the international markets targeted, similar to that likely in the domestic market, forces an assessment of the entry strategy to select that marketers addressing only the domestic market need not consider.

Examples

Carrefour

The Carrefour brand, originally from France, has clearly demonstrated its ability to cross national boundaries. From its early days in France in the 1960s, Carrefour has spread its hypermarket concept through Europe and the rest of the world. By the end of the 1990s, with a presence in 26 countries and following a merger with Promodes, Carrefour had become the world's second biggest retailing group and Europe's largest. The company's commitment to global expansion that has resulted in this position stemmed partly from the saturation of the domestic French retailing market, where there were restrictions on retailing growth designed to protect existing outlets. For Carrefour, the obvious expansionist route was, therefore, through acquisition. By acquiring local retailers, both in France and in other markets, the company was able to step around some of the rules and regulations. The Euromarche Group and the Montlaur retailing chain are just two of these acquisitions that have helped Carrefour continue its growth. However, Carrefour's impressive global expansion has not only been through acquisition. In many countries it has created its own hypermarket networks, while in the United Arab Emirates, Qatar, Romania, Santo Dominguo, Tunisia and Egypt it operates through franchises and partnerships. Via this mix of entry options, Carrefour has now established itself in 30 countries with over 9600 stores, and is the leader in hypermarkets worldwide.

(*Sources:* M. Laurent Noel, 'Carrefour has Czech Mate', *Chain Store Age*, 1999, 75 (8), pp. 44–8; Sally Dibb and Lyndon Simkin, *The Marketing Casebook*, London: Thomson, 2001; www.carrefour.com, 2004)

Unilever

FMCG giant Unilever has just conducted a five-year plan to improve its structure and overhaul its marketing strategy. For one of the world's largest companies and a leading supplier of fast moving consumer goods, this was a necessary process of refocusing involving a major reorganization of the company's activities leading to a rationalization of Unilever's portfolio of 1600 brands. The intention was to build growth by focusing on around 400 of the business's strongest brands. This has allowed Unilever to rid itself of its unprofitable brands, leaving greater resources to devote to the stronger parts of its portfolio. The remaining brands have been organized into two global divisions: (a) foods, and (b) home and personal care.

Associated with this strategic review, the brands have been categorized. 'International' brands are those such as *Lipton* tea, *Magnum* ices and *Calvin Klein* perfume that have a standard global name and appeal to consumers in different parts of the world. Then there are 'international brand positionings', that have different names in different locations, but which are none the less consistently positioned. An example is *Flora* spread, which in Germany has the brand name *Becel*. Finally, there are brands that have a strong national presence, but are not recognized internationally. *Wishbone* salad dressing and *Persil* washing powder are examples from the US and the UK. *Bird's Eye* is used in the UK for frozen foods, but *Findus* in Italy and *Iglo* in many other European countries. With this three-level approach to global branding, Unilever believes it can benefit from economies of scale while also reflecting localized trading conditions.

In order to achieve this new strategy, Unilever has been actively engaged in restructuring its businesses, with many international acquisitions and disposals. Bestfoods was acquired in 2000, bringing *Knorr* into Unilever's portfolio, a brand worth 2.5 billion euros and sold in over one hundred countries. *Ben & Jerry's* ice cream was recently added to ice cream brands *Algida* and *Wall's*. At the same time, the company has reorganized its marketing. By creating the home/personal care and food divisions, each with its own marketing supremo, Unilever is trying to move away from its previously fragmented structure. A number of global brand directors now handle the company's international marketing activity which, Unilever believes, is resulting in better communication and stronger links between brand management and marketing activities.

(*Sources:* Harriet Marsh, 'Unilever a year down the path', *Marketing*, 22 February 2001, pp. 30–1; Unilever Annual Report, 2000; www.unilever.com, 2004; www.unilever.co.uk, 2004)

Test yourself

Case question

1 Why does a global company such as Unilever need three different categories of brands?

Quick questions

2 Explain the different levels of involvement in international marketing.
3 What role does marketing intelligence play for a business deciding to enter a new international market?

Applied question

4 You work for a frozen food manufacturer that has previously only sold its merchandise domestically. The business is considering taking advantage of the reduction of trade barriers in the EU to trade internationally. Prepare a report exploring the different environmental forces that must be considered before your business enters a new non-domestic market.

Extra readings

Bradley, F. (2002) *International Marketing Strategy.* Harlow: FT Prentice Hall.
Bridgewater, S. and Egan, C. (2002) *International Marketing Relationships.* Basingstoke: Palgrave Macmillan.
Jeannet, J.-P. and Hennessey, H.D. (2001) *Global Marketing Strategies.* Boston, MA: Houghton Mifflin.
Paliwoda, S. and Ryans, J.K. (1995) *International Marketing Reader.* London: Routledge.
Paliwoda, S. and Thomas, M.J. (1998) *International Marketing.* Oxford: Butterworth-Heinemann.
Terpstra, V. and Sarathy, R. (2000) *International Marketing.* Cincinnati, OH: South Western.

42: Consumer Marketing

Key definitions

Consumer markets are those in which the targeted customer is the end-user private consumer.

Customers in consumer markets are private individuals or families, typically in the home situation.

Key issues

- Marketing was created by the consumer goods companies of North America in the 1950s and 1960s.
- The marketing toolkit described throughout this book is applicable to consumer marketing.
- The consumer is the end-user private customer generally purchasing products for self-consumption or use in the household.
- Consumer goods include: (a) inexpensive, frequently bought convenience products; (b) shopping goods; (c) speciality goods; and (d) unsought goods. FMCGs (fast moving consumer goods) are those items typically purchased in a supermarket or convenience store.
- Consumer goods marketing requires clear target marketing, product and brand positioning, and differentiation from rival products. Strong brand identities, brand awareness and wide-spread distribution are core requisites.
- The standard consumer buying process includes: (a) recognition of need; (b) information search; (c) evaluation of alternatives; (d) selection and adoption; and (e) post-purchase evaluation. Influencing factors are social, person-specific and psychological.
- Distribution may involve agents or brokers, wholesalers or retailers between the producer and the consumer. Shelf space allocation and product prominence in-store are particularly important.
- Keen (competitive) prices are important, and the full promotional mix typically is utilized in order to achieve brand awareness and create interest in the product.

Conceptual overview

Marketing *per se* was established by the leading consumer brands in the United States, such as Ford, Kellogg's and Kodak. The marketing toolkit and the marketing process described in *Marketing Briefs* (and any leading marketing text) apply to the marketing of consumer-oriented products and services. The marketing of services specifically is addressed in Brief 44. This Brief reiterates the key issues concerning the marketing of consumer goods.

Marketers of consumer goods practise the full extent of marketing and require clear target market strategies, product differentiation, distinct brand positioning and fully specified marketing mixes. Strong brand awareness and identities (Briefs 14 and 20), plus prominent shelf space and extensive distribution (cf. Briefs 28 and 46) are core requisites for effective marketing. The product must satisfy clearly identified customer needs and reflect consumers' buying behaviour.

The 'standard' consumer buying behaviour decision-making process (cf. Brief 6) involves: (a) recognition by a consumer that there is a problem for which the purchase of a product or service is the likely solution; (b) the seeking of information to assist in selecting viable product or service options; (c) the evaluation of the evoked set of likely options; (d) the final selection and purchase of one product or service; and (e) the on-going post-purchase subjective assessment of whether the specific product purchased was the 'right' one. This final stage will impact on the process next time around.

It is important to recognize that not all purchases pass through all five stages. A brand loyal and contented consumer may start at stage (c). For low risk, cheap, frequently purchased items such as cigarettes or a newspaper, there will be a quick progression from stage (a) to stage (d), with possibly no utilization of stages (b) or (c). The greater the risk (owing to cost, duration of consumption, unfamiliarity, uncertainty), the more likelihood there is of all five stages coming into play. By understanding which stages feature, a marketer can better tailor a marketing mix programme to appeal to the targeted consumers.

All consumers are different, however, and this in part is a result of their social influences – social class, culture, family roles, reference group membership and grasp of marketing messages in the media. Person-specific influences such as demographics and situational factors are very important, as are psychological influences such as perceptions, motives, attitudes towards what and how they purchase, plus the personality of the consumer.

Consumer products include: (a) inexpensive, frequently purchased, low involvement convenience products, such as bread, drinks, cigarettes or newspapers; (b) more carefully selected shopping goods, such as lower-priced appliances, stereo equipment and clothing; (c) speciality goods demanding much deliberation owing to their value, length of ownership, visibility to peers or novelty, including expensive jewellery, cars, holidays and computing equipment; (d) unsought goods purchased when a sudden problem occurs or when aggressive selling generates interest, for example pension policies or life insurance. FMCGs are fast moving consumer goods, such as most products retailed in supermarkets. Branding, keen pricing, brand awareness – necessitating extensive promotional activity and shelf space allocation – are fundamental to the marketing of FMCGs.

In consumer markets, distribution may involve movements from producers, agents or brokers, wholesalers and retailers to consumers. One producer may use several channels. For example, Mars distributes its confectionery products through two principal channels: direct to the warehouses of the national supermarket chains which in turn sell these products to the ultimate customers, and to wholesalers and cash and carry operators which in turn supply corner shops, CTNs (newsagents) and forecourt shops.

Consumer marketing requires a clear understanding of the market, notably customer needs, brand awareness, buying behaviour; competitive propositions and pricing; distinct product differentiation; brand identity and brand awareness programmes; competitive pricing; shrewd product development, and appropriate distribution for the target market that ensures readily available products and good shelf space allocation in retail outlets (cf. Brief 33). The consumer marketer must determine a clear target market strategy, brand positioning and differential advantage, and develop marketing mixes appropriate to the targeted markets (cf. Brief 32).

Examples

Taco Bell

US advertising for Taco Bell is based around a lively Chihuahua called Dinky. The well-loved dog is renowned for his statements about the product. 'Yo quiero Tac Bell', for example, means 'I want Taco Bell'. Consumers particularly like the fact that the dog can talk, but it seems that Dinky's popularity runs much deeper than simply the comments with which he is associated. Marketers for Taco Bell have worked hard to develop a character that consumers feel is both endearing and funny. The company's efforts to understand their target market also mean that they understand that teenage lads, who are big purchasers of Taco Bell, feel a connection with the creature, who has been described as 'a 19-year-old guy in a dog's body who thinks about food and girls'. As well as enhancing the Taco Bell brand, one surprising result of the little dog's popularity is that ownership of Chihuahuas has actually increased!

(*Sources:* C. Bidwell, 'Taco Bell says, "Ay, Chihuahua" ', *Austin American Statesman*, 6 March 1998, p. E5; W.D. Hoyer and D.J. MacInnis, *Consumer Behaviour*, 2001, Boston: Houghton Mifflin)

Island and Ocean Village

Island was jointly launched by holiday companies First Choice and Royal Caribbean, in order to attract a new group of customers to cruise ship holidays. This kind of holiday has been traditionally associated with older couples, a fact generally reflected in tour operators' marketing materials for cruises. Targeting those in their 30s, the *Island* initiative stemmed from a conviction that younger people, if provided with a suitable proposition, would also enjoy the cruise liner experience. This group also provided an opportunity to extend the potential market size for cruises. *Island* is 'the four-star way to see the seas with no standing on ceremony'.

Developing an attractive proposition involved careful consideration of the target group's characteristics and holiday preferences. The positioning of the offering, away from the 'mature' perception of the market, was particularly important. For example, the *Island* marketing team believed that this younger target market would be less interested in the formality of 'dressing for dinner' or set meal times. The new customer group also needed to be offered a range of on-board services with which they could relate. In an innovative move, it was decided that companies familiar to the target market could provide on-board services. Focus-group research helped the company to identify suitable providers, such as *Oddbins*, *Costa Coffee* and fitness-company, *Holmes Place*. The style of promotion for the cruises was also developed to reflect the kind of holiday that thirty-somethings enjoy. Traditional images of evening sunshine were avoided, as were pictures of the ship. Cruise prices were set at a level that was accessible to this younger age-group, with starting prices of around £500 a week. *Island*'s approach has now been emulated by various rivals. 'Your world, your way! *Oceania Cruises* welcomes you aboard a new cruising experience sailing in stylish luxury and offering a higher level of service combined with intimacy and informality' and, 'A brand new take on holidays at sea, *Ocean Village* is for people who like to go flat out at sports and activities one minute and be flat out by the pool the next. Easy going and informal in style, dressing down not up, is what *Ocean Village* is all about'.

(*Sources:* Lucy Barrett, 'Island sets course for greener waters', *Marketing Week*, 19 April 2001, pp. 19–20; Ocean Village, 2004; www.cruisecontrolcruises.co.uk, 2004)

Test yourself

Case question

1 Why was it important for *Island* to carry out consumer research and what role did this play in the development of its holiday proposition?

Quick questions

2 In what ways is the marketing mix for consumers different to that for business customers?
3 'Television advertising is the most appropriate promotional tool for targeting consumers.' Discuss this statement, using examples to illustrate your answer.

Applied question

4 In your role as marketing manager for mobile phone company Orange, you have to develop marketing programmes for consumers and business customers. Prepare a report outlining the features of a marketing programme for consumers and explain how this might differ from one for business customers.

Extra readings

Assael, H. (1998) *Consumer Behaviour and Marketing Action.* Cincinnati, OH: South Western.

Blackwell, R.D., Miniard, P.W. and Engel, J.F. (2001) *Consumer Behaviour.* Fort Worth, TX: West.

Desmond, J. (2003) *Consumer Behaviour.* Basingstoke: Palgrave Macmillan.

Dibb, S., Simkin, L., Pride, W. and Ferrell, O.C. (2001) *Marketing: Concepts and Strategies.* Boston, MA: Houghton Mifflin.

Peter, J.P. and Olson, J.C. (1998) *Consumer Behaviour and Marketing Strategy.* Homewood, IL: Irwin.

Solomon, M., Bamossy, G. and Askegaard, S. (2001) *Consumer Behaviour.* Harlow: Pearson/FT.

43: Business-to-Business Marketing

Key definitions

Organizational marketing, *industrial marketing*, or *business-to-business marketing* is marketing activity targeting other organizations rather than end-user consumers.

An *organizational business-to-business market* is made up of individuals or groups that purchase a specific type of product for re-sale, for use in making other products, or for their use in daily operations.

Business-to-business customers are other organizations and not end-user consumers: manufacturers; channel members such as retailers, wholesalers, agents, brokers, distributors and dealers; public sector bodies; not-for-profit organizations; other companies, or government departments.

Types of *business-to-business purchases* are new task, modified re-buy or straight re-buy.

Key issues

- Business-to-business marketing involves exchanges and transactions between companies or organizations, including manufacturers, channel member organizations, public sector bodies, not-for-profit bodies, government departments and other companies.
- The terms business-to-business marketing, industrial marketing and organizational marketing are often used interchangeably.
- Products include raw materials, major equipment, component parts, accessory equipment and supplies, process materials and business services.
- There are often fewer customers in target markets than in consumer markets, and a great deal of data are routinely collected about organizational markets. In some respects, therefore, it is often stated that target marketing is relatively more straightforward in business-to-business markets than in consumer markets.
- Customer grouping for targeting used to be based on the industrial sectors into which customers fell. More and more businesses are now practising market segmentation, based on customer need and customer buying behaviour.
- The business-to-business buying behaviour process emulates the consumer buying process, but with the inclusion of a specification stage and the caveat that the selection of the right supplier (particularly when an on-going relationship is likely) is of paramount importance. The buying process tends to be more formalized owing to the risks involved and several customer managers may be involved in the buying centre.
- The marketing mix is loosely similar to that deployed by consumer marketers, but with a few key differences. Service and advice often are integral to the business-to-business product proposition. Personal selling and sales promotion dominate the promotional mix, with the nature of any advertising being more technical and less emotional. Pricing tends to be negotiated, pre-set, or based on tenders. Marketing channels still involve intermediaries, but often there are direct customer-supplier relationships.

Conceptual overview

Business-to-business marketing involves activities (exchanges) between businesses as suppliers and businesses as customers. Customers are companies, government departments or institutions, not the general public as consumers. Industrial or business-to-business markets include several categories of products: (a) raw materials; (b) major equipment; (c) component parts; (d) accessory equipment; (e) process materials; and (f) business-to-business services (cf. Brief 15).

Many textbooks claim that target marketing is straightforward in business-to-business markets. While there are generally fewer customers in business-to-business markets than in consumer markets and more official data tend to be collected for industrial markets, to glibly state that target marketing is easy is to gravely under-estimate the reality of the task. In most countries there is significant industrial census data collected for government purposes, known in the UK and US as SIC (Standard Industrial Classification) data. Unfortunately, many SIC codes are too broad to be useful in this way. However, compared with consumer markets, it is reasonable to argue that target marketing is sometimes *relatively* more straightforward than for targeting consumer goods or services.

Market segmentation (cf. Brief 11) is often poorly practised in business-to-business markets. Historically, businesses have classified their customers by industry sector or the product group purchased, rather than utilizing variables based on customer need and behaviour, as in market segmentation. This situation is changing, but slowly.

It is important to remember that the buying behaviour of businesses as customers differs from the buying behaviour of consumers (cf. Briefs 6 and 7). The buying process is more formalized and includes more stages, there are different influencing factors, and typically more personnel (the buying centre) are involved in the purchase decision. Types of business-to-business purchases include: (a) new task, (b) modified re-buy and (c) straight re-buy.

Compared with the marketing of consumer products, there are relatively few variations in the marketing practices for business-to-business products, unlike for services (cf. Briefs 19 and 44). For business-to-business marketing, the core marketing mix as deployed in consumer markets loosely still applies, although there are some important caveats.

The product is more broadly defined than the actual component or finished good being sold on from one company to another. Very often service, as part of the overall 'product' proposition, is very important. Key elements, in addition to the core and actual product, of importance in business-to-business marketing include: on-time delivery; quality control; custom/bespoke design; technical advice before a sale; product specification advice; installation application support; on-going maintenance and warranties; and parts distribution.

Depending on the product in question and the target market's characteristics, when compared with the distribution of consumer goods, there often are not as many stages in the marketing channel. Direct marketing channels or carefully selected distributors are common. Significant levels of technical advice are required during the product specification stage, supply process and installation. Occasionally agents are used in order to field enquiries and handle general administration, particularly for seasonal products.

Marketing communications activity is very different from consumer marketing. In particular, the utilization of the ingredients of the promotional mix varies from consumer goods marketing. Fewer customers, technical products, high cost products and repeat purchases place greater emphasis on personal selling and telemarketing in the promotional mix. There is relatively little advertising when compared with consumer marketing, but it is used to create general awareness, brand identity and to support a personal selling effort or sales promotion campaigns, through technical journals, trade directories and trade associations. Advertising is less emotive than in consumer goods marketing. Sales promotion is particularly important through catalogues and print material, sample merchandising and trade shows, often tied to personal selling and the activities of the sales force. Direct mail is a very popular ingredient of the promotional mix for many business-to-business products. Public relations is utilized by marketers of all types. Business-to-business marketers, notably through the support of sports events and theatre productions, have frequently used sponsorship. The growth of direct marketing has led to rapid take-up of the Internet in these businesses' promotional mixes (cf. Brief 26).

There are specific issues for pricing, too. Legal and economic constraints are quite prevalent in many business-to-business markets. For example, EU agreements prohibit price fixing, low price imports and dumping of discounted obsolete products. Low pricing used to be the fundamental selling platform in industrial marketing, but now the need to create a differential advantage (cf. Brief 35) is the focus, often involving customer service. This sometimes helps to justify an above-average market price. The common pricing methods are: pre-set or administered pricing; bid pricing with invitations to tender; negotiated pricing, when business-to-business customers expect to be able to negotiate on price. Payment terms, such as 90 days' credit, are particularly important to most business-to-business customers.

Increasingly, marketers for business-to-business products recognize the need to develop marketing strategies similar in complexity to those instigated by FMCG and consumer goods companies. Business-to-business companies are no longer in the market simply to supply raw materials/components/services to other producing/service businesses as a base price operation. There is a need to steal an edge in terms of product innovation and selling techniques over competitors, and to perpetually update positioning and product imagery. The creation of a differential advantage, through customer service, selling/distribution methods or through product innovation, is very much a focus for most business-to-business companies. Many have turned to customer service and the building of on-going, mutually beneficial relationships as a means of creating an edge over rivals (cf. Briefs 2 and 8).

Examples

Sony

Many companies market directly to consumers and also to business clients. Sony, for example, primarily focused on the consumer market with televisions, video cameras, Walkmans and hi-fi systems. However, a separate sales and marketing operation marketed presentation systems and audio devices to businesses, for meeting rooms and business presentations. Recently, the company has targeted the growing PC and laptop sectors with its excellent Vaio range. While of interest to students and home office users, the take-up of this innovative range of computers has been particularly strong among business users, with many companies specifying the Vaio range as the preferred model to purchase. Sony Europe has re-examined its marketing activity, creating a top brand marketer as head of both consumer and business-to-business marketing. Sony believes that in an already highly competitive marketplace, new entrants will increasingly position themselves as being at the cutting-edge. This is similar to Sony's brand positioning, so Sony recognizes the importance of strengthening its marketing activity. The *You make it a Sony* brand strategy will continue, and expectations are that Sony's business-to-business target markets will become much more important to the company, as Sony devotes more attention to servicing these markets.

(*Sources:* Sony; *Marketing Week*, 27 November 2003, p. 8)

St Andrew's Hospital

St Andrew's Hospital in Northampton is the market leader in mental health care in the UK. Its divisions address everything from adolescent learning difficulties through to major behavioural problems with patients requiring secure accommodation and lengthy treatment programmes. It has a specialist unit dealing with brain injuries and, through an on-site partner, also offers clinic facilities for patients needing to 'dry out'. Its staff are recognized as being leading-edge thinkers. St Andrew's brand reputation is based on the quality of its care, its multiple care pathways and its ability to relate to patients, their families and to the medical staff or personnel in social services who refer patients to the hospital. St Andrew's has charitable status, but strives to set its fees sufficiently high to permit it to provide the high-quality care that is at the core of its ethos, and to continually reinvest in its facilities and treatment programmes.

While some patients deal directly with the charity, the vast majority of patients are referred from the National Health Service (NHS). St Andrew's has a reputation for being able to deal with difficult patients suffering from complex problems. However, the NHS is increasingly moving towards centralized buying, with numerous

Trusts joining forces in order to be able to purchase services – such as those offered by St Andrew's – at lower rates. In addition to the medical staff who diagnose the patients' problems and recommend appropriate courses of treatment, the NHS has risk assessors, financial managers and professional purchasing executives, who all are involved in the decision concerning which treatment programme to purchase from which provider. For St Andrew's and other suppliers to the NHS, such formalized purchasing and group decision-making complicate the marketing activity and the engagement programmes the charity runs with its customers. For the patient, to his/her family, to the referring medical staff and the numerous administrators involved, St Andrew's must develop bespoke messages, marketing communications and client handling programmes. This complex buying centre must be addressed for St Andrew's to operate with full bed occupancy, in order to fulfil its mission to truly help those suffering with mental health problems.

(*Sources:* St Andrew's Hospital, 2004; James Watkins, Director of Marketing and Strategy, St Andrew's Hospital, 2003)

Test yourself

Case question

1 What implications are there for St Andrew's Hospital in there being formalized NHS purchasing through a complex buying centre?

Quick questions

2 Why is personal selling so heavily used in business-to-business markets?
3 Using an example of your choice, explain how the business-to-business marketing mix differs from that for consumer products.

Applied question

4 Your company specializes in providing marketing training for small and medium-sized enterprises. You are currently developing a one-week training programme for managers from the business-to-business sector. One day of the course will be devoted to explaining the characteristics of the business-to-business marketing mix. Write a short case study to help you explain the key features of the business-to-business marketing mix that can be used as the basis for an interactive course exercise. You can base the case study on a company or industry of your choice.

Extra readings

Chisnall, P. (1995) *Strategic Business Marketing.* Harlow: Pearson.

Ford, D. (2001) *Understanding Business Markets and Purchasing.* London: Thomson Learning.

Ford, D., Gadde, L-E., Hakansson, H. and Snehota, I. (2003) *Managing Business Relationships.* Chichester: Wiley.

Hart, N. (1994) *Effective Industrial Marketing*. London: Kogan Page.

Hutt, M.D. and Speh, T.W. (2003) *Business Marketing Management: Strategic View of Industrial and Organizational Markets.* Cincinnati, OH: South Western.

Naude, P., Michel, D., Salle, R. and Valla, J-P. (2003) *Business-to-Business Marketing.* Basingstoke: Palgrave Macmillan.

Webster, F.E. (1995) *Industrial Marketing Strategy.* New York: Wiley.

44: The Marketing of Services

Key definitions

A *service* is an intangible product involving a deed, performance or effort that cannot be stored or physically possessed.

Service characteristics include intangibility, a direct organization–client relationship and inseparability, consumer participation in the production process and complexity.

The *marketing mix for services* includes product, price, promotion and place, but additionally people, physical evidence and process.

Service quality is a customer's perception of how well a service meets or exceeds expectations.

Key issues

- The marketers of services have a challenging marketing remit owing to the core characteristics of the services product, notably its intangibility and dependence on people. The services marketer must manage an extended marketing mix, comprising '7Ps' of people, physical evidence and process, alongside the traditional ingredients of product, price, promotion and place.
- It is imperative that service quality is maintained, requiring a thorough understanding of customer needs and expectations; the setting and policing of service quality criteria; careful employee recruitment, training, motivation and control; plus the management of operational factors affecting service provision.
- All marketers strive to create differentiation for their products, clear brand positioning and a differential advantage over competitors' products. Owing to the nature of services, for marketers handling services, these tasks are particularly important but they are prone to immense difficulties.
- Branding, distinctive positioning and control of personnel are central to the effective marketing of services. An appreciation of the additional marketing mix ingredients (people, physical evidence or ambience and the process of transaction) is also an essential requisite.

Conceptual overview

The marketing of services is difficult owing to the characteristics of the service product, the need to ensure service delivery quality, the complexity of branding the intangible, plus the increased difficulty in creating a differential advantage or competitive edge for a service. The marketer's definition of product includes physical goods, services and ideas. Services differ from other products in marketing because of the core characteristics of the service product: intangibility, a direct organization–client interaction and inseparability, consumer participation in production, and complexity (cf. Brief 19).

Services marketers realized many decades ago that people are integral to the service product and that people should be a fifth ingredient of the marketing mix. The marketers of consumer and business-to-business products have since emulated their colleagues in services and have also incorporated people in their marketing mixes. In addition to people, services marketers have added physical evidence or ambience and process to the marketing mix for services, which is then the '7Ps':

- People
- Physical evidence
- Process
- Product
- Price
- Promotion
- Place

A customer in a bank may be withdrawing cash, paying bills, enquiring about a mortgage, arranging life assurance or negotiating a loan. The bank, be it ABM Amro, HSBC or Lloyds TSB, will have a range of products to offer such a customer, all branded and promoted extensively through promotional mix activity. To the customer in the branch at the moment of enquiry, however, the 'product' is only as good, appealing and effectively positioned as the bank staff offering the advice, guidance and providing the customer service. The customer also will be keenly aware of the surrounding ambience and of how easy and straightforward the enquiry process has been. In this situation, as in most services, the additional ingredients of the services marketing mix will be pivotal in the customer's perception of product quality and ultimately in the level of customer satisfaction experienced. The traditional marketing mix ingredients of product, price, promotion and place, are also important. The services marketer has a much broader marketing mix to specify, action and control than the marketer of consumer or business-to-business products.

Marketers must devote significant management time and resources to controlling service quality. This involves: (a) properly understanding customer expectations; (b) thoroughly specifying service quality criteria; (c) monitoring the delivery of the service, benchmarked against these criteria; (d) employee performance control, motivation and remedial activity; plus (e) management's control of the service's operational requirements.

A core aim of marketing is achieving product/brand differentiation with a real or perceived differential advantage/competitive edge (cf. Briefs 14 and 35). For any product this is difficult, but in services the characteristics of the service product and transaction add to the complexity of the task. Once achieved, a differential advantage and differentiation are hard to sustain, owing to low barriers to entry and the problems of protecting an intangible product. The reasons are simple but varied:

1 No product differentiation.
2 No patent protection.
3 Few barriers to entry: easy for competitors to enter and to copy.
4 Difficult to control the customer interface.
5 Problems of growth: key personnel can only be spread so far.
6 Irregular service quality, largely resulting from human activity.
7 Difficult to improve productivity and lower the cost to the consumer.
8 Problems in innovation: services can be copied and are 'people-based'.
9 Restrictive regulations, particularly in the professions.

The key implication is that marketing in services has had to adopt all the key practices from consumer and business-to-business marketing, in particular the development of brands, clear product differentiation, strong promotional imagery and brand identity. This has been true for many years in the financial services sector and tourism industry, but is growing in other sectors, ranging from leisure and health through to education and government units. Branding, distinctive positioning *vis-à-vis* rivals and control of personnel are pivotal to the success of most services businesses.

Examples

Express Carriers

Companies offering express carrying services such as UPS, Federal Express and TNT are involved in so much more than simply delivering letters and packages. As competitiveness in the sector has increased, company buyers' expectations have also risen. Now they are looking for a proposition based on a finely tuned process that offers a range of value added services. In addition to providing the likes of express delivery, bar-coded tracking and customs clearance, many customers expect their carriers to respond to customer queries, handle inventory and even become involved in the packing process. Some aspects of this enhanced service offer have been made possible by improvements in information technology. Now both buying and supplying parties are able to use the Internet to keep tabs on their packages, from the point of dispatch to the point of receipt.

(*Source:* 'Value-added takes on a new meaning', *Purchasing*, 120 (15 February 1996), pp. 68–9)

Club Med

For Club Med, which offers resort-based holidays at over 100 locations, the service proposition is based upon transporting customers from their busy lives to a calm and enjoyable atmosphere, in a variety of exotic locations. A particular strategic objective for the company is also to ensure that customers keep coming back to its holiday villages. According to Club Med's research, a typical visitor will enjoy five visits to the company's resorts. These figures highlight the importance of customer loyalty to the company, and help explain why Club Med goes to so much trouble to encourage re-visiting.

Loyalty to the company's particular style of holidays is achieved in a variety of ways. First, visitors to Club Med resorts pay a small joining fee and annual subscription to become members of the holiday company's club. Thereafter, they receive regular information about the company's resorts, together with discount offers and newsletters. This helps increase visitors' feelings of involvement with the brand. Club Med also ensures continuity of its service offer by making certain that each of its villages shares certain similar characteristics, irrespective of where they are located. Good weather, natural beauty, tranquillity and the potential for recreation (e.g. for water sports), are just some of the required features. The Club Med concept is also based on the notion of social interaction and guests are strongly encouraged to mix with other visitors, both at mealtimes and during sporting and other recreational activities. Finally, the company's promotional material emphasizes that its holidays are good value, with guests paying an all-inclusive price for facilities and meals. This feature, the company believes, helps further accentuate feelings of detachment from the hustle and bustle of everyday life.

(*Source:* M. Kotabe and K. Helsen, 'Club Med: The party is over', in *Global Marketing Management*, New York: Wiley, 2001, pp. 633–8)

Test yourself

Case question

1 In what ways has Club Med attempted to develop a distinctive holiday product?

Quick questions

2 Why is the services marketing mix extended?
3 Using appropriate examples to illustrate your answer, explain the elements of the marketing mix for services.

Applied question

4 Assume that you work for an international advertising agency and are responsible for a leading hotel operator's account. Your team is trying to develop an advertising campaign that focuses on the *people*, *physical evidence* and *process* aspects of the hotel offer. You are required to make a presentation to the hotel company's board of directors explaining why you have chosen to focus on these aspects. What information should your presentation cover?

Extra readings

Gilmore, A. (2003) *Services Marketing and Management*. London: Sage.
Gronroos, C. (2000) *Service Management and Marketing*. Chichester: Wiley.
Kasper, H., van Helsdingen, P. and de Vries Jr, W. (1999) *Services Marketing Management: An International Perspective*. Chichester: Wiley.
Lovelock, C.H. (2001) *Principles of Services Marketing and Management*. Englewood Cliffs, NJ: Pearson.
Palmer, A. (2000) *Principles of Services Marketing*. Maidenhead: McGraw-Hill.
Zeithaml, V. and Bitner, J. (2002) *Services Marketing*. New York: McGraw-Hill.

45: Non-Business Marketing

Key definitions

Non-business marketing activities are conducted by individuals or organizations to achieve goals other than profits, return on investment or possibly market share.

A *target public* is a collection of individuals with an interest in or concern about an organization, a service or a social cause.

Not-for-profit marketing is the application of marketing practices for organizations endeavouring to appeal to target markets but without profit motives.

Social marketing is the use of marketing to influence the acceptability of ideas or principles.

Key issues

- Many non-commercial organizations practise marketing, notably in the public sector, utility and voluntary sectors.
- There are two categories of not-for-profit marketing: (a) not-for-profit and (b) social marketing. Not-for-profit is the application of marketing practices for organizations such as hospitals and colleges, which still endeavour to appeal to target markets but do not have profit motives. Social marketing is the use of marketing to influence the acceptability of social ideas, such as waste recycling or care in the community.
- The exchange in the marketing transaction within non-business marketing stems from negotiation and/or persuasion, rather than a monetary exchange for a product. The exception is the exchange of money implicit in a charitable donation.
- The aim of non-business marketing is to obtain a desired response from a target market, whether it is the acceptance of an idea, awareness of an institution or charitable donation. It is important a non-business marketer understands the mission of the organization and that this is communicated to the target market.
- Target marketing differs from that deployed in commercial organizations practising market segmentation, in that often many diverse target publics must be served and satisfied.
- The marketing mix is quite different from that developed for a commercially marketed product. The product will be generally an idea or service, distribution will be often direct, price is more likely to be a donation or opportunity cost rather than monetary value, promotion will be varied and pivotal, with the additional ingredients of the services marketing mix tending to be very important.

Conceptual overview

Not all marketing occurs in commercial entities seeking to make profits or increase their market share. In recent years the charity sector has adopted the principles of marketing to good effect, as have utilities (not-for-profit ones still exist outside the UK), health and education. The use of marketing in these, and many more non-business sectors, requires some modification to the core practices prevalent in consumer goods, commercial services and business-to-business organizations. Non-business marketing takes two forms: (a) not-for-profit marketing, such as in charities or public sector bodies and (b) social marketing, when the intention is to successfully convey and market an idea or principle.

Target publics are the target markets for non-business marketers: those individuals or organizations with an interest in an organization, its cause or its product. Client publics are the direct consumers of the organization's activity, while general publics are the indirect consumers. A hospital's client publics are its patients and staff, while its general publics are the relatives of its patients and the community in general.

The marketing mix tends to be different from that devised by most commercial businesses. The product often is an idea or a service, rather than a physical good, and therefore reflects the aspects of the services marketing product (cf. Briefs 19 and 44). The product tends to be difficult to specify, but thought must be devoted to identifying the benefit being offered to the target publics. Promotion is an important part of the marketing mix in order to convey the benefit and mission of the organization or idea, but available budgets typically are not large. Publicity, personal selling (often by volunteers), direct mail and sales promotions in the form of competitions and demonstrations, dominate the promotional mix. Distribution channels tend to be direct, not requiring the services of marketing intermediaries. Price is more likely to be in the form of a voluntary donation or the time given up to support the activity, than a monetary price. The people, physical evidence and process ingredients of the services marketing mix invariably will be important (cf. Brief 44).

Without a tangible product or commercial operating structures, it is difficult for managers to control the marketing activities inherent in non-business marketing. Control is designed to identify activities that have taken place and ensure these reflect the mission of the organization and the intentions of its leadership. Corrective action, as in any marketing situation, may be required if there is not a good fit between actions and strategic intent. The standards against which performance is judged must reflect the ethos and goals of the non-business organization.

Examples

Shelter

Some non-business organizations are turning to the commercial sector for help with their marketing activity. Shelter, the charity that highlights the plight of the homeless, previously used other agencies before signing up Saatchi & Saatchi to guide its advertising. One of the first outputs was a London-based poster campaign designed to draw attention to the paucity of cheap accommodation in the area. Efforts to raise awareness are just part of the Shelter story. The charity also has housing aid centres and runs a 24-hour telephone helpline aimed at people with housing problems. In addition, Shelter organizes appeals in support of those needing its services. Marketing plays an important role in drawing attention to these services and to the plight of the individuals Shelter supports.

(*Source:* Mark Kleinman, 'Shelter picks Saatchis for "hardship" ad work', *Marketing*, 15 February 2001, p. 5)

Red Nose Day

Comic Relief's *Red Nose Day* is a biennial fund-raiser featuring the best of comedy and enjoying the support of a large number of well-loved comedians and other celebrities. During the event, comedians and celebrities take over a television channel for the evening, screening a mix of entertainment, fund-raising events and poignant pieces relating to some of the charity's good causes. Members of the public are also encouraged in the weeks and months running up to *Red Nose Day* to organize their own fund-raisers. Over the years, the event has proved to be a popular feature with the public. In 1999, around £35 million was raised in total. The 2001 and 2003 events exceeded this sum. One-third of the money goes to UK-based projects, with the rest heading for Africa. Over £250 million has been raised since the charity first started in 1985.

The public can make their donations to the Comic Relief cause in a variety of ways. With over 15 000 volunteers manning 7000 telephone lines, coordinated from 99 call centres, this is not-for-profit marketing on a large scale. In addition, donations can be made through certain high street retail outlets, by post and over the Internet via the Comic Relief website, which is capable to dealing with around 200 donations every minute. The marketing activity associated with this major event is not confined to Red Nose Day itself. Indeed, Comic Relief has its own Marketing Director and it is difficult to avoid the numerous television trailers and print advertisements featured in the run-up to the entertaining evening. When coupled with the strong word-of-mouth communication and excitement leading up to the event, this is a powerful illustration of the relevance of marketing in non-business organizations.

(*Sources:* Joanna Witt, 'Comic touch', *Marketing*, 15 March 2001, p. 15; www.payrollgivingonline.org.uk, 2004; BBCi, 2004)

Test yourself

Case question

1 Outline some marketing objectives for Comic Relief. How might these differ from the marketing objectives of a commercial organization?

Quick questions

2 What is non-business marketing?
3 Give three different examples of non-business organizations and for each say what the marketing objective might be.

Applied question

4 As Marketing Director for an education establishment, you have years of experience of marketing in the not-for-profit sector. You have recently recruited a Marketing Manager to help with the preparation of promotional materials for your college. The new recruit has a background in the marketing of consumer goods, so is unfamiliar with the education sector. You decide to have a meeting to outline the key differences between commercial and non-business marketing. Prepare some notes to identify the areas you intend to cover.

Extra readings

Adkin, S. (1999) *Cause-Related Marketing*. Oxford: Butterworth-Heinemann.
Gronroos, C. (2000) *Service Management and Marketing*. Chichester: Wiley.
Hill, E., O'Sullivan, T. and O'Sullivan, C. (2003) *Creating Arts Marketing*. Oxford: Butterworth-Heinemann.
Lovelock, C.H. (2001) *Principles of Services Marketing and Management*. Englewood Cliffs, NJ: Pearson.
Palmer, A. (2000) *Principles of Services Marketing*. Maidenhead: McGraw-Hill.
Zeithaml, V. and Bitner, J. (2002) *Services Marketing*. New York: McGraw-Hill.

46: Retail Marketing

Key definitions

Retailing is all transactions in which the purchase is intended to be consumed by consumers through personal, family or household use.

Retailers are businesses that purchase products for the purposes of re-selling to consumers in order to make a profit.

Non-store retailing is the selling of goods or services outside the confines of a retail facility.

Direct retailing is the omission in the marketing channel of retail stores, with suppliers or e-retailers instead utilizing the tools of direct marketing to interact with prospective customers.

Key issues

- Retailers provide place utility by having products where consumers want to buy them; time utility by trading at times when consumers want to buy; possession utility by facilitating transfer of ownership or use of products to consumers; or form utility, in the case of retail services.
- Retail locations include the central business district (CBD) or traditional town centre hub, suburban shopping centres, edge-of-town centres, retail parks or retail villages (often based on crafts or selling seconds and discontinued lines). In any shopping centre, the prime pitch is the area with the principal shops, highest customer footfall and peak rents or land values.
- Major store types include department and variety stores; hypermarkets, superstores and supermarkets; discount sheds and category killers; warehouse clubs; speciality shops; factory outlets; markets and cash and carry warehouses; plus catalogue showrooms.
- The standard categories of retailing include most merchandise categories, such as groceries, clothing, furniture and so forth, but also in-home retailing, non-store retailing, mail order and automatic vending.
- Non-store retailing is retail activity outside the confines of a store. Mail order retailing has witnessed renewed fortunes in recent years. E-commerce and the growth of direct marketing have added an extra dimension to retailing, with on-line retailers growing in number, doing without the need for physical stores and shops.
- Franchising is an arrangement whereby the franchisor or supplier grants a franchisee or dealer the right to sell the franchisor's products in exchange for a payment. Franchising is commonly used to initiate rapid expansion or to take advantage of non-domestic opportunities. Many branches of Benetton and McDonald's are franchised.
- The core strategic issues in retailing include location, property ownership versus leasing, product assortment decisions, retail brand positioning, in-store atmospherics, store image, scrambled merchandising, the use of retail technology such as EPoS and inventory control, CRM systems and

loyalty cards, the coordination of available marketing channels, the balance of power with suppliers, regulation of company ownership, the growth of e-retailing, and the trend towards global retailing.

- The extended marketing mix for services, notably people, physical evidence and the process of transaction, are particularly important to retail marketers.

Conceptual overview

Retail marketing involves managing marketing activity in the retail sector. Retailing is where the purchase is intended to be consumed by consumers through personal, family or household use, and involves: (a) retail stores or (b) non-store retailing. Retail stores include the large mixed retailing department and variety stores; hypermarkets, superstores and supermarkets; discount sheds; traditional speciality shops; markets and cash carries; and recently, warehouse club outlets, factory outlets and catalogue showrooms. Non-store retailing is the selling of goods or services outside the confines of a retail facility through mail order, in-home retailing or increasingly via e-commerce. The growth of the Internet and dot.com businesses has increased the use of direct marketing by retailers, many of which do not require retail stores.

Retailers are businesses that purchase products for the purposes of re-selling them to consumers in order to make a profit. Mail order and automatic vending are also classed as being part of retailing. Retailers provide: (a) place utility, by having products where consumers want to buy them; (b) time utility, by trading at times when consumers want to buy; (c) possession utility, by facilitating transfer of ownership or use of products to consumers; and (d) form utility, in the case of retail services – such as hairdressers, dry cleaners or restaurants – which 'do' something to or for the consumer.

Retail stores tend to cluster together in order to attract sufficient customer traffic, in traditional town centre (central business district) locations, suburban shopping centres, edge-of-town, on retail parks or in retail villages. The standard categories of retailing include:

- Food and grocery
- Men's and women's wear
- Children's wear
- Footwear and leather goods
- Chemist/druggist
- Books and greetings cards
- CTN (confectionery, news and tobacco)
- Furniture, carpets and soft furnishings
- Toys

- Music and computer games
- Jewellery
- Off-licence beverages
- Electrical (appliances, brown and white goods)
- Hardware and DIY (do-it-yourself)
- Mixed retail business

Often included are:

- Restaurants, cafes and catering
- Mail order
- Hotels
- In-home retailing
- Automatic vending
- Banking and financial services
- Telemarketing

Fundamental strategic issues in retailing include:

- The use of franchising – many brands are franchised to other businesses who run stores or retail merchandise carrying the well-known franchised brand.
- The types of locations to occupy – expensive city centre prime pitches, secondary sites, edge-of-town retail parks or free-standing superstores.
- Property portfolio ownership – whether to acquire (own) or rent sites, with the associated financial implications.
- Product assortment (mix) decisions (cf. Briefs 15 and 17) – how far to extend or diversify.
- Retail brand positioning, store image and in-store atmospherics – retailers devote significant attention and resources to developing differentiated and desirable brand identities.
- Scrambled merchandising – the addition of unrelated products to the product mix.
- The use of retail technology – such as EPoS and inventory management tools, CRM systems and loyalty schemes (cf. Brief 8), and in-store displays.
- Channel coordination – how to harness the possibilities of e-commerce alongside more traditional channels.
- Regulation – increasing government regulation over monopoly ownership.
- Supply chain power – the balance of power and/or cooperation between retailers and their suppliers.
- Global retailing – more and more retail companies are acquiring businesses in other countries or spreading their brands into new territories through organic growth.

The growth of direct marketing and e-commerce are currently major strategic issues. Some retailers have embraced e-commerce alongside their store networks, while others have opted to focus on either stores or Web-based selling but not both. Some have integrated available channels through 'callnet retailing': orders made on line or via direct TV are collected in-store. As with any other type of marketing activity, retail marketers must understand their markets, customer needs and competitive pressures; develop clear target market strategies and well considered brand positionings; and devote a great deal of attention to their marketing mix, which is the extended services marketing mix (cf. Brief 44). People, physical evidence (in-store atmospherics) and processes are particularly important. These issues are just as pertinent to non-store retailers as to retail chains utilizing stores.

Examples

Tesco *Clubcard*

Even Tesco, the UK's market leading supermarket, needs to ensure that it keeps its customers satisfied. The company's loyalty programme, *Clubcard*, has played an important part in this process, providing the focal point for Tesco's marketing activity. Estimates suggest that 14 million individuals from 10 million households have a Tesco *Clubcard*. Under the scheme, customers receive points according to their shopping expenditure. These points can be exchanged for a variety of leisure activities and gifts. Once customers achieve a certain number of points within a particular reward period, they are rewarded further, this time by becoming a *Clubcard Key Holder* or *Premium Key Holder*. These privileges provide access to a further range of offers and gifts. In return, Tesco builds both customer loyalty and its database about its customers and their spending behaviour. This in turn enables Tesco to fine-tune its merchandising and its marketing communications, while cementing its position as the UK's dominant retailer. As Tesco expands into Asia-Pacific and central Europe, there are plans to use Clubcard in Tesco's burgeoning overseas markets.

(*Sources:* Mark Kleinman, 'Tesco to offer profiles of Clubcard customers', *Marketing*, 8 February 2001, p. 8; Tesco Clubcard marketing material; Tesco website, 2004; Tim Mason, Tesco plc)

New Look

Originally founded in 1969, New Look has enjoyed considerable recent success in fashion retailing. By 1998, the once small chain had acquired 200 sites, enjoyed expansion into France with Mim and been floated on the Stock Exchange. Now there are over 500 UK stores, close to 150 in France and annual sales of £650m. Operating at the value end of ladies' fashion and aimed primarily at trendy teenagers and women in their twenties or thirties, the company has achieved a steady increase in market share. New Look now has 13% brand share of the wallets of 12- to 45-year-old women in the UK, according to Millward Brown Research. This puts New Look ahead of rivals such as Next (10% share), Dorothy Perkins (9%), Top Shop (9%) and M&S (7%), built on the back of a strong low price proposition and continually changing stock to reflect the latest fashion trends.

However, at the start of 2000, some industry pundits were suggesting that New Look had lost some of its edge. A blip in profits was put down to the fact that the retailer had been offering too many overlapping designs, thus watering down its trendy personality. There have also been suggestions that the business relied too strongly on price promotions at a time when other discount retailers abounded. In this respect, it was crucial that New Look continued to be able to differentiate itself from the likes of value-based rivals such as Matalan and TK Maxx.

In an attempt to revive its fortunes, New Look management looked at a variety of initiatives associated with its stores and product range. Among the suggestions were plans to increase store size, improve in-store atmospherics and ambience, plus the addition of more variety in the products on offer. For example, the company considered adding a range of lifestyle goods to its other lines. However, in a market dominated by intense competition, the key for New Look was to ensure that any mooted changes would not damage aspects of the retailer's brand previously so popular with consumers. In redesigning its stores, up-dating merchandising and improving store ambience, while preferring high street and mall locations, New Look has proved the pundits wrong by achieving record sales and increasing profit margins. By refreshing its marketing mix so successfully, New Look has remained true to its fashion at low prices ethos. Unlike many competing retail brands, New Look has managed to achieve a broad appeal, with 37% of customers under the age of 20, 32% between 20 and30, and 31% over 30.

(*Sources:* Verdict on Womenswear Retailers, 2001; Harriet Marsh, 'Why New Look must take stock', *Marketing*, 29 March 2001, p. 17; www.newlook.co.uk, 2004)

Test yourself

Case question

1 Why are the atmospherics and layout of fashion retailers such as New Look so important?

Quick questions

2 Why must retailers determine their store location with care?
3 Does the importance of atmospherics vary for different types of retail outlet?

Applied question

4 As a consultant specializing in retailing, you are preparing a report to explain how the retail marketing mix is changing. What areas would you explore in your report and why?

Extra readings

Fernie, J., Moore, C. and Fernie, S. (2003) *Principles of Retailing.* Oxford: Butterworth-Heinemann.

Ghosh, A. (1997) *Retail Management.* Orlando, FL: Dryden.

Gilbert, D. (2002) *Retail Marketing Management.* Harlow: Pearson/FT.

Hasty, R.W. and Reardon, J. (1996) *Retail Management.* New York: McGraw-Hill.

Howe, S. (2002) *Retailing in the European Union.* London: Routledge.

Jones, R. and Murphy, D. (2002) *Retail Therapy.* Basingstoke: Palgrave Macmillan.

McGolderick, P.J. (1997) *Retail Marketing.* Basingstoke: McGraw-Hill.

Varley, R. (2001) *Retail Product Management.* London: Routledge.

47: Social Responsibility in Marketing

Key definitions

Social responsibility is an organization's obligation to maximize its positive impact and minimize its negative impact on society.

Reaction strategy is a business's decision to allow a condition or potential problem to go unresolved until the public learns about it.

Defence strategy is a business's decision to try to minimize or avoid additional obligations linked to a problem.

Accommodation strategy is a business's decision to take responsibility for its actions when encouraged by special interest groups or threatened by government intervention.

Proactive strategy is a business's decision to assume responsibility for its actions and respond to accusations made against it without outside pressure or the threat of government intervention.

Green marketing is the specific development, pricing, promotion and distribution of products that do not harm the environment. It is a response to the increasingly popular green movement and consumers' growing concerns.

Key issues

- More and more businesses are developing policies to ensure their commercial activities do not harm the broader community.
- Corporate responsibilities include economic (be profitable), legal (obey the law), ethical (be ethical) and philanthropic (be a good corporate citizen). Social responsibility is a recent extension of these corporate responsibilities.
- Not all organizations are so enlightened, instead choosing to adopt either a reactive or defence strategy to social responsibility issues. The former involves denial and a failure to face up to responsibilities, while a defensive approach entails a marked avoidance to fully address a problem or face up to the consequences.
- A far better approach is to be aware of problems or endeavour to avoid them occurring. The unexpected, though, can never be totally pre-empted. A business can choose to accommodate an emerging problem by responding positively and willingly to external pressure to rectify a situation it has caused or to which it has contributed in part.
- Without any external pressure from consumers, stakeholders, lobbyists or government, a fully socially responsible business will opt to face up to a problem and rectify the situation with a proactive strategy.
- A specific sub-set of social responsibility is *green marketing*, created in part by the pressure of consumers who are committed to increasing environmental awareness and bringing about changes in production and marketing consumption in order to safeguard the natural environment.

Conceptual overview

Marketing ethics (cf. Brief 48) concern the separate decisions and acts of individual managers. Social responsibility refers to a business's obligation to strive to have a positive impact on society. Retailers refusing to stock GM-modified foods until consumers have been shown they are safe is an example of a set of businesses acting in an overtly socially responsible manner. Organizations must balance their commercial objectives with a need to avoid acting in a manner that may jeopardize the environment or external groups. Businesses have an obligation to be profitable, to obey the law, be ethical and to be good corporate citizens. Social responsibility is a recent extension of these corporate responsibilities.

Consumer issues and lobbying groups promoting consumer rights have done much in recent years to create awareness of social responsibility issues. These include safety, employment conditions, pollution, as well as terms and conditions of purchases. Many organizations now recognize they are part of the broader community and that it is to everyone's benefit if they 'put something back'. McDonald's support of family accommodation near children's hospitals or Tesco's computer vouchers for local schools, are examples. A more dramatic aspect of social responsibility has been the upsurge of green marketing, with many businesses developing products, marketing mix programmes and manufacturing processes with the intention of safeguarding the planet and reducing any harmful impact on the environment. The rapid growth of low-emission fuels for vehicles, or LPG and electric cars, is an example of green marketing.

There are four basic strategies for social responsibility in marketing:

- Reaction: a business adopting this strategy does nothing until forced to after someone finds out what it has done. It will typically then react by denying knowledge or blame and trying to appease individual victims privately.
- Defence: once a problem has arisen – under this strategy a business minimizes additional obligations and strives to contain the problem through legal moves and lobbying.
- Accommodation: a business assumes responsibility and endeavours to rectify the problem. After all, unanticipated problems do occur, so there is no need to pretend otherwise.
- Proactive: this strategy sees a business respond to a problem and rectify the situation when feasible without external pressure to do so. The most enlightened and socially responsible of the possible strategies.

It is open to debate which of these is preferable: many would argue for accommodation or proactive approaches. Even with these approaches, a business may need to adopt a defence strategy also under certain circumstances. The reactive stance is not desirable.

Examples

Body Shop

The first Body Shop store was opened in Brighton in 1976. The outlet's founder, Anita Roddick, built the retail concept around the belief that businesses must be socially responsible and accountable for their actions. This vision is reflected in all aspects of the Body Shop's marketing and trading practices. The cosmetics on sale are made from biodegradable, natural ingredients. Packaging is recyclable and animal testing is taboo. There is an emphasis on educating customers about the products and how they are made. The business pursues trade opportunities which do not exploit the poor or under-privileged and has been active in setting up trade exhibitions and sponsoring events that boost local economies around the world. As part of Body Shop's *Trade Not Aid* programme, Roddick has travelled extensively to identify socially responsible trade opportunities. The business also supports a number of environmental good causes, including those that protect the rain forests and support endangered species. Roddick is currently exposing sweat-shop labour used in developing economies to produce big brands' clothing products. Human rights are part of the Body Shop corporate ethos, as are concerns for the sustainability of the natural environment. However, the company is proactive in developing programmes and business practices that enable it to have a clear conscious. How many other businesses may claim to have similar codes?

(*Sources:* Amanda Wilkinson, 'Cause for Concern', *Marketing Week*, 11 February 1999, pp. 28–31; David Benady and Amanda Wilkinson, 'Nestle Acts to Boost its Corporate Image', *Marketing Week*, 13 May 1999, p. 26; www.thebodyshop.com, 2004)

Ben & Jerry's

The zany flavours of Ben & Jerry's ice cream have become a familiar sight in supermarket freezer cabinets. Set up by Ben Cohen and Jerry Greenfield, this multimillion dollar success story is based on a socially responsible corporate mission: 'We're not part of the economic machine that makes profits and oppresses people. We think there should be a spiritual aspect to business. As we help others, we cannot help but help ourselves.' This underlying philosophy has shaped the 'caring capitalism' which is at the heart of how the business operates. The philosophy extends to Ben & Jerry's concern for the local, national and international community, as well as to its own employees.

Now that the Ben & Jerry's operation is owned by the mighty Unilever (Wall's, Ola etc.), it remains to be seen the extent to which these founding business ethics and socially responsible practices will hold fast. Certainly the signs are that the company's mission has remained intact, as described on the company's website:

> Ben & Jerry's is founded on and dedicated to a sustainable corporate concept of linked prosperity:
>
> 1 To make, distribute and sell the finest quality all-natural ice cream and euphoric concoctions with a continued commitment to incorporating wholesome, natural ingredients and promoting business practices that respect the Earth and the Environment.
> 2 To operate the Company on a sustainable financial basis of profitable growth, increasing wealth of our stakeholders and expanding opportunities for development and career growth for our employees.
> 3 To operate the company in a way that actively recognizes the central role that business plays in society by initiating innovative ways to improve the quality of life locally, nationally and internationally.

Central to the mission of Ben & Jerry's is the belief that all three parts must thrive equally in a manner that commands deep respect for individuals in and outside the company and supports the communities of which they are a part.

The company, therefore, is involved in many charitable causes and attempts to offer economic opportunities to people deprived of them, to minimize waste problems caused by its manufacturing, to support sustainable farming and production methods of its ingredients, to support non-violent ways of achieving peace and justice, and to demonstrate respect for people inside and outside the business.

(*Sources*: Ferrell, O.C. and Fraedrich, J., *Business Ethics*, Boston, MA: Houghton Mifflin, 1997; Ben & Jerry's website, 2004)

Test yourself

Case question

1 Ben & Jerry's stance on social responsibility issues is summarized above. Why is this stance so important to the company's success?

Quick questions

2 Explain what is meant by social responsibility in marketing.
3 Explain the key differences between ethics and social responsibility in marketing.

Applied question

4 Assume the role of a newspaper reporter. Your editor has asked you to prepare a feature that focuses on how businesses are handling social responsibility issues in their marketing. Using a range of examples, prepare a report that explains how businesses are dealing with social responsibility issues. You should consider *reaction*, *defence*, *accommodation* and *proactive* strategies for dealing with social responsibility concerns.

Extra readings

Charter, M. and Polonsky, M.J. (1999) *Greener Marketing: A Global Perspective on Greener Marketing Practice.* Sheffield: Greenleaf.

Dibb, S., Simkin, L., Pride, W. and Ferrell, O.C. (2001) *Marketing: Concepts and Strategies.* Boston, MA: Houghton Mifflin.

Goldberg, M.E., Fishbain, M. and Middlestadt, S.E. (eds) (1997) *Social Marketing: Theoretical and Practical Perspectives.* Mahwah, NJ: Lawrence Erlbaum Associates.

Ferrell, O.C. and Fraedrich, J. (2000) *Business Ethics.* Boston, MA: Houghton Mifflin.

Manley II, W.W. (1992) *The Handbook of Good Business Practice.* London: Routledge.

48: Marketing Ethics

Key definitions

Marketing ethics are the moral philosophies that define right and wrong behaviour in marketing.

Moral philosophies are the rules that guide individuals and help determine their behaviour.

Corporate culture is a set of values, beliefs, goals, norms and rituals that members or employees of an organization share.

An *ethical issue* is an identifiable problem, situation or opportunity requiring an individual or organization to choose from among several actions that must be evaluated as right or wrong, ethical or unethical.

Codes of ethics are formalized rules and standards that describe what is expected of employees.

Key issues

- Well-publicized news stories concerning unethical practices have helped bring marketers' behaviour into the public domain.
- Increasing numbers of organizations are creating codes of ethics and management controls to monitor ethical issues. Most professional bodies have created codes of conduct to include ethical considerations.
- Adverse publicity resulting from unethical behaviour can seriously damage a business's or a brand's reputation.
- Marketing ethics direct good and bad behaviour in marketing and are important for safeguarding consumers, employees and other stakeholders.
- Much depends on the moral philosophies guiding individuals in an organization.
- Utilitarianism as a moral philosophy maximizes the greatest good for the largest number of people.
- Ethical formalism as a moral philosophy is based on rules of behaviour that can be consistently enforced across an organization to control an individual staff member's actions.
- Marketing ethics increasingly go hand-in-hand with the social responsibility stance adopted by a business and its marketers (cf. Brief 47).

Conceptual overview

Various high profile news stories – such as product failures causing injury, unscrupulous time-share selling, misleading sales promotions with fictitious prizes and poor consumer protection – have brought bad marketing behaviour to the attention of the general public. This, coupled with growing professionalism and standards in marketing, has led to more organizations monitoring the behaviour of their personnel and the impact of their marketing campaigns. Consumer pressure groups, such as the Consumers' Association, have similarly assessed marketers' behaviour more publicly. Although not uniform, the result has been a trend towards more concern for ethical behaviour in marketing.

There are also selfish reasons for marketers devoting greater attention to marketing ethics. Adverse publicity arising from unethical behaviour can do much harm to a brand's standing or to the company in question, creating an opportunity for competitors to exploit this weakness. Poor handling of ethical issues causes customer dissatisfaction and the public increasingly expects businesses to behave well and at the very least to do nothing that harms its customers, employees or the environment.

Moral philosophies are the rules followed by organizations or private individuals that guide their behaviour. There are two basic options:

- Utilitarianism focuses on maximizing the greatest benefit for the largest number of people. It would, under this approach, be unethical to act in a way that leads to personal gain at the expense of society in general. Does a car manufacturer made aware of a potentially flawed component re-call vehicles as a costly precaution? Or, does the manufacturer adopt a 'wait and see' stance, instead only acting after several related crashes have occurred? Most consumers would hope the car producer would act ethically and immediately instigate a product re-call, but the car manufacturer may not act in such a utilitarian manner.
- Ethical formalism adopts a different approach to marketing ethics. Under this approach, rules for behaviour are based on whether or not actions can be consistently taken as a general rule without on each occasion considering alternative options. The issue is whether or not enforceable and consistent practices can be specified, communicated and actioned repeatedly. Most marketers are influenced by their colleagues' attitudes, senior managerial practices, corporate codes of conduct and by the prevalent corporate culture: values, beliefs, goals, norms, rituals. It is unlikely unethical practices in one company will ever be identically replicated in a competing business owing to the rival business's culture and ethical stance.

Codes of ethics are being produced by increasing numbers of organizations. To be meaningful, management must take decisive action to enforce these codes of conduct. The trend nevertheless, in marketing-oriented businesses, is towards consideration of ethical issues, with practices implemented to enforce ethical behaviour. Social responsibility is also a growing concern in many Boardrooms (cf. Brief 47).

Examples

Alcopops

The UK launch of alcoholic soft drinks, which became known as 'alcopops', proved very popular with 18–24-year-olds. Before long, brands such as *Hooper's Hooch* (Bass) and *Two Dogs* (Merrydown) were firm favourites with this age group. However, consumer groups and some politicians quickly objected to the way in which these alcoholic fizzy drinks were being promoted, arguing that the marketing was, wrongly, too appealing for under-age drinkers. Before long, manufacturers like Whitbread were responding to the demands for more ethical behaviour by modifying the branding and packaging of the drinks to position them away from soft drinks aimed at youngsters. The Portman Group, the industry body responsible for promoting sensible drinking, played an important role in guiding the manufacturers' behaviour, which was modified to reflect a more utilitarian stance.

(*Source:* David Benady, 'Whitbread rejigs alcopop launch for "adult" appeal', *Marketing Week*, 9 February 1996)

Nestlé

Since 1999, Nestlé has been involved in a major public relations exercise following accusations of unethical behaviour surrounding the marketing of baby formula. That year the Advertising Standards Authority (ASA) upheld a complaint against an advertisement the company placed in a student newspaper. The advertisement, which opposed a consumer boycott of its products, was the latest round in a dispute between Nestlé and consumer pressure groups. At the heart of the fracas was a protest by the *Infant Formula Action Coalition* which opposes Nestlé's promotion of baby formula to developing nations. The pressure group highlights World Health Organization figures that suggest the deaths of 1.5 million babies each year could be prevented by reversing the trend that has seen a move away from breast feeding. Nestlé has also been accused of being slow to sign up to the 1981 International Code of Marketing of Breast-Milk Substitutes. It was only in 1984 that Nestlé agreed to comply with the code. By 1988, the company was once again falling foul of consumer groups and there were renewed calls for a consumer boycott. At this time the *International Baby Food Action Network* (IBFAN) accused Nestlé of failing to follow the code.

The reason for the ASA's ruling against Nestlé stemmed from claims in the advertisement that, '... even before the WHO International Code of Marketing Breast-Milk Substitutes was introduced in 1981, Nestlé marketed infant formula ethically and responsibly, and has done so ever since'. According to ASA, Nestlé could not support this statement. The company had, for example, continued distributing free baby milk samples in developing countries as late as 1994. As Nestlé continues the attempt to overcome consumer hostility, other businesses should beware of such ethical minefields.

(*Sources:* Amanda Wilkinson, 'Cause for Concern', *Marketing Week*, 11 February 1999, pp. 28–31; David Benady and Amanda Wilkinson, 'Nestlé Acts to Boost its Corporate Image', *Marketing Week*, 13 May 1999, p. 26)

Test yourself

Case question

1 In the Nestlé example, this multinational fell foul of consumer groups because of how it marketed baby formula. What action should Nestlé have taken to handle the concerns of the pressure groups?

Quick questions

2 What are marketing ethics?
3 Why should businesses consider marketing ethics when making marketing decisions?

Applied question

4 As marketing manager of a large furniture retailer, you have been asked to prepare a report about some of the ethical issues facing the business. Your report should consider a range of product, promotion, pricing and distribution issues.

Extra readings

Dibb, S., Simkin, L., Pride, W. and Ferrell, O.C. (2001) *Marketing: Concepts and Strategies*. Boston, MA: Houghton Mifflin.

Donaldson, T. (1992) *The Ethics of International Business.* New York: Oxford University Press.

Ferrell, O.C. and Fraedrich, J. (2000) *Business Ethics.* Boston, MA: Houghton Mifflin.

Goldberg, M.E., Fishbain, M. and Middlestadt, S.E. (eds) (1997) *Social Marketing: Theoretical and Practical Perspectives.* Mahwah, NJ: Lawrence Erlbaum Associates.

Jones, C., ten Bos, R. and Parker, M. (2004) *Business Ethics.* London: Routledge.

Megone, C. and Robinson, S.J. (2002) *Case Histories in Business Ethics.* London: Routledge.

49: Value-Based Marketing

Key definitions

Value-based marketing is the inclusion of the value of marketing strategy and marketing activity in an organization's financial analysis of shareholder value.

Marketing shareholder value analysis (SVA) divides the estimation of the value to the business created by a marketing strategy into two components: (a) the present value of cash flows during the strategizing and planning phases and (b) the continuing value of the business at the end of the planning phase.

Key issues

- Most senior managements, particularly of publicly quoted companies, focus on shareholder value as their driving performance measure. This calculation has tended to be undertaken by the finance function, excluding marketing activities.

- Many marketing activities are longer-term and resource-demanding: building up brand awareness, creating customer satisfaction, investing in emerging opportunities, competing with hostile brands. In traditional shareholder value analysis, such expenditures penalize marketing activity: profitability rises immediately if marketing budgets are slashed!

- The notion of shareholder value in marketing has been expounded in recent years in order to gain credibility for marketing's remit, but also to encourage senior managers to realize the genuine importance of marketing to the strategic drivers for the business that accelerate growth, increase profit margins over time and leverage investments. Marketing, after all, is often the visionary function that understands the marketplace and impending changes.

- Shareholder value analysis (SVA) in marketing enables the strategies and tactics of marketing to be incorporated within this financial appraisal. The value to the business of a marketing strategy is estimated, based on (a) the present value of the business during the strategizing and planning stage, and (b) the continuing value of the business after the plans have been implemented and actioned.

Conceptual overview

Most Boards of businesses focus on shareholder value as a performance goal. Until recently, marketing has focused on brand awareness, customer satisfaction, market share and profitability measures (cf. Brief 39). While these measures all impact upon shareholder value, some marketing experts argue that marketing as a discipline has failed to adequately address shareholder value and the factors of most concern to Boards of Directors. The concept of value-based marketing has recently emerged in order to rectify this inadequacy.

Effective marketing *is* seen as important by Boards and investors in larger businesses. Few directors or shareholders would disagree with marketing's desire to build long-term relationships (cf. Briefs 2 and 8), achieve competitiveness or create value to the customer and other stakeholders. However, few CEOs are marketers and marketing practitioners have failed to establish themselves in the upper echelons of very senior management. Some marketers have attempted to demonstrate their worth by persuading senior colleagues to understand the importance of satisfying customers, only to find other business functions claim, rightly, that they too help to satisfy a business's customers. Other marketers have justified their activities by showing a causal link with corporate earnings or return on capital employed. Unfortunately, a reduction in marketing expenditure is the easiest way in which a business can boost immediate-term profitability.

Modern finance, to cite value-based marketing expert Peter Doyle, is based on four principles: (a) the importance of cash flow; (b) the time value of money; (c) the opportunity cost of capital; and (d) the concept of net present value. All too often these lead to short-termism and the desire to minimize outlays. Marketing, by contrast, strives to invest in the future by building up the profile of brands, nurturing customer loyalty and seeking to combat competitors' moves. These marketing goals require expenditure.

Shareholder value analysis (SVA) divides the estimation of the value to the business created by a marketing strategy into two components: (a) the present value of cash flows during the strategizing and planning phases and (b) the continuing value of the business at the end of the planning phase, after implementation of the recommended strategy. SVA provides a means of demonstrating the contribution of marketing to the business's financial performance. This also enables marketing assets, such as marketing knowledge, brands, customer loyalty and strategic relationships, to be included in the SVA, as each can be shown to have quantifiable financial value to the business. SVA enables marketers to communicate the expected results of their marketing strategies in terms comprehended by top management. It supports marketers' requests for budgets, notably those traditionally most at risk to cost-cutting in times of reduced demand, such as advertising and marketing research.

In many organizations, the lack of a true marketing orientation has allowed the finance function to take over the notion of shareholder value analysis (SVA). By focusing on short-term profits and ignoring intangible assets, such as brand awareness and customer satisfaction, traditional accounting practices marginalize marketing activity. However, SVA can in fact bring the core strategic drivers of marketing to the fore. Until now, marketing has struggled to quantify its results to demonstrate its value. By adopting SVA, marketers can reverse this state of affairs.

SVA can help justify marketing actions in terms of their propensity to bring financial value to the business. SVA offers marketing a greater theoretical base and encourages profitable marketing investment. SVA also penalizes arbitrary cuts to the marketing budget, something encountered regularly by marketers when a company's fortunes decline suddenly. Without SVA including the work of marketers, it is not possible for senior managers to identify and develop the strategic value drivers for the business that accelerate growth, increase profit margins and leverage investments. It is likely that the incorporation within SVA of marketing and the use by marketers of SVA will increase significantly.

Examples

Vodafone

In recent years, 'dot.com' businesses have been a focus of many city analysts and investors. Leading US stockbroker Charles Schwab recognized the opportunity and launched global Internet services. In just 12 months, the business trebled its market capitalization. A decade or so ago, UK telecoms giant BT was the star of investors and mobile phone operator Vodafone was simply a UK-focused start-up business for a larger electronics company. Now, BT's share price has plummeted as investors recognize its debt mountain and its focus on non-growth markets, while Vodafone has become one of the world's largest brands and dominates global mobile telecommunications. Investors have followed Vodafone's growth and its stock market value has shot up. These examples illustrate well the fickleness of investors who seek short-term and assured returns. The need for marketers to demonstrate their worth is nicely demonstrated by Vodafone's impressive marketing strategy and business performance.

(*Sources:* Vodafone; Peter Doyle, *Value-Based Marketing*, Chichester: Wiley, 2000)

Whitbread

Whitbread is very clear about its strategic aims, as described on its website:

> Our business is focused on growth sectors of the leisure market – lodging, eating out and active leisure. Our priorities, on behalf of our shareholders,

are to grow our business and to achieve annual improvements in the return on their capital. We are doing this by:

- Growing the profitability, scale and market share of our leading brands;
- Developing new brands that have the potential to reach significant scale;
- Managing our business so that shareholder value is added to by each of our activities;
- Ensuring that each of our brands is a leader in its field for customer service;
- Becoming the employer of choice in the UK leisure industry;
- Working to meet our responsibilities to the wider stakeholders in our business, including commercial partners and the communities in which our brands operate.

A decade ago, Whitbread was one of the UK's largest operators of pubs, an activity that stemmed from the company's heritage as a brewer of beer. Now there is no involvement in what had been the core of the business, pubs and brewing. Today Whitbread is a leisure business targeting growing and emerging markets in the leisure industry. This involves:

- Hotels
  - — Whitbread operates more than 60 four-star *Marriott* hotels under franchise.
  - — *Travel Inn* is the UK's biggest hotel brand, with over 16 600 rooms in 292 budget-led hotels.
- Restaurants
  - — Whitbread is the UK's largest full-service operator, with more than 1400 restaurant outlets.
  - — Brands include *Brewers Fayre*, *Beefeater*, *Brewsters*, *Pizza Hut* in the UK and *TGI Friday's*, plus the leading coffee shop brand, *Costa*.
- Racquets, health and fitness
  - — With more than 300 000 members and 55 outlets, *David Lloyd Leisure* is the market leader in this growing sector and is also the principal commercial tennis operator, with over 500 courts.

The change of focus away from brewing was led by an analytical evaluation of the use of leisure time by consumers and by the importance of demonstrating shareholder value. The many brand champions within the Whitbread empire know that they, too, must demonstrate the value of their brand to the Board of Directors if their part of the business is to continue.

(*Source:* www.whitbread.com, 2004)

Test yourself

Case question

1 Why should Whitbread's marketers identify measures for verifying their performance that relate to creating financial value for the company's stakeholders?

Quick questions

2 What is the core reasoning behind marketing shareholder value analysis?
3 How would you sum up the notion of value-based marketing?

Applied question

4 As a financially oriented Managing Director, how would you expect your marketing colleagues to demonstrate their contribution to your business's fortunes? Outline your response with specific examples.

Extra readings

Aaker, D.A. (1999) *Managing Brand Equity.* New York: Free Press.

Black, A., Wright, P. and Bachman, J.E. (1998) *In Search of Shareholder Value.* Harlow: Pearson/FT.

Butterfield, L. (1999) 'Advertising and Shareholder Value', in *Excellence in Advertising.* Oxford: Butterworth-Heinemann.

Doyle, P. (2000) *Value-Based Marketing.* Chichester: Wiley.

Mather, S.S. and Kenyon, A. (2001) *Creating Value: Successful Business Strategies.* Oxford: Butterworth-Heinemann.

50: One-to-One Marketing

Key definitions

One-to-one marketing is the segment of one: bespoke marketing messages and propositions targeted at individual customers.

One-to-one marketing utilizes *advances in marketing databases and technology* to strive to build relationships with individual customers within target market segments.

Key issues

- Marketers have argued that neither mass marketing (an undifferentiated marketing mix aimed at the overall marketplace) nor treating individual customers uniquely was the most effective manner in which to satisfy customers or use resources. Market segmentation based on groups of customers sharing common needs and buying behaviour was the preferred route.
- Recent advances in technology have enabled better database management and the capture of information about customer characteristics and purchasing behaviour. Coupled with increasing use by customers of technology in buying (for example, e-commerce), there has been a recent move to one-to-one marketing.
- Market segmentation tends still to be deployed to identify broadly defined groups of customers, with individuals in a particular segment sharing needs and buying characteristics. The individuals within a particular market segment, though, can then be targeted with bespoke messages and marketing propositions, apparently customized to each individual.
- Different authors have adopted various terms to describe one-to-one marketing, notably the 'segment of one' or 'customer-centric marketing'. The underlying rationale stems from the basis of relationship marketing, popularized during the 1990s.
- It is likely that one-to-one marketing will grow in the near future, but is unlikely to be widespread in all markets and for all products. It is particularly prevalent in markets witnessing a growth in e-commerce, such as mail order, book and music retailing, financial services and tourism.

Conceptual overview

The benefits associated with market segmentation are numerous (cf. Brief 11). Segmentation is, therefore, strongly propounded in the academic literature and widely recognized by marketing practitioners. The principal assumption is that customers are too numerous and varied in their product needs and buying requirements to be satisfied by a single offering. Market segmentation allows businesses to satisfy this heterogeneity in a resource-effective manner. Instead of treating all customers the same with a single mass market offering, or stretching resources unrealistically to offer individual consumers bespoke marketing mixes, market segmentation groups customers into segments in which customers share similar needs, expectations and buying behaviour.

At a time when rapid developments in information technology (IT) are providing better access to usable customer data than ever before, further developments in target marketing have been possible in certain markets and product categories. Better customer information and the IT systems to capture, analyse and utilize this information (cf. Brief 8), have led to what has been termed one-to-one marketing or the segment of one. One-to-one marketing is the use of advances in marketing databases and technology to strive to build relationships with individual customers within target market segments. As with relationship marketing, an aim is to capture a greater proportion of an individual customer's purchasing by better understanding his or her evolving needs, purchasing patterns and buying behaviour, and by tailoring marketing communications to the individual.

Customers' propensity to use new media for shopping illustrates an increasing confidence and flexibility. On-line Internet shopping is growing significantly. This coincides with some customers apparently being too pressurized to engage in traditional shopping activities: time is a diminishing resource. New media are therefore altering how customers make familiar purchases. Individuals, who previously visited insurance brokers to purchase car insurance, today buy direct from one of the many telephone-based or Internet operations. Businesses booking airline flights are increasingly using the Internet, while families selecting annual holidays are buying from a wider array of marketing channels than ever before.

These developments in the marketing environment, and the subsequent impact upon consumer behaviour, are changing the way in which segments are determined and managed. In many businesses, database improvements are allowing access to a wider range of segmentation variables. In particular, the popularity of demographics and other consumer-related variables is being replaced with more sophisticated schemes built upon behavioural characteristics (cf. Brief 11). Many marketing practitioners, who see these behavioural variables as a better basis for building lasting customer relationships, have traditionally favoured such schemes. Improvements in data management technology are increasing the opportunities for segmentation based on product-related factors, such as benefits and product usage patterns. In turn, this enables marketers to more accurately hone their marketing propositions and to tailor better their marketing communications.

Taken to their logical conclusion, these advances in data capture and management allow marketers to record and respond to the needs and wants of *individual* customers. The impact of this development on market segmentation theory is potentially substantial. Now, marketers can apparently target the individual needs of customers in markets where previously it was only possible to satisfy the requirements of an entire segment or group. Marketers still define target market segments and targeting priorities, but can now adopt the practices of one-to-one marketing to appear to interact with the individual customer.

The terms *customer-centric marketing*, the *segment of one* and *one-to-one marketing* have all been used to describe this development.

The underlying rationale is that marketers can use their enhanced technological capability to capture and satisfy the needs of individual customers, rather than dealing either at the segment or mass market level. A particular attraction of the approach is that it can improve an organization's chances of building resource-rich, long-term customer relationships. Indeed, the conceptual foundations of one-to-one marketing are in relationship marketing theory (cf. Brief 2). One-to-one marketing allows partnerships to be developed between suppliers and customers and these interactions can be used as the basis for deep and adaptive relationships. This aspect of relationship marketing is currently more commonly referred to as *customer relationship management* (CRM), which uses technology-enhanced customer interaction to shape appropriate marketing offers (cf. Brief 8). One-to-one depends on using technology to achieve communication, a continuous dialogue leading to an on-going 'learning' relationship, clear incentive for such a dialogue, plus acknowledging the privacy of the customer and other demands on his/her time.

Not surprisingly, the concept of the 'segment of one' is attracting considerable academic and practitioner curiosity. Whether one-to-one marketing is market segmentation taken to its logical conclusion, or even segmentation at all, remains open to debate. After all, previous definitions of the segmentation concept have centred on the notion of a 'group' of customers or entities. According to this definition, the segment of one cannot be regarded as a segment at all. The key questions are whether the traditional view will be swept aside and to what extent the segment of one can be regarded as the new panacea of marketing. It is probable that one-to-one marketing will anyway be more appropriate for certain customers and products than others.

Examples

Amazon

Amazon, the on-line provider of books, music and other products, works hard to retain its customers. The company offers an extremely wide product range at competitive prices through a seamless and responsive shopping experience. By updating and responding to customer purchase information, Amazon is able to recommend other products customers might like to buy. In the case of books, for example, this is achieved by matching titles purchased by an individual with the buying patterns of other customers who bought the same title. Thus a customer who purchases a celebrity chef cook book might on a subsequent visit to the site be offered an alternative cooking title which proved popular with other customers buying the celebrity chef cook book. In the words of the company's Chief Executive, Amazon 'is a place where (customers) can buy anything they might want to buy on-line. This notion is that you take customers and put them at the centre of their own universe.' If customers do not frequently access the Amazon site, emails notify customers of new titles or current leading sellers that match their apparent purchasing interests. Without the IT capability to track an individual's purchases, such one-to-one marketing would not be possible.

(*Sources:* Wheatley, M. (2000) 'Amazon out of the jungle?', *Business Life*, September, pp. 54–7; Reed, D. (2000) 'Payback time', *Marketing Week*, 20 January, pp. 43–9)

Egg

When Prudential set out to develop a new kind of bank, few could have forecast the impact of *Egg* on the financial services scene. Targeted at young professionals and better-off older customers, a key objective has been to attain a slice of the burgeoning electronic sales of financial products. The new bank's operation is strongly grounded in customer relationship management (CRM) principles. As *Egg*'s website points out, this Internet bank is keen to ensure that customer encounters are managed with care, stating that, 'every conversation and interaction with a customer needs to set up the opportunity for the next'. This notion of a 'learning' relationship is a fundamental principle of customer relationship management and one-to-one marketing. The logic is clear, by remaining attuned to customer requirements, *Egg* is more likely to be ready to provide the financial products needed, at the appropriate time in an individual's life. Whether it be a first mortgage for a young single, a personal loan for a couple seeking to decorate a nursery for a first child, or pensions advice for someone in their early 40s, the ultimate success of the bank will lie partly in its ability to be able to predict and satisfy these customer needs.

Financial services companies have long had access to the kind of customer data that should make such responsiveness possible. However, it is only relatively recently that businesses such as *Egg* and *First Direct* have demonstrated the kind of versatility that genuinely flexible data capture and management make possible. Even here, there have been problems. Senior management at *Egg* could not have predicted the enormous attention that greeted its launch. The company was quickly overwhelmed by applications from prospective customers, causing initial problems with service levels. This has meant that *Egg* must continue to work hard to achieve the kind of learning relationship it seeks with its customer base of more than one million.

(*Source:* http://www.egg.com)

Test yourself

Case question

1 For what reasons must Egg develop a learning relationship with its customers? Why is a learning relationship crucial to one-to-one marketing?

Quick questions

2 What is one-to-one marketing?
3 Why is good data management essential in one-to-one marketing?

Applied question

4 You have been asked to make a presentation to your Board of Directors explaining how one-to-one marketing might be implemented in your business. Prepare a draft presentation that highlights the key points that you will cover.

Extra readings

Chaffey, D., Mayer, R., Johnston, K. and Ellis-Chadwick, F. (2000) *Internet Marketing.* Harlow: FT/Pearson.

Doyle, P. (1995) 'Marketing in the New Millennium', *European Journal of Marketing*, 29 (13), pp. 23–41.

Foley, D., Gordon, G.L., Schoebachler, D.D. and Spellman, L. (1997) 'Understanding Consumer Database Marketing', *Journal of Consumer Marketing*, 14 (1), pp. 5–19.

Gummesson, R. (2002) *Total Relationship Marketing: Rethinking Relationship Marketing Management.* Oxford: Butterworth-Heinemann.

Peppers, D. and Rogers, M. (1999) *The One-to-One Manager.* New York: Currency Doubleday.

Peppers, D. and Rogers, M. (1993) *The One-to-One Future.* London: Piatkus.

Sheth, J.N., Sisodia, R.S. and Sharma, A. (2000) 'Customer-Centric Marketing', *Journal of the Academy of Marketing Science*, 28 (1), pp. 55–66.

Stone, M. and Foss, B. (2001) *Successful Customer Relationship Marketing: New Thinking, New Strategies, New Tools for Getting Closer to Your Customers.* London: Kogan Page.

Answers to Questions in the Marketing Briefs

Answer schemes for the four set questions in each Brief. They provide an opportunity to:

- Test your knowledge
- Assess your own exam answers

Answers to Questions in the Marketing Briefs

These answers are not totally comprehensive, but they are fully complete regarding the essential themes that should be covered when addressing such questions under examination conditions. Individual tutors may have 'personal favourites' they additionally would include, but the core relevant concepts are detailed in these specimen answer schemes. Remember to use appropriate examples. However, most examiners seek primarily a clear understanding of relevant concepts and frameworks from an examination answer and not an overly-detailed discussion of an example.

Brief 1: Defining Marketing

1. Marketing is all about understanding customers in order to be able to satisfy their needs and expectations. A marketing team should, therefore, regularly undertake marketing research to gain this understanding. In the case of Nectar, this was particularly important as research identified growing consumer dissonance. Consumers were becoming overloaded with too many loyalty cards and store payment cards. Nectar grew out of such research findings in an attempt to offer customers a loyalty card accepted by many brands. Marketing research was also important in the formation of the Nectar alliance, as member brands had to be non-competing while also complementary. Two rival petrol brands could not both be members, and if BP appeals to a middle market as opposed to discount shoppers, the other partner brands had to be similarly positioned. As the alliance expands its membership, research will be required to ensure the new brands' customer profiles match those of the existing member brands.
2. Marketing has been defined in various ways – there is no single 'correct' definition. However, the ability to satisfy customers and understand their changing needs, in order to expedite the exchange of a product or service, is fundamental to any definition. In addition, the ability to create an edge over competitors, identify favourable marketing opportunities, utilize resources effectively and achieve the organization's goals, are important aspects.
3. Marketing strategy involves an understanding of the marketplace in order to prioritize opportunities. It then requires a clear specification of target markets, appropriate brand positioning and the determination of a competitive advantage over rivals. Marketers must then specify a marketing mix to implement the recommended target market strategy.
4. A business report should contain concise and clearly defined sections that reflect the characteristics of the target audience. This answer should, therefore,

be in a suitable format for the chosen example. A good business report balances brevity with sufficient explanation and detail to avoid ambiguity. The key points that the report should make in this instance are those covered in answers 2 and 3 above. There will also need to be a clear attempt to link these themes explicitly to the chosen example. This could be achieved by either including a discrete section in the report, or by citing frequent examples throughout.

Brief 2: Relationship Marketing

1 The various exponents of relationship marketing explain that in order to build on-going relationships with customers, there are additional target groups to consider. Figure 2.1 suggests a variety of these. A good answer should address each of these additional audiences, suggesting ways in which mutually beneficial relationships would benefit Chrysler. For example, Chrysler requires the backing of financial investors and analysts, which would be part of the Influence markets. This might be achieved by regular briefings and site visits with leading analysts.
2 Relationship marketing experts believe that traditional marketing focuses on the single transaction and seeking new customers. Relationship marketing develops on-going relationships with customers by focusing on links between marketing, quality and customer service and the various audiences suggested in Figure 2.1.
3 Relationship marketing hinges on the concept of on-going loyalty and seeking a greater proportion of existing customers' purchases. The focus is the lifetime value of the customer relationship rather than one-off transactions. Loyalty programmes are designed to aid customer retention.
4 Figure 2.1 explains that in addition to customers, marketers should devote time and resources to conveying their message to additional target audiences in order to facilitate on-going relationships that are mutually beneficial. The six markets model suggests six target audiences: customers, internal markets (e.g. the workforce), referral markets (e.g. brokers), supplier markets, employee (recruitment) markets and 'influence' markets (e.g. city investors). It is necessary to clearly link the discussion of these markets explicitly to the chosen example. This could be achieved by either including a discrete section in the report, or by referring to frequent examples throughout.

Brief 3: Marketing Orientation

1 At the heart of marketing orientation is the assumption that being customer focused drives organizational performance. The answer should define what is meant by marketing orientation, explaining the various other components, before focusing on the role of customer orientation in Dow. The company's innovative products gave it an initial edge over rivals. In order to maintain its market share,

the company shrewdly assessed how customers used its Ziploc bags, responding with relevant product offers. This understanding of customer usage revealed marked national differences to which Dow was able to respond.

2 Marketing orientation involves a clear customer focus, understanding and staying in touch with customer needs and buying behaviour so that appropriate product offerings can be developed. In achieving a marketing orientation, competitor orientation and interfunctional coordination are also key.

3 Research suggests that businesses with a marketing orientation enjoy enhanced business performance. By achieving customer closeness and understanding the competitive environment, companies are better placed to satisfy customers and fend off competitive threats. By contrast, a production orientation is driven by the desire to cut product costs and 'sell' products to whoever will have them. This latter approach is not necessarily conducive to developing long-term customer relationships.

4 Business presentations need to be carefully designed to reflect the requirements and characteristics of the intended audience. A good presentation balances coverage of key points with illustrative examples and sufficient explanation. The topic should be introduced to demonstrate its importance, before a systematic review of the key areas is undertaken. The presentation should end with a summary of key points and/or recommendations. Answer 2 explains the principles of a marketing orientation. A sales oriented approach involves a company devoting resource to selling as many products as it can. The focus is on maximizing the number of individual transactions rather than on building long-term customer relationships. The recommendations about how the chosen business could become more marketing orientated should be based around the requirement for a customer focus. This means getting to know the needs and buyer behaviour of the target audience. A sound appreciation of the competitive situation is also required if an appropriate competitive edge is to be developed. Finally, the importance of interfunctional coordination in achieving a marketing orientation must be considered (cf. Brief 37).

Brief 4: The Marketing Environment

1 The marketing environment is made up of the external forces that influence an organization's capability to undertake its business. In the case of F1, there are several macro forces at play. These include the social pressures of anti-smoking, regulatory pressures from the EU and British governments, the economic downturn in the Tiger Economies, plus the micro competitive pressures upon individual tobacco companies and racing teams.

2 The forces of the marketing environment create strategic windows and threats for all businesses. Companies without an understanding of such external forces are likely to suffer, while competitors that do have an appreciation are likely to gain an advantage.

3 The elements of the marketing environment generally are broken down into two categories. The macro marketing environment forces include political, legal, regulatory, societal/green, technological and economic. The micro marketing environment forces include more company specific aspects, such as types of competition, supplier power, buyer power and the influence of a business's other publics. Make sure that the answer uses the chosen examples throughout the explanation.
4 A business report should contain concise and clearly defined sections that reflect the characteristics of the target audience. This answer should, therefore, be in a suitable format for the chosen example. A good business report balances brevity with sufficient explanation and detail to avoid ambiguity. The report needs to outline what is meant by the marketing environment and what the forces might be. Certain forces are likely to be more prevalent in the airline industry, requiring detailed discussion. For example, economic factors significantly impact upon the amount of passenger traffic. Political forces, such as the Gulf War, often reduce air traffic. Current health concerns about long-haul flying are an example of a social factor. In such a highly competitive industry, inevitably the micro forces of the competitive environment will be very significant. It is important that the report demonstrates the relevance of the highlighted forces.

Brief 5: PEST and SWOT Analyses

1 A core part of marketing is the identification and analysis of emerging marketing opportunities. The SWOT analysis is one of the simpler tools marketers deploy to understand emerging opportunities and their capability to address them. The defence business in question has a strategic mission to broaden its product applications into non-defence target markets. In order to understand what opportunities there might be outside its core defence business, it is essential for this company to conduct a thorough opportunity analysis.
2 Environmental scanning is the process of collecting information about the forces of the marketing environment. Utilizing such information, marketers can conduct an opportunity analysis and endeavour to identify strategic windows.
3 The elements of the marketing environment generally are broken down into two categories. The macro marketing environment forces include political, legal, regulatory, societal/green, technological and economic. The micro marketing environment forces include more company-specific aspects, such as types of competition, supplier power, buyer power and the influence of a business's other publics. Scanning of the environment identifies emerging opportunities and allows marketers to refine their target market strategy.
4 A business report should contain concise and clearly defined sections that reflect the characteristics of the target audience. This answer should, therefore, be in a suitable format for the chosen example. A good business report balances brevity with sufficient explanation and detail to avoid ambiguity. Without a SWOT analysis, marketers are unable to concisely and thoroughly determine

be in a suitable format for the retailing example. A good business report balances brevity with sufficient explanation and detail to avoid ambiguity. Many retailers have readily adopted the practices of direct marketing. For most, this has included using the Internet as both a distribution channel and a marketing communications vehicle. Many, such as Tesco or Iceland, have set up e-commerce Web-based marketing: the use of the Internet for commercial transactions.

Brief 28: Marketing Channels

1 Many businesses are involved at only one level in the marketing channel. A producer may depend on separate organizations to distribute and retail its products. In a few situations, however, companies have adopted vertically integrated marketing channels. While this significantly adds to operational complexity and costs, it enables a vertically integrated business to maintain direct control over its product throughout the distribution chain. Fuel companies such as Shell, Esso and BP extract oil, refine it into saleable products and distribute these to their own retail outlets.

2 The group of interrelated intermediaries that direct products to customers within a channel of distribution includes businesses that all must maintain financial viability. This means they all have their own corporate goals and objectives, plus unique operational characteristics. Inevitably, the longer marketing channels tend to involve a greater number of marketing intermediaries, each displaying certain inefficiencies and exhibiting possibly conflicting objectives. For these reasons, shorter distribution channels may be seen as more efficient. However, as described in Brief 29, the intermediaries may provide specialist services: if the channel were reduced, these might be undertaken less efficiently by the few remaining players.

3 In consumer markets, the marketing channel usually involves two or more of the following stages: producer, agents or brokers, wholesalers, retailers, and then the consumer. Some products, such as confectionery, may pass through all five stages, whereas factory outlets have only two: producer direct to consumer. Any other combination is possible.

4 One of the key factors to consider would be the targeted customers' readiness to accept direct marketing. When selecting a suitable channel for a target market, a marketer should consider various factors, including: company objectives, available resources, market characteristics and expectations, competitor activity, the buying behaviour of the end-user and channel intermediaries, product attributes, plus marketing environmental forces. The marketer should also consider the appropriateness of the market coverage policy: intensive, selective or exclusive. Make sure that frequent links are made to the holiday market.

Brief 29: Wholesaling and Physical Distribution Management (PDM)

1 When selecting packaging material, companies must consider the functionality of the packaging for end-users, stockists and distributors. Packaging must protect the product, while also facilitating its easy use, storage and handling (cf. Brief 18). In addition, 'green' concerns and technological advances in materials handling must be taken into account.

2 Materials handling is the physical handling of products and is important for efficient warehousing, as well as in transport from the point of production to the point where an item is consumed. Materials handling should raise the usable capacity of a warehouse, reduce the number of times an item is handled, improve customer service and increase customer satisfaction with the product.

3 The core categories of wholesalers are merchant wholesalers, taking title to goods and assuming risks associated with ownership and stock handling (full service or limited service merchant wholesalers); agents and brokers, which are functional middlemen performing limited marketing tasks in return for a commission; and manufacturers' own sales branches and field offices.

4 A business report should contain concise and clearly defined sections that reflect the characteristics of the target audience. This answer should, therefore, be in a suitable format for the example and recipient. A good business report balances brevity with sufficient explanation and detail to avoid ambiguity. Possible transport modes for moving flowers include motor vehicles, railways, ships and inland waterways, air, and pipelines (although the last might not be too easy for flowers!). Some of the essential criteria include: cost, transit time, reliability, capability, accessibility, security, traceability and ease of operational coordination.

Brief 30: Pricing Concepts

1 Price is the value placed on the product exchanged in the marketing process. It is intrinsically linked to the consumer's perception of value for money. Price should reflect the selected brand positioning, target market characteristics, and the nature of the other marketing mix ingredients. In the case of the leading fragrance houses, a premium price is required to support the upscale brand positioning, exclusive distribution and promotional imagery adopted.

2 Pricing objectives include: corporate survival, profitability, return on investment, market share levels, cash flow, maintaining the status quo, or supporting product quality.

3 Marketers adopt either a policy of price or non-price competition. Under the former, the marketer emphasizes price in the marketing mix and endeavours to match or beat the prices set by competitors. Under a policy of non-price competition, a

marketer instead opts to emphasize other ingredients in the marketing mix rather than keen pricing.

4 The document should present information concisely in clearly defined sections. It is important that the document also reflect the characteristics of the target audience. Key factors affecting pricing include: organizational and marketing objectives, pricing objectives (cf. Answer 2), cost, the fit with other marketing mix ingredients, channel member expectations, buyers' perceptions, perceived value for money, plus competitive, legal and regulatory issues.

Brief 31: Setting Prices

1 In this market, the leading brands have built up reputations for product reliability and quality. Consumers, therefore, make a trade-off between brand-led perceived quality and the low price of retailer own-label offerings. It is also likely that a particular shopper's preferred brand will be affected by where he/she shops. Thus, Tesco shoppers may be prepared to sample an own-label can of beans, whereas a consumer who shops at one of the budget retailers may prefer to purchase a brand with which they are more familiar.

2 Fixed costs are those costs that do not vary with changes in the number of units produced or sold (e.g. factory rents). Variable costs are those costs that vary directly with changes in the number of units produced or sold (e.g. the wages for a second production shift required to meet drastically increased demand).

3 Setting prices involves eight core stages: setting objectives; assessing the target market's view of price; determining demand; analysing the relationship between demand, cost and profitability; evaluation of competitors' prices; selection of a pricing policy; developing a pricing method; and determining a specific price.

4 Price elasticity of demand is a measure of the sensitivity of demand to changes in price. For example, in Figure 31.1 in Brief 31, customers' need for electricity results in inelastic demand: quantity sold varies relatively little with price. Whereas non-essential purchases, such as cinema tickets, are very prone to changes in demand following price fluctuation. This latter phenomenon arises because consumers have plenty of choice about how they spend their leisure time and disposable income, plus cinema attendance is not an essential need. The briefing sheet prepared for the small businesses should convey these messages, taking particular care to explain relevant terms and provide examples.

Brief 32: The Marketing Mix

1 The NSPCC, as a non-business organization promoting a good cause, depends heavily on the promotional ingredient of the marketing mix. The *Full Stop* campaign included public relations, direct mail, television advertising, posters,

email requests for donations and events. The 'product' being promoted was a hard-hitting message featuring abused Action Men and Spice Girl figures to raise awareness of child cruelty. Had the NSPCC not adopted such a carefully specified marketing mix, the *Full Stop* campaign would not have been as effective.

2 The core ingredients of the marketing mix are: product, price, place (distribution) and promotion. The marketers of services, owing to the characteristics of the service product (cf. Brief 44), include three additional elements: people, physical evidence and process. Many marketers outside of the service sector have also now adopted these elements.

3 In certain situations, different managers are responsible for determining specifications for separate ingredients of the marketing mix. It is important that the composite marketing mix presented to customers is consistent, with all components meshing. For example, an upmarket restaurant would not be viable in a seedy part of town with cheap prices. Answers should refer to examples that explain why consistency between the elements is important.

4 A discussion document should contain concise and clearly defined sections that reflect the characteristics of the target audience (some assumptions may need to be made about these). Make sure the document is in a suitable format for the chosen audience and context. A good discussion document balances brevity with sufficient explanation and detail to avoid ambiguity. The focus in this answer is the traditional '4Ps' of the marketing mix, as retailers stocking the shampoo would have the onus for determining the extended marketing mix for services. The answer should examine each of the principal '4Ps', outlining the key issues. For example, pricing must reflect the company's objectives, cost base, brand positioning, customer expectations, competitors' pricing, and the need for retailers to also make a profit. Depending on the characteristics of the target market and the chosen brand positioning for the shampoo, certain retailers and channels of distribution would be more appropriate than others. Product attributes, packaging and branding would require specification, and it is possible that a customer support helpline might be provided. Promotional activity would be very important in such a competitive market, and it is highly likely that all ingredients of the promotional mix would be used.

Brief 33: Marketing Strategy

1 The Irish Industrial Development Authority (IDA) pinpointed attractive economic sectors for growth, by examining long-term economic prospects for different commercial sectors. With a focus on consumer products, electronics, health care and financial services, the IDA then identified countries with concentrations of leading international producers of such products. A roadshow and marketing campaign sought to attract these businesses to Ireland.

2 Marketing strategy indicates the specific markets towards which activities are to be targeted and the types of competitive advantage to be exploited. Implicit in the development of a marketing strategy is an analysis of marketing opportunities

and organizational assets. A target market strategy is a core element of a marketing strategy.

3 Without a marketing strategy, tactical marketing mix activity is unlikely to make optimum use of an organization's strengths and resources, will probably not achieve an organization's goals and mission, and there will be very little cohesion to a business's functions. This issue is inexorably linked with the requirements for achieving a marketing orientation (cf. Brief 3). A marketing strategy is essential for identifying which target markets to exploit, with what brand positioning and differential advantage.

4 A business report should contain concise and clearly defined sections that reflect the characteristics of the target audience, in this case, colleagues. The document should also be tailored to the industry example. A good business report balances brevity with sufficient explanation and detail to avoid ambiguity. Marketing strategy indicates the specific markets towards which activities are to be targeted and the types of competitive advantage to be exploited. A marketing strategy should identify the most beneficial market segments to target, specify the appropriate brand positioning and seek a competitive advantage over rivals. Strategic marketing planning is a process for specifying the methods and resources required to achieve an organization's goals and mission within the specified target markets, while coordinating all of a business's functions to this end. Strategic marketing planning leads to a marketing strategy that directs the tactical recommendations at the heart of a marketing plan (cf. Brief 36).

Brief 34: Competitive Forces and Strategies

1 In what has become an established market sector, there are now numerous strong players, such as O2, Orange and leader Vodafone. To enter the market on a cost basis, striving to undercut rivals, would be suicidal as the global share of Vodafone would provide scale economies that would be difficult to match. Differentiation, too, would be hard to achieve, with the existing players, notably Orange, developing highly individual brand identities that seem to have significant appeal to their targeted consumers. Focus would perhaps be a possibility, in terms of selecting niche market segments or the choice of retail partners. Note Porter's generic strategies (cf. Brief 35).

2 Marketing strategists argue that most marketing practitioners wrongly define competitors as only major like-for-like rivals. Porter argues that the threat of new entrants, substitute solutions to customers' needs, power of suppliers and buyers, plus a business's other publics, all are important aspects of the micro marketing environment (cf. Brief 4).

3 Without an understanding of competition, a marketer cannot realistically differentiate his/her products from those of competitors. Without monitoring rivals' strategies, it is not evident which rivals pose the greatest threat and how, or which competitors are the most vulnerable to attack.

4 The feature should reflect the expectations of the target audience, while presenting an informative account of the Porter framework (cf. Figure 34.1). It is important the feature reviews each of the separate components, citing examples (cf. this Brief), with a comment to the effect that most companies only monitor like-for-like direct rivals, and even then, do so poorly.

Brief 35: Competitive Advantage

1 Porter suggests the routes to competitive advantage include focusing on only tightly defined markets or products, developing cost-based advantage in order to trade on the basis of price, and differentiation. In practice, all three options are possible in this market. Small and larger manufacturers focus on niche markets (underwear for the sports enthusiast, the elderly or infirm, saucy lingerie, cross-dressers!), but only larger organizations are likely to have the scale economies to offer a cost focus. Most leading brands strive for differentiation: witness the enviable reputation of the Wonderbra.
2 Competitive advantage is the creation of a perceived or real advantage for a product or brand over rival products in the eyes of the target market.
3 There are various options available for creating a competitive advantage, including Porter's generic strategies of cost leadership, focus and differentiation. Companies also utilize their marketing assets (cf. Briefs 5 and 33), strengths (cf. Brief 5) and differential advantages to create a basis for competing. A differential advantage is an attribute of a brand, product or service, or marketing mix that is unique to one organization and desired by targeted customers.
4 A business report should contain concise and clearly defined sections that reflect the characteristics of the target audience. This answer should, therefore, be in a suitable format for the chosen example. A good business report balances brevity with sufficient explanation and detail to avoid ambiguity. The core steps include understanding the possibilities for adopting one or more of Porter's generic strategies, plus the establishment, if possible, of a differential advantage. This requires identifying the segments in a marketplace; ascertaining the needs and wants of customers in each segment; an assessment of which rivals offer these; determining rivals' strengths; assessing gaps between customers' expectations and competitors' offers; matching the organization's own capabilities and strengths with these gaps; and checking that the emerging differential advantage is plausible and able to be communicated to targeted customers.

Brief 36: Marketing Planning

1 Effective marketing planning requires a process of analysis, strategizing and tactical programme recommendations designed to achieve the determined strategy.

The management of *Crayola* identified the nature of declining sales and instigated research to understand better the needs and expectations of its target markets: children and their parents. The research findings led to a revised product mix and the move into related educational toys. The marketing plan then specified a marketing mix designed to take these new products effectively to the targeted customers.

2 Marketing planning is a systematic process involving assessing marketing opportunities, devising marketing strategies and specifying marketing objectives, determining marketing mix programmes, allocating resources and developing a plan for implementation and control. Companies practising marketing planning revise regularly their understanding of the dynamics of the marketplace, up-date strategies accordingly, and develop marketing programmes that reflect the up-to-date understanding of the marketplace and the latest strategic thinking. They tend to ruthlessly allocate resources accordingly and develop marketing controls to more effectively manage their marketing activity.

3 Marketing is often in a dynamic environment caused by market trends, the forces of the macro-marketing environment, competitor moves and fickle customers. Marketers must continually strive to stay abreast of developments and revise their strategies and tactical programmes accordingly. The marketing planning cycle (cf. Figure 36.1) enables this to be achieved, typically annually.

4 A report should contain concise and clearly defined sections that reflect the characteristics of the target audience. A good business report balances brevity with sufficient explanation and detail to avoid ambiguity. The report for the pitch should explain the benefits available from marketing planning and outline the core aspects of the analysis, strategizing and tactical programmes and controls inherent in thorough marketing planning. A suitable managerial process could be suggested, as outlined in Figure 37.2 (cf. Brief 37). This Brief outlines the essential stages of the marketing planning process, including: the analysis of markets and the trading environment; determination of core target markets; identification of a competitive advantage; statement of specific goals, objectives, priority target markets and desired brand positionings; development of marketing mix programmes; and determination of the required budgets, allocation and scheduling of tasks, plus on-going monitoring of performance.

Brief 37: Implementation and Controls

1 Without this research, the types of organizations utilizing radio could not effectively assess its worth, while those organizations not using radio as a media option in their promotional activities could not assess its potential. For all organizations, any view as to the trade-off potential between various media options would only have been subjective judgements. The on-going monitoring of promotional campaigns utilizing radio could not possibly be thoroughly evaluated without some use of research findings.

2 Too few businesses overtly attempt to control the on-going implementation of their marketing activities. Controls involve clear objectives, on-going monitoring of performance, remedial actions as required, as well as managerial and operational processes designed to facilitate the implementation of marketing recommendations.
3 The common barriers relate to poor managerial practices and processes, managerial culture and resource utilization. The most frequently cited impediments to implementation are detailed in Figure 37.1 in the Brief. These are evident in most situations and organizations, to varying degrees, but answers should cite examples.
4 A report should contain concise and clearly defined sections that reflect the characteristics of the target audience, in this instance the client managers the marketing consultant is advising. A good business report balances brevity with sufficient explanation and detail to avoid ambiguity. The answer should highlight the importance of creating the necessary infrastructure to enable effective implementation of recommendations (cf. Figure 37.1), relevant managerial processes (cf. Figure 37.2), and the importance of controls and monitoring procedures, such as audits, specification of tasks, set-up orientation and facilitation, authorization and empowerment, plus on-going reviews.

Brief 38: The Marketing Audit

1 Sky has utilized a marketing audit to assess the manner in which consumers sign-up to or learn about product options. The audit also revealed the benefits rival broadcasters have had, such as the BBC with *BBCi*, in attracting customers and building brand awareness through Internet activities. Internally, the audit demonstrated the need to improve marketing planning processes within Sky and to more formally manage its marketing operations. The audit, therefore, included sales data, customer contact profiles, competitor information, budgetary data, and information concerning the operation of the sales and marketing functions.
2 A marketing audit, popularized by Philip Kotler, is a systematic examination of the marketing function's objectives, strategies, organization and performance. The marketing audit generally includes: a market audit, marketing strategy audit, marketing organization audit, marketing systems audit, marketing productivity audit, plus an audit of the marketing mix/functions.
3 The marketing audit benchmarks performance, identifies deficiencies and reveals areas in which the marketing-led organization excels. Repeated regularly, the audit provides a check of how well deficiencies have been tackled and the extent to which strengths are being properly leveraged. The marketing audit's real benefits stem from its ability to help track progress and remedy problems, but these benefits stem from regular repetition of the audit.

4 Business presentations need to be carefully designed to reflect the requirements and characteristics of the intended audience. A good presentation balances coverage of key points with illustrative examples and sufficient explanation. The topic should be introduced to demonstrate its importance, before a systematic review of the key areas is undertaken. The presentation should end with a summary of key points and/or recommendations. In this instance, the presentation should define what is meant by the marketing audit (cf. Answer 2) and outline its core benefits (cf. Answer 3). The specific ingredients should then be explained (cf. Figure 38.1), with illustrative examples linked to the car parts industry.

Brief 39: Performance Measures in Marketing

1 Most organizations worry about their financial viability and use of resources. Marketing-oriented businesses set performance goals that additionally include marketing-related variables, such as customer satisfaction or brand awareness. For Chester Zoo, these factors are important and are assessed, but the Zoo must also adopt measures commonly used within the leisure sector for comparative analysis: membership levels, dwell time, value for money and visitor levels. The nature of the Zoo and its corporate mission add very peculiar variables to the measures used, including issues of breeding levels. The Zoo adopts an impressive array of performance measures that genuinely are used to direct future plans.

2 Marketing performance is the effectiveness of marketing programmes in implementing recommended strategies, matching objectives and satisfying targeted customers. Performance measurement is the assessment of these performance measures.

3 Qualitative measures are those assessing subjective or judgemental variables, such as customer satisfaction and brand awareness. Although these variables can be scored and quantified, they are still based on subjective opinions. Quantitative measures tend to be factors based on larger samples and numerical records, such as sales volumes, profitability, return on investment and other popular accounting measures. Most businesses should strive to adopt a balanced 'basket' of performance measures.

4 A report should contain concise and clearly defined sections that reflect the characteristics of the target audience, in this instance the brand manager's colleagues and senior executives. A good business report balances brevity with sufficient explanation and detail to avoid ambiguity. The report should define what is meant by marketing performance (cf. Answer 2), explain the options (cf. list in the Brief, plus also Brief 49), suggest a basket of factors suitable for the business, and outline ways in which these measures can be put into practice.

Brief 40: Internal Marketing

1 As described in Brief 37, an accepted way for ensuring take-up by managers is to involve them in the process leading up to recommendations being made and marketing mix programmes being developed to facilitate their implementation. This is a lesson promoted also by internal marketing experts. There was greater chance of the different Fujitsu business functions – such as product development and sales – and senior managers accepting the new scheme, if they participated in the strategizing process.

2 Internal marketing is the application of marketing practices and programmes within an organization. Utilizing programmes and guidance targeted at employees – rather than the external customers more generally the target for marketing activity – responsiveness and a unified sense of purpose among employees can be fostered.

3 In Brief 2, it was explained that relationship marketing focuses on developing on-going relationships with customers rather than seeking only initial transactions. The aim is to gain a greater slice of a customer's on-going purchasing. The leading exponents of relationship marketing argue that this requires more than nurturing links with customers, suggesting the six markets model (cf. Figure 2.1 in Brief 2). One of these additional markets is the internal audience within the organization. Staff cooperation, understanding, commitment, goodwill and ability, are essential requisites for building effective relationships with customers.

4 The consultant should first explain what is meant by internal marketing (cf. Answer 2) and how it can benefit an organization by creating a more effective and oriented workforce, better able to satisfy customers in the long term. The consultant should then explain some of the associated key requisites, including: information sharing, orientation of staff, multi-functional team interaction, internal marketing communications, debrief sessions, staff motivation and training programmes, empowerment of line personnel to deal with emergent problems, successes to champion, plus effective management and controls. Staff selection, training, motivation and reward are core aspects. The answer should touch on the cited example in the question.

Brief 41: International Marketing

1 As described in Briefs 15 and 17, companies tend to have finite resources. Unilever's portfolio has expanded over the years by organic growth and through the acquisition of brands and companies. The company, sensibly, is retrenching in order to properly resource its core and most important brands. However, Unilever operates globally and many national markets have powerful market leading brands unique only to their territory. Reflecting differing customer tastes, competitor activity, the forces of the marketing environment (cf. Brief 4) and market trends

in these different markets, Unilever must maintain some non-global brands in order to reflect target market needs and expectations. In between its global 'international' brands and these local-only brands, is an insightful category of 'international brand positionings'. These are products with a more global brand identity and positioning, but marketed using locally focused marketing mix programmes, reflecting the needs of local target markets.

2 International marketing involves seeking sales outside domestic markets. At one extreme, there is straightforward export marketing, using domestic products to sell outside the domestic market. At the other extreme is global marketing, with a commitment to using assets outside the domestic market and making investments in other countries. Between these extremes are international marketing, involving some direct involvement in non-domestic markets; or multinational marketing, with the adaptation of certain marketing activities to reflect local tastes outside the domestic market.

3 An understanding of the forces of the marketing environment and local customer requirements is crucial for effective non-domestic marketing. This understanding requires marketing intelligence in order for marketers to properly reflect customer needs and develop appropriate marketing strategies outside their domestic market.

4 A report should contain concise and clearly defined sections that reflect the characteristics of the target audience, in this instance the manager's colleagues and senior executives. A good business report balances brevity with sufficient explanation and detail to avoid ambiguity. The report should explain why a business should adapt its marketing strategy and marketing programmes outside its domestic market. The core reasons involve understanding different customer, competitor and distribution issues in unfamiliar territories, and the ability to customize the marketing mix to properly reflect local needs. In order to develop effective strategies and tactics, marketers must be aware of marketing environment issues. The report should mention each of the macro and micro marketing environment forces cited in Brief 4.

Brief 42: Consumer Marketing

1 Consumers opting for cruise ship holidays tended to be older and affluent. The industry desired to attract younger consumers. The First Choice and Royal Caribbean joint venture *Island* targeted a different market segment than normally sought by cruise liners: those in their 30s, particularly couples. Without an understanding of the expectations, perceptions, needs and likely buying behaviour of these different targets, *Island* could not possibly have developed a product specification and brand positioning likely to appeal to these current non-category users. The research identified the *angsts* and dislikes inherent in these consumers, enabling the marketing mix to instead communicate reassuring and appealing propositions.

2 The business-to-business marketing mix varies in several ways, although fundamentally it is based on the same core elements as in consumer marketing. The business-to-business product often involves large elements of customer service and support, distribution tends to include less stages in the channel, marketing communications centres on personal selling and sales promotion, while pricing is very different: few companies pay an advertised list price as in consumer markets (cf. Brief 43).

3 As highlighted in Brief 20, there are many types of advertising and several other important aspects of the promotional mix. Where budgets allow and target markets are sufficiently large, TV advertising is a very effective way for creating brand awareness for consumer products, establishing a positive brand attitude, and communicating the desired brand positioning. TV advertising for consumer goods tends to be highly emotive and image enhancing.

4 A report should contain concise and clearly defined sections that reflect the characteristics of the target audience, in this instance the marketing manager's colleagues and senior executives. A good business report balances brevity with sufficient explanation and detail to avoid ambiguity. The report needs first to clarify what is meant by business-to-business and consumer markets. The different ways of creating segments (cf. Brief 11) and targeting (cf. Brief 12) should be outlined, before focusing on the different marketing mix requirements (cf. Answer 2). Business users want easy billing, composite financial records, personal call exclusion, international access, easy menu operation and memory access, plus hands-free capability. Consumers tend more to focus on price, free minutes per month, off-peak rates, insurance packages for theft, texting capabilities and ease of use.

Brief 43: Business-to-Business Marketing

1 In many business-to-business situations, the customer is in fact composed of a mix of personnel. These managers often have very different buying criteria from each other and the influencing factors vary (cf. Brief 7). To market only to one person within such a buying centre runs the risk that either that person is not the sole decision-maker or the influence of colleagues interested in a rival's marketing mix might be hard for that person to ignore. It is important to fully understand the composition of the client's buying centre, developing messages within the marketing mix to satisfy all of those involved. This is the challenge facing mental health hospital St Andrew's.

2 Fewer customer numbers in many business-to-business target markets, compared with consumer markets, make personal contact more viable. The nature of the buying process (cf. Figure 7.1) and the characteristics of the product (often high risk, complex, costly for the customer), require the direct involvement of personnel in order to reassure customers, explain product attributes and usage, maintain on-going relationships and facilitate repeat purchases.

3 The business-to-business marketing mix varies in several ways, although fundamentally it is based on the same core elements as in consumer marketing. The business-to-business product often involves large elements of customer service and support, distribution tends to include less stages in the channel, marketing communications centres on personal selling and sales promotion, while pricing is very different: few companies pay an advertised list price as in consumer markets (cf. Brief 43). Answers should contrast a consumer product's marketing mix with that deployed by a business-to-business marketer.

4 The case study should be concise, punchy yet informative. It should reflect the time pressures and multi-tasking often evident in smaller businesses. The case should scene-set by defining what is meant by business-to-business marketing, highlighting the types of markets and products involved. It should then examine the different buying decision-making process inherent in most business markets, mentioning the role of the buying centre and the likely influencing factors (cf. Brief 7). The manner in which customers are targeted and the nuances of the marketing mix should then be explained in detail. Mention should be made of how important it is to adhere to the core marketing process of analysis, strategizing and marketing programme specification. Although the core message should centre on the detail of the business-to-business marketing mix, without addressing these other themes, the nuances of the marketing mix discussion will be lost and incomplete.

Brief 44: The Marketing of Services

1 The characteristics of the service product, notably its intangibility, place great emphasis on creating a distinctive branding in services. Club Med has created a product proposition based on the club notion, focusing on all-in services targeting families and adults desiring plenty of leisure activities. The concept is intended to transport customers from their busy lives into a calm, fun, enjoyable atmosphere, in exotic locations. The Club Med concept is uniform across its one hundred locations, ensuring regular customers visiting a different Club Med find reassuring familiarity. This, linked with carefully managed customer service levels and the payment of a joining fee to the club, ensures on-going loyalty and repeat buying.

2 Brief 19 details the characteristics that distinguish the service product from the consumer good, particularly its intangibility, involvement of a direct customer interface, customer participation in the production of the service, complexity and the role of personnel. These characteristics have forced marketers to add additional ingredients to the services marketing mix: people, physical evidence and process.

3 The '7Ps' of the services marketing mix include: product, price, promotion, place (distribution), people, physical evidence and process. Any service exhibits these

attributes, but popular examples include airlines, financial services and medical treatment. Ensure the answer given utilizes examples to illustrate the discussion.

4 Business presentations need to be carefully designed to reflect the requirements and characteristics of the intended audience. A good presentation balances coverage of key points with illustrative examples and sufficient explanation. The topic should be introduced to demonstrate its importance, before a systematic review of the key areas is undertaken. The presentation should address the characteristics of the target market customers and their requirements. The marketing mix, after all, must reflect these customer needs. As is so important in all services, the marketing mix must strive to establish a credible competitive advantage (cf. Brief 35) and convey a strong and well-differentiated brand positioning (cf. Brief 13). The presentation should then focus on the '7Ps' of the services marketing mix (cf. Answer 3), showing a link for the hotel company's Board with target market needs, competitive advantage and brand positioning.

Brief 45: Non-Business Marketing

1 Comic Relief's marketing objectives involved raising more donations than previously, increasing awareness for both its night on TV and the good causes it supports, improving the image for the charity and ensuring viewers were satisfied with the night's programming and the use of donors' money. This mix of financial and marketing oriented objectives is no different to those adopted by many non-business organizations. Brief 39 outlines the measures often used by marketers to measure performance: these often closely reflect core marketing objectives.

2 Non-business marketing involves organizations that do not have a commercial ethos and do not focus on financial profitability measures for success. Non-business marketing activities are conducted by individuals or organizations to achieve goals other than profits, return on investment or market share.

3 Non-business organizations might include hospitals, colleges, charities, political parties or voluntary organizations. A hospital's marketing objectives may include prudent use of resources, high volume turnaround of patients, reduced waiting lists and improved patient care. Colleges may focus on increased student enrolment, increased external fund raising and improving brand image. Charities seek to increase target public awareness of their activities and causes, recruit volunteer and celebrity support, while increasing donor income and more effectively using available budgets to support their needy targets. Voluntary groups often have similar objectives. Political parties strive to improve brand awareness, communicate effectively their propositions, instil voter loyalty and gain greater share of voice during election campaigns.

4 The notes should first define what is meant by non-business marketing, establishing the very different objectives sought to be achieved by commercial and

non-business organizations. There still must be an exchange, so a proposition and distinctive positioning must be developed that plausibly reflect target audience expectations. The smaller budgets evident in the non-business sector often place greater emphasis on public relations and sponsorship, voluntary-led personal selling and some direct marketing activity, as opposed to advertising. The ingredients of the services marketing mix are very important (cf. Brief 44).

Brief 46: Retail Marketing

1 Retailing is often classified as being part of the service sector, and as such, the ingredients of the services marketing mix matter (cf. Brief 44). In a fashion retailer, the target market is typically narrowly defined in terms of age, income, lifestyles and the aspirations of the target market segment. New Look targets a value-conscious, young adult and teenage, middle to lower social class, female target market. These customers have very specific expectations in terms of trends, fashion clothing attributes, the atmosphere of a store and its image. The atmospherics and layout are part of the physical evidence ingredient of the services marketing mix, but to a lifestyle and trend oriented target market, they are particularly important considerations for New Look's marketers.

2 Non-store retailing is growing, notably through mail order and e-commerce. Nevertheless, the majority of retail sales occurs in-store. Location is a fundamental issue for retail marketers, who must find sites with high footfall, easy access, viable rents and in proximity to associated stores and key trader magnets.

3 Atmospherics are integral to the retail store's marketing mix (cf. Answer 1), but the requirement will vary by retail category and will depend on the nature of the target market. New Look must appeal to value conscious consumers seeking little customer service in vibrant outlets. An up-scale perfumery, on the other hand, must create an ambience befitting its brand positioning, the brand values of the products stocked and characteristics of its target market segment. The importance of atmospherics is consistently high across most types of retailing, but the specific application varies dramatically.

4 A business report should contain concise and clearly defined sections that reflect the characteristics of the target audience. This answer should therefore be in a suitable format for the chosen example. A good business report balances brevity with sufficient explanation and detail to avoid ambiguity. The retail marketing mix is based on the services marketing mix (cf. Brief 44), but key strategic trends are altering the manifestation of these mix issues. For example, e-commerce has implications for the retail product, channel of distribution, promotional mix and physical evidence ingredients of the marketing mix (cf. Briefs 26 and 27). The strategic issues outlined in this Brief all have some impact on the marketing mix.

Brief 47: Social Responsibility in Marketing

1 Few businesses so explicitly state their social values as Ben & Jerry's did over a decade ago. These values, as stated in the example, dictated the very proposition marketed and also helped shape the business's target market strategy. More specifically, they directly impacted on Ben & Jerry's selection and deployment of marketing mix activities, from product ingredient selection, packaging choices, the use of promotional mix elements and brand positioning. There were also implications for the company's internal marketing (cf. Brief 40).

2 Social responsibility in marketing is an organization's obligation to maximize its positive impact and minimize its negative impact on society. While not confined to the marketing function, these policies and obligations directly impact on the activities of marketers. There are four strategies that can be followed: reaction, defence, accommodation and proactive.

3 Social responsibility in marketing is an organization's obligation to maximize its positive impact and minimize its negative impact on society. While not confined to the marketing function, these policies and obligations directly impact on the activities of marketers. Marketing ethics are the moral philosophies that define right and wrong behaviour in marketing. Marketers are daily faced with a choice of actions, some of which may be deemed unethical. The individual manager should be guided to avoid unethical behaviour.

4 A newspaper feature should contain concise and clearly defined sections that reflect the characteristics of the target audience. A good business feature balances brevity with sufficient explanation and detail to avoid ambiguity. The feature should first define what is meant by social responsibility in marketing (cf. Answer 2), expanding on this definition to outline the four core options available. The use of illustrative examples is critical to this answer. The focus of the feature report should then be on discussing the four options: (a) reaction, all too common, when a business fails to tackle a problem until the public finds out; (b) defence, when a business strives to deflect attention, minimize its obligations or avoid additional problems; (c) accommodation, when a business takes responsibility once encouraged to do so by pressure groups or regulators; and, (d) proactive, when a business accepts responsibility without external pressure and attempts to remedy the situation.

Brief 48: Marketing Ethics

1 Nestlé should have accommodated the pressure groups at the very least (cf. Brief 47), and ideally have proactively tackled the situation. This should have involved more watertight guidance to its staff in terms of publishing codes of ethics and policing employee activities, particularly in terms of marketing activity. Instead news headlines continued to carry accusations concerning Nestlé's

US-based marketers allegedly breaking the International Codes attempting to control the marketing and distribution of breast milk substitutes.

2 Marketing ethics are the moral philosophies that define right and wrong behaviour in marketing. An ethical issue is an identifiable problem, situation or opportunity, requiring an individual or organization to choose from among several actions that must be evaluated as right or wrong, ethical or unethical.

3 The adverse publicity facing Nestlé is a prime reason for addressing ethical issues routinely, rather than having to react to events as they unfold. Marketing ethics drive good and bad behaviour; the latter can prove very costly in terms of lost sales, compensation and lost customer, employee and stakeholder confidence. A reputation for behaving ethically can bolster significantly a company's image and the customer perceptions of its brands.

4 A business report should contain concise and clearly defined sections that reflect the characteristics of the target audience. This answer should, therefore, be in a suitable format for the chosen example. A good business report balances brevity with sufficient explanation and detail to avoid ambiguity. The report should define ethical behaviour in marketing, citing good and bad practice examples. The link should be made with social responsibility (cf. Brief 47). Moral philosophies – utilitarianism and ethical formalism – should be outlined. The detail must then address the marketing mix elements within furniture production and retailing. For example, the need to source replenishable raw materials (not from the rain forests), fire-safe and hypoallergenic materials; promotions that do not mislead on price or payment terms; pricing policies that are not erroneous or unfair; and so forth.

Brief 49: Value-Based Marketing

1 Marketing performance is the assessment of the effectiveness of marketing programmes to implement recommended marketing strategies, satisfy marketing objectives, fulfil corporate expectations and achieve the required levels of customer satisfaction (cf. Brief 39). Value-based marketing argues that an organization's financial analysis of shareholder value should include the financial value resulting from the company's marketing strategy. For a holding company such as Whitbread, there is an increasing need for the marketing function to demonstrate its financial contribution. In the specific case of Whitbread, the company's withdrawal from its historical origins in pubs and brewers signalled a commitment to align with evolving growth opportunities in the leisure sector. Under-performing brands and operations in stagnant or declining markets are unlikely to be supported by the Board!

2 The basic rationale behind shareholder value analysis (SVA) is the inclusion of the value of marketing strategy and marketing activity in an organization's financial analysis of shareholder value. SVA divides the estimation of the value

to the business created by a marketing strategy into two components, the present value of cash flows prior to the implementation of a marketing strategy, and the continuing value of the business post implementation.

3 Value-based marketing is an attempt to add objectivity and rigour to the assessment of marketing performance and financial contribution to the organization (cf. also Brief 37).

4 The answer should address the more standard performance measures popular in marketing, such as profitability, sales volumes, market share, return on investment, return on capital employed, customer satisfaction, customer retention and brand awareness. Clearly all but the last three of these measures relate to financial performance. The finance function in most businesses has for many years supported senior directors in demonstrating to stakeholders the value of the business. Traditionally, such shareholder value analysis (SVA) has ignored the marketing function. Marketers must endeavour in the future to more overtly demonstrate the financial contribution to their business, as described in this Brief. The financially oriented Marketing Director in question would no doubt endeavour to do this using SVA.

Brief 50: One-to-One Marketing

1 One-to-one marketing aims to take bespoke marketing messages and propositions to individual customers. The notion is related to relationship marketing (cf. Brief 2) and customer relationship management – CRM (cf. Brief 8). One-to-one marketing depends strongly, therefore, on an effective dialogue with individual customers. This dialogue should be continuous and lead to an 'on-going' learning relationship, so that marketers continually up-date their proposition and marketing mix to reflect the evolving expectations of these individual customers. In so doing, the intention is to maximize the lifetime value of customers, rather than focus on the level of individual transactions.

2 One-to-one marketing is the segment of one: bespoke marketing messages and propositions targeted at individual customers. This is based on the principle of mass customization.

3 Database improvements and marketers' increasing capability to use customer data have been fundamental in the development of what has become known as customer relationship management – CRM (cf. Brief 8), and more recently, one-to-one marketing. Without the use of technology to better understand and monitor individual customers, the role of technology in facilitating marketers' ability to communicate with customers, and the impact of technology (e.g. e-commerce) to alter shopping behaviour, one-to-one marketing would not be feasible.

4 Business presentations need to be carefully designed to reflect the requirements and characteristics of the intended audience. A good presentation balances coverage of key points with illustrative examples and sufficient explanation.

The topic should be introduced to demonstrate its importance, before a systematic review of the key areas is undertaken. The presentation should end with a summary of key points and/or recommendations. The presentation should first define what is meant by one-to-one marketing, highlighting its link with customer relationship management (CRM) and relationship marketing principles (cf. Briefs 2 and 8). The presentation should then focus on the key requisites for effective one-to-one marketing, which include using technology to achieve the capture of customer data and communication, a continuous dialogue leading to an on-going 'learning' relationship, the provision of a clear incentive to the customer for such a dialogue, plus acknowledging the privacy of the customer and other demands on his/her time.

Revising for Examinations: Tips and Guidance

This section offers you some observations about how examinations are generally set and a series of tips that are designed to help you handle the examination experience including answers to the following questions:

- How should I decide which topics to revise?
- How long should my examination answer be?
- How should I structure my answer?
- Can I prepare examples in advance?
- What should I do if I run out of time?

Revising for Examinations: Tips and Guidance

Very few people enjoy sitting examinations. It is not unusual to feel stressed, anxious or just plain scared when faced with the prospect. With a great deal resting on examination results and the need to devote considerable time and energy to the process, it is obvious why people become stressed. Do not despair. You can do a great deal to put yourself more in control of the examination situation and make the experience less threatening. With this in mind, there are two objectives for this section in *Marketing Briefs*. The first is to provide some observations about how examinations are generally set. This should provide some comfort during the difficult revision period! The second objective is to present a series of tips that are designed to help you handle the examination experience. These tips are presented in a question and answer format (just to get you in the mood!). We offer some specimen trial examination papers, with suggested answer schemes, in the next section of the book. This section concludes with 'ten golden rules' for tackling examinations.

How examination papers are set

Tutors understand the stresses and strains of exam time. In fact, it is in the interests of tutors or an examination body for students to be successful in their exams. In most cases tutors do not try to set 'trick' questions or examine areas not covered by the syllabus. This means you can be pretty sure that the examination papers you face will focus on the concepts presented during lectures and covered by course readings. It is self-evident, therefore, that there is no substitute for attending prescribed classes, keeping up to date with necessary readings and properly following the course throughout the period of study.

Ten tips for handling the examination experience

How long should my examination answer be?

A simple answer to this question is impossible to provide. The quantity and quality of an answer are not necessarily correlated. Individuals' handwriting also varies considerably, so generalizing is difficult. Experience suggests that for a typical essay style question to which 45 minutes have been devoted, someone with average size handwriting might turn in an answer of between three and five pages. However, the relevance and quality of the content matter more than the quantity of pages!

What format should I use for my answers?

Make sure that you check out the expectations of your tutors and closely follow the guidance from the examining body. Also follow the instructions given on the exam paper itself! For example, many professional examinations expect business report format to be adopted. Other examining bodies ask for essay style answers. Alternatively you might be asked to prepare a memorandum, develop a business proposal or even outline some slides for a presentation. It is vital that you respect any such format requests and it is sensible to practise using them in advance of the examination. Use examples if asked to do so: failure to incorporate these will lead to a loss of marks. Bear in mind that there are plenty of questions to try in this book. Some examining bodies will be able to offer sample exam answers that will give you an indication of the appropriate format to adopt. Most institutions offer revision sessions: attend them! Also try to remember that tutors with the job of marking examination papers are often faced with a daunting pile of scripts, so clear, readable and unambiguous answers are advantageous.

How should I structure my answer?

First of all, think before you begin to write. Plan. Ask yourself which components of the marketing theory the question is trying to examine. Check to see what kinds of examples you are being asked to include and whether there is any guidance about how your answer should be presented. Make some notes to remind yourself about these key issues so you do not forget (a rough answer plan). You should refer back to these notes once you have completed your answer to ensure that you have satisfied these criteria. Different examining bodies have different expectations about the structure that answers should take. Make sure that you have a clear understanding of your examining body's expectations prior to sitting the examination. As a general rule, it makes sense to ensure that your answer begins with a 'scene-setting' introduction, has a discernible structure throughout, and finishes with a conclusion or summary. This final section plays an important role in reminding you and the examiner about what exactly has been covered in your answer. Remember, the marketing concept(s) mentioned in the question must dominate your answer.

Should I include other concepts?

All questions are set with the expectation that specific issues and concepts will be raised in response (see the answer guidelines given to the specimen exam questions in the next section of *Marketing Briefs*). These key requisites must be included in your answer. No matter how accurately you discuss other concepts, if those at the heart of the question are not the focus of the answer, you will not gain good marks. If additional concepts are cited, you must show their relevance to your answer and to the question: failure to do so will give the impression that you were not certain what to include in your answer so you have cited everything you could remember from the course! A related problem is that of tangents. All too often an answer starts on track, but then detours into irrelevant territory. An essay plan helps in this respect. Ensure you answer the specific question as set. Do not 'make up' your own question, presenting an answer that does not overtly answer the real question.

Should I use diagrams in my answers?

Diagrams can be an extremely useful element of an effective exam answer and can be used to illustrate models or summarize key points and relationships. But use them wisely. For example, diagrams should be simple and quick to reproduce. A multi-coloured and artistic rendition of a model, taking many minutes to draw, will receive no more marks than a basic sketch covering the key points. Be warned, the sight of a student carrying a large clutch of felt-tipped pens into an exam room can make some tutors weep! Make sure you overtly link any diagrams used to the question's theme and the main body of your answer.

Should I use examples in my answers?

Marketing is a practical business subject and it is important to use examples to illustrate how the theoretical components work in practice. Many of the questions you face will probably specify that examples are needed. Even if they do not, you can assume that examples will probably be required. They always help to demonstrate a student's understanding of the concept and the subject of marketing.

Can I prepare examples in advance?

Some exam questions ask you to use examples of your choice. Others refer to a particular product, brand or industry and instruct you to make use of them in your answer. Some institutions give advanced warning of the examples that will be featured in the exam. Irrespective, it is a great idea to prepare some examples before you sit the examination. Although you cannot always predict which products and industries you might be asked about, you will almost certainly be able to apply some of your prepared examples in certain questions. You might also find it a welcome break from book-based revision. For instance, why not look around the supermarket for ideas? Alternatively you could search for product examples in magazines and advertisements. You might find it useful to refer to one or other of the professional marketing journals. For example, *Marketing*, *Marketing Week* and *Campaign* all include topical and interesting articles about on-going marketing campaigns and newly launched and existing products. This book contains many small case examples that might also be useful in an examination situation. The process of thinking about all of these examples and considering how they might be applied to various components of marketing theory will be also be useful in its own right.

In what other ways can I make my answer as accessible as possible?

First, check out your handwriting. As people increasingly rely upon word processing, writing skills are in decline! Test out your handwriting by preparing a sample written at a time when you were tired and under pressure. Ask a friend, work colleague or relation to give you an honest view about whether or not it is legible. Contrary to popular belief, most tutors are no better equipped to decipher the indecipherable than anyone else! So if you think there is a problem with your writing, do whatever you can to work it out before the examination sitting. Secondly, beware of 'wallpaper syndrome'. This is the production of numerous pages of unstructured script, without paragraphs, headings or illustrations. If you prepare a simple answer plan and use sub-headings to link your answer to it, structuring your answer will be much easier. Clarity is essential.

What should I do if I run out of time?

Begin by telling yourself (over and over if necessary) that there is no excuse for running out of time. If you understand the examination rubric before going in to sit the paper, you should have a clear idea of how long to devote to each question. The key is to adhere to this schedule RUTHLESSLY. If the unthinkable happens, which it sometimes does, and you do run out of time, adopt a damage limitation strategy. If you know that the end of the examination is fast approaching, you could try to complete as much of the paper as possible in brief note form. At the very least, this will indicate to your examiner that you had an appreciation of the required areas. Although this strategy will not generate as many marks as a more considered approach, you should at least recoup some of the marks you would otherwise have lost.

How should I decide which topics to revise?

Questions about the prioritization of topics for revision purposes are also difficult to answer. It is important to balance revision efficiency with appropriate coverage of the required syllabus. It is self-evident that as topics are cut out of the revision process, the coverage of the syllabus worsens. This may leave you quite exposed if there happens to be a compulsory question that falls into one of the areas you have omitted. A suitable balance can be to ensure that all areas of the syllabus receive some revision time, with additional time devoted to a proportion of key topics. This strategy is obviously less risky for examination papers where students can choose among a range of questions. Tutors rarely refer to previous papers or adhere to a pattern of questions, so 'question spotting' based on previous years' exam papers is generally not worthwhile.

Ten golden rules for examinations

- ***Revision and preparation.*** There is no substitute for understanding the subject.
- ***Awareness of exam requirements and the rubric.*** Effective preparation requires an understanding of the paper's format and requirements before you sit the exam.
- ***In-exam planning.*** Understand the required format and take time out initially in the exam to properly plan your answers.
- ***Concept comprehension.*** The examiners are primarily concerned with your grasp of the concepts cited in the questions: never lose sight of this.
- ***Examples.*** Illustrative examples demonstrate your understanding of the concepts.
- ***Clarity.*** A well-structured answer counts for much; clarity of thinking in the answer is essential.
- ***Legibility.*** Examiners must be able to easily grasp your message: ensure your layout, writing and structure assist in this.
- ***Focus.*** The concept at the heart of the question set is of paramount concern to the examiner, so avoid drifting off on tangents.
- ***Time management.*** Too many students fail to finish their answers in the time permitted or allow too much time for their earlier answers at the expense of later ones.
- ***Calmness.*** Do not be fazed by those around you: remain calm and collected, adhering to your answer plans.

Specimen Examination Papers and Answer Guides

To succeed in an examination you need to:

- Fully prepare and revise
- Adhere to the examination instructions
- Consider carefully your answers and write them as clearly as possible
- Focus on the marketing concept(s) at the heart of the question
- Remain calm during the examination
- Do your best

Specimen Examination Papers and Answer Guides

A good examination paper should be challenging but also a true reflection of the level of the course offered to the student. Most institutions employ independent external examiners to check on standards and the appropriateness of the examination paper for the relevant candidates and syllabus coverage. Second marking of a sample of scripts, to verify the principal marker's judgement of answers and range of marks, is also widely deployed by education establishments. The institution, after all, has every reason to seek fairness and rigour. The chances are that your examination will be thoroughly processed in an equitable manner. The only parts you should play are to (a) fully prepare and revise, (b) adhere to the examination instructions, (c) consider carefully your answers and write them as clearly as is possible, (d) remain calm during the examination and (e) do your best.

Students often learn concepts, models or frameworks verbatim, and can reproduce such frameworks or checklists quite readily in examination conditions. This does not equate to their fully grasping the concepts and understanding their application. Requesting that answers cite examples is an effective way for examiners to identify candidates with a genuine understanding. Examples can be requested in two ways: (a) by setting a question in the context of a particular market or brand, or (b) by requesting the candidate refers to appropriate examples of the candidate's choice (see the following examples). It is important that if asked to cite examples, you do so. Failure to use relevant examples will cost you a significant proportion of marks. If a question names a market, company or brand, you should refer to it during your answer. Even if examples are not expressly requested, consider incorporating them in your answer in order to demonstrate your understanding of the concept. Do not overly focus, however, on the details of the particular market, company or brand cited, as the examination primarily is concerned with your grasp of the concepts. Never feel you know more about a stated market, company or brand than the examiner, presenting overly detailed real-world information that detracts from your specific answers to the questions set.

This section of *Marketing Briefs* owes much to the authors' preparation of materials for their website that accompanies their mainstream marketing textbook, *Marketing: Concepts and Strategies*, published by Houghton Mifflin, 4th edition, 2001.

You may find the examination guidance offered on this website to be of benefit:

http://users.wbs.warwick.ac.uk/dibb_simkin/index/html

Select the *student site* from the home page.

An extension of the use of examples is the inclusion in the examination of a mini-case study. This approach presents some information relevant to the questions set, but still expects candidates to draw on their knowledge of marketing. The following illustrative examination papers contain compulsory case studies. If your institution does not utilize cases in examinations, simply ignore this part of the paper and progress to the essay section of each of these specimen examination papers.

XXXX
University of XXXXXX

Marketing Management
December XX, 20XX

Sample Instructions

1. **This is a closed book examination.**
2. **Time allowed: 2 hours.**
3. **Candidates are required to answer 2 questions only, which are equally weighted. Question 1 – the case study – is compulsory. Answer only one question in the essay section (Questions 2 to 7).**
4. **Read the instructions on the answer book and complete the required particulars on each answer book used.**

Question 1: Compulsory Case Question

McDonald's Controls

Mighty McDonald's was established in 1940 when Dick and Mac McDonald opened up in San Bernadino in California. Ray Kroc, credited with the chain's global ambitions, bought the rights to develop the brand in 1955 and created McDonald's Corporation and the famous Golden Arches. Every day, from Moscow to Hong Kong, McDonald's serves over 38 million people, including a million in the UK where the company enjoys a 75% share of the hamburger market. Nearest rival Burger King, despite massive recent expansion, can manage only 15%. There are 23 000 McDonald's restaurants in 110 countries producing sales of close to £25 billion. Leading branding consultancy Interbrand ranked McDonald's as the most recognized brand in the world, beating even Coca-Cola.

Whether in Lisbon, Chicago or Manchester, a McDonald's restaurant is instantly evident, with its familiar layout, ambience, design and 'feel' the envy of most services marketers. The menus change slightly to reflect local tastes, but overall there is consistency in the product the world over. Alcohol is available in Lausanne, while incredible ice cream desserts are on offer in Porto, but everywhere the core dishes are the same: The Big Mac, chicken nuggets and Filet-O-Fish. McDonald's is available as eat-in or as a drive-through take-away. McDonald's caters for a wide range of customers: single adults snacking, sales reps lunching, children partying or teenagers dining before going to a movie.

Page 1 of 3

When McDonald's first came to the UK, it had to educate its customers to expect unbuttered rolls, no knives or forks and no table service. This may seem strange to a generation that has grown up in fast food restaurants, but it was a major marketing task. Staff, too, had to be trained and managed to perform effectively their duties. Behind the scenes, internal marketing programmes still ensure staff grasp the fundamentals of the McDonald's trading concept and ideals.

Controls are central to the trading practices of the company. Every customer ordering a Big Mac must receive a similar meal every time: cooked identically, with similar relish, wrapping, pricing and a smile. With 70% of McDonald's restaurants franchised to independently owned companies and operators, such uniformity does not occur by accident. McDonald's promotes the whole restaurant experience and establishes performance standards to maintain a consistent customer offer. As the company continues to grow, with innovative outlets on ferries, at football grounds and even in hospitals, internal operational controls are crucial. McDonald's understands the importance of maintaining high standards and of integrating the brand, people, design, ambience, technology and food to create a winning experience.

While ice creams are a more prominent part of the menu in Portugal, beer and wine lead the Swiss selection inside a McDonald's, and salads are popular in the USA, the core McDonald's proposition is focused around the burgers, chicken nuggets and fries popular with young and old. To the customer, though, the uniformity of the brand and the marketing proposition is apparent, thanks to the internal controls, operational standards and the effective internal communications and procedures of the McDonald's empire.

(*Sources:* 'Progressive not McDesperate', Letters, *Marketing Week*, 22 April 1999, p. 32; 'Aroma therapy', *Marketing Week*, 8 April 1999, pp. 28–9; Ian Darby, 'Big Mac blunder hits McDonald's', *Marketing*, 7 January 1999, p. 1; Claire Murphy, 'How McDonald's conquered the UK', *Marketing*, 18 February 1999, pp. 30–1; McDonald's, London)

Case Questions – Compulsory

Q1a. Why is it important for McDonald's to have a tightly unified brand and marketing proposition?

(60% of the case question marks)

Q1b. Why and how is internal marketing so important to McDonald's?

(40% of the case question marks)

Page 2 of 3

Essay Questions – Answer Only One

Q2. For Rover, as it comes to terms with its challenging trading environment in isolation of former parent company BMW, which aspects of the competitive arena will be the most significant? Why?

Q3. The understanding of the marketing environment is poor in many organizations. Taking a single product/brand example, outline the most important facets of the marketing environment that should be assessed.

Q4. Market segmentation is often cited as the most important aspect of marketing strategy. Discuss this assertion, illustrating your answer with examples of your choice.

Q5. What must be considered to ensure the effective up-take of marketing planning in an organization? Utilize examples of your choice to illustrate your answer.

Q6. Which ingredients of the marketing mix are the most difficult to control in a service business? Use examples to illustrate your views.

Q7. For the brand manager of a railway business, which aspect of buying behaviour is the single most important piece of information for a marketer to understand?

Page 3 of 3

Answer guides: Marketing Management

Q1a The question expected the candidate to identify the benefits inherent in strong branding, describe McDonald's brand characteristics, then go on to explore why in a service business, strong branding is so important (little product differentiation, low barriers to entry, customer awareness, etc.). A good answer should go on to expand on McDonald's franchise arrangement and the importance of harmonizing a strong brand to create a competitive edge.

Q1b The question focused on internal marketing. A good answer should expand on the need to control staff in order to ensure consistent service delivery and branding, internal communications and management controls. In a service business, the product includes personnel, and McDonald's brand status, image and performance depend significantly on its staff. Internal marketing programmes orientate these personnel, ensure service delivery quality and help motivate and control those delivering the service. Added value in the answer could stem from nicely linking the *six markets model* of relationship marketing.

Q2 Competition in marketing is examined here: a 'hobby-horse' during any thorough marketing course. The answer should utilize the core concepts, such as Porter's five forces and basis for competing, or the work of Aaker, Hooley and Saunders. It is particularly important answers recognize that competitive threats stem not only from like-for-like rivals and that effective marketing strategy requires an understanding of which competitors are vulnerable to attack and which pose the greatest threat. A competitive edge over rivals is highly desirable in marketing. A poor answer will be one that fails to link into Rover as the example.

Q3 The question focused on the marketing environment. The answer should properly explore the macro and micro forces and nicely incorporate detailed examples. The answer should demonstrate that students comprehend the differences between the macro and micro marketing environment, that they can remember the principal components and that they recognize the importance of this concept in marketing opportunity analysis and marketing strategy development. Inevitably certain forces of the marketing environment will matter more than others to the product example selected, but answers should still reveal that the student knows what are all of the forces.

Q4 Another course favourite should be segmentation. The answer should debate the segmentation process – segmentation, targeting and positioning – and its benefits – improved customer focus and satisfaction, prudent use of resources and clarity in direction – then address the specific question, putting segmentation in the broader context of marketing strategy. The other ingredients of marketing strategy – the identification of opportunities, targeting priorities, positioning and the creation of a competitive advantage, etc. – matter, too, but market segmentation's benefits are significant and anyway dovetail with these other ingredients of marketing strategy.

Q5 This question considered marketing planning. The initial requirement is to summarize the key requisites for effective marketing planning and the core ingredients of the planning process. The answer should then examine the implementation barriers (internal operational issues and so forth), which are the main focus of the question! The marketing planning literature and implementation literature both contain many checklists of requisites, as detailed in *Marketing Briefs*, and these should be cited in a sound answer to this question.

Q6 Services marketing often is a course focus, addressing the characteristics of the service product and their implications for the extended marketing mix and the difficulties in creating a differential advantage. An answer should define what is meant by services in marketing, highlight the core characteristics that make the service product different to the physical good (intangibility, inseparability, customer participation, complexity, etc.), detail the additional ingredients of the services marketing mix – the '7Ps' – and outline the strategic implications in terms of how these characteristics and additional 'Ps' create problems in creating a sustainable competitive advantage, and the importance of establishing a strong brand identity. The focus should be on people, physical evidence and process, but that is not to say the traditional '4Ps' are irrelevant.

Q7 An examination was expected of customer profiles, KCVs, buying processes and influencing factors, set in the context of a particular train travelling segment. The answer must demonstrate a grasp of the core aspects of buying behaviour, rather than immediately focusing on those aspects deemed most important in this particular context. Such a discussion will be simplified if the standard buying process models and checklists of influencing factors are presented. The answer only then should select the key elements in this example, justifying why they matter and why they are more important than the excluded elements.

XXXX
University of XXXXXX

Marketing Analysis
July XXXX

Sample Instructions

1. **This is a closed book examination.**
2. **Time allowed: 2 hours.**
3. **Candidates are required to answer 2 questions only, which are equally weighted. Question 1 – the case study – is compulsory. Answer only one question in the essay section (Questions 2 to 7).**
4. **Read the instructions on the answer book and complete the required particulars on each answer book used.**

Question 1: Compulsory Case Question

Cars Go Electric

The UK Government's Green Paper *Transport: The Way Ahead* indicated a projected growth in traffic of up to 80% by the year 2025. With increasing use of vehicles and journey length, there are congestion and environmental problems. A combination of rising levels of carbon dioxide, nitrogen dioxide and sulphur dioxide have already caused acid rain, global warming problems and an increase in respiratory disease. A variety of UK and EU legislation has drawn attention to the environmental difficulties associated with road usage trends. The European Commission's *Auto Oil Package* has focused attention on air quality standards, demanding considerable reductions in vehicle emissions. The expectation is that the future will bring increasingly stringent national and EU legislation.

It is possible that European moves to reduce vehicle emissions will follow a similar pattern to that seen in California. There, strict environmental legislation required that by 2003, 10% of all new vehicles (some 800 000) must be zero-emission. Not surprisingly, car manufacturers have invested heavily in developing a range of alternative fuel technologies in their drive towards more environmentally friendly vehicles. Currently, only battery-powered electric vehicles (EVs) are able to achieve zero emissions. Other fuels under investigation include the use of alcohol, compressed natural gas, hydrogen, liquefied petroleum gas, coal derived liquid fuels and fuels derived from biological materials such as soya beans. Chrysler, Ford, General Motors, Honda, Nissan and Toyota are just some of the manufacturers which have actively developed EVs for the Californian market.

In Europe too, the move towards more environmentally friendly vehicles continues apace. PSA Peugeot/Citroen has been a major player in the *Coventry Electric Vehicle Project*. This £400 000 joint initiative with the Energy Saving Trust involved five fleet operators – Coventry City Council, East Midlands Electricity, Peugeot, PowerGen and the Royal Mail – testing electric-powered Peugeot *106* cars and vans. The aim was to increase awareness of EVs. Peugeot's involvement in electric vehicle development is long established. Following early developments of technology in 1968, the company became the first European car manufacturer to offer EVs to its customers. Now the company is looking to establish the electric *106* through its dealer network. This fits with PSA Peugeot/Citroen's long-term strategy to introduce electric versions of the Peugeot *106* and the Citroen *Saxa* throughout Europe.

Despite the ecological benefits of these innovative vehicles, many consumers remain unconvinced. Images of slow electric milk floats and the *Sinclair C5* electric trike are commonly associated with EVs. It is true that EVs require frequent re-charging and do not have high top speeds. Nevertheless, many consumers desire more environmentally friendly vehicles. EVs are very quiet on the roads and, with no clutch or gears, are relatively straightforward to drive. They are highly manoeuvrable and easy to park. EV batteries are currently expensive but running costs are remarkably low. The tasks facing the car manufacturers are to identify which types of consumers are likely to purchase an EV and to determine the product features and image necessary to stimulate sufficient demand to make such models commercially viable. The target market segments need to be defined and clear positioning strategies designed to appeal to these targeted consumers.

(*Sources:* C.D. Haywood, 'An analysis of the market potential for electric vehicles in the United Kingdom', MBA dissertation, University of Warwick, 1997; J.M. Dunne, 'Status of emissions legislation', Vehicles Standards and Engineering Department of Transport, London; 'Nissan switches to electricity', *Coventry Evening Telegraph*, 7 January 1997, p. 48; P. Foster, 'Air pollution exceeds limits every five days', *The Times*, 26 September 1997, p. 4; 'Positively all my own work', *Auto Express*, 3 January 1997; 'Selling fuel cells: electric cars', *Economist*, 25 May 1996; 'Survey on living with the car: a partly electric future', *Economist*, 22 June 1996; http://www.aqmd.gov/monthly/white.html (the case for electric vehicles); http://www.ford.com/electricvehicle/qvm.html (Ford's electric vehicle site); http://www.bsi.ch/vel/velen01.htm (the light electric vehicle project, Mendrisio Switzerland))

Case Questions – Compulsory

Q1a. How might a company such as Ford research consumer attitudes to electric vehicles?

(50% of the case question marks)

Q1b. When determining core target markets, what criteria should be utilized by Ford in judging the attractiveness of electric vehicle purchasers?

(50% of the case question marks)

Page 2 of 3

Essay Questions – Answer Only One

Q2. 'Brand positioning is the most important aspect of marketing strategy.' Discuss this assertion, illustrating your answer with examples of your choice.

Q3. Is it correct that for any product – consumer, industrial or service – the augmented product is a critical ingredient of the marketer's marketing mix? Support your discussion with relevant examples.

Q4. As BA's profits nose-dived, its marketers re-examined the airline's competitive position. What must they examine and why?

Q5. In the car fuel market, the influencing factors are more pertinent than the decision-making process in understanding consumers' buying behaviour. Do you agree or disagree with this view?

Q6. The marketing environment is often ignored by marketing managers. For an example of your choice, suggest why it is important to consider the forces of the marketing environment when assessing marketing opportunities.

Q7. Marketing planning is a fruitful means for properly analysing market developments. Does marketing planning always adequately assess the marketplace? Demonstrate your views with examples of your choice.

Page 3 of 3

Answer guides: Marketing Analysis

Q1a A straightforward marketing research question: the answer should cover the marketing research process (from problem definition, through data collection to presentation of conclusions), the differences between secondary and primary data collection; discussion of all possible/relevant primary tools with pros/cons; then selection of certain tools shown to be relevant to the case product (EVs). In a good answer there should be a discussion of relative pros/cons and an explanation of why certain tools should be discounted in this instance. Such an innovative product that is unfamiliar to consumers requires in-depth research utilizing focus groups, clinics/trials and individual depth interviews. Much has been written, though, so a secondary data trawl first would prove productive.

Q1b Target marketing. The answer should offer at the least the targeting considerations from the S–T–P process (such as resources, market size, financial viability, competition, etc.). A better answer would include market attractiveness issues from portfolio tools such as the DPM, enabling a more diverse set of factors to be considered, balancing short-term returns and resource utilization against longer-term market trends and likely take-off of this type of product. A poor answer would wrongly focus on only one or two variables and would fail to acknowledge that this product category currently is unattractive in terms of sales performance, but in the longer term is more attractive.

Q2 There are many aspects of marketing strategy, including marketing opportunity analysis and the development of a strategic focus, the fit with a corporate mission, the need to identify a competitive advantage, plus the fundamental need to prioritize target markets. An examination of positioning is required, but in addition positioning must be related to the other facets of marketing strategy in order to address the specific question. It is arguable that these other components of marketing strategy must be addressed before attention turns to positioning. Without an effective positioning strategy, however, the marketing strategy will not be fully successful.

Q3 The augmented product concept is the focus, and this implies the answer should overview the three levels of a product. The answer should use examples and must detail the core components of the augmented product (such as customer service, warranty, aftermarket back-up, etc.). A poor answer will be one that fails – despite the question's wording – to refer to the three core markets: consumer, industrial and service. A fundamental aspect of the augmented product is the role of customer service personnel. This notion links with the basics of services marketing, where *people* is a core ingredient of the marketing mix. Most other types of business, though, have recognized the importance of providing customer support in order to build up on-going relationships with existing customers (as well as reassuring potential customers).

Q4 Competition is poorly understood in most organizations. The answer should utilize the core concepts, such as Porter's five forces and basis for competing, or the work of Aaker, Hooley and Saunders. It is particularly important that answers recognize that competitive threats stem not only from like-for-like rivals and that effective marketing strategy requires an understanding of which competitors are vulnerable to attack and which pose the greatest threat. A competitive edge over rivals is highly desirable in marketing. A basic answer will merely utilize Porter's concepts, while a better answer will also incorporate Aaker-style checklists. These ideas should be adequately linked to BA. The strongest answers will include the notion of warfare strategies – head-to-head, flanking, guerrilla attacks; defence; knowledge of whom to fight and whom to avoid – popularized by Hooley and Saunders or Aaker.

Q5 A buyer behaviour question designed simply to draw the distinction between the process and influencing forces. The answer must, therefore, present a model of the consumer (not business-to-business) buying decision process and categorize the possible influencing forces. Both the buying process and influencers must be related to the chosen market – fuel buying – and then the answer should 'cherry pick' the most important stages in the process and influences. Only then can the choice be made between buying process and influencers, as demanded in the question. In practice, most consumers buy fuel based on brand loyalty, location, price or as a crisis purchase. Irrespective, it is a routine re-buy with very limited decision-making. The influencers are, therefore, likely to be more important.

Q6 It should be obvious why marketers must monitor the marketing environment: identification of strategic windows of opportunity and the pre-emption of threats. Poor understanding of the marketing environment and its associated threats/opportunities is, unfortunately, more often the norm. The answer should address the macro forces and Porter's micro forces – demonstrating awareness of the differences between these two levels and the core components of both – and also integrate examples effectively. The effective use of illustrative examples is crucial in this answer.

Q7 The answer should indicate that marketing planning should involve analysis, strategy development, then tactical implementation programmes. This planning process involves marketing opportunity analysis, assessment of the marketing environment and market trends, and an objective evaluation of which strategic direction to take in the context of such analyses. Too many plans leap straight into marketing mix tactics. Good planning includes analysis. The production of the annual marketing plan in many businesses provides the only 'sanity check' assessment of market developments. Examples should be used in the answer effectively.

XXXX
University of XXXXXX

Marketing Analysis
July XXXX

Sample Instructions

1. **This is a closed book examination.**
2. **Time allowed: 2 hours.**
3. **Candidates are required to answer 2 questions only, which are equally weighted. Question 1 – the case study – is compulsory. Answer only one question in the essay section (Questions 2 to 7).**
4. **Read the instructions on the answer book and complete the required particulars on each answer book used.**

Question 1: Compulsory Case Question

Private Health Care

For many employees, a benefit offered by their employers is private health insurance. Until the 1980s, BUPA dominated this market with health insurance policies and a network of private hospitals and clinics. The primary benefits to customers were claimed to be speedy consultations and treatment – avoiding state hospital queues – and hotel-like facilities in hospitals for patients and their relatives. However, in recent years demand has levelled off, with only around 12% of the population buying private health cover. Competitors to BUPA have been far from inactive. Private hospital operators have proliferated and many new sites have opened. Many mainstream insurance companies have launched their own private health insurance schemes: Norwich Union, Legal & General, Royal and Sun Alliance and Abbey National's *Abbey Healthcare* have combined to erode BUPA's market share from 60% to 40%. Market challenger PPP has really made in-roads, taking 30% of the £2 billion market.

For all companies operating in this market, the fundamental problem is the complexity of the 'product' being offered. BUPA's group marketing director, Pat Stafford, believes that consumers – as with all financial services – are not sure what they have bought. The product needs simplifying and its benefits stressing.

Accordingly, BUPA invested £50 million in developing *Call BUPA First*, its paperless system of claims. Customer service became a priority, with better training of personnel, new procedures and a responsive attitude to customer requirements. A brand-building initiative was launched to explain policy benefits. The strapline *You're Amazing* was at the centre of this brand-building, emphasizing the importance of customers being able quickly to deal with any ailments or medical concerns without undue inconvenience or delay. To ensure BUPA is fully customer oriented, the business was divided into five distinct divisions: health care, nursing homes, hospitals, the Spanish subsidiary Sanitas, plus dental/travel insurance. Each SBU was allocated top level marketers from consumer goods and services backgrounds.

Research identified the general public to be largely cynical about health insurance, creating a significant challenge for BUPA's expanding team of marketers. The situation was further complicated for BUPA because it targeted both consumer and business-to-business market segments. A growing number of householders are being enticed into the private health care market by seductive television advertising, direct mail and offers 'piggy-backing' on existing contents, motor or home insurance schemes. The core market remains, though, the corporate sector with large and small businesses providing policies for their employees along with pension schemes and company cars. The marketing packages required to entice a private consumer at home into protecting his or her family and the proposition necessary to persuade ICI or JCB to buy into a scheme for thousands of their employees, are both quite different. BUPA intends not only to effectively defend its position against the growing band of competitors, but to successfully attract new category users into the private health sector.

(*Sources:* BUPA; 'BUPA looks for better health', Claire Murphy, *Marketing*, 3 December 1998, p. 21; Lisa Campbell, 'BUPA axes O&M for direct focus', *Marketing*, 26 November 1998, p. 1)

Case Questions – Compulsory

Q1a. Why is customer service so important to BUPA's product offer?

(50% of the case question marks)

Q1b. Why must BUPA develop separate marketing mix executions for its consumer and business target markets? How might these marketing mixes differ?

(50% of the case question marks)

Page 2 of 3

Essay Questions – Answer Only One

Q2. Why is it necessary to extend the marketing mix for services? Can industrial marketers benefit from including any of these additional ingredients of the services marketing mix in their marketing mix programmes? Use examples to illustrate your views.

Q3. For Rover, as it comes to terms with its challenging trading environment in isolation of parent company BMW, which marketing analyses will be most critical? Why?

Q4. Formalized marketing planning encourages a re-appraisal of marketing opportunities and target market strategies. Utilizing examples of your choice, consider other circumstances in which a marketing team might adopt the A–S–P process of marketing.

Q5. The understanding of competition is a major deficiency in most Board rooms. What should be known about the competitive environment in order to develop realistic marketing strategies? Use appropriate examples to illustrate your discussion.

Q6. 'It is essential to "get into the heads" of targeted customers in order to satisfy them and also to minimize competitive threats.' To what extent do you agree with this assertion? For a marketer of a glossy magazine such as *Cosmopolitan*, what must be known about target market customers?

Q7. Target marketing is often cited as the most important aspect of marketing strategy. Discuss this assertion, illustrating your answer with examples of your choice.

Answer guides: Marketing Analysis

Q1a The answer should discuss that this is a highly competitive environment with a plethora of competing offers, all lacking the tangibility of 'real' products. The characteristics of the service product (intangibility, inseparability, etc.) therefore play an important part, and, to the customer, the ease of transaction, people providing the service and general level of customer care matter and may prove differentiators for the rival brands.

Q1b The private consumer taking out private health cover is more value-conscious and will annually – at renewal – assess the benefits versus the costs. Mailers offering low-price alternatives might well attract their interest. High profile brand-building campaigns, such as BUPA's or PPP's TV advertising, help to maintain loyalty. For business users, the individual is not directly involved in the selection of service provider, and for the central corporate buyer, the overall cost of the package for the entire workforce will be critical. There may be various decision-makers involved – the buying centre – such as human resource staff, finance managers and senior directors. Therefore the two – consumers and businesses – have different needs, expectations and buying processes. There need to be bespoke marketing mix executions aimed at each group. The answer should suggest a few likely examples of such mix executions, drawing out contrasts between consumer and business needs.

Q2 The four core characteristics of services, notably intangibility, lead to greater emphasis on people, process and physical evidence in the marketing mix. The answer should address the reasons – the characteristics of the service product – for adding these 3Ps, as well as the components of the extended marketing mix. The second part of the question makes the point that most marketers now recognize the importance of staff in relationship-building and providing customer service, and that customers in all types of markets appreciate ease of transaction (process) and the environment in which they receive the product being appropriate. Good examples to illustrate these points are crucial.

Q3 What are the components of the macro and micro marketing environment that are so challenging for Rover as it parts from parent BMW? Additional competitive pressures, general economic stresses on all car producers, green trends towards low-emission vehicles, supplier issues as companies worry about Rover's viability, dealer defections, Internet trading and imports, buyer pressures forcing down Rover's prices. The list goes on! The core analyses would seem, therefore, to be (a) the marketing environment and its implications, (b) customer perceptions, needs and buying behaviour, (c) competitor strategies and impact on Rover, (d) Rover's capabilities.

Q4 The answer should demonstrate an appreciation that marketers often 'fire fight' and devote the lion's share of their efforts to day-to-day operational issues, rather than marketing analyses or strategizing. Crises – low sales, dealer defections, environmental impact, competitor attack – may stimulate the

Analyses–Strategy–Programmes aspect of marketing. Target market strategy reformulation, the identification of new segments or territories to enter/leave, new product development/launch, branding and MarComms are other popular spurs to analysis and strategizing.

Q5 At the very least the answer should talk about Porter's competitive forces (direct, new entrant, substitute, supplier and buyer power) and these issues of competition. The ideas of Porter or Aaker in tackling an understanding of competition could usefully be cited. The answer would benefit from a discussion of the information and thinking required to be able to seek a competitive advantage.

Q6 While good students often can disagree with an assertion in an examination question and provide a solid response, it is difficult to see how any candidate could safely disagree with the need for marketers to understand customers' needs, expectations, decision-making buying behaviour and the influencing factors at work during such buying behaviour. In a competitive arena such as lifestyle magazines, with promotional pressures, fashion trends, the need to differentiate while maintaining a loyal following, with decreasing margins, this is very true. This is a straightforward buyer behaviour question.

Q7 What is target marketing? The answer has to address the essentials of market segmentation and should cite all phases: segmenting, targeting and positioning. Good use of examples should easily demonstrate the worth of this approach and the lack of mass market undifferentiated products available. The question has a second core element, though: is segmentation the most important aspect of marketing strategy? There is a large list of other ingredients on which the answer could draw, including market opportunity analysis, branding, Ansoff's strategic options, strategic focus issues and differential advantages, corporate mission versus marketing objectives, and so forth. The answer needs to include mention of some other issues in addition to market segmentation and to agree or disagree with the implicit statement in the question.

Glossary of Key Terms

A comprehensive survey of the key marketing terms to help revision and quicker learning. For example:

- **Marketing** is the management process responsible for identifying, anticipating and satisfying customer requirements profitably.
- **Marketing** consists of individual and organizational activities that facilitate and expedite satisfying exchange relationships in a dynamic environment through the creation, servicing, distribution, promotion and pricing of goods, services and ideas.

Glossary of Key Terms

ABC sales : contribution analysis examines the financial worth to a company of its products, brands or target markets.

Accommodation strategy a business's decision to take responsibility for its actions when encouraged by special interest groups or threatened by government intervention.

Advertising a paid form of non-personal marketing communication about an organization and/or its products that is transmitted to a target audience through mass media.

Advertising campaign a series of advertisements, utilizing various media, to reach a target audience.

AIDA a persuasive sequence aimed at the target audience: attention, interest, desire and action.

Basis for competing a combination of a company's strengths plus any differential advantage; it should form the leading edge of a marketing strategy.

BCG (Boston Consulting Group) growth-share matrix a proprietary portfolio model that considers market growth rate and the product's relative market share.

Brand an established product name, term, symbol, design, wholly of a proprietary nature, usually officially registered.

Brand awareness a qualitative measure of marketing performance that determines whether a company's brands adequately capture the attention of their target markets; one of the core marketing communications effects.

Brand equity the marketing and financial value associated with a brand's strength in the market.

Brand extension a company's use of one of its existing brand names for an improved or new product, usually in the same product category.

Brand insistence the degree of brand loyalty persuading a customer to accept no substitute.

Brand loyalty a strongly motivated and long-standing decision to purchase a particular product or service.

Brand positioning the creation of a clear and distinctive image in the minds of targeted customers for a brand.

Brand preference the degree of brand loyalty and preference for the brand over competing brands.

Brand recognition a customer's awareness that a brand exists and is an alternative purchase option.

Brand success brand success requires prioritization on quality, superior service, first mover advantage, differentiation, unique positioning, strong marketing communications, consistency and reliability.

Branding policies the options for marketers include: individual branding, overall family branding, line family branding and brand extension.

Branding types three core categories include: manufacturer, retailer own label and generic.

Break-even point the point at which the costs of producing a product equal the revenue made from selling the product.

Business-to-business buying behaviour the purchase behaviour of producers, re-sellers, government units and institutions, and not that of end-user private consumers.

Business-to-business buying decision process includes six key stages: problem recognition, product/requirement specification, search for suitable products/suppliers, evaluation of options *vis-à-vis* the specified requirement, selection of a supplier and order placement, and finally the evaluation of product and supplier performance.

Business-to-business customers other organizations and not end-user consumers: manufacturers; channel members such as retailers, wholesalers, agents, brokers, distributors and dealers; public sector bodies; not-for-profit organizations, government departments.

Business-to-business market a market made up of individuals or groups that purchase a specific type of product for re-sale, for use in making other products, or for their use in daily operations. Also termed an organizational or industrial market.

Business-to-business marketing marketing activity targeting other organizations rather than end-user consumers. The customers are manufacturers; channel members such as retailers, wholesalers, agents, brokers, distributors and dealers; public sector bodies; not-for-profit organizations; or government departments. Also termed organizational or industrial marketing.

Business-to-business products items bought for use in a company's operations or to produce other products. There are raw materials, major equipment, accessory equipment, component parts, process materials, consumable supplies and industrial services; also known as industrial products.

Business-to-business purchases these are purchase types such as purchases by individuals or organizations of a specific type of product for re-sale, for use in making other products, or for their use in daily operations. Purchase types are new task, modified re-buy or straight re-buy.

Buying centre the group of people within an organization who are involved in making business-to-business purchase decisions.

Causal forecasting a set of techniques used to examine changes in sales due to fluctuations in one or more market variables: examples are barometric, surveys of buyer intentions, regression analysis and other econometric models.

Codes of ethics formalized rules and standards that describe what is expected of employees.

Communication the sharing of meaning through the transmission of information.

Communications effects effects of marketing communications, including advertising; they are considered to be category need, brand awareness, brand attitude, brand purchase intention and purchase facilitation.

Competing products/services/brands those that a targeted customer could select as an alternative to a business's own product or service.

Competition oriented pricing a pricing strategy that considers costs and revenue to be secondary to competing with rivals' pricing.

Competitive advantage the achievement of superior performance *vis-à-vis* rivals, through differentiation, to create superior customer value or by managing to achieve lowest delivered cost. The generic strategies for creating a competitive advantage are cost leadership, differentiation and focus, and are not mutually exclusive.

Competitive forces industry rivals, new entrants, substitute solutions, plus the bargaining power of customers and of suppliers.

Competitive positions these influence marketing warfare strategies and tactics; the positions are market leader, market challengers, fast movers, followers and nichers.

Competitors generally viewed by a business as those companies that market products similar to, or substitutable for, its products when aimed at the same target market.

Concentration strategy the process by which a business directs its marketing effort towards a single market segment through one marketing mix.

Consumer buying behaviour the decision processes and acts of individuals involved in buying and using products for personal or household use.

Consumer buying decision process the process involves five stages: problem recognition, information search, evaluation of alternatives, purchase and post-purchase evaluation. Possible influences on the consumer decision process include personal, psychological and social.

Consumer markets markets in which the targeted customer is the end-user private consumer, either private individuals or families, typically in the home situation.

Consumer products items purchased to satisfy personal or family needs. There are convenience products, shopping goods, speciality products, unsought products and consumer services products.

Consumer sales promotion an activity encouraging or stimulating consumers to patronize a specific retailer or to try/purchase a particular product.

Corporate culture a set of values, beliefs, goals, norms and rituals that members or employees of an organization share.

Corporate strategy determines direction and the utilization of resources in all core business functions, not just marketing: production, finance, research, personnel, sales and marketing.

Cost leadership one of the generic strategies for competitive advantage; economies of scale in production and marketing enable a business to compete on the basis of low price.

Cost oriented pricing a process of adding a monetary amount or percentage to the cost of producing and marketing a product.

Crisis management a PR process in which a company responds to negative events by identifying key target publics for which to provide publicity, developing a well-rehearsed contingency plan, reporting facts quickly and accurately with no attempt to cover up, and providing ready access for journalists.

Customer relationship management (CRM) the use of (technology-enhanced) customer interaction to shape appropriate marketing offers designed to nurture on-going relationships with individual customers within an organization's target markets. The intention is to gain a greater proportion of an existing customer's purchases.

Customer satisfaction the degree to which the marketing mix satisfies customer needs and expectations; a qualitative measure of marketing performance involving surveying customer views over time and benchmarking results against competitors' scores.

Customer-centric marketing see *One-to-one marketing.*

Decline the final stage of the product life cycle, during which sales fall rapidly.

Defence strategy in the context of social responsibility, a business's decision to try to minimize or avoid additional obligations linked to a problem.

Defensive warfare a policy striking a balance between awaiting market developments or competitor activity and proactively parrying competitors' actions.

Demand oriented pricing pricing based on the level of demand for a product: high prices when demand is high; low prices when demand is weak.

Derived demand demand for industrial products arising from demand for consumer products (a surge in house building creates demand for construction equipment purchased by house builders).

Descriptor variable those variables used to describe or label the determined market segments.

Differential advantage an attribute of a brand, product, service or marketing mix that is desired by the targeted customer and is provided by only one supplier.

Differentiation one of the generic strategies for creating competitive advantage; the ability to create a product or marketing mix that creates a distinctive identity and – in the minds of targeted customers – the ability to satisfy a need.

Direct mail printed advertising material delivered to a prospective customer's or donor's home or work address.

Direct mail package comprises the mailing envelope, attention-getting device, explanatory letter, response and return devices.

Direct marketing the use of a marketing channel that avoids dependence on marketing channel intermediaries, focusing marketing communications activity on promotional mix ingredients that contact directly targeted customers.

Directional policy matrix (DPM) the market attractiveness–business strength model; helps to determine growth and divestment opportunities by considering many aspects of market attractiveness and business position.

Distribution the 'place' ingredient in the marketing mix, involving the selection of a marketing channel or channels. See also *Physical distribution.*

Domestic marketing activity directed exclusively to a business's home market.

E-commerce the use of the Internet for commercial transactions and interaction with customers.

Elastic demand important in pricing decisions: if demand falls or rises when price increases or decreases, demand is deemed elastic.

Environmental scanning the process of collecting information about the forces of the marketing environment.

Ethical issue an identifiable problem, situation or opportunity requiring an individual or organization to choose from among several actions that must be evaluated as right or wrong, ethical or unethical.

Evoked set the group of products a buyer views as possible alternatives after conducting an information search.

Exclusive distribution the use of only one outlet (or channel) in a relatively large catchment to distribute a product.

Export marketing taking advantage of opportunities outside of the home market through exports, but focusing production and product development on domestic markets.

Extensive decision-making occurs for unfamiliar, expensive, infrequent or high risk purchases, where much information-gathering and deliberation will be required.

Facilitating agencies organizations such as transport companies, insurers, financiers, marketing services businesses, warehouse operators, and trade market organizations performing activities that facilitate marketing channel operations.

Focus one of the generic strategies for creating competitive advantage; the ruthless focus on narrowly defined markets, target market segments or product mixes; often termed niching.

Forecasting the prediction of future events on the basis of historical data, opinions, trends or known future variables. There are three core categories of marketing forecasting: *causal*, *judgemental* and *time series projections*.

Generic strategies the generic strategies for creating a competitive advantage according to Michael Porter are cost leadership, differentiation and focus, and are not mutually exclusive.

Global marketing total commitment to international marketing, in which a company applies its assets, experience and products to develop and maintain marketing strategies on a global scale.

Green marketing the specific development, pricing, promotion and distribution of products that do not harm the environment. It is a response to the increasingly popular green movement and consumers' growing concerns.

Growth the product life cycle stage in which a product's sales rise rapidly and profits reach their peak.

Heterogeneous market a market in which all customers have different requirements.

Impulse purchases purchases involving little conscious planning and resulting from a powerful urge to make the purchase.

Industrial market see *Business-to-business market.*

Industrial marketing see *Business-to-business marketing.*

Industrial products see *Business-to-business products.*

Inelastic demand demand that is not significantly affected by a price increase or decrease.

Integrated marketing communications (IMC) the coordination and integration of all marketing communication tools, avenues and sources within a company into a seamless programme that maximizes the impact on consumers and other end-users at a minimal cost. Integration of the whole promotional mix and business-to-business, marketing channel, customer-focused and internally directed communications.

Intensive distribution the use of all available outlets or channels for distributing a product.

Internal marketing the application of marketing within the company, utilizing programmes of communication and guidance targeted at internal audiences to develop responsiveness and a unified sense of purpose among employees.

International marketing involves the reduction of reliance on intermediaries and the establishing of direct involvement in non-domestic target markets.

Internet a chain of computer networks stretching across the world, linking computers of different types to the websites of commercial businesses, not-for-profit organizations, public bodies, private individuals and social groups. Increasingly used for e-commerce.

Intranets internal, in-company Internet networks for routine communications, fostering group communications, providing uniform computer applications, distributing the latest software, or informing colleagues of marketing developments and new product launches.

Introduction the first product life cycle stage: a product's first appearance in the marketplace, before any sales or profits develop.

Intuition the use by marketers of their experiences and instincts to make decisions, often negating the use of marketing research.

Joint demand demand occurring when two or more products are used in combination to produce a product.

Judgemental forecasting the use of subjective opinions of managers, aggregated and averaged, to predict future events and sales levels. Sales force composite, expert consensus and the delphi approach are types of judgemental forecasting.

Judgemental sampling see *Sampling.*

Labelling a packaging ingredient that is used to distinguish a product and to convey product or legally required information to customers and distributors.

Level of involvement the level of interest, emotional commitment and time spent on a particular purchase.

Levels of a brand these are: the tangible product, the basic brand and the augmented brand.

Levels of a product these are: the core product, actual product and the augmented product.

Limited decision-making occurs for products purchased occasionally, for which some information-gathering and deliberation are needed, and there is only limited risk perceived by the customer.

Macro marketing environment see *Marketing environment.*

Managing products involves new product development, product modification and product deletion. Most marketers manage a portfolio of products.

Market an aggregate of people who as individuals or as organizations have a need for certain products and the ability, willingness and authority to purchase such products.

Market attractiveness–business strength model see *Directional policy matrix.*

Market positioning arranging for a brand or product to occupy a clear, distinctive and desirable place in the minds of targeted customers relative to competing products or brands.

Market segmentation grouping heterogeneous customers in a market into smaller, more similar homogeneous customer groups. The customers in a specific segment should share similar product needs and buying characteristics.

Market segmentation process this involves: (a) grouping customers into segments; (b) targeting those segments a business deemed to be the focus for its sales and marketing activity; and (c) positioning the product or service with a distinctive image in the minds of those customers targeted.

Marketing (i) individual and organizational activities that facilitate and expedite satisfying exchange relationships in a dynamic environment through the creation, servicing, distribution, promotion and pricing of goods, services and ideas; (ii) the management process responsible for identifying, anticipating and satisfying customer requirements profitably.

Marketing assets organizational capabilities that managers and the marketplace view as being beneficially strong.

Marketing audit a systematic examination of the marketing function's objectives, strategies, organization and performance.

Marketing channel a channel of distribution, a group of interrelated intermediaries that direct products to customers.

Marketing cost analysis the breakdown and classification of costs to determine which are associated with specific marketing activities to determine their worth.

Marketing environment the external forces that directly or indirectly influence an organization's capability to undertake its business; the *macro marketing environment* consists of six core forces: political, legal, regulatory, societal/green, technological, plus economic/competitive issues; the *micro marketing environment* includes more company-specific forces: types of competition, supplier power, buyer power, and a business's other publics.

Marketing ethics the moral philosophies that define right and wrong behaviour in marketing.

Marketing implementation a process involving activities to put marketing recommendations into action. Implementation requires necessary infrastructure, processes and managerial controls.

Marketing information system (MIS) the framework for managing and accessing internal and external data, utilizing data processing, retrieval and transmission technology.

Marketing intelligence the composite of all the data, findings, ideas and experience available within a marketing function.

Marketing intermediary a 'middleman' who links producers to other middlemen or to those who ultimately use the product.

Marketing mix the tactical toolkit of product, place, price and promotion (the 4Ps) that marketers manipulate in order to satisfy their customers and implement their target market strategies. Services marketers have extended the mix to 7Ps, the additional elements being people, physical evidence/ambience and process of transaction.

Marketing opportunity analysis an appraisal of the marketplace and organizational assets to identify circumstances and timing that enable a business to effectively reach its selected target markets.

Marketing orientation involves a clear customer focus, understanding and staying in touch with customer needs and buying behaviour so that appropriate product offerings can be developed; entails customer orientation, competitor orientation and inter-functional coordination.

Marketing oriented pricing pricing that takes into account marketing strategy, competition, value to the customer, price–quality relationships, explicability, costs, product line pricing, negotiating margins, political factors and the impact on distributors or retailers.

Marketing performance the assessment of the effectiveness of marketing programmes to implement recommended marketing strategies, satisfy marketing objectives, fulfil corporate expectations and achieve the required levels of customer satisfaction.

Marketing plan a written document or blueprint for implementing and controlling an organization's marketing activities related to the specified marketing strategy.

Marketing planning a systematic process involving assessing marketing opportunities, devising marketing strategies and specifying marketing objectives, determining marketing mix programmes, allocating resources and developing a plan for implementation and control.

Marketing research a formalized means of obtaining/collecting information to be used to make sound marketing decisions when addressing specific problems. The marketing research process involves: defining the problem or task, developing associated hypotheses to be examined, data collection, analysis and interpretation of the findings, and the reporting of the findings to the decision-makers.

Marketing shareholder value analysis (SVA) divides the estimation of the value to the business created by a marketing strategy into two components: (a) the present value of cash flows during the strategizing and planning phases and (b) the continuing value of the business at the end of the planning phase. SVA places a financial value on a business's marketing activity.

Marketing strategy indicates the specific markets towards which activities are to be targeted and the types of competitive advantage to be exploited.

Maturity the product life cycle stage at which a product's sales curve peaks and starts to decline; profits continue to decline.

Micro marketing environment see *Marketing environment.*

Mission the broad, long-term tasks the organization wishes to achieve and the overall standing *vis-à-vis* its publics that it intends to cement.

Moral philosophies the rules that guide individuals and help to determine their behaviour.

Multinational marketing the adaptation of some of a company's marketing activities to appeal to local culture and differences in taste outside of the home market.

Multi-segment strategy the process by which a business directs its marketing effort towards two or more market segments by developing a bespoke marketing mix for each separate targeted market segment.

New product development (NPD) the NPD process entails: idea generation, screening, concept testing, business analysis, product development, test marketing and commercialization.

Non-business marketing activities conducted by individuals or organizations to achieve goals other than profits, return on investment or market share.

Not-for-profit marketing marketing practices for organizations endeavouring to appeal to target markets but without profit motives.

Offensive warfare a policy whereby challengers aggressively seek market share gains by identifying weaknesses in the market leader's and other rivals' marketing mixes and developing corresponding strengths.

One-to-one marketing the segment of one; bespoke marketing messages and propositions targeted at individual customers. Utilizes advances in marketing databases and technology to strive to build relationships with individual customers within target market segments.

Opinion leader a member of a reference group who appears to those in his/her peer set to be knowledgeable about the particular product in question.

Organizational market see *Business-to-business market.*

Organizational marketing see *Business-to-business marketing.*

4Ps product, place, price and promotion; the original constituents of the marketing mix, the tactical toolkit that marketers manipulate in order to satisfy their customers and implement their target market strategies.

7Ps extension by services marketers of the 4Ps of the marketing mix (product, place, price and promotion) to include people, physical evidence/ambience and process of transaction.

Packaging a product's container(s), label and graphic design.

People as part of the marketing mix, people provide customer service, are part of the augmented product and interact with customers in order to facilitate the exchange process.

Perceived value for money the benefit consumers believe to be inherent in a product or service, weighed against the price demanded.

Performance standard an expected level of performance against which actual performance can be measured.

Personal selling a process of informing customers and persuading them to purchase products through personal communication in an exchange situation.

PEST analysis analysis of the market/marketing environment conducted by economists, examining political, economic, social and technological forces.

Physical distribution a set of activities used in the movement of products from producers to consumers: order processing, materials handling, warehousing, inventory management and transportation. In terms of physical distribution management (PDM), customer service focuses on product availability, promptness and quality.

Physical evidence in the marketing mix is the environment in which a service is offered, its ambience and physical utility.

Pioneer pricing the setting of a base price for a new product; options include price skimming and penetration pricing.

Place that aspect of the marketing mix that relates to selection of a distribution or marketing channel.

PLC see *Product life cycle.*

Positioning the process of creating an image for a product or brand in the minds of targeted customers. See also *Brand positioning; Market positioning.*

Positioning statement a plausible, memorable image-enhancing summation of a product's or brand's desired stature.

PR see *Public relations.*

Price the value placed on the product being exchanged in the marketing process.

Price elasticity of demand a measure of the sensitivity of demand to changes in price.

Primary marketing research data bespoke information collected for specific marketing research requirements; e.g. observation and surveys.

Principal influencing factors on a buying centre these include environmental, organizational, interpersonal and individual factors.

Proactive strategy a business's decision to assume responsibility for its actions and respond to accusations made against it without outside pressure or the threat of government intervention.

Probability sampling see *Sampling.*

Process in the marketing mix, the interaction of staff with customers; flows of information to customers, ordering, delivery and payment mechanisms, and systems for handling customers.

Product a core ingredient of the marketing mix; a product is everything – favourable and unfavourable, tangible and intangible – received in the exchange of a physical good, an idea, or a service.

Product adoption process the process by which a product is purchased by the consumer, it includes five key stages: awareness, interest, evaluation, trial and then adoption (purchase).

Product item specific version of a product that can be designated a distinct offering amongst a company's portfolio of products.

Product life cycle (PLC) stages in the life of a product, viewed as emulating the human life cycle: the stages are introduction, growth, maturity and decline.

Product life cycle options options available to marketers to alter the product portfolio as existing products move through the PLC; they are product deletion, product modification or new product development/introduction.

Product line a group of closely related product items that are considered a unit through marketing, technical or end-use considerations.

Product mix the composite group of products that a company makes available to customers in its target markets.

Product portfolio analysis a strategic planning tool that analytically takes a product's (brand's) performance and market standing into consideration when determining a marketing strategy and allocating the marketing budget.

Product positioning activity directed towards creating and maintaining a company's intended product concept and image in the minds of targeted customers.

Professional pricing a strategy deployed by experts with significant experience in a particular field to utilize their knowledge when setting prices.

Promotion communication with individuals, groups or organizations in order to facilitate exchanges by informing and persuading an audience to accept the business's products.

Promotional mix comprises advertising, public relations, personal selling, sales promotion, direct mail, sponsorship and the Internet.

Promotional pricing pricing linked to the short-term promotion of a product.

Psychological pricing pricing designed to encourage purchases based on emotional rather than rational responses.

Public relations (PR) the planned and sustained effort to establish and maintain goodwill and understanding between an organization and its publics.

Public relations programme on-going, lengthy duration, awareness building or awareness maintaining multi-technique PR activity.

Publicity communication in news story form about an organization and/or its products that is transmitted through mass media at relatively no charge.

Pull policy promotion by a manufacturer directly to the intended ultimate consumer. See also *Push policy.*

Push policy promotion to only the next stage in the marketing channel. See also *Pull policy.*

Qualitative marketing research findings or information that may be difficult or expensive to reliably quantify; e.g. value judgements typically stemming from focus groups and in-depth personal interviews.

Quantitative marketing research findings or information that can be analysed and expressed numerically; e.g. large sample surveys from mailed questionnaires or telephone interviewing, Web-based surveying, or analysis of sales data and market forecasts.

Reaction strategy a business's decision to allow a condition or potential problem to go unresolved until the public learns about it.

Reference group that with which a consumer identifies and to which consumers look for their values. See also *Opinion leader.*

Relationship marketing seeks to develop on-going relationships with customers by focusing on maintaining links between marketing, quality and customer service. See also *Six markets of relationship marketing.*

Reputable partnership reputable and ethical sponsorship dealings between a recognized, welcome and acceptable recipient organization and a sponsoring organization.

Routine response behaviour occurs when purchasing frequently bought, low cost, low risk items, requiring little search and decision effort.

Sales analysis the use of sales figures to evaluate a business's performance.

Sales management the determination of sales force objectives, forecasting and budgeting, sales force organization and sales territory planning, sales force selection, recruitment, training, reward and motivation, and sales force evaluation and control.

Sales promotion activity and/or material inducing sales through added value or incentive for the product to resellers, sales people or consumers.

Sampling selection of survey targets that reflect their overall larger populations. *Probability sampling* can be random, stratified or area, while *judgemental sampling* is more subjective and is often quota-based.

Secondary marketing research data 'second hand' information previously collected or published for another purpose but readily available to consult; e.g. internal reports or external sources such as information libraries or websites.

Segment of one one-to-one marketing; bespoke marketing messages and propositions targeted at individual customers within a target market segment.

Segmentation base variables dimensions or characteristics of customers and their buying behaviour used to divide a total market into market segments.

Selective distribution the use of only some available outlets or channels to distribute a product.

Service an intangible product involving a deed, performance or effort that cannot be stored or physically possessed.

Service characteristics these include intangibility, a direct organization–client relationship and inseparability, consumer participation in the production process, and complexity.

Service quality a customer's perception of how well a service meets or exceeds expectations.

Services marketing mix see *7Ps.*

Six markets of relationship marketing customer markets, influencers, referral, employee recruitment, suppliers and internal markets within the business.

Social marketing the use of marketing to influence the acceptability of ideas or principles.

Social responsibility an organization's obligation to maximize its positive impact and minimize its negative impact on society.

Sponsorship financial or material support for an event, activity, person, organization, product or cause by an unrelated organization or donor. Funds are made available to the recipient of the sponsorship deal in return for the prominent exposure of the sponsor's name or brands.

Strategic marketing plan an outline of the methods and resources required to achieve an organization's goals and mission within specified target markets; it coordinates all of a business's functions to this end.

Strategic window a major development or opportunity (often temporary) to take advantage of a market opportunity ahead of competitors, triggered by change in the marketing environment.

SWOT analysis evaluation of an organization's strengths, weaknesses, opportunities and threats.

Target audience the marketing communications practitioner's term for the target market segment intended as the principal recipient of the advertising's message.

Target public a collection of individuals with an interest in or concern about an organization, a service or a social cause.

Target publics the organization's target audiences in its public relations: customers, employees, shareholders, trade bodies, suppliers, referral bodies, financial institutions, government officials and society in general.

Targeting prioritizing the segment or segments on which an organization should focus its sales and marketing activities.

Teleselling uses telecommunications for sales and marketing activity, focusing on one-to-one communication between the sales person and the customer prospect.

Time series projection forecasting based on a set of observations, such as monthly or annual sales returns, that is examined and extrapolated to produce predictions for the future.

Total market approach see *Undifferentiated market approach.*

Trade sales promotion activity encouraging wholesalers, retailers or dealers to carry and market a producer's products.

Undifferentiated market approach this assumes that all customers have similar needs and wants and can be served by a single marketing mix.

Value-based marketing the inclusion of the value of marketing strategy and marketing activity in an organization's financial analysis of shareholder value.

Website a coherent document readable by a web browser, containing simple text or complex hypermedia presentations, generally promoting the views of the website host or brand.

Wholesaler an individual or business engaged in facilitating and expediting exchanges between producers and business-to-business customers within the distribution channel.

Index